Evening Standard

Children's London

LYDIA CONWAY

SIMON & SCHUSTER
A VIACOM COMPANY

To Paul, without whose unquestioning support, unfailing encouragement and epic stamina there would have been no book. And to Jake, Benja, Sasha and Tara, without whom there would have been no point.

First published in Great Britain by Simon & Schuster UK Ltd, 1998
A Viacom Company

Simon & Schuster Ltd
Africa House
64-78 Kingsway
London WC2B 6SX

A CIP catalogue record is available from the British Library

ISBN 0-671-02203-2

Design: Neal Cobourne and Moore Lowenhoff
Typesetting: Stylize Digital Artwork
Cover photograph: Andrew Stewart

Simon & Schuster Australia
Sydney

Printed and bound in Italy

Also published in this series:
The London Pub & Bar Guide

All information was checked and correct at press time but opening days, times and prices are subject to change. It is therefore advisable to check details in advance, especially before setting out on a long journey.

CONTENTS

INTRODUCTION

If you think children and London mix like oil and water, you might be in for a surprise. There are, in fact, few better playgrounds than the capital. Since the first edition of this book, London has become one of the most child-friendly cities in Europe. Most parks and gardens now offer year-round entertainment, while shops and restaurants have improved their facilities and added new attractions for children.

Museums and art galleries are no longer places in which you have to whisper or behave as if you are at Great Auntie Ethel's funeral. There are buttons to push, trails to follow, quizzes to answer, prizes to win, costumes to wear, interactive exhibits, old-fashioned games, and workshops galore. Children can experience the sites, sounds and even smells of medieval England, war-torn France and Roman London, and really feel what it was like to live in different times, places and even different dimensions.

What stops most people from enjoying London with children is not knowing what to expect before they arrive. For this reason, I have emphasised the things that will be specifically relevant to children. For example, is there anywhere to picnic? How long are the queues? How can I avoid hidden expenses? What do we do if it rains?

As a mother of four children I know how difficult it can be to find places suitable for the whole family. Many of those described in this book are old favourites that we have been visiting for years. Others have been recommended by friends and their children.

Each entry takes into account differences in children's ages, interests and physical abilities, helping you to plan your trip in advance. Going on a 5-mile nature trail with a baby or toddler in a pushchair might be rather taxing, as would taking a diminutive 5-year-old to a theme park, where there might be height restrictions. A trip to Godstone Farm, however, could be great fun for everyone. Older children might be doing a special project at school or have an interest in a particular subject, like fans or medicine, in which case they would enjoy a visit to the Fan Museum or the Old Operating Theatre.

Attention span can also vary with age, so I have tried to give an indication of how long to spend at each venue. The weather can, of course, ruin a day out, so activities that are particularly suitable for rainy days are clearly indicated. Where possible, there are also suggestions for what to do and where to go if you are caught in the rain.

Children's London is a very emotive subject. Some things have been left out of this book from choice, others from ignorance. There are always new venues opening and old ones being revamped, so if you have any suggestions based on your own experience of London with children – pleasant or unpleasant – please do write in about them.

Finally, I hope you and your children will enjoy exploring London and the South-east of England as much as we did.

Lydia Conway, 1998

EROS AWARDS

AUTHOR'S ACKNOWLEDGEMENTS

The real authors of this book have been the children, whose fads and foibles, views and voices can be heard throughout. The babies have been breast-fed on benches and put to sleep in dark corners; the toddlers have thrown tantrums up towers, fallen in ponds and climbed on exhibits; the older children have been variously loud, stubborn, quiet, cynical, enchanted, bemused and, above all, honest, as only children know how.

I would also like to thank all the staff at the many tourist attractions, museums, galleries, theatres, parks, shops and restaurants who helped with my research, often well beyond the call of duty.

My special thanks to Jo Bowlby at the Evening Standard, who believed in me in the first place, and to all those at Simon & Schuster who have continued to do so.

KEY

☺	Suitable for under-5s
E	Free admission
☼	Suitable for fine weather
☁	Suitable for rainy days
☁	Suitable whatever the weather
◐	Suitable for less than 3 hours
◑	Suitable for half a day
●	Suitable for a whole day
⊖	Underground
DLR	Docklands Light Railway

GETTING AROUND

Travelcard: a daily, weekly or monthly Travelcard allows unlimited travel in Greater London on the rail network, buses, Underground and Docklands Light Railway. You can then travel on any combination of tube, train, bus and DLR within your selected zone/s as many times as you wish, for as long as your ticket is valid (on weekdays only after 9.30am; not on night buses).

Buses: will stop automatically at Compulsory bus stops (white background). At Request stops (red background) buses will stop if you signal to the driver by sticking your arm out or, if you are aboard the bus, ringing the bell. Under-14s travel at a reduced flat fare (until 10pm). Under-5s travel free. It is advisable to have the correct fare in change.

London Underground: trains run every few minutes, 20 hours a day so you don't need a timetable but you should pick up a tube map (free from ticket offices). Tickets must be purchased before you travel (penalty for travelling without a valid ticket, £10). Tube and bus fares are based on a six-zone system, and the most economical way of getting around is to buy a Travelcard (see above). Under-14s travel at a reduced-rate fare (15- and 16-year-olds need to carry a Child Rate Photocard, available free from all tube stations and London post offices). Under-5s travel free. If you are with young children, try to avoid rush hour (Monday to Friday, 7-10am and 5-7pm). *Access to the Underground* is a booklet for disabled people that details lifts and ramps at each station and is also useful for buggy users (available at Travel Information Centres or from London Regional Transport, Unit for Disabled Passengers, 55 Broadway, SW1H 0BD).

Docklands Light Railway: the DLR runs on raised tracks from Tower Gateway (near Tower Hill) and Bank stations to the Isle of Dogs. This is a good way to see the Docklands but service is limited in the evenings and at weekends.

Railways of London and the Southeast: phone Rail Travel Enquiries 24-hour information on 0345 484950 for details of fares, maps, timetables, etc. Toilets and mother-and-baby rooms can be found at: Euston, King's Cross, Liverpool Street, Paddington, St Pancras, Victoria and Waterloo.

Taxis: black-cab drivers know central London very well as they have to complete a rigorous two-year course to learn the whereabouts of every street and the quickest route to it before they can be registered. They can be booked by phone (0171 286 0286, 0171 253 5000 or 0171 272 0272) or hailed in the street when the yellow Taxi sign is lit. Tipping is not obligatory but a tip of 10 to 15 per cent is common. When hailing a taxi in the street, remember that black cabs are not obliged to accept a hiring of over 6 miles, but if they do and the journey is wholly within the London area the fare payable is shown on the meter. If a driver accepts a hiring to a destination outside the London area, the fare becomes negotiable (with the exception of journeys to Heathrow Airport). Cabs are now fitted with rear seat-belts but the law seems to be rather hazy when in comes to babes in arms – you just sit with them on your lap.

Minicabs: are unlicensed and drivers often do not know even the local area well. They cannot be hailed in the street (either phone for one or go in person to the cab office). The standard of driving can vary considerably. However, they usually work out cheaper than black cabs, especially for longer journeys. Negotiate a fare when you phone. There are several companies in London who offer women drivers for women and children (see local telephone directory).

Car: on-street parking in central London can be expensive and difficult. Gone are the days when traffic wardens didn't work in the rain (their excuse used to be that their pens didn't write). Illegally parked cars may also be clamped or removed. Restrictions are shown by yellow lines on the road and kerb and an accompanying yellow plate on lampposts. Parking restrictions are usually in force between 8.30am and 6.30pm, Monday to Friday, and 8.30am-1.30pm on Saturday, and meters cost anything from £2 per hour. The stay is often limited to two hours (check details on individual meters). Watch out for Parking Permit Holders Only signs – wardens are very strict about illegally parked non-permit holders. Charges for off-street parking vary enormously from the expensive to the exorbitant. For a free map of National Car Parks in London, write to or phone the Map Office, NCP Ltd, 21 Bryanston Street, W1 (tel: 0171 499 7050). Listed below is a selection of central London, 24-hour car parks:

Arlington Street, W1 (tel: 0171 499 3312)
Audley Square, W1 (tel: 0171 499 3265)
Brewer Street, W1 (tel: 0171 734 9497)
Park Lane, W1 (tel: 0171 262 1814)
Young Street, W8 (tel: 0171 937 7420)

LONDON BY SEASON

From Trooping the Colour to burning the Guy, from teddy-bear, doll's-house and model-train fairs to Christmas lights and Santa's grotto, there is something for children in London every week of the year. Whether you want to join a pancake race, watch an Easter parade, attend a clown service, or sing carols in Trafalgar Square, this quick-reference section will guide you in the right direction.

DAILY CEREMONIES

CEREMONY OF THE KEYS 🔲 ☀ ◐

ADDRESS Tower of London, Tower Hill, EC3
PHONE 0171 709 0765
The gates of the Tower of London are locked every evening by the Chief Warder of the Yeomen Warders, who is ceremonially challenged by a sentry as he approaches the Bloody Tower, in one of the oldest continuous military ceremonies in the world. For your free tickets you must apply in writing, with a stamped addressed envelope, to: The Resident Governor, Queen's House, HM The Tower of London, EC3N 4AB. State the number of people (not more than seven) and required date.
TRAVEL ⊖ *Tower Hill* • **HOURS** *Daily, 9.40pm*

CHANGING OF THE GUARD ☺ 🔲 ☀ ◐

ADDRESS Buckingham Palace, SW1
PHONE 0839 123411 for recorded information
Every child reading AA Milne should see this event at least once, if not with Alice. If you can't face the crowds outside Buckingham Palace, other good vantage points can be found outside St James's Palace, at Wellington Barracks in Birdcage Walk, or by walking behind the Old Guard to Buckingham Palace. The ceremony lasts 40 minutes and takes place inside the palace railings, with the public viewing it from outside. The procession, usually accompanied by a military band, leaves Wellington Barracks at 11.27am and marches to the Palace via Birdcage Walk. It also takes place at **Horse Guards** Parade Whitehall, SW1, and **Windsor Castle**, Windsor, Berks.
TRAVEL ⊖ *Hyde Park Corner or Green Park (Buckingham Palace);*
⊖ *St James's Park or Charing Cross (Horse Guards Parade); Windsor rail (Windsor Castle)* • **HOURS** *Daily Apr-Aug, alternate days Sep-Mar, 11.30am (Buckingham Palace); Mon-Sat 11am, Sun 10am (Horse Guards Parade); Mon-Sat 10.30am (Windsor Castle). Cancelled in wet weather and on some state occasions.*

JANUARY
LONDON PARADE ☺ 🅴 ☼ ◗

PHONE Parade hotline 0181 566 8586

Nine-storey-high inflatable characters, including Mighty Mouse and Betty Boop, marching bands, colourful floats, and cheer- leading groups from around the world in the biggest New Year's Day party in Europe. Over 10,000 performers, headed by the Lord Mayor of Westminster watched by around one million spectators. Starts at noon from Parliament Square, along Whitehall to Trafalgar Square, then Lower Regent Street to Piccadilly at around 3pm.

TRAVEL ⊖ *Westminster, Embankment or Green Park* • **WHEN** *1 Jan, noon*
• **PRICES** *Free street view. Seats in grandstand at Piccadilly Circus adults £15, children and concs £10*

INTERNATIONAL BOAT SHOW ☀ ◑

ADDRESS Earl's Court Exhibition Centre, Warwick Road, SW5
PHONE 0171 385 1200

The largest sailing and power-boat show in Europe, with a colourful Central Harbour scene where you can see boats of all shapes and sizes, plus equipment from complex radar to simple yatching shoes.

TRAVEL ⊖ *Earl's Court* • **WHEN** *Early Jan for one week*

TOY AND TRAIN COLLECTOR'S FAIR ☀ ◗

ADDRESS Alexandra Palace, Alexandra Park, N22
PHONE 0181 365 2121

Large sale of collectors' toys and model trains. A similar fair is also held in June.

TRAVEL ⊖ *Wood Green, then bus W3* • **WHEN** *Mid- to late Jan*

CHINESE NEW YEAR FESTIVAL ☺ 🅴 ☼ ◗

The area of Soho around Newport Place and Gerrard and Lisle Streets comes to life with fire crackers, papier-mâché dragons and paper lanterns adorning windows and balconies. Young men dressed in colourful lion costumes dance the famous lion dance through the streets, receiving gifts of money and food from local restaurants, shops and residents. There is often a stage in Leicester Square on which performers re-enact scenes from Chinese history.

TRAVEL ⊖ *Leicester Square* • **WHEN** *Late Jan or early Feb on Sun nearest to New Year's Day, 11am-6.30pm*

FEBRUARY
GUN SALUTE 🅴 ☼ ◗

ADDRESS Hyde Park, opposite the Dorchester Hotel, Park Lane, W1
and Tower of London, Tower Hill, EC3

On Ascension Day a 41-gun salute takes place in Hyde Park, where the King's Troop, Royal Horse Artillery, gallop down the park pulling the gun carriages before firing them. Also on the Queen's Birthday (21 Apr), Coronation Day (2 Jun), the Duke of Edinburgh's birthday (10 Jun) and the Queen Mother's birthday (4 Aug). A 62-gun salute is fired at the Tower of London at 1pm by the Honourable Artillery Company. If the occasion falls on a Sunday, the guns are fired on the following day.

TRAVEL ⊖ *Green Park (Hyde Park) or Tower Hill (Tower of London)* • **WHEN** *6 Feb, noon (Hyde Park) and 1pm (Tower of London)*

SOHO PANCAKE-DAY RACE ☺ 🖪 ☼ ◑

ADDRESS Carnaby Street, W1

PHONE Alternative Arts 0171 287 0907

Watch the teams run with their frying pans, tossing pancakes as they go, or join in the bizarre ritual. To take part, call one week before.

TRAVEL ⊖ *Oxford Circus* • **WHEN** *Shrove Tuesday, phone for time*

THE GREAT SPITALFIELDS PANCAKE RACE ☺ 🖪 ☼ ◑

ADDRESS Old Spitalfields Market, Brushfield Street, E1

PHONE 0171 375 0441

Entry is free. Teams of four or more should bring their own frying pan (phone for entrance forms).

TRAVEL ⊖ *Liverpool Street* • **WHEN** *Shrove Tuesday, 12.30pm*

MARCH

DAILY MAIL IDEAL HOME EXHIBITION ☺ ☔ ◑

ADDRESS Earl's Court Exhibition Centre, Warwick Road, SW5

PHONE 0171 385 1200; box office 0895 677677

Europe's greatest consumer show. Kids love browsing round the show houses, while adults can hunt for the latest labour-saving gadgets and gizmos.

TRAVEL ⊖ *Earl's Court* • **WHEN** *Mid- to late Mar for 3 weeks, daily, phone for details* • **PRICES** *Adults £9-£10, children £5-£6 (under-5s free)*

ORANGES AND LEMONS SERVICE 🖪 ☔ ◑

ADDRESS St Clement Danes, Strand, WC2

PHONE 0171 242 8282

The church of the Royal Airforce (full of RAF symbols, memorials and monuments). The bells are rung to the tune of 'Oranges and Lemons' at 9am, noon, 3pm and 6pm daily and there is an annual Oranges and Lemons Service in March for schoolchildren, in which each child is given an orange and lemon.

TRAVEL ⊖ *Temple* • **WHEN** *Phone for date*

HEAD OF THE RIVER RACE ☺ 🖪 ☼ ◑

PHONE 0181 940 2219

The Head of the River Race runs from Mortlake to Putney. The **Oxford and Cambridge Boat Race** may be more famous, but for children this race is more fun, easier to see, and more colourful. The eight-man boats set off 10 seconds apart and the race takes over an hour. It's fun trying to guess which boat has won – the race is timed so the results aren't known until the end.

TRAVEL ⊖ *Putney Bridge or Mortlake rail* • **WHEN** *Last Sat in March, phone for time*

OXFORD AND CAMBRIDGE BOAT RACE 🖪 ☼ ◑

PHONE 0171 379 3234

If you actually want to see this famous race, it is far better watched on TV, but you can't beat the carnival atmosphere as thousands of people turn out to catch a glimpse of the two boats battling their way along the 4½-mile stretch between Putney Bridge and Mortlake. Best vantage points are Putney Bridge, Bishop's Park, Dukes Meadows and Chiswick Bridge but

those with small or numerous children should take a picnic and a radio and head for the less crowded river banks. Go early for a good view.
TRAVEL ⊖ *Putney Bridge or Mortlake rail* • **WHEN** *Usually Sat before Easter, or Sat of Easter weekend, phone for date and times*

EASTER

BUTTERWORTH CHARITY ▣ ☀ ◑
ADDRESS St Bartholomew-the-Great, Smithfield, EC1
PHONE 0171 606 5171
Traditionally, poor widows were presented with money and their children with buns. Now hot cross buns are presented to children (and anyone else who would like one) in the churchyard before a service.
TRAVEL ⊖ *Barbican* • **WHEN** *Good Friday, 11.30am*

EASTER FUNFAIR ☺ ☀ ◑
ADDRESS Alexandra Palace, Wood Green, N22
PHONE 0181 365 2121
Fairground rides and stalls over the Easter weekend.
TRAVEL ⊖ *Wood Green, then bus W3*

EASTER KITE FESTIVAL ☺ ▣ ☀ ◑
ADDRESS Blackheath, SE3
Single-line, box, stunt and sport kites, kite ballet and 'rokkuku' (Japanese-style kite flying). Lots of colourful stands so if you forget your own kite you can buy one for as little as £1 or splash out on a custom-made kite for considerably more.
TRAVEL *Blackheath rail* • **WHEN** *usually 10am-dusk*

EASTER PARADE ☺ ☀ ◑
ADDRESS Battersea Park, SW11
A colourful carnival with a fairground, stalls and stage acts such as stunt riders, freefall parachute team and motorcycle display teams. A special children's village has bouncy castle, slides, clowns and puppets (and baby-changing facilities). There is also an arts and craft marquee.
TRAVEL *Battersea Park or Queenstown Road rail* • **WHEN** *Easter Sunday, 10am-9pm, parade starts at 3pm* • **PRICES** *Adults £5, children £2 (under-10s free)*

LONDON HARNESS HORSE PARADE ☺ ▣ ☀ ◑
ADDRESS Regent's Park, NW1
PHONE 01733 234451
The judging of horses and carts, drays and brewers' vans is followed by a parade twice round the Inner Circle.
TRAVEL ⊖ *Baker Street or Regent's Park* • **WHEN** *Easter Monday, judging starts at 9.45am*

APRIL

APRIL FOOL'S DAY ☺ ▣
In France they pin paper fish to your back. (Remember the opening scene of *French Connection II*?) The British just play bizarre practical jokes – our kids still laugh every year at the up-turned, empty boiled-egg joke. Scan all the newspapers today and try to work out which story is the April Fool.
WHEN *1 Apr*

LONDON MARATHON ☺ 🅴 ☀ ◑

PHONE Sportsline 0171 222 8000

This 26-mile race attracts over 25,000 runners. It starts at Blackheath (just outside Greenwich Park gates), goes via the Isle of Dogs, Victoria Embankment and St James's Park, and finishes on Westminster Bridge. Kids love cheering the athletes, and it's fun for the tiny tots to see the fancy-dress brigade (there is always a gorilla or two and a man in a tutu), while older kids can celebrity-spot. The best place to watch is at the start or finish but anywhere along the route is fun.

TRAVEL *Blackheath rail for start,* ⊖ *Westminster for finish* • **WHEN** *phone for date, 9am onwards*

QUEEN'S BIRTHDAY GUN SALUTE 🅴 ☀ ◑

Hyde Park and Tower of London (21 Apr). See **Gun Salute**

MAY

FA CUP FINAL

ADDRESS Wembley Stadium, Wembley, Middx
PHONE 0181 900 1234

The showpiece event of the English football season. Phone for ticket prices.

TRAVEL ⊖ *Wembley Park or Wembley Central* • **WHEN** *Early May*

LONDON DOLL'S HOUSE FESTIVAL ☁ ◑

ADDRESS Kensington Town Hall, Hornton Street, W8
PHONE 0171 937 5464/0171 361 2827

Collectors' fair with wonderful display of doll's houses and stalls selling everything from sterling-silver coffee pots and hand-painted porcelain to curtains, wallpaper and whole kits. Not suitable for very young children.

TRAVEL ⊖ *High St Kensington* • **WHEN** *Early May*

OAK APPLE DAY 🅴 ☀ ◑

ADDRESS Royal Hospital, Chelsea, SW1

Commemorates King Charles II's escape from Oliver Cromwell's Parliamentary forces in 1651, when he hid in a hollow oak. Today the colourful uniformed Chelsea Pensioners decorate his statue at the Chelsea Hospital with oak leaves and branches.

TRAVEL ⊖ *Sloane Square* • **WHEN** *Thurs after 26 May*

PUNCH AND JUDY FESTIVAL ☺ 🅴 ◑

ADDRESS St Paul's Churchyard, Covent Garden, WC2
PHONE 0171 240 2255

Annual festival held on nearest Sunday to 9 May to commemorate the date Samuel Pepys watched the first recorded Punch and Judy show in 1662.

TRAVEL ⊖ *Covent Garden* • **WHEN** *nearest Sunday to 9 May*

LONDON TO BRIGHTON HISTORIC COMMERCIAL VEHICLES RUN 🅴

PHONE Crystal Palace Park Events Line 0181 778 9496

Annual drive from Crystal Palace to Brighton by historic commercial vehicles, including vintage lorries, buses and vans.

TRAVEL *Crystal Palace Park rail* • **WHEN** *usually mid-May*

JUNE

CORONATION-DAY GUN SALUTE (2 JUN)
E ☀ ☽

Hyde Park and Tower of London. See **Gun Salute**

BEATING THE RETREAT ☀ ☽

ADDRESS Horse Guards Parade, SW1

A military display of marching and drilling bands, with trumpeters, massed bands, pipes and drums. The 'retreat' or setting of the sun is beaten on drums by soldiers on foot and horseback in a colourful ceremony popular with older children. Floodlit performances. Call for tickets, which become available from 1 Mar. Tickets available from Premier Box Office, 1b Bridge Street, SW1 (opposite Big Ben).

TRAVEL ➌ *St James's Park or Charing Cross* • **WHEN** *Daily, 9.30pm during fortnight preceding the **Trooping of the Colour**, which is on Sat nearest 11 Jun*

TROOPING OF THE COLOUR **E** ☀ ☽

The route goes from Buckingham Palace, along the Mall to Horse Guards Parade, Whitehall, and back again in honour of the Queen's official birthday. The route to Horse Guards Parade is very crowded but there is usually space on the Mall (Green Park side). At about 1pm the Queen watches a Royal Air Force jet display from her balcony. For tickets to the event, or the full-scale dress rehearsals which are on the two preceding Saturdays (at which the Queen is not present), apply, enclosing an SAE, to the Brigade Major, Household Division, Horse Guards, Whitehall, SW1. Tickets are awarded by ballot so if you wish your application to be included in the ballot for the dress rehearsal, state this with your application. Only two tickets per application, which should be in before the end of February.

TRAVEL ➌ *Hyde Park Corner* • **WHEN** *Sat nearest 11 Jun*

BIGGIN HILL INTERNATIONAL AIR FAIR ☺ **E** ●

ADDRESS Biggin Hill Airfield, Biggin Hill, Kent

PHONE 01959 540959

An annual aviation spectacle held on the famous RAF airfield, where squadrons of Spitfires and Hurricanes defended London in the Second World War. International flying displays, ground events, a funfair and exhibition stands. Alternatively, park as near the airfield as possible and picnic on the surrounding greens and grassy areas while watching the planes for free.

TRAVEL *Biggin Hill rail* • **WHEN** *Two days in mid-June* • **PRICES** *Adults £8.50, under-15s £3, family ticket (1 car and up to 6 occupants) £19*

SUMMER KITE FESTIVAL ☺ **E** ☀ ☽

ADDRESS Blackheath, SE3

Lots of kite trading stalls, kite trains, fighting kites, stunt kites and parachuting teddy bears.

TRAVEL *Blackheath rail* • **WHEN** *Sun in Jun, 10am to dusk*

PRACTICAL CLASSICS BROMLEY PAGEANT OF MOTORING ☺ ※ ●

ADDRESS Norman Park, Hayes Lane, Bromley, Kent
PHONE 01959 541444 for bookings
The biggest one-day car show in the world has over 3,500 exhibits and attracts 35,000 visitors. There are also hot-air balloons, arena events, a children's funfair and a rock 'n' roll band.
TRAVEL Hayes rail • **WHEN** Late Jun • **PRICES** Adults £6 (or £4 in advance), children £2.50 (or £2 in advance)

HENLEY ROYAL REGATTA ▤ ※ ◑

PHONE 01491 572153
Take a picnic, arrive early and find a good viewpoint along the tow-path to watch the world's oldest rowing regatta. All except the last third of a mile of the course is open to the public for free, and if the wind is in the right direction you can hear the commentary.
TRAVEL Henley rail • **WHEN** Late Jun or early Jul, Wed-Sat, first race usually 8.30am

KENWOOD LAKESIDE CONCERTS ※

ADDRESS Kenwood House, Hampstead Lane, NW3
PHONE 0171 413 1443
Older children or those with an interest in music will love these outdoor concerts of popular classics in the delightful lakeside setting among the trees. Concerts end with a fireworks display. Take a picnic and a rug to keep warm, and pray for fine weather. Call the box office or buy tickets two hours before concert begins.
TRAVEL ⊖ Archway, Hampstead or Highgate, then bus 210 or 271 • **WHEN** Jun-Aug, every Sat • **PRICES** phone for prices

JULY

STREETS OF LONDON FESTIVAL ☺ ▤ ※ ◖

PHONE Zap Productions 01273 821588
Drama, mime, juggling, clowning and dancing on the streets and in shopping centres throughout London.
WHEN July, August and September

GREENWICH FESTIVAL ☺ ▤

PHONE 0181 305 1818
This popular arts festival has various free events for children and kicks off with an opening-night fireworks display.
TRAVEL Greenwich rail or Island Gardens DLR, then foot tunnel • **WHEN** Ten days in mid-Jul

ROYAL TOURNAMENT ✿ ◑

ADDRESS Earl's Court Exhibition Centre, Warwick Road, SW5
PHONE 0171 373 8141
This popular military spectacle includes mast manning, cutlass swinging, absailing, paragliding, marching displays and very noisy massed brass bands. There are also forces' competitions and re-enactments of historic events. The whole show lasts for two and a half hours.
TRAVEL ⊖ Earl's Court • **WHEN** Two weeks in mid-Jul • **PRICES** £5-£25 (concs available)

DOGGETT'S COAT AND BADGE RACE ⛶ ☼

PHONE 0171 626 3531

Founded in 1715, this sculling race for six Thames watermen runs from London Bridge to Cadogan Pier, Chelsea. Best view is from London Bridge.

WHEN *Late Jul*

AUGUST

QUEEN MOTHER'S BIRTHDAY GUN SALUTE
⛶ ☼ ◖

Hyde Park and Tower of London (4 Aug). See **Gun Salute**

NOTTING HILL CARNIVAL ⛶ ☼ ◐

PHONE 0181 964 0544

Europe's largest, and noisiest, street festival, where steel bands, flamboyantly costumed dancers and pulsating lorries throb their way through the streets of Notting Hill. Dazzling colour and blaring music blend with the tantalising smells of Caribbean food to make an exciting day out for older children (Monday is *the* day but Sunday is best for kids). Anyone with small or even medium-sized children should avoid the main festival area and beat a hasty retreat to the relative safety of the Notting Hill Carnival Family Events, where small fry can enjoy the atmosphere without getting lost in the crush. Events include the ubiquitous face painting, juggling, mural painting, puppet and mask making at the Meanwhile Gardens, Great Western Road near Westbourne Park tube.

TRAVEL ⊖ *Westbourne Park; no car access* • **WHEN** *Bank Holiday Sun and Mon all day*

AUGUST BANK HOLIDAY FUNFAIRS

ALEXANDRA PARK Wood Green, N22 (⊖ Wood Green, then bus W3)
COVENT GARDEN PIAZZA WC2 (⊖ Covent Garden)
EALING COMMON Gunnersbury Ave, W5 (⊖ Ealing Common)
HAMPSTEAD HEATH NW3 (Hampstead Heath rail or ⊖ Hampstead)

SEPTEMBER

COVENT GARDEN FESTIVAL OF STREET THEATRE ☺ ⛶ ☼ ◐

ADDRESS Covent Garden Piazza, WC2

PHONE 0171 240 2255

A week of aerial trapeze artists, stilt walkers, jugglers, escapologists, physical comedy and improvisation from performers from the UK and Europe.

TRAVEL ⊖ *Covent Garden* • **WHEN** *Early Sep*

GREAT RIVER RACE ☺ ⛶ ☼ ◖

PHONE 0181 398 9057

Over 200 traditional craft, including cutters, whalers and gigs, race 22 miles from Richmond to Island Gardens, opposite Greenwich Pier. Boats competing include Chinese dragonboats, Hawaiian war canoes, Viking longboats, Irish curraghs, shallops, wherries, whalers, gigs and skiffs. Children aged 10 and over can take part (accompanied by an adult). Fun to watch the end.

WHEN *Early Sep*

HORSE OF THE YEAR SHOW
ADDRESS Wembley Arena, Wembley, Middx
PHONE 0181 900 1234 for details; 0171 900 1919 for tickets
Annual equestrian event with top showjumpers, dressage, shires, hunters and hacks. Call for times and prices.
TRAVEL ⊖ *Wembley Park or Wembley Central* • **WHEN** *Four days in late Sep or early Oct*

HORSEMAN'S SUNDAY 🅴
ADDRESS St John's Church, Hyde Park Crescent, W2
PHONE 0171 262 3791
Annual blessing of horses performed by the vicar, followed by showjumping, a gymkhana and other events in Kensington Gardens Paddock (western end of Kensington Gardens). Free.
TRAVEL ⊖ *Lancaster Gate or Paddington* • **WHEN** *Sun in late Sep, noon* • **PRICE** *Free*

SPITALFIELDS SHOW 🅴
ADDRESS Old Spitalfields Market, Brushfield St, E1
PHONE Alternative Arts 0171 375 0441
Entries include anything from herbs and flowers to preserves, with special sections for children's entries.
WHEN *Mid-Sep* • **PRICE** *phone for prices*

OCTOBER

COSTERMONGER'S PEARLY HARVEST FESTIVAL 🅴 ◓
ADDRESS St Martin-in-the-Fields, Trafalgar Square, WC2
PHONE 0171 930 0089
Over a hundred pearly kings and queens, all wearing clothes decorated with thousands of pearl buttons, gather for the harvest-festival service.
TRAVEL ⊖ *Leicester Square or Charing Cross* • **WHEN** *1st Sun in Oct, 3pm*

PUNCH AND JUDY FELLOWSHIP FESTIVAL ☺ 🅴
ADDRESS Covent Garden Piazza, WC2
All-day festival of Punch and Judy shows
TRAVEL ⊖ *Covent Garden* • **WHEN** *1st Sun in Oct, 10.30am-5.30pm*

NOVEMBER

LONDON TO BRIGHTON VETERAN CAR RUN 🅴
ADDRESS Hyde Park, Park Lane, W1
The popular annual run commemorates Emancipation Day, when it became legal for 'horseless carriages' to travel at more than 4mph and without being preceded by a man waving a red flag or lamp. Motorists celebrate by destroying their red flags before they drive off in a collection of cars, all of which were built before 1905. Spectators can watch anywhere along the route (via Westminster Bridge and Croydon, on the A23).
TRAVEL ⊖ *Hyde Park Corner or Marble Arch* • **WHEN** *1st Sun in Nov, 7.30am; first cars due at Brighton, 10.30am*

FIREWORKS NIGHT

PHONE London Tourist Board Fireworks Service 0839 123410 (call from mid-Oct)
Look in your local paper for details of displays, which are often accompanied by a funfair and side-shows.
WHEN *5 Nov*

LORD MAYOR'S SHOW ☺ 🄴 🕒

PHONE 0171 606 3030 or 0171 332 1455 for details
Starting at the Mansion House and finishing at the Royal Courts of Justice, this is the biggest ceremonial event in the City, celebrating the beginning of the Lord Mayor's year in office. It involves 5,000 participants and over 70 floats. There is a state procession, military parade, a fair in Paternoster Square, a firework display from a barge moored on the Thames (best vantage points are Victoria Embankment, Blackfriars Bridge or Waterloo Bridge) and the Lord Mayor's gilded 18th-century coach pulled by six shire horses.
TRAVEL ⊖ *Victoria, Blackfriars or Waterloo* • **WHEN** *2nd Sat in Nov, 11am*

REMEMBRANCE SUNDAY 🄴 🕒

ADDRESS Cenotaph, Whitehall, SW1
Service to remember the dead of past wars, with a salute of guns. Poppy wreaths are laid on the Cenotaph by the Queen, the Prime Minister and other major dignitaries.
TRAVEL ⊖ *Westminster* • **WHEN** *2nd Sun in Nov, 11am*

CHRISTMAS LIGHTS 🄴

In mid-November the Bond Street Christmas lights twinkle into action, switched on by a celebrity on the corner of Clifford Street and New Bond Street. The lights are often best on Regent Street. Look out for the elaborate Christmas decorations in Oxford Street, Regent Street, Carnaby Street, Covent Garden Market, Piccadilly and the Burlington Arcade.

CHRISTMAS PARADE 🄴

PHONE London Tourist Board Christmas Information Service 0891 50 54 55
American-style parade with floats and marching bands through the shopping streets of the West End.
TRAVEL ⊖ *Oxford Circus, Piccadilly Circus or Bond Street* • **WHEN** *Sun in late Nov*

DECEMBER

For information on Christmas events around London, call the London Tourist Board Christmas Information Service. For details of Christmas shows and pantomimes, call one of the following numbers from a fax machine and you will receive fax-back details: London and the Southeast 0660 600592; rest of England 0660 600593; Scotland, Wales and Northern Ireland 0660 600594.

CAROL SERVICES 🄴

St Paul's Cathedral, Ludgate Hill, EC4 (tel: 0171 236 4128).
Usually Christmas Eve service of lessons and carols led by the cathedral choir. ⊖ St Paul's
Southwark Cathedral, Montague Close, SE1 (tel: 0171 407 3708).
⊖ London Bridge

Westminster Abbey, Broad Sanctuary, SW1 (tel: 0171 222 5152/7110). Lessons and carols by the Abbey choir, usually Christmas Eve. ⊖ Westminster

CAROL SINGING **E**

Trafalgar Square, WC2, every evening before Christmas from mid-December to Christmas Eve. ⊖ Westminster

CHRISTINGLE **E**

This service, which originated in 18th-century Germany, features a nativity play usually performed by a local school, carols and a procession for children around the church. Each child carries a Christingle, or small candle, in a satsuma. For details of local churches with a Christingle service, call the Children's Society on 0171 639 1466.

CHRISTMAS TREE **E**

ADDRESS Trafalgar Square, WC2
PHONE 0171 211 6393
A giant Norwegian spruce (an annual present from the people of Oslo to thank Britain for liberating them from the Nazis) is lit each evening until 6 January. Carols sung around the tree each evening until Christmas Eve.
TRAVEL ⊖ *Charing Cross* • **WHEN** *3 Dec-6 Jan, 3pm-10pm*

ERNEST READ CONCERTS FOR CHILDREN

ADDRESS Royal Festival Hall, South Bank, SE1
PHONE 0171 928 8800
The Ernest Read Symphony Orchestra presents a programme of Christmas music, plus carols for choir and audience. (See also Stage and Screen).
TRAVEL ⊖ *Waterloo or Embankment* • **WHEN** *programme starts mid-Dec*

ROYAL INSTITUTION CHRISTMAS LECTURES FOR YOUNG PEOPLE

ADDRESS 21 Albermarle Street, W1
PHONE 0171 409 2992
Series of five lectures for older children. Broadcast on BBC2.
TRAVEL ⊖ *Green Park* • **WHEN** *Tickets available in August for filming in December* • **PRICES** *Adults £14, children £6*

TREE DRESSING

Organised by the London Wildlife Trust, tree-dressing ceremonies usually take place over the first weekend in December. Adults and children can help decorate the trees and join in various related festivities. For details of the event nearest you, call one of the following: Camley Street Natural Park (tel: 0171 833 2311), Richmond, Twickenham and Kingston Nature Reserve (tel: 0181 898 9582), London Wildlife Garden Centre (tel: 0171 252 9186).

FATHER CHRISTMAS

DRUSILLAS ☺ ● ◑

ADDRESS Drusillas Zoo Park, Alfriston, E Sussex
PHONE 0323 870656
See Santa getting ready for Christmas in his workshop; after Christmas you can see how Santa and Mrs Claus relax after all their hard work. Children's Christmas parties also available for ages 3-10.
TRAVEL *Berwick or Polegate rail* • **PRICES** *phone for prices*

HARRODS ☺ 🄴 ◖

ADDRESS 87 Brompton Road, SW1
PHONE 0171 730 1234
Free visit to Santa's grotto will yield a badge and gift, but queues at this famous store are invariably long.
TRAVEL ⊖ *Knightsbridge* • **PRICE** *Free*

LONDON TOY AND MODEL MUSEUM ☺ ◑

ADDRESS 21-23 Craven Hill, W2
PHONE 0171 262 9450
Santa events, toy-making with the elves, a Christmas treasure hunt, carol singing and Santa's grotto (included in the ticket price).
TRAVEL ⊖ *Paddington* • **HOURS** *Daily 9am-5.30pm* • **PRICES** *Adults £5.50, children £3.50 (under-4s free), family ticket (2+2) £15*

LONDON ZOO ☺ ☀ ●

ADDRESS Regent's Park, NW1
PHONE 24-hour information 0171 722 3333; Zoo-line 0891 505767
Children can volunteer to play leading roles in the Living Nativity Play, starring with a donkey, sheep and camels in the Christmas story. Santa's grotto and a visit from a real reindeer included in the usual admission price.
TRAVEL ⊖ *Camden Town or Baker Street, then bus 274; London Water Bus along Regent's Canal; car park and meter parking near zoo entrance* • **HOURS** *Mar-Oct: daily, 10am-5.30pm; Nov-Apr: daily, 10am-4pm (closed Christmas Day)* • **PRICES** *Adults £8, children and concs £6 (under-4s free), OAPs and students £7, family ticket £24*

SANTA SPECIAL FLIGHT

PHONE Steve on 01344 640112
Avia Tours organise a 45-minute flight from Heathrow. Price includes drinks, snack and a gift from Father Christmas.
PRICE *£89*

SELFRIDGES ☺ 🄴 ◖

ADDRESS Oxford Street, W1
PHONE 0171 629 1234
It's free to meet Santa during shopping hours in his top-floor grotto, but go early in the season as queues are enormous by mid-December.
TRAVEL ⊖ *Bond Street or Marble Arch* • **PRICE** *Free*

SYON PARK CHILDREN'S DAY ☺ ◑

ADDRESS Syon Park, Brentford, Middx
PHONE 0181 560 0881
Father Christmas arrives on a horse-drawn dray. Face painting, miniature railway rides, a magician, free balloons and craft demonstrations. Call for times and dates.
TRAVEL *Syon Lane rail* • **PRICE** *phone for prices*

TEN DAYS OUT

The following days out have been designed to group attractions together in small areas that can easily be covered on foot. Some are precise step-by-step guides that could be done in a day and are especially suited to families with small children or babies. Others are more flexible, offering several alternatives along the way, and can be followed fully or partly, depending on time, specific interests and stamina. Some 'days out' have been included that could not possibly be completed in a single day, allowing you to plan a route to suite your family. There are also alternative places of interest for younger or older children, as well as suggestions for where to rest and eat, what to do if it rains, and things to look out for on the way.

CRYSTAL PALACE AND HORNIMAN MUSEUM AND GARDENS ☺ ⼤ ❖ ●

Crystal Palace itself might no longer be there, 99 fire engines having failed to save the original glass exhibition centre from a terrible fire in 1936, but **Crystal Palace Park** is one of the best-serviced family parks in London.

The park is so jam-packed with things for children of all ages to do and see that your first stop should be the information centre near the Penge entrance. Plan your day over coffee at the nearby café or let your children run riot in the large, enclosed children's playground while you spread your map and leaflets over the picnic tables provided.

At weekends and on summer holidays there is a small children's funfair between the car park and playground (suitable for under-8s) along with cart rides drawn by two of the farmyard shire horses.

If you are here on a weekday on your own with an infant, head for the excellent, free One O'clock Club near the start of the miniature railway ride. From the playground, head south past the *pétanque* pitch (rules and boules available at the information centre), following signs to the 'Monsters', 29 huge model dinosaurs made in the 1850s and now lurking among the undergrowth. The paths, which are all accessible by buggy, take you across wooden bridges, past waterfalls, near hilly slopes where children can scramble up for a better view, and round to the boating lake. From here you can backtrack up to the small Palace Farmyard, which is full of both rare and common farm animals, including Gertie the 5-ft-long pig and some very friendly goats. There is a picnic table here but I wouldn't rate your chances of eating your food before the goats do.

From here, you can retrace your steps, keeping the sports stadium on your left, and head up the hill to the tea maze. (The maze has hedges just short enough for anxious parents to look over to keep track of young offspring; there is also a special escape gate.) Alternatively, if you are here on a Sunday or Bank Holiday with older children, head west past

Station Gate for the Crystal Palace Museum (southwest corner of the park), charting the fated history of the great glass exhibition centre.

All the main attractions are on the east side of the park, with the tea maze out on a limb. However, if you plan your day so you finish by the maze, you can cut across the park, past the site of the old palace, to Crystal Palace Parade and catch the 122 bus up to Forest Hill, from where the **Horniman Museum and Gardens** is a 10-minute walk (alternatively, the 176 bus from the Penge Entrance or Sydenham Gate will drop you right outside the museum).

WET-WEATHER ALTERNATIVE

You could easily spend a day in the park but if it rains or you want something different, head for the **Horniman Museum and Gardens**. This delightful, informal and highly diverting anthropological museum houses a vast, eclectic array of items ranging from Javanese shadow puppets, African masks and Native American headdresses to a mummified crocodile, half a fruit bat and a pair of Arabian shoes with flaps to scare away scorpions (see Museums and Galleries for further details). If the sun comes out again, there are lovely gardens offering outdoor activities.

LISTINGS

CRYSTAL PALACE PARK (tel: 0181 778 7148): See The Great Outdoors
HORNIMAN MUSEUM AND GARDENS (tel: 0181 699 1872): See Museums and Galleries
JOANNA'S (tel: 0181 670 4052): See Eating Out

NEARBY

DULWICH PICTURE GALLERY (tel: 0181 693 5254): See Museums and Galleries
FREE RANGE (tel: 0181 693 5008): See Eating Out

GREENWICH ☺ ☂●

Arrive by boat at Greenwich Pier and you sail straight into the view Canaletto made famous and which has changed little since 1755. As the boat rounds the pier you will get an uninterrupted view through Wren's spectacular Royal Naval College, built in two halves so that from the **Queen's House** royalty would still have a gateway to the river, and beyond up the tree-clad hill of **Greenwich Park** to Charles II's **Old Royal Observatory**, which marks longitude zero, the baseline of world time.

Once off the boat you cannot miss the majestic **Cutty Sark**, the famous tea clipper. You can see the sailors' living quarters as they were when she transported tea from China – note the stark difference in conditions for officers and crew – and a colourful collection of ships' figure heads in the lower hold.

Moored a little further along the waterfront is the tiny **Gypsy Moth IV**, the 54-ft yacht in which Sir Francis Chichester circumnavigated the world single-handedly. It is particularly popular with young children, who are fascinated by the cramped conditions in which Chichester lived for 274 days while still managing to find room for books, a celebratory bottle of champagne, and some wonderfully antiquated-looking cooking equipment.

Note the enormous domed lift of Brunel's foot tunnel, which links Greenwich Pier to the Isle of Dogs. You could use this to reach Island Gardens DLR for your return journey. Children love running along the pedestrian tunnel, built in 1900 to give south-London labourers access to

Millwall Docks. Even if you are not using the DLR it is worth walking through the tunnel to the Isle of Dogs for the views back across the river to Wren's and Jones's skyline – and on really wet days your kids can always count the 200,000 tiles lining the tunnel.

If curiosity gets the better of you, you could take the riverside path from here to the Millennium Dome on Greenwich Peninsula but it is a long way past corrugated-iron fencing, barbed-wire-protected junkyards and graffiti-strewn concrete walls to see an as-yet unfinished product. Best wait until the Millennium, when it should be tidied up and there will be a shuttle service from here to the Peninsula and, hopefully, something worth seeing when you get there.

Instead, if you head inland and into the town centre you will come to the popular weekend Greenwich Covered Arts and Craft Market, which is good for anything from wooden toys and hand-knit baby clothes to découpage loo seats and flavoured ground coffee (try the vanilla or double chocolate fudge). Prices are reasonable compared to Covent Garden and standards are high. Permanent shops within the covered market that are also open during the week include a Peruvian shop, an excellent children's book shop and a candle shop. The market gets very crowded, especially on Sundays, so try to arrive early.

Lunch at Goddard's Pie and Mash Shop is a very traditional affair. The restaurant is run by Jeff and Kate Goddard, whose family have been in the business since 1890 (although, despite being a listed building, its existence is threatened with a compulsory purchase order). Their 'winter warmers', such as 'minced beef and onion pudding 'n' mash, with gravy/liquor', priced £2.10, are served to locals and tourists seated at wooden benches. Even fussy kids love the choice of fruit pies served with ice-cream or custard.

From here, head for the **National Maritime Museum**, which brings vividly to life British maritime history and has plenty of hands-on interactivity and weekend children's events. Outside, next to the Bosun's Whistle Café (a missable but conveniently situated restaurant serving full meals, light snacks or just a cup of tea), children can climb aboard their own ship-shaped climbing frame.

If you have young children with you, make your way to the well-equipped park playground (to the left of Bosun's) and small boating pond but don't let them run off too much steam – it is an arduous climb up to the Old Royal Observatory even without having to push an occupied buggy. If you have older children who are interested in history and architecture, they might enjoy the sumptuous 17th-century splendours of Inigo Jones's Queen's House (to your right as you leave the museum), where you can see how royalty really lived.

Make sure you leave plenty of time for the attractions at the top of the park. In addition to a splendid view of London beneath the Wolfe Monument, the Meridian Line, the Millennium Clock and the Old Royal Observatory itself, there is a bandstand with Sunday-afternoon band performances and children's entertainment and, beyond that, the beautiful enclosed flower gardens with duck pond (and some of the most over-fed ducks in London), deer enclosure and a host of squirrels, to say nothing of some of the oldest and largest trees in London, some surviving from the 1660s.

From here you can leave by Blackheath Gate for a stroll across the heath to the village train station, or make your way back down the hill for the return journey. If you are planning to go across Blackheath, remember to bring your kite.

LISTINGS

CUTTY SARK (tel: 0181 858 3445): See Museums and Galleries

FAN MUSEUM (tel: 0181 305 1441): See Museums and Galleries

GODDARD'S YE OLD PIE HOUSE, 45 Greenwich Church Street, SE10 (no phone). Greenwich rail. Open Jul-Sep, Tue-Sun 11am-3pm; Oct-Jun, Wed-Sun 11am-3pm.

GREENWICH PARK (tel: 0181 858 2608): See The Great Outdoors

GREENWICH FOOT TUNNEL, linking Greenwich Pier, SE10, and the Isle of Dogs, E14. Greenwich rail or Island Gardens DLR. Open 24 hours daily (lift daily, 5am-9pm; wheelchair and buggy access when lift open). Free.

GYPSY MOTH IV (tel: 0181 853 3589): See Museums and Galleries

NATIONAL MARITIME MUSEUM (tel: 0181 858 4422): See Museums and Galleries

OLD ROYAL OBSERVATORY (tel: 0181 858 4422): See Museums and Galleries

QUEEN'S HOUSE (tel: 0181 858 4422): See Museums and Galleries

ESCAPED (tel: 0181 692 5826): See Eating Out

CAFÉ SOL, 13 Nelson Road, SE10 (tel: 0181 853 4385)

HAMPSTEAD AND HIGHGATE ☺ ▣ ☀ ●

Highgate Cemetery is a good starting point if you are coming by tube to Archway. The cemetery is a wonderfully atmospheric Victorian Valhalla of funereal follies, memorials and monuments. Follow the Circle of Lebanon passageway, lined with catacombs, at the heart of which is a large cedar tree. Search among the undergrowth for the sleeping stone lion on the tomb of menagerie owner George Wombwell or the stone dog on the tomb of Tom Sayers, the last of the bare-fist prizefighters. And don't forget to see the final resting place of Karl Marx.

Continue on to the Whittington Stone on Highgate Hill which, according to tradition, marks the spot where Dick Whittington heard the chiming of Bow Bells – on top perches a cat, his legendary companion. Then stop for a spot of lunch at **Lauderdale House**. You should aim to arrive by noon unless you have booked in advance. Alternatively, you can eat their home-cooked Italian take-away food on the lawn. There are often puppet shows or craft fairs in the building adjacent to the café.

Next, either walk round the historic grounds (originally for locals without their own gardens) or head for any part of Hampstead Heath for a wander round. Most of the Heath is accessible by buggy. If you go on a weekday on your own with under-5s, try the One O'clock Club at Parliament Hill, which has attractive gardens, a playground, and is a favoured spot for kite-flying.

Save some energy for a quick look round **Kenwood House** at the top of Hampstead Heath, with its Gainsboroughs and Rembrandts (free, leave buggies at entrance). Look out for the portrait of the eccentric 18th-century inventor John Joseph Merlin, who built the first roller skates and demonstrated them by making a grand entrance at a masquerade ball in 1760, skating into the ballroom while playing a violin. Unable to stop, he smashed into a large mirror, breaking it and injuring himself.

Those with older children might prefer to concentrate on the historic houses in the area. The Freud Museum is in the house where the father of psychoanalysis moved after fleeing Nazi-occupied Austria in 1938 and has various artefacts and furnishings, including his famous couch. You can also visit Keats House, where the poet came to live in 1818. The house has been preserved as it was in Keats's day.

There is a local-history museum in Burgh House, off Well Walk. This is also the site of a spring where water was bottled at the beginning of the 18th century (note the initials WG on the gates for the physician Dr William Gibbons).

Fenton House has several pieces of 18th-century furniture, English and Chinese porcelain, paintings and a large collection of early musical instruments kept in playing order for use by students and occasional musical recitals. In summer Shakespeare is sometimes performed here.

LISTINGS

BURGH HOUSE, New End Square, NW3 (tel: 0171 431 0144). Open Wed-Sun, noon-5pm. Free.

FENTON HOUSE, Hampstead Grove, NW3 (tel: 0171 435 3471) Closed Mondays. Open Wed-Fri 2-5pm, Sat-Sun 11am-5pm.

FREUD MUSEUM, 20 Maresfield Gardens, NW3 (tel: 0171 435 2002). ⊖ Hampstead. Open Wed-Sun, noon-5pm. Adults £3, concs £1.50, under-12s free.

HIGHGATE CEMETERY, Swain's Lane, N6 (tel: 0181 340 1834). ⊖ Archway or Highgate. Eastern Cemetary, open daily, 10am-4pm (in winter), 10am-5pm (in summer). Western Cemetary, open for guided tours only, weekdays at noon, 2pm and 4pm, and on weekends hourly from 11am-4pm. (No weekday tours during December, January or February). Adults £1, accompanied children free.

KEATS HOUSE, Keats Grove, NW3 (tel: 0171 435 2062). ⊖ Hampstead. Opening times vary. Free.

KENWOOD HOUSE, Hampstead Lane, NW3 (tel: 0181 348 1286). ⊖ Golders Green. Open daily, 10am-6pm (winter to 4pm). Free.

LAUDERDALE HOUSE, Waterlow Park, Highgate Hill, N6 (tel: 0181 341 4807). ⊖ Archway. Café open Tues-Sun, 8am-7pm for snacks, hot and cold meals. See Workshops

REGENT'S CANAL WALK � ☀ ●

To avoid the crowds (which by 1pm in the summer can be unbearable, especially for toddlers), begin your walk at Camden Lock Market, where you can watch the stallholders setting up shop from 8.30am (trading usually starts at 9.30am on Saturdays and Sundays). Walk over the hump bridge, from where you can see the drawbridge of the **Pirates' Castle Watersports Centre** (over-8s can have a go at canoeing in summer at this water-sports centre), or pause for home-made ice-creams and sorbets, as well as Italian food, at **Marine Ices** before weaving your way up to Primrose Hill for a fine view of the city, and a helpful viewing panel at the summit.

Back down the hill you can rejoin the canal at **London Zoo**. Going by the back of the zoo and the Snowdon Aviary, you pass under Blow-up Bridge, reduced to rubble in 1874 when a working narrowboat carrying gunpowder and benzol exploded as it was towed underneath it. For a visit behind the scenes at Lords, take the tow-path exit off Park Road. Tours are also available at the gold-domed mosque (booking is essential). Continue along the tow-path, past the brightly painted canal boats, to the Lisson Grove exit for lunch at the **Sea Shell**, which does delicious chips and large portions of fish (share portions if you are on a budget).

If it's a Sunday, drop in at the Church Street Market. The **Puppet Theatre Barge** is moored in Little Venice until June for children's shows which, if you haven't lingered for too long at any of the sights, you should have plenty of time to catch (shows usually start at 3pm).

ALTERNATIVE ROUTE

An alternative to this walk is to join the Regent's Canal in Hackney, at Victoria Park, and follow the canal through Old Ford Lock and down to the Thames, with a stop-off at the **Ragged School Museum**, where you can catch a glimpse of the lives of Victorian schoolchildren in the East End. Then head down to Limehouse Basin, where the canal joins the Thames.

WET-WEATHER ALTERNATIVE/YOUNGER CHILDREN

If it is raining, hop on one of the covered narrowboats which run between Camden Lock and Little Venice. Cruises last 45 minutes and you can get off at **London Zoo** and pick up a later boat (see Waterways for full details).

LISTINGS

LONDON CENTRAL MOSQUE, 146 Park Road, NW8 (tel: 0171 724 3363). ⊖ Baker Street. Open dawn to dusk daily. Free. Visitors must remove shoes before entering. Women, for whom there is a separate gallery, should cover their heads.

LONDON ZOO (tel: 0171 722 3333): See Animal Attractions

LORD'S CRICKET GROUND: See Behind the Scenes

MARINE ICES: See Eating Out

PIRATES' CASTLE WATERSPORTS CENTRE: See Sports and Leisure

PUPPET THEATRE BARGE (tel: 0171 249 6876 or mobile 0836 202 745): See Stage and Screen

RAGGED SCHOOL MUSEUM (tel: 0181 980 6405): See Museums and Galleries

REGENT'S CANAL, NW1 and NW8. ⊖ Camden Town, St John's Wood or Warwick Avenue. Tow-paths open dawn to dusk daily. For free *Canal Walks in London* brochure with maps, send SAE to: Canal Information, British Waterways Board, The Toll House, Delamare Terrace, London W2 6ND.

REGENT'S CANAL INFORMATION CENTRE, Camden Lock, NW1 (tel: 0171 482 0523). ⊖ Camden Town or Chalk Farm. Narrowboat trip from here.

REGENT'S PARK: See The Great Outdoors

SEA SHELL: See Eating Out

SOUTH KENSINGTON ☺ ⛅ ●

Most of the museums here are linked to South Kensington tube station by a long tunnel, making this an ideal day out when it is cold and raining.

First stop is the **Science Museum**, which houses the world's most comprehensive collection of scientific, technological, industrial and medical inventions, hundreds of working exhibits and lots of interactivity for even very young children.

Next door is the **Natural History Museum** with its enormously popular dinosaur exhibition and the spectacular new Earth Galleries. Although the two are linked, you should enter the Earth Galleries by going outside and back in through the entrance on Exhibition Road for the full dramatic effect. Beyond six imposing statues of Earth's inhabitants, both mythical and real, is an escalator that ascends through the middle of a vast rotating metal sphere, which changes colour as you pass through. The new multi-million pound exhibition is divided into six galleries, and covers everything from volcanoes and earthquakes to wind and water, with plenty of interactive exhibits to amuse and educate all ages.

A quick dash across the road brings you to the **Victoria & Albert Museum** for all things decorative. Not only does it have the most stupendous collection of fine and applied arts but, more prosaically, it has an excellent café for rainy days. If the sun comes out, head for **Kensington Gardens** at the top of Exhibition Road for a picnic and fresh air.

If you are feeling really piggy, take the bus along the Brompton Road to **Harrods** for a blow-out tea in the Georgian Restaurant on the fourth floor. This famous store used to sell anything from hairpins to elephants, but now more modestly claims to provide 'anything within reason'. The spectacular food halls are especially popular with children as is, more obviously, the toy department.

LISTINGS

HARRODS (tel: 0171 730 1234): See Shopping and Services; Eating Out
KENSINGTON GARDENS: See The Great Outdoors
NATURAL HISTORY MUSEUM: (tel: 0171 938 9123): See Museums and Galleries
SCIENCE MUSEUM (tel: 0171 938 8000/8080): See Museums and Galleries
VICTORIA & ALBERT MUSEUM (tel: 0171 938 8500): See Museums and Galleries

SOUTH BANK ☺ ☀ ●

From Westminster tube, cross Westminster Bridge for a quiet, traffic-free walk along the river with lots of things for small children to do and see. Look back across the bridge for the most impressive view of the **Houses of Parliament** and Big Ben before visiting the **London Aquarium** in County Hall. When you have had your fill of fish, head for Jubilee Gardens, looking out for the striking memorial to the International Brigade of the Spanish Civil War. Here you can picnic and let the little ones run off steam before taking in a free lunchtime concert or evening foyer event in the South Bank complex.

Beyond the concert halls, the National Film Theatre, National Theatre and LWT building, you come to the Coin Street development and the Jubilee Walkway, which leads you past the market at Gabriel's Wharf and Blackfriars Bridge. From here, if time and energy allow, you can cross the bridge and continue down river to **Shakespeare's Globe** Theatre just before Southwark Bridge.

Children over four will enjoy visiting **MOMI (the Museum of the Moving Image)**, where actors playing movie characters make for very diverting guides. The museum traces the history of film and television in a highly imaginative, challenging way. There are baby-changing facilities in the Royal Festival Hall (first floor) and a playground in Jubilee Gardens. The National Film Theatre riverside café is fun and reasonably priced, and those with older children can take out day membership (50p per person) and catch a matinee.

LISTINGS

MUSEUM OF THE MOVING IMAGE/MOMI (tel: 0171 928 3232): See Museums and Galleries
NATIONAL FILM THEATRE (tel: 0171 928 3232). ⊖ Waterloo or Embankment

NATIONAL THEATRE (tel: 0171 928 2252). Free foyer music Mon-Sat from 6pm until performances start. See Stage and Screen

ROYAL FESTIVAL HALL, South Bank, SE1 (tel: 0171 921 0682). ⊖ Waterloo or Embankment. Free music daily 12.30-2pm, jazz Fridays from 5.15pm. Education department publishes list of special events for children (tel: 0171 921 0886).

TRAFALGAR SQUARE ☀ ●

Starting from Charing Cross Station, walk into Trafalgar Square, where the fountains spurt into action at 10am daily, climb onto the lions (something every London child must do, if only to test their parents' washing powder against the stains of pigeon droppings) and crane your neck for a view of Nelson on his column, depicted correctly without an eye patch, and with only one arm.

Before Nelson's statue was erected, 14 stonemasons held a dinner on top of the 145-ft high column. The significance of Nelson's Column was recognised by Hitler, who planned to remove it to Berlin after the conquest of Britain as a mark of world domination. The brass reliefs around the bottom show scenes from Nelson's four great battles and every year on 21 October there is a service here to commemorate him. Look out for London's smallest police office – a small hollow pillar built as an observation post for one policeman to monitor political rallies. The lamp on the top allegedly came from Nelson's flagship *Victory*.

Also look for the brass plaque on the north wall, which shows the British imperial standards of length. The statue of Charles I on horseback, looking down Whitehall where the king was beheaded in 1649, marks the original site of Charing Cross, from which all distances from London are measured. Here you can feed the pigeons (in summer you can buy pigeon feed for rather more than tuppence a bag).

At the northeast end of the square stands the church of St Martin-in-the-Fields, which has free lunchtime concerts on Tuesdays and is home to the London Brass Rubbing Centre. The church also houses the popular Café in the Crypt, which has home-made snacks and delicious cakes.

At the north side of the square is the **National Gallery**, where you can follow one of the amusing family quiz trails or devise your own tour, using the touch-screen computers in the Micro Gallery (for those in a hurry, the quick-visit guide directs you to the 16 greatest masterpieces).

For Sunday lunch, head north, up the Strand to **Smollensky's**, an exceptional restaurant which bends over backwards to accommodate and entertain children. Alternatively, head southwest from Trafalgar Square, through Admiralty Arch into The Mall and St James's Park, a picturesque spot for picnicking and birdwatching by the water.

On the other side of The Mall is the ICA, a good place to introduce children to contemporary art. Beyond the ICA is the (Grand Old) Duke of York's Column, paid for by docking a day's pay from every soldier in the British Army (adding to his unpopularity, which had already given rise to the derisory nursery rhyme).

From St James's Palace you get a less crowded view of the Queen's Guard marching to Buckingham Palace for the **Changing of the Guard** (but you might have missed this by now unless you were up at the crack of dawn, as it takes place at 11.30am daily, alternate days in winter).

If you are with older children interested in the Second World War, your final stop should be the **Cabinet War Rooms**, Churchill's secret underground headquarters.

LISTINGS

CABINET WAR ROOMS (tel: 0171 930 6961): See Museums and Galleries
CAFE IN THE CRYPT (tel: 0171 839 4342): See Eating Out
CHANGING OF THE GUARD: See London by Season
ICA (tel: 0171 930 3647)
LONDON BRASS RUBBING CENTRE (tel: 0171 437 6023): See Workshops
NATIONAL GALLERY (tel: 0171 839 3321): See Museums and Galleries
ST JAMES'S PARK: See The Great Outdoors
SMOLLENSKY'S (tel: 0171 497 2101): See Eating Out

ALEXANDER PALACE TO FINSBURY PARK ☀●

Running alongside the old railway line between the palace and the park is a 4-mile country nature trail with leafy detours through woods. (For a free map and booklet, call 0181 889 6737 or 0181 348 6005.) At both ends of the walk there are bank-holiday funfairs, boating lakes and rainy-day alternatives (ice-skating at Alexandra Palace and ten-pin bowling at Finsbury Park). **Alexandra Palace** is best suited to young children; it has a pitch-and-putt golf course, a children's playground, an animal area and summer-holiday children's events.

Finsbury Park, despite its noisy and congested roads and its litter-strewn pavements, is a fun area for older kids. Behind the tatty and tattered façade lie a wealth of excellent eateries, ranging from Afro-Caribbean, Greek and Cypriot to Mauritian.

Gunners fans come to buy the latest home strip from **Arsenal's World of Sport** shop before visiting the club's museum at Arsenal Stadium, while those after participatory sport head for Rowan's Ten Pin Bowling or a spot of plate-smashing at the Greek restaurant **Apollo**. There is a pretty boating lake in the park and a good children's adventure playground.

LISTINGS

ARSENAL MUSEUM (tel: 0171 704 4000): See Museums and Galleries
ARSENAL WORLD OF SPORT (tel: 0171 272 1000): See Shopping
FRANCES' FRESH FISH SHOP, 99 Stroud Green Road, N4 (tel: 0171 263 9767). Unicorn fish, barracuda, doctor fish, parrot and dameberry are just a few of the dozens of varieties available in this famous fish shop, which imports direct from the Seychelles, Mauritius and the West Indies. For any child doing a project on fish this is a diverting stopping-off point and there is also a vast range of sauces and fishy accoutrements to inspire even the most timid cook.
ROWAN'S TEN PIN BOWLING, 10 Stroud Green Road, N4 (tel: 0181 800 1950). Open-all-hours venue offering ten-pin bowling, snooker and American pool. Fast food is available all day.
COCO TOWN TAKE-AWAY, Restaurant and Wine Bar, 1-3 Stroud Green Road, N4 (tel: 0171 263 7440). Excellent ground-floor take-away counter sells saltfish fritters, Steak in Egusi and barbecued chicken; basement restaurant offers authentic Nigerian cooking.
APOLLO, 134 Seven Sisters Road, N7 (tel: 0171 263 4687): See Eating Out

THE CITY OF LONDON ••

There is a surprising amount to interest and amuse children in the City –
from the Bank of England Museum, where the intriguing story of England's
financial system is vividly displayed, to the Whispering Gallery of St Paul's
Cathedral – and it's all contained in a relatively small space. Those
interested in architecture will enjoy the contrast between the shiny modern
offices and the old banks with their stately pillars and marbled halls. The
following day out is best suited to children over 8 years old.

Start at **St Paul's Cathedral** and climb up to the Whispering Gallery,
then outside to the Stone Gallery for views of the capital, taking plenty of
change to feed the telescopes. The fit and the brave can continue up to the
Golden Gallery for an even better view of the surrounding skyscrapers.

Leaving St Paul's, any philatelists among you should head north to King
Edward Street and the **National Postal Museum** (closed weekends),
which houses one of the world's most important stamp collections as well
as extensive archives and a reference library. Younger children might
enjoy a quick run around **Postman's Park** opposite the National Postal
Museum, which is home to a unique and very sentimental memorial wall of
ceramic tiles, dedicated to ordinary people who died in acts of heroic self-
sacrifice. The youngest of these was 'William Fisher, aged nine, [who] lost
his life on Rodney Road, Walworth, while trying to save his little brother
from being run over, July 12, 1886.'

From here you can either double back on yourself and head down
Cheapside to the **Bank of England Museum** (opposite Bank tube
station) or head north for the **Museum of London**, where you can while
away a good few hours with children of all ages (toddlers particularly
enjoy running up and down the various ramps and levels). If you are with
under-5s you are probably badly in need of a rest and a train home. Stop
for a cup of tea at the café opposite the museum then head home (via the
Barbican Centre, if you have any energy left) from Barbican station.

If you wish to save the Museum of London for another day, head west
from the National Postal Museum, via Fleet Street and Prince Henry's Room
(the oldest domestic house in the City, and one of the few to survive the
Great Fire, it has its original Elizabethan timbered façade, a well-
preserved interior and now exhibits Samuel Pepys memorabilia) to Dr
Johnson's Memorial House. Here in Gough Square is the home in which
Johnson lived and compiled his famous Dictionary, the first definitive and
comprehensive English dictionary (the first edition is on display in the
dining room).

Next stop could be the Public Records Office Museum on Chancery
Lane, which houses the national archive of central-government and legal
documents, the oldest and most valuable of which is the Domesday Book,
the first comprehensive survey of England, ordered by William the
Conqueror in 1085. It is on permanent display along with temporary
displays of other famous documents such as William Shakespeare's will,
Nelson's log book from HMS *Victory* and Guy Fawkes's confession.

Alternatively, have a look at Sir John Soane's Museum. Once the home of
the celebrated designer and architect, it now houses his eclectic collection of
funerary objects and some wonderful paintings in the unusual Picture Room.
Designed to hold enough pictures to fill a gallery nearly four times its size,
the room has walls made up of a series of hinged panels which open out to
reveal pictures hung behind them, thus making the most of the confined
space. From here you can catch the tube home from Holborn station.

LISTINGS

BANK OF ENGLAND MUSEUM, Bartholomew Lane, EC2 (tel: 0171 601 5545).
See Museums and Galleries

DR JOHNSON'S MEMORIAL HOUSE, 17 Gough Square, Fleet Street, EC4
(tel: 0171 353 3745). ☻ Aldwych. Mon-Sat, 11am-5pm.

MUSEUM OF LONDON, 150 London Wall Walk, EC2 (tel: 0171 600 3699).
See Museums and Galleries

NATIONAL POSTAL MUSEUM, King Edward Street, EC1 (tel: 0171 239 5420).
See Museums and Galleries

POSTMAN'S PARK, off King Edward Street, EC1. ☻ St Paul's.
Open daily, 9am-dusk.

PRINCE HENRY'S CHAMBERS, 17 Fleet Street, EC4 (tel: 0171 353 1190).
☻ Aldwych Mon-Sat, 11am-2pm. Free.

PUBLIC RECORDS OFFICE MUSEUM, Chancery Lane, WC2 (tel: 0181 876 3444).
☻ Chancery Lane. Mon-Fri, 9.30am-5pm. Free.

ST PAUL'S CATHEDRAL, Ludgate Hill, EC4 (tel: 0171 248 2705).
See Museums and Galleries

SIR JOHN SOANE'S MUSEUM, 12-14 Lincoln's Inn Fields, WC2
(tel: 0171 430 0175). ☻ Holborn. Tues-Sat, 10am-5pm. Free.

COVENT GARDEN ☺ ☀◐

There are plenty of street performers here, ranging from mime artists, fire-
eaters and jugglers to Chinese string quartets. Climb the narrow stairs to
Benjamin Pollock's wonderful first-floor toyshop (in the central covered
market section between Hobbs and The Body Shop) before visiting the
Theatre Museum or the **London Transport Museum**. Make sure you
leave enough time for the **Cabaret Mechanical Theatre**, a magical
world of automata which will beguile toddlers and teenagers alike.

Around Covent Garden Piazza, you can watch candles being made in
the candle shop and have a go at making some yourself, or have a look
round the doll's house shop.

To the west of the market square is St Paul's, the 'actors' church', under
the portico of which George Bernard Shaw's creation Eliza Doolittle was
selling flowers when she was first seen by Henry Higgins. There's also a
memorial to the English composer Thomas Arne, who wrote 'Rule Britannia'.
There is nearly always a busker or two entertaining the crowds in front of
this magnificent building.

A stroll up Neal Street will take you past several shops with cheap
novelties to amuse kids, to Neal's Yard and the Neal's Yard Clock, created
by cartoonist Tim Hunkin, which fills with water and on the hour tips it via
a system of bells and watering cans onto flowers that appear to grow.

LISTINGS

CABARET MECHANICAL THEATRE: See Museums and Galleries

CANDLE SHOP (tel: 0171 836 9815). See Shopping and Services

COVENT GARDEN (tel: Alternative Arts on 0171 375 0441 for forthcoming
events)

COVENT GARDEN MARKET: See Shopping and Services

THE LONDON DOLL'S HOUSE COMPANY (tel: 0171 240 8681) See Shopping
and Services

LONDON TRANSPORT MUSEUM: See Museums and Galleries

THEATRE MUSEUM: See Museums and Galleries

MUSEUMS AND GALLERIES

Uncover medieval London, find a mummified crocodile, sample cooking from Roman and Tudor times, play Victorian games, examine a dinosaur fossil, or follow the children's foot trail. There is a wealth of treasure – and a little trivia – to entice children into London's many museums and art galleries.

ALEXANDER FLEMING LABORATORY MUSEUM ☀ ◑

ADDRESS St Mary's Hospital, Praed Street, W2
PHONE 0171 725 6528
Small, friendly museum devoted to the father of penicillin on the site of the original, cramped laboratory where in the 1920s Alexander Fleming discovered a Petri dish contaminated with a mysterious mould – an event marking the beginning of a whole new antibiotic age. The role penicillin then played in the fight against bacteria and disease is retraced through meticulously arranged displays and a video. Children over 8 years with an interest in science, or those doing projects on Fleming, will love this museum, and it looks just the way one would imagine an old-fashioned laboratory to look. Toilets and baby-changing area. No wheelchair or buggy access.
TRAVEL ⊖ *Paddington* • **OPEN** *Mon-Thurs, 10am-1pm (or by appointment for parties of 6 or more)* • **PRICES** *Adults £2, children and concs £1*

ARSENAL MUSEUM ☀ ◑

ADDRESS Arsenal Stadium, Avenell Road, N5
PHONE 0171 704 4000
Fans come from miles around to see Charlie George's double medals and Alf Kirchen's kit. You can test your knowledge on the interactive video games and wallow in Arsenal's history while watching the club on film. The dedicated can also take the one-and-a-half-hour stadium tour (£4; book in advance).
TRAVEL ⊖ *Arsenal* • **OPEN** *Fri, 9.30am-4.30pm* • **PRICES** *Adults £2, children £1*

BANK OF ENGLAND MUSEUM ▣ ☀ ◐

ADDRESS Threadneedle Street (entrance Bartholomew Lane), EC2
PHONE 0171 601 5545
A fascinating insight into the 'Old Lady of Threadneedle Street', this well-planned, engaging museum is ideal for children aged 8 or over (they need to have at least some understanding of money). There are interactive videos in the Banking Today gallery, as well as a dealing desk at which you can work the colour-coded keyboard or use the telephone for up-to-the-minute data about markets and exchange rates. There are question-and-answer sessions and group activities for ages 5-10 and ages 11-14

(usually in groups of 12 or more). Shop sells chocolate gold bars, paperweights made from used notes, pens, postcards. Toilets. Some wheelchair and buggy access.

TRAVEL ⊖ *Monument, Bank or Cannon Street* • **OPEN** *Mon-Fri, 10am-5pm, closed weekends (except Lord Mayor's Show)* • **PRICE** *Free*

HMS *BELFAST* ☺ 🄴 🄶

ADDRESS Morgan's Lane, off Tooley Street, SE1
PHONE 0171 407 6434

Moored on the Thames near Tower Bridge, this Second World War cruiser is Europe's largest preserved warship. From the Captain's bridge to the boiler rooms, you see the mess decks, galley, sick bay, gun turrets and punishment cells. Experience a four-minute recreation of surface action – what might have happened if the ship had been hit by a shell and how it would have controlled the danger. See what the sailors ate for breakfast or hunt for the ship's cat. Look out from the bridge and imagine what it would have been like to have navigated by relying only on visual observation, then see the huge guns which have a range of 14 miles (from its present mooring, it could take out Hampton Court Palace). Half-term activities include Battle Damage, a damage-control exercise for children. Confined spaces and stepladders. Toilets for the disabled. Wheelchair access to some parts. Leave buggies on quarter-deck.

TRAVEL ⊖ *London Bridge or Tower Hill; Tower Gate DLR; ferry from Tower Pier* • **OPEN** *Mar-Oct: daily, 10am-6pm; Nov-Feb: daily, 10am-5pm (closed 25 Dec)* • **PRICES** *Adults £4.70, children £2.40 (under-5s free), concs £3.60*

BETHNAL GREEN MUSEUM OF CHILDHOOD ☺ 🄴 ✿ 🄶

ADDRESS Cambridge Heath Road, E2
PHONE 0181 983 5200; recorded information 0181 980 2415

Not surprisingly, this delightful collection of toys, dolls, games and puppets is always overrun with excited kids but there is plenty of space in its large interior to accommodate everyone. Tom liked the 1880 toy butcher's shop, complete with split carcasses glistening with blood, and Alice was intrigued by the complete wardrobe of Henrietta Byron (including a tiny set of stays) in the collection of children's clothes. But it is the doll's houses that are the perennial favourites – 46 of them in two long 'streets', ranging from a 15-room Victorian mansion to little home-made cottages. Not only do they capture everyone's imagination but they are a novel way to learn about social history (check out the flash modernist 1930s model). The temporary exhibitions, including the annual Spirit of Christmas exhibition, are excellent and are usually linked to the popular weekly two-hour Saturday Arts workshops. Also holiday activities. Café, toilets and baby-changing facilities. Some wheelchair and buggy access. Nearby: The Cherry Orchard, 241 Globe Road, E2 (tel: 0181 980 6678); open Mon 11am-3pm, Tues-Fri 11am-7pm. Reasonably priced vegetarian restaurant with cakes, hot and cold salads and baked potatoes.

TRAVEL ⊖ *Bethnal Green or Cambridge Heath rail; bus 8, 309, 106, 253 or D6. Limited parking near Bethnal Green tube station* • **OPEN** *Mon-Thurs and Sat, 10am-5.50pm (including bank holidays); Sun, 2.30-5.50pm (closed Fri, May Day Bank Holiday, 24-26 Dec and 1 Jan). Weekly Saturday Arts workshops (11am and 2pm)* • **PRICE** *Free*

BLACK CULTURAL MUSEUM ⬛ 🌧 ☽

ADDRESS 378 Coldharbour Lane, SW9
PHONE 0171 738 4591
This local museum charts every aspect of the history of black people in Britain. Changing exhibitions.
TRAVEL ⊖ *Brixton* • **OPEN** *Mon-Sat, 10.30am-6pm* • **PRICE** *Free*

BRAMAH TEA AND COFFEE MUSEUM 🌧 ☽

ADDRESS Maguire Street, Butler's Wharf, SE1
PHONE 0171 378 0222
If you have ever questioned why Britain is such a great tea-drinking nation or wondered about the origins of the coffee house, this is the place to come. The collection of over 1,000 teapots and coffee makers alone serves to illustrate the different ways tea and coffee have been made since they were first introduced in the 17th century. Follow the events that culminated in the Boston Tea Party of 1773 and led to the great clipper races of the 1860s (See also **Cutty Sark**). See how Nestlé and General Foods persuaded the public to make coffee by introducing it as an instant powder and bombarding them with television advertising, which has promoted the product almost every night since 1956. Café serves Bramah blends, scones and cakes. Shop sells tea and coffee and related items. Toilets. No baby-changing facilities. Disabled access: phone in advance.
TRAVEL ⊖ *Tower Hill* • **OPEN** *Daily, 10am-6pm* • **PRICES** *Adults £4, under-14s and concs £2.50, family ticket (2+4) £9*

BRITAIN AT WAR THEME MUSEUM 🌧 ☽

ADDRESS Tooley Street, SE1
PHONE 0171 403 3171
Starting with an elevator descent to underground bunkers, where dummies shelter from an air raid, you can relive the drama of everyday life on the home front, experiencing the sounds, smells and visual effects of the London Blitz. In the Blackout, you wander through a London street that has just been hit by a doodlebug. It all gets a bit gory, with a man whose face has been blown off and a woman half-buried beneath a pile of rubble but, needless to say, the kids like those details best. Families or small groups of children can play the Blitz Zone, a game where volunteers are transformed into ARP wardens, complete with gas masks and tin helmets. They then embark on a two-and-a-half-minute race against time to find an unexploded bomb buried in the street rubble, while the sights, sounds and smells of the Blitz rage around them. This is a superb museum for children, making history really come alive, although the noises might frighten toddlers. Toilets (no disabled or baby-changing facilities). Wheelchair access.
TRAVEL ⊖ *London Bridge* • **OPEN** *Apr-Sep: daily, 10am-5.30pm; Oct-Mar: daily, 10am-4.30pm (closed 25-26 Dec)* • **PRICES** *Adults £5.95, under-15s £2.95 (under-3s free), concs £3.95 (disabled in wheelchairs free), family (2+2) £14*

BRITISH MUSEUM ☺ ⬛ 🌧 ◑ ●

ADDRESS Great Russell Street, WC1
PHONE 0171 636 1555; recorded information 0171 580 1788
This vast museum houses the national treasury of art and artefacts from all over the world, all periods and all civilisations, and the 4 million items increase daily with new bequests and recent finds. You cannot possibly do even a quarter of the museum in one visit – to walk through all 94

galleries you would cover nearly 3 miles – but you can always come back. Start with the Ancient Greeks and Romans, and the Egyptians – every aspect of life and death is examined and explained with easy-to-read information cards. The Egyptians are particularly popular, with their mummified fish, falcons and cats as well as humans. The jars of human organs standing next to the mummies, carefully preserved for the afterlife, seem to hold a particular fascination for children. Also popular with kids is the Lindow man (room 35), who was found in a Cheshire peat bog 2,000 years after having been murdered, probably by Druids. Pick up a free Treasure Trail at the information desk. We have done the Big and Little Cats Trail, which covers the Egyptian rooms and shows you how to make a lion-faced pizza when you get home, and the Chinese Animals and Monsters Trail, which takes you round the Joseph E Hotung Gallery. Café and restaurant. Shop and children's shop (room 27, ground floor). Toilets for the disabled and baby-changing facilities. Wheelchair access by prior arrangement. Buggy access (but stairs to each floor).

TRAVEL ⊖ *Holborn, Russell Square or Tottenham Court Road* • **OPEN** *Mon-Sat, 10am-5pm; Sun, noon-6pm (closed Christmas Day, New Year's Day, Good Friday, 1st Mon in May). Café and restaurant close 30 mins earlier* • **PRICE** *Free (charge for some temporary exhibitions)*

BRUCE CASTLE MUSEUM ⊟ ☀ ◑

ADDRESS Lordship Lane, N17
PHONE 0181 808 8772

Excellent local-history museum for those wanting to know more about the area in which they live. Good for children doing projects on the postal system, as there is an important exhibition on the subject. Toilets. No disabled or baby-changing facilities. Wheelchair and buggy access to ground floor only.

TRAVEL ⊖ *Seven Sisters, Wood Green or Tottenham Hale or Bruce Grove rail* • **OPEN** *Wed-Sun, 1-5pm* • **PRICE** *Free*

BRUNEL'S ENGINE HOUSE ☀ ◑

ADDRESS Railway Avenue, Rotherhithe, SE16
PHONE 0171 231 3314 or 0171 252 0059

The engine house contains the sole surviving example of a compound horizontal V, steam pumping engine, built in 1885, as well as the exhibition Brunel's Tunnel and Where It Led. No toilets or baby-changing facilities. Restricted access for wheelchairs and buggies.

TRAVEL ⊖ *Rotherhithe or bus P11, 47 or 188* • **OPEN** *1st Sun of every month, noon-4pm* • **PRICES** *Adults £2, children and concs £1*

BUCKINGHAM PALACE ☀ ◑

PHONE 0171 839 1377

Since 1993 the Queen's official residence has been opened to the public for two months each year, allowing visitors to see the Grand Hall, Throne Room, Green Drawing Room, State Dining Room, Silk Tapestry Room and Music Room. In all, 18 out of the palace's 600 rooms are on show. The children I took were somewhat disappointed. In the Throne Room, rather than a stately throne, they saw two pink chairs marked ER and P. The State Dining Room, with its scarlet and gilt, looks like a palace dining room should; the vaulted Picture Gallery is spectacular, and Nash's Blue Room is breathtaking, but it might be better to allow the sacred portals to live in your offspring's imagination. Most tickets sold on day of entry. (Wheelchair users and those with special needs must register by 1 July; forms available from Royal Collection Enterprises Ltd, St James's Palace, SW1A 1JR, tel: 0171 839 1377 ext 4204.)

TRAVEL ⊖ *St James's Park, Victoria or Green Park* • **OPEN** *Aug-Oct* • **PRICES** *Adults £9.50, under-17s £5, under 4's free, OAPs £7*

CABARET MECHANICAL THEATRE ☺ ♣ ◐

ADDRESS 33-4 The Market, Covent Garden Piazza, WC2
PHONE 0171 379 7961

If you are shopping in Covent Garden, a visit to this delightful museum will revive even the most jaded of spirits. The Cabaret Mechanical Theatre is hugely popular with children of any age – and plenty of office workers can be found idling away their lunch hours in the tiny, cave-like space. All you will hear are the squeals of delight as this bizarre world of moving wood and metal sculptures comes to life. There is a man eating spaghetti all day, a bucking bronco in a bath, a typing tiger, a brightly painted Noah's Ark, flying dodos and a pirate ship. My favourite is the man flogging a dead horse – the only exhibit inside the museum that requires a donation to bring it to life to meet the museum's high costs – the allusion is self-explanatory. While older children are fascinated by the mechanics of the automata, all of which can be seen working, as well as the puns and witty play on words, the museum is particularly suitable for really young children, who can make each of the hundred or so hand-carved, moving models operate by pushing buttons without any help from adults. Little ones are provided with stools to stand on so they can reach the higher exhibits, and there are even some buttons low enough for buggy-bound children to press. Outside you can chance your luck with the mechanical chiropodist, who will tickle your foot for a few pence. No toilets or baby-changing facilities. No wheelchair access.

TRAVEL ⊖ *Covent Garden* • **OPEN** *Mon-Sat, 10am-6.30pm; Sun, 11am-6.30pm (until 7pm in summer; closed Christmas Day)* • **PRICES** *Adults £1.95, children and concs £1.20 (under-5s free), family ticket (2+3) £4.95*

CABINET WAR ROOMS ♣ ◐

ADDRESS Clive Steps, King Charles Street, SW1
PHONE 0171 930 6961

Churchill's secret underground headquarters are a great place for older children or those with some interest in or understanding of the Second World War, but there is no interactivity for younger children. There are 21 rooms, including the Cabinet Room, Transatlantic Telephone Room, Map Room and Prime Minister's Bedroom, all just as they were left at the end of the war. Among the maps, telecommunication equipment and scrambling devices, there are also more personal things belonging to Churchill – the desk from which he made his famous broadcasts and his chamber pot (there were no loos in this cramped bunker). The audio guides are good value for money. Shop. Toilets for the disabled. Baby-changing facilities in men's and women's toilets. Wheelchair access.

TRAVEL ⊖ *St James's Park or Westminster* • **OPEN** *Daily, 10am-6pm (last admission, 5.15pm; closed 24-26 Dec), Apr-Sep, 9.30am-6pm* • **PRICES** *Adults £4.60, children £2.30 (under-5s free, various other concs)*

CUMMING MUSEUM ▣ ❦ ◔

ADDRESS 155-7 Walworth Road, SE17
PHONE 0171 701 1342

Award-winning museum which charts Southwark's history from the Roman settlement to the present day and includes displays on medieval life, Shakespeare's Bankside theatre and the Southwark of Charles Dickens. Often has themed, hands-on exhibits and holiday workshops. No toilets. No wheelchair or buggy access.

TRAVEL ⊖ *Elephant & Castle; bus 12* • **OPEN** *Tues-Sat, 10am-5pm* • **PRICE** *Free*

CUTTY SARK CLIPPER SHIP ☺ ☀ ◔

ADDRESS King William Walk, Greenwich Pier, SE10
PHONE 0181 858 3445

Now standing in dry dock, the *Cutty Sark*, which was launched in 1869, was the fastest, most famous tea clipper ever built and the only one to survive. The history of the *Cutty Sark* is told through pictures and models on the 'tween deck and figure heads are housed in the lower hold. Toilets nearby on Greenwich Pier. Wheelchair access to deck only. In summer you can also visit the **Gypsy Moth IV**. See also Ten Days Out.

TRAVEL *Greenwich or Island Gardens DLR, then walk through foot tunnel* • **OPEN** *Summer: Mon-Sat, 10am-6pm, Sun, noon-6pm; winter: Mon-Sat, 10am-5pm, Sun, noon-5pm* • **PRICES** *Adults £3.50, children and concs £2.50 (under-5s free), family tickets (2+3) £8.50*

DESIGN MUSEUM ❦ ◑

ADDRESS Butler's Wharf, Shad Thames, SE1
PHONE 0171 403 6933

Displays everyday things and explains why and how mass-produced consumer objects, from cars to toothbrushes, work and look as they do. Day-long museum workshops run June-October (included in price of admission). Bookshop and library. Bar, café, toilets (baby-changing facilities in men's and women's toilets). Full wheelchair and buggy access.

TRAVEL ⊖ *Tower Hill or London Bridge; bus 15 or 47* • **OPEN** *Mon-Sun, 11.30am-6pm* • **PRICES** *Adults £5.25, children, OAPs and students £4 (under-5s free) family ticket (2+2)*

DULWICH PICTURE GALLERY ☀ ◔

ADDRESS College Road, SE21
PHONE 0181 693 5254

The oldest art gallery in the country exhibits works by Rembrandt, Gainsborough, Rubens and Murillo. It is rarely crowded and there is a nearby park, making it a good way to introduce quite young children to art. Holiday art workshops. Tea tent in summer. Toilets (no disabled or baby-changing facilities). Buggy and wheelchair access.

TRAVEL *North Dulwich or West Dulwich rail* • **OPEN** *Tues-Fri, 10am-5pm; Sat, 11am-5pm; Sun, 2-5pm but closed Dec 31 1998-May 2000* • **PRICES** *Adults £3.50, children 7-16, disabled, students and OAP £2.50, under-7's free, family ticket (2+3) £10, OAP and disabled free (Tues from 2pm until closing only)*

FAN MUSEUM ❦ ◔

ADDRESS 12 Crooms Hill, SE10
PHONE 0181 305 1441

The only venue in the world devoted entirely to the art of the fan, with over 2,000 fans on display. Demonstrations on the craft of fan-making and restoration. Also changing exhibitions. Shop. Toilets for the disabled; baby-changing surface. Wheelchair access.

TRAVEL *Greenwich rail* • **OPEN** *Tues-Sat, 11am-4.30pm; Sun, noon-4.30pm (winter); Tues-Sat, 11am-5pm; Sun, noon-5pm (summer)* • **PRICES** *Adults £5, children £3 (under-7s and disabled free)*

FLORENCE NIGHTINGALE MUSEUM 🐛 🕐

ADDRESS 2 Lambeth Palace Road, SE1
PHONE 0171 620 0374

Located at St Thomas's Hospital, the museum tells the history of the famous 'Lady with the Lamp', using original objects, audio-visuals, period settings and a life-size reconstruction of a ward scene from the Crimean War. Florence Nightingale lived in a world where women had virtually no influence, yet her achievements were inspirational. She is remembered today not only for her heroic deeds during the Crimean War, but also for her pioneering work over the next twenty years, when she created the modern professions of nursing and midwifery, setting standards of hygiene and good medical practice, and establishing formal training for nurses. The museum is ideal for primary-school children doing projects on the Victorians, as well as for any budding young nurses. Take a picnic to eat overlooking the Thames in Jubilee Gardens or Lambeth Palace Gardens. Shop. Toilets (no baby-changing facilities). Facilities for the disabled. Wheelchair and buggy access.

TRAVEL ⊖ *Westminster or Waterloo* • **OPEN** *Tues-Sun and bank holidays, 10am-4pm* • **PRICES** *Adults £3.50, children, OAPs and students £2.50, family ticket (2+2) £7*

GEFFRYE MUSEUM 🅴 🕐

ADDRESS Kingsland Road, E2
PHONE 0171 739 9893

The new £5.3 million extension, which should be finished by 1999, will double the size of this deservedly popular museum, bringing the interiors up to 1995, giving more space for the museum's innovative programme of workshops and temporary exhibitions, and providing a restaurant. Children love nosing round the rooms, which are decorated in different period styles from the 1600s to 1939 and give a real insight into the way homes looked in the past and the type of people who lived in them. There is a walled herb garden and lots of imaginative holiday and weekend activities for all ages. In addition, there are often summer-evening events, plus music and picnics on the lawns. Café. Shop. Toilets for disabled and baby-changing facilities. Wheelchair access to ground floor only.

TRAVEL ⊖ *Liverpool Street, then bus 242, or Old Street, then bus 243* • **OPEN** *Tues-Sat, 10am-5pm; Sun and bank holidays, 2-5pm (closed Good Friday, Christmas Day and 1 Jan)* • **PRICE** *Free (under-8s must be accompanied by an adult)*

THE GOLDEN HINDE ☺ ☀ 🕐

ADDRESS St Marie Overie Dock, Cathedral Street, SE1
PHONE 0171 403 0123

This full-size reconstruction of Sir Francis Drake's flagship is a real treat for all would-be pirates and distressed damsels. The crew, dressed in Elizabethan costume, will regale visitors with stories of stormy nights sleeping on the hard deck and the cruel punishments given to those sailors who dared to steal food to supplement their meagre rations. Children love having free rein to explore the five cramped levels, from Drake's cabin to the cannon gun deck. Also Living History overnight stays. **NEARBY: Shakespeare's Globe** Theatre.

TRAVEL ⊖ *Monument or London Bridge* • **OPEN** *Phone for opening times. In summer: Tues-Fri, 11am-5pm; Sat, 10am-5pm; Sun, 2-5pm, 2.30-3.30pm free children's entertainment.* • **PRICES** *Adults £2.30, children £1.50, under-4s free, concs £1.90, family ticket (2+4) £6. Children's birthday parties (exclusive use of ship) from £150 for 15 children.*

GRANGE MUSEUM OF COMMUNITY HISTORY ☺ 🄴 ✿ ◐

ADDRESS Neasden Roundabout, Neasden Lane, NW10
PHONE 0181 452 8311

A great place to bring kids for an hour or two to explore the history of Brent. The museum is crammed full of old photos, costumes and the stories of local people's lives from the 1920s to the present day. Try on the old-fashioned hats; imagine having to wear the corsets and suspenders on display; gawp at the ludicrous longjohns; draw your favourite exhibits on the drawing paper provided, or fill in a quiz. Take a picnic to eat in the enclosed garden, where you can search for unusual plants, identify herbs in the Victorian herb garden, or toss pennies in the old well from the original farm. Free activity sheets. Changing and feeding facilities on request. Wheelchair and buggy access to ground floor and garden.

TRAVEL ⊖ *Neasden or bus 316, 112, 182, 245, 297 or 302; by car on North Circular and park on the roundabout* • **OPEN** *Mon-Fri, 11am-5pm; Sat, 10am-5pm (open Sun, 2-5pm, May-Sep only)* • **PRICE** *Free*

GUARDS MUSEUM ◐

ADDRESS Wellington Barracks, Birdcage Walk, SW1
PHONE 0171 414 3271

The story of the Foot Guards is told through a collection of uniforms, weapons and memorabilia spanning 350 years. The **Changing of the Guard** starts from here, so try to time your visit to coincide with this (see London By Season). No toilets.

TRAVEL ⊖ *St James's Park* • **OPEN** *Daily, 10am-4pm (last admission, 3.30pm) but phone ahead because it is closed on ceremonial days* • **PRICES** *Adults £2, children and concs £1, family ticket (2+3) £4*

GUNNERSBURY PARK MUSEUM ☺ 🄴 ✿ ◐

ADDRESS Gunnersbury Park, W3
PHONE 0181 992 1612

Popular local museum where captions to the exhibits have been specially written to appeal to children and there are lots of kids' activities. You can dress up in Victorian sailor suits or pinafores, try on hats, play hopscotch and parlour games, and colour in penny-plane pictures. Imagine yourself a Victorian child as you copy work onto a slate at an old school desk, then become a chimney sweep and climb the replica chimney. The library now houses costumes from Victorian times to the 1930s and the drawing room has a collection of carriages. Regular programme of weekend and holiday workshops. There is a café but if it's fine weather, take a picnic to the park, which has a boating pond, lake, playgrounds, a pitch-and-putt course, an orangery and mock ruins, erected by a next-door neighbour to hide the Rothschild stables. Wheelchair and buggy access.

TRAVEL ⊖ *Acton Town; free on-site parking* • **OPEN** *Apr-Oct: Mon-Fri, 1-5pm, Sat-Sun and bank holidays, 1-6pm; Nov-Mar: daily, 1-4pm; Apr-Oct: Victorian Kitchens, Sat-Sun and bank holidays, 1pm-6pm* • **PRICE** *Free*

GYPSY MOTH ☺ ☀ ◐

ADDRESS King William Walk, SE10

PHONE 0181 858 0786

This is the tiny vessel in which Sir Francis Chichester made the first single-handed voyage around the world in 1966-7 in order to beat the records set by the old sailing clippers. Toilets nearby on Greenwich Pier.

TRAVEL *Greenwich or Maze Hill rail, or Island Gardens DLR then Greenwich foot tunnel* • **OPEN** *Easter-Oct: Mon-Sat, 10am-6pm; Sun, noon-6pm (last admission, 5.30pm)* • **PRICES** *Adults 50p, children 30p*

HORNIMAN MUSEUM AND GARDENS ☺ 🅴 ❀ ◑

ADDRESS 100 London Road, SE23

PHONE 0181 699 1872

Delightful, informal and indispensable anthropological museum with an eclectic collection started by Frederick Horniman, a 19th-century tea merchant who made his fortune as the first man to sell tea in packets, then spent a good deal of it shipping back bizarre and wonderful artefacts gathered on his travels. The dozens of masks, headdresses and Egyptian mummies are always a hit with young children. Our family favourite is the Punch and Judy selection, whose annotations can be read like a story. The Living Waters aquarium has Perspex tanks that reach right down to the ground so even toddlers can eyeball piranha and angel fish. The impressive array of animals in the Natural History section is displayed to illustrate the story of evolution and the history of flight, as well as according to species, offering an invaluable study source for older children. Presided over by a spectacular 100-year-old stuffed Canadian walrus, the glass cases are full of huge elephant skulls, stuffed vultures, an ancient mummified crocodile, ostriches, eagles and, though not for the squeamish, dogs' heads. There are massive scale models of insects and even half a fruit bat and the foot of an orang-utan. In the Music Room children can explore the making, playing and physics of a French horn, and look for an armadillo guitar, a Peruvian whistling pot, nose flutes or musical glasses. Of the 6,000 instruments in the collection, 1,500 have been included in revolutionary hands-on displays, with touch-screen technology and simple graphics showing the history, geography and techniques of the instruments, which can be listened to on headphones. It is easy to spend a whole day here, having lunch in the café or a picnic in the delightful gardens. Some people dislike the old-fashioned glass cases but these are one of our favourite displays, not least because really young children cannot knock anything over; they can also see everything on their own level, and the wide variety on offer never fails to fascinate. There is an ambitious series of weekend and holiday workshops and plenty to see in the beautiful Horniman Gardens, which have nature trails, formal and water gardens, an animal enclosure, and the new Centre for Understanding the Environment, a futuristic building with a living grass and wild-flower roof.

TRAVEL *Forest Hill rail or bus 176, 185, 94, 122, 63; parking in roads off London Rise* • **OPEN** *Mon-Sat, 10.30am-5.30pm; Sun, 2-5.30pm (closed 24-26 Dec)* • **PRICE** *Free*

HOUSE OF DETENTION ❧ ◓

ADDRESS Clerkenwell Close, EC1
PHONE 0171 253 9494

Aided by a dramatisation of a prisoner chatting to you through a personal stereo, you can see the horrors of London's criminal history in these dark, eerie prison cells (a series of passageways and tunnels beneath Kingsway College in Clerkenwell). Toilets. Some wheelchair and buggy access.

TRAVEL ⊖ *Farringdon* • **OPEN** *Daily, 10am-6pm* • **PRICES** *Adults £4, children £2.50, concs £3, family ticket (2+2) £10*

HOUSES OF PARLIAMENT 🄴

ADDRESS Palace of Westminster, Parliament Square, SW1
PHONE 0171 219 4272; House of Lords, 0171 219 3107

All that remains of the medieval royal palace is Westminster Hall, with its impressive hammer-beam roof decorated with massive carved angels. You can look at, but not go into, the Hall at the first of a series of security checks before being ushered through St Stephen's Hall and Central Hall, and into a small room where all visitors have to sign a form promising not to cause a disturbance. From here you go up steep staircases to the Strangers' Gallery above the chamber. You get a guide to the House, explanatory diagrams, notes on procedure and a Points of Order sheet so you can follow what is being debated. Worksheets. Shop. Post Office. Toilets for the disabled. Wheelchair access. To find out more about Parliament and its workings, send a postcard with your name and address to The Parliamentary Education Unit, Room L210, 1 Derby Gate, SW1A 2DG, requesting one of the following publications: The Palace of Westminster, The Work of an MP, Education Sheets on Parliament or The Glorious Revolution 1688-89.

TRAVEL ⊖ *Westminster* • **HOURS** *Opening times of each house vary (phone for details). Victoria Tower Gardens: daily, 7am-dusk. To sit in on Question Times (Mon-Fri, 2.30-3.30pm; Prime Minister's Question Time, Wed, 3-3.30pm), you must obtain a ticket by applying in writing to your local MP. Long queues form (St Stephen's entrance), especially in summer, so either apply for an advance ticket or go after 5pm on the appropriate days to avoid the queues. House of Lords open Mon-Wed, 2.30pm, Thurs, 3.00pm, and some Fri, 11am* • **PRICE** *Free for both houses (when house is sitting)*

IMPERIAL WAR MUSEUM ☺ ❧ ◑

ADDRESS Lambeth Road, SE1
PHONE 0171 416 5000

This museum does a superb job, telling the story of war from Flanders to the Gulf as tastefully as is possible, with thousands of exhibits, from ration books to rockets, all beautifully lit, labelled and mounted. You can see the large exhibits like tanks, planes and submarines from above and below. The Home Front display is popular with children of any age and you can watch archive film and listen to sound-recordings of people's wartime experiences. The Blitz and Trench Experiences are multi-sensory displays where you can see, hear and feel what it was like to be at the front or to be in London during the Blitz. For a small additional charge you can go on a simulated fighter plane and take part in Operation Jericho, flying with the RAF on a secret mission. There is nothing crass or voyeuristic but the museum comes closer than any other to conveying the true horror of war. Special events and workshops during school holidays. Restaurant and picnic area. Shop is well stocked with recruitment posters, books, and 'photo packs' and 'document packs' based on the museum's collection.

Toilet for the disabled, breast-feeding and baby-changing facilities. Wheelchair and buggy access.

TRAVEL ⊖ *Elephant & Castle or Waterloo or Lambeth North* • **OPEN** *Daily, 10am-6pm* • **PRICES** *Adults £5, children £2.50 (under-5s free), concs £4, family ticket (2+4) £13 (free admission 4.30-6pm daily)*

‖EWISH MUSEUM 🍴🕐

ADDRESS Raymond Burton House, 129-31 Albert Street, NW1
PHONE 0171 284 1997

Well-laid-out museum of all things Jewish, with a comprehensive programme of children's events throughout the year, which are free with admission.

TRAVEL ⊖ *Camden or bus 31, 274 or C2* • **OPEN** *Sun-Thurs, 10am-4pm; closed Fri, Sat, Jewish festivals and public holidays* • **PRICES** *Adults £3, children and concs £1.50, family ticket (up to 4 members) £7.50, OAP £2*

‖EW BRIDGE STEAM MUSEUM ☺🍴🌓

ADDRESS Green Dragon Lane, Brentford, Middx
PHONE 0181 568 4757

While children press buttons, pull levers, open and shut doors and operate pumps in the new Water For Life gallery, they might think they are just having fun, but they are actually learning everything there is to know about London's water. From Roman toilets, through the cholera epidemic, the growth of public sanitation and private bathrooms to the massive London ring main, the gallery features interactive displays, working models and intriguing artefacts. Did you know Dick Whittington had a public lavatory built for 64 men and 64 women? Or what the Romans used toilet spoons for? Visitors can see, hear and even smell inside a Victorian sewer – watch out for the rat – or discover how they coped with sanitation in the Middle Ages. Sift into Sewage invites children to put their hands inside gloves which hang in a cesspit and try to discover the hidden object that has dropped in. In the modern section, children can control a robot as it moves down a pipe in order to find hidden messages along the pipe walls. Finally, the Pump It Up section shows just how a pump works and forms a natural link with the steam museum itself, home to the largest collection of steam-powered, water-pumping beam engines in the world.

TRAVEL ⊖ *Gunnersbury then bus Richmond 391, 237 or 267; Kew Bridge rail; car park* • **OPEN** *Daily, 11am-5pm. Engines in steam at weekends and bank holidays* • **PRICES** *Weekends: adults £3.80, children £2, concs £2.50, family ticket (2+3) £10.50; weekdays: adults £2.80, children £1 and concs £1.50, family ticket £7*

‖IVESEY MUSEUM ☺🅴🕐

ADDRESS 682 Old Kent Road, SE15
PHONE 0171 639 5604 (updated info on changing exhibitions)

Excellent small local-history museum with changing, hands-on exhibitions particularly suited to children under 12. Past exhibitions have included Use Your Loaf, focusing on food, with feely boxes, kitchen curiosities, fun food facts and a chance to grind your own corn, and Optical Confusions, an array of optical tricks and illusions. The museum also has a soft corner with cushions, toys and books for under-5s. Picnic area in courtyard. Shop with toys, cards, games and small gifts. Toilets for the disabled. Disabled access to ground floor.

TRAVEL ⊖ *Elephant & Castle, then bus 53 or 177; free parking in side streets* • **OPEN** *Tues-Sat, 10am-5pm* • **PRICE** *Free. All children must be accompanied.*

LONDON CANAL MUSEUM ☀ ☾

ADDRESS 12-13 New Wharf Road, N1

PHONE 0171 713 0836

Beside Regent's Canal on Battlebridge Basin, the museum is a good starting point before a canal walk or boat trip, and children get a real insight into what it would have been like living in the cramped quarters of a barge's cabin – the pull-down bed was for adults, and the children had to sleep upright on hard wooden benches after an 18-hour day leading the horses, steering the boats and helping with the daily chores. Toilets. Baby-changing on request.

TRAVEL ⊖ *King's Cross* • **OPEN** *Tues-Sun, 10am-4.30pm (last admission, 3.45pm; closed Dec 24, 25, 26 but open on bank holiday Mondays)* • **PRICES** *Adults £2.50, children £1.25*

LONDON DUNGEON ☔ ☾

ADDRESS 28-34 Tooley Street, SE1

PHONE 0171 403 0606

Dreamt up by London housewife Annabel Geddes, whose children were disappointed by the lack of 'blood and thunder' to be found at the Tower of London, the vaults under London Bridge Station are full of gruesome scenes of torture, murders and executions. An 11-year-old Canadian friend who stomped unimpressed around the rest of London reading Spiderman comics was really 'wowed', especially when Anne Boleyn is beheaded: 'And she was in the middle of talking – that shut her up!' As well as historic figures such as Boadicea, Richard the Lion-Heart, Anne Boleyn et al., there are exhibits detailing the history of the Great Plague, Newgate Prison and the Norman Conquest. Look out for the hapless St George, who was tied to a cross while his skin was scraped with iron combs, then nailed to a table and poisoned. Refusing to die, he was sawn up by sharp wheels, boiled in a pot of molten lead and finally beheaded. Hanging was always a popular spectator sport but so were the stocks, the pillory, flogging, branding and boiling alive (allowed by law until 1531). Not suitable for young children or those prone to nightmares (best for over-8s). Go Mon-Thurs before noon to avoid crowds. Café. Toilets.

TRAVEL ⊖ *London Bridge* • **OPEN** *Daily, 10am-4.30pm* • **PRICES** *Adults £8.95, children £6.50, students £7.95, concs £6.50. No unaccompanied children.*

LONDON PLANETARIUM ☔ ☾

ADDRESS Marylebone Road, NW1

PHONE 0171 935 6861

Wander through the gallery of astronomy and space travel before taking your reclining seat for the audio-visual star show. As you gaze up into the dome of stars, the usually impossible-to-comprehend habits of the planets, of time and the universe are explained before your very eyes. The images are created by the Zeiss Planetarium Projector, which can recreate the night sky as seen from any place on Earth and at any time through history. No prior knowledge of astronomy necessary. Shows last 30 minutes and start every 40 minutes. Phone for exact times. Wheelchair access (book in advance). See also **Madame Tussaud's**.

TRAVEL ⊖ *Baker Street* • **OPEN** *Daily, 9am-5pm, closed 25 Dec;* • **PRICES** *Adults £5.85, under-16's 3.85, OAP £4.50, under-5's free. Reduced*

*prices if combined with tickets for Madame Tussaud's – but please give
at least 24hr notice: adults £12, under-16's £8.05, OAP £9.25, under-5's
free. Preferably no children under 5, no buggies or pushchairs allowed
but baby carriers are provided, under-16's must be accompanied by
an adult.*

LONDON TOY AND MODEL MUSEUM

ADDRESS 21-3 Craven Hill, W2
PHONE 0171 402 5222 or 0171 706 8000
This wonderful museum started life as two large Victorian houses. These
were joined together to create a labyrinth of small rooms with the best
collection in Europe of dolls, teddies, dinky toys, Meccano, clockwork
planes, model cars and shops, regiments of soldiers, nursery toys and
doll's houses. Despite a £4 million facelift, the museum has managed to
retain its eccentricity, while the themed galleries on five floors mean more
space to display the 7,000 or so toys and models, ranging from an
ancient Roman gladiator doll to a modern toy robot. The collection of
scale models includes a highly decorated, fully functioning 1920s funfair
and the miniature Axford village. There's a wooden Noah's Ark with
90 pairs of animals, and a showcase displaying that most famous of
London bears – Paddington. From the simplest wooden peg dolls to the
child-sized working model of a Cadillac car, presented to the King of
Siam in 1912, the displays are informative and imaginative. A model
railway circles the garden, and there is a also a miniature railway that
trundles children through tunnels and across the pond and is steam
driven at weekends. Under-10s can ride the highly decorated, hand-
cranked vintage fairground carousel for just 10p, before playing the
end-of-pier penny slot machines with their older siblings. Summer events
include a model-boat regatta, a teddy bears' picnic and a train fair.
Not suitable for double buggies.
TRAVEL ⊖ *Lancaster Gate, Bayswater, Queensway or Paddington* • **OPEN**
Daily, 9am-5.30pm (including bank holidays) • **PRICES** *Adults £5.50,
children £3.50 (under-4s free), concs £4.50, family ticket (2+2) £15*

LONDON TRANSPORT MUSEUM ☺ 🌸 ◖

ADDRESS 39 Wellington Street, WC2
PHONE 0171 379 6344; recorded information 0171 836 8557
Designed specifically with children and families in mind, this museum
offers plenty to do and see for even very young children. There are
horse-drawn, motor and trolley buses, trams and underground trains,
illustrating London public transport from 1829 to the present day, housed
within the impressive, ornate, cast-iron arched frame and glazed roof of
the 1870s Flower Market. Sit on an old bus and imagine what it was
like to go to work in days gone by during one of London's famous 'pea-
soupers'. On the horse-drawn buses, look for the 'decency boards', the
panels along the upstairs seats guarding ladies' ankles from the gaze of
uncouth passers-by. Look at the evolution of the driver's cab, from the
introduction of such luxuries as a windscreen, which first appeared in
1927, to the almost fully insulated cab of the NS-type bus. Don't miss the
'Padded Cell', an 1890 carriage that has no windows because designers
thought that passengers might be frightened at seeing the tunnel walls
flashing by so fast, or the ladies-only carriage on the Metropolitan
Underground train. For toddlers and younger children, a new clamber-on

Fun Bus has a soft play area, a see-through engine and lots of noisy buttons to push and pull. There is also plenty of room for toddlers to run around. Fifteen giant, hands-on Kids' Zones mark an easy-to-follow route around the museum. Each zone has a fun activity with buttons to press and levers to pull. Lots of holiday events. Café for snacks and good coffee. Shop (with good selection of transport posters and postcards). Toilets for the disabled. Baby-changing facilities. Allow one hour for under-5s, two or more for over-7s, then head for the **Cabaret Mechanical Theatre** across the Piazza, which both toddlers and teenagers will enjoy.

TRAVEL ⊖ *Covent Garden* • **OPEN** *Sun-Thurs, 10am-6pm; Fri, 11am-6pm (last admission, 5.15pm; closed 24-26 Dec)* • **PRICES** *Adults £4.95, children and concs £2.95 (under-5s free), family ticket (2+2) £12.85, family season ticket £19.95*

MADAME TUSSAUD'S ☺ ❄ ◐

ADDRESS Marylebone Road, NW1
PHONE 0171 935 6861

Madame Tussaud's is the world's most famous waxwork museum, with over 2 million visitors every year. I have never understood the attraction, especially for children who don't know who half the models are meant to be. However, if you fancy rubbing shoulders with figures from the world of politics, history, entertainment and art, this is the place to be (even if they are in wax). Most children like the 'brilliantly gory' Chamber of Horrors. Our 4-year-old enjoyed the sights and sounds of the seaside at the Promenade Pier Café and 'meeting' the Royal Family in all their finery, despite not knowing who anyone was. Jake recognised a rather grey-looking Henry VIII surrounded by his six wives and we all laughed at the 'man in the grey suit' in the selection of modern prime ministers. The Spirit of London dark-ride finale takes you off on a whistle-stop tour of London's history in a 'time taxi', visiting Elizabeth I, Shakespeare, Sir Christopher Wren, Queen Victoria, Charles Dickens, Churchill, Twiggy and Benny Hill. But don't blink. Toilets for the disabled and baby-changing facilities.

TRAVEL ⊖ *Baker Street* • **OPEN** *Daily, 9am-5.30pm, closed 25 Dec* • **PRICES** *Adults £9.75, under-16's £6.90, OAPs £7.45, under-5's free. Under 16's must be accompanied. No buggies or pushchairs allowed but baby carriers are provided. Beat the queue by booking a day ahead and give at least 24hrs notice if a joint ticket including the London Planetarium is required: adults £12, under-16's £8.05, OAP £9.25, under-5's free.*

MUSEUM OF LONDON ☺ ❄ ◑

ADDRESS London Wall, EC2
PHONE 0171 600 3699

See what a Roman room would have looked like; stand in an 18th-century debtor's prison cell and walk through the door of Newgate Prison; wander down a Victorian street and look into the grocer's and pawnbroker's shops. Listen to the sounds of London at war and imagine what it was like to spend the night in an air-raid shelter. Marvel at the ornate splendour of the Lord Mayor of London's 1757 stagecoach. Look out for a pair of leather bikini-style trunks dating from Boadicea's sacking of London in AD 61 and the skulls of some of her decapitated victims. Displays are imaginative and there are numerous changing exhibits from an extensive collection. Among the museum's most treasured possessions are those recovered from the remains of Londinium's Temple of Mithras, built in about AD 250 (the foundations of which have been restored and can be seen on Queen Victoria Street, EC4). The new London Now gallery brings the story of London up to the present day, exploring big issues faced by Londoners since the Second World War. Seasonal events. Workshops. Picnic area on nearby lawns. Restaurant next door (closes 5pm). Shop. Toilet and baby-changing facilities. Wheelchair and buggy access with lift between floors.

TRAVEL ⊖ *St Paul's, Barbican or Moorgate* • **OPEN** *Tues-Sat, 10am-5.50pm (last admission, 5.30pm); Sun and bank holidays, 12pm-5.50pm* • **PRICES** *Adults £4, children £2, family ticket (2+3) £9.50. Admission free after 4.30pm*

MUSEUM OF THE MOVING IMAGE (MOMI) ☺ ♥ ◑

ADDRESS South Bank, SE1
PHONE 0171 928 3535; recorded information 0171 401 2636
Popular hands-on museum which tells the story of moving images from Chinese shadow puppets through to film, television, video, satellite and holograms. Children can be interviewed by a televisual Barry Norman then watch themselves on the TV monitor, make their own cartoons in the animation room; read the News at Ten from Autocue, go for a Hollywood audition, take part in a cowboy film or fly across London like Superman. Actors are on hand to liven up the proceedings and the museum is packed with original film and television clips, posters, memorabilia and costumes. Excellent programme of workshops, events, lectures, films and magic-lantern shows. Café. Shop. Toilet for the disabled and baby-changing facilities. Wheelchair access. Buggy access restricted.

TRAVEL ⊖ *Waterloo or Embankment* • **OPEN** *Daily, 10am-6pm (closed 24-26 Dec)* • **PRICES** *Adults £6.25, children and concs £4.50 (under-5s free), family ticket (2+4) £17*

MUSEUM OF RUGBY ♥ ◑

ADDRESS RFU, Rugby House, 21 Rugby Road, Twickenham, Middx, TW1 1D5
PHONE 0181 892 2000
The history of rugby, with models of players, interactive video footage and a scrum machine. Combined ticket includes a tour of the stadium.

TRAVEL *Twickenham rail* • **OPEN** *Tues-Sat, 10.30am-5pm, Sun 2pm-5pm; Tour times: Tues-Sat, 10.30am, noon, 1.30pm, 3pm, Sun 2pm, 2.30pm* • **PRICES** *Adults £4, children and concs £2.50, family ticket (2+3) £10*

MUSICAL MUSEUM ☺ ♥ ◑

ADDRESS 368 High Street, Brentford, Middx
PHONE 0181 560 8108
One of the world's most comprehensive collections of automatic musical instruments, including musical boxes, pianos and pipe organ systems, which play recordings made famous by musicians early this century. The Regal Cinema Wurlitzer plays a wonderful range of sound-effects from the age of the silent movie, from church bells to horses' hooves. Demonstration tour lasts one-and-a-half hours. Although some say it's best for older children, 3-year-old Sam went with his grandmother and was mesmerised from start to finish.

TRAVEL ⊖ *South Ealing or Gunnersbury, then bus 237 or 267* • **OPEN** *Apr-Oct: Sat-Sun, 2-5pm; July-Aug: Wed, 2-4pm* • **PRICES** *Adults £3.20, children and concs £2.50, family ticket (2+2) £10*

NATIONAL ARMY MUSEUM ☺ 🇪 ❀ ◐

ADDRESS Royal Hospital Road, Chelsea, SW3

PHONE 0171 730 0717

The emphasis is on the lives of individual soldiers, from the first men to join Henry VIII's Yeomen of the Guard (who still guard the Tower of London) to the present-day men and women of action. Particularly popular is the 400-sq-ft model of the Battle of Waterloo, complete with over 70,000 model soldiers, and the skeleton of Napoleon's horse Marengo. Look out for uniforms worn by Sir Winston Churchill and Edward VIII and a lamp used by Florence Nightingale. Read the original handwritten order from Supreme Commander Lord Raglan that sent the Light Brigade to the worst-ever massacre in English cavalry history – of the 607 men who rode into the Valley of Death, 278 never rode out (poetically recounted in Tennyson's famous poem 'The Charge of the Light Brigade'). There is a chilling reconstruction of trench warfare, with a section made from original materials from the battlefield of Ypres. On a lighter note, you can hear soldiers' songs at the push of a button or see if you can find the telescope used by Wellington at the Battle of Waterloo. Summer-holiday activities include model-making, drawing, trails, films. Café. Shop. Baby-changing facilities. Wheelchair and buggy access.

TRAVEL ⊖ *Sloane Square, then bus 11, 19 or 22 to Smith Street* • **OPEN** *Daily, 10am-5.30pm* • **PRICE** *Free*

NATIONAL GALLERY ☺ 🇪 ❀ ◐

ADDRESS Trafalgar Square, WC2

PHONE 0171 839 3321

As you cannot possibly see everything in one go, your first stop should be the high-tech micro-gallery in the Sainsbury Wing, where colour touch-screen computer terminals allow you to explore the collection then plan and print out your own personalised tour. While you are at it, you can also unearth information on individual paintings, artists, techniques and themes from the complete catalogue of over 2,000 pictures. It is worth investing in the *National Gallery Children's Book* and/or the *Twenty Great Paintings* booklet rather than joining a guided tour. Alternatively, simply let younger children roam around – you will be surprised by what they find, the way the see paintings and what they like. Playing I-spy helps to keep younger children amused while the older ones do one of the popular children's quizzes. Those in a hurry should pick up the information sheet, *A Quick Visit to the National Gallery*, which directs you to the 16 greatest masterpieces. The rooms are laid out in broadly chronological order so older children can get a real feel for the development of art through the ages. Budding architects should note the designs for the Sainsbury Wing. Prince Charles decried the early plans as 'a monstrous carbuncle on the face of a much-loved and elegant friend', but the extension that was finally built blends well with the original building while still paying homage to modernity. Wheelchair access (Sainsbury Wing or Orange Street entrance). Buggy access. Baby-changing facilities.

TRAVEL ⊖ *Leicester Square, Charing Cross or Embankment* • **OPEN** *Mon-Sat, 10am-6pm; Sun, 2-6pm* • **PRICE** *Free (charge for special exhibitions)*

NATIONAL MARITIME MUSEUM ☺ ❀ ◑

ADDRESS Romney Road, SE10

PHONE 0181 858 4422

The National Maritime Museum galleries include the Navy Board Models, Captain Cook Explorers, Barge House, Nelson Gallery and 20th-century Sea Power. In the Neptune Hall you can walk round the engine room of the steam tug *Reliant*, go aboard a steam liner, and peak into the luxury steam yatch of biscuit baron Alfred Palmer, where the table is set for tea with china cups and Bourbon biscuits. Watch the lighthouse signal flashing across the hall or ring the bell of the *Mauretania*. Adjust your eyes to the dimly lit barge house, home to Queen Mary's barges, with their richly carved and gilded exteriors and luxurious, deep-red upholstery, and find the uniform Nelson wore at the Battle of Trafalgar. The 20th-century rooms are fascinating – submarines, radar, battleships and lots more. This is a wonderful museum for all things nautical, with the most friendly, helpful and entertaining staff we've come across. Toilets for the disabled and baby-changing facilities. Wheelchair access to ground floor only. Buggy access (steps between floors).

TRAVEL *Greenwich or Maze Hill rail, DLR Bank to Island Gardens or DLR Stratford to Island Gardens, then walk through foot tunnel; boats from Westminster, Charing Cross or Tower Pier to Greenwich Pier* • **OPEN** *Phone for details since much of it will be closed for refurbishment until Easter 1999. The Children's Interactive All-Hands Gallery and the Nelson Exhibition will remain open, Mon-Sun, 10am-5pm* • **PRICES** *Adults £5.00, children £4 (under-5s free), concs £4.00. Tickets also give entry to the* **Old Royal Observatory** *and the* **Queen's House***, and are valid for a second visit within one year of the first.*

NATIONAL PORTRAIT GALLERY ▤ ☂ ◐

ADDRESS St Martin's Place, WC2
PHONE 0171 306 0055
Anyone wishing to put faces to historic figures, especially those doing projects on the Tudors and Stuarts, should come here. There are also plenty of contemporary icons such as Jagger and Geldof for added interest. The top floor is full of Tudor royalty, notorious traitors, po-faced prelates and the only painting of Shakespeare for which he actually sat. Look out for a rather tired-looking Charles II next to a room housing portraits of his many mistresses, including the orange-seller-turned-actress Nell Gwyn. We found it best suited to children age 9 and over. Quiz and worksheets available. No café but there is one next door in the National Gallery. Shop. Toilets for the disabled and baby-changing facilities. Wheelchair access.

TRAVEL ⊖ *Leicester Square or Charing Cross* • **OPEN** *Mon-Sat, 10am-6pm; Sun, 2-6pm* • **PRICE** *Free (charge for special exhibitions)*

NATIONAL POSTAL MUSEUM ▤ ☂ ◐

ADDRESS King Edward Building, King Edward Street, EC1
PHONE 0171 776 3636
Although this cramped museum is not particularly child-friendly, it does have a superb collection of almost every stamp issued anywhere in the world since 1878, as well as letter boxes, franking machines and other post-office artefacts. Stamps are kept in glass drawers that pull out for viewing, and include the Penny Black, the most valuable square inch of paper in the world, and the 1913 Express Delivery of China, the largest stamp ever issued at just under 10 x 3 in. You can begin your own collection in the shop, which also sells model post vans and pillar boxes, postcards and books.

TRAVEL ⊖ *St Paul's* • **OPEN** *Mon-Fri, 9.30am-4.30pm (closed weekends and bank holidays)* • **PRICE** *Free*

NATURAL HISTORY MUSEUM ☺ 🍂 ◑

ADDRESS Cromwell Road, SW7
PHONE 0171 938 9123

The giant skeleton of a Diplodocus marks your arrival in the great Central Hall of this monolithic, neo-Gothic bastion of Victoriana. The fusty, dusty and distinctly dull museum I remember as a child is unrecognisable now. The bones, rocks and fossils are still there but the mahogany-and-glass display cases have given way to moving beasts, press-button gadgets and 3D video magic. You can't go wrong with the ever-popular Dinosaurs gallery, which has some bloodthirsty scenes to enjoy, or Discovering Mammals, a display of the biggest, tallest and most rare animals in the world, including the blue whale. The Creepy Crawlies gallery teems with spiders, insects, centipedes and other arthropods, while Wonders introduces visitors to the museum's more unusual exhibits – a 40-million-year-old spider trapped in amber, an extinct giant ground sloth, and an elephant-bird egg. The Discovery Room (Easter and summer holidays) is aimed at 7- to 11-year-olds but younger children will also have fun here, trying to guess what's inside the 'feely box' by touch alone, or collecting data about their bodies. To visit the wonderful new Earth Galleries, which explore the history of the earth and the forces that have shaped it, leave the main museum and re-enter through the Galleries' own entrance on Exhibition Road. The effect is extraordinary as you travel up the long escalator, which ascends right through the centre of a giant suspended earth. On the slate-lined walls of the very high, very narrow space, above which is a glass-domed atrium, are maps of the night sky and the planets, and portholes illuminating the museum's most prized possessions. Once inside, there is plenty to see and lots of interactivity. The Earthquake Experience, set in a recreated Japanese supermarket, shows you what happened in Kobe in 1995, while Restless Surface explores the action of wind, rain, waves and ice in a very dramatic, hands-on display. Films. Café and restaurant. Shop. Toilets for the disabled. Baby-changing facilities. Wheelchair and buggy access.

TRAVEL ⊖ *South Kensington* • **OPEN** *Mon-Sat, 10am-5.50pm; Sun, 11am-5.50pm* • **PRICES** *Adults £6, under-18s £3 (under-5s free), concs £3.20, family ticket (2+4) £16. Free Mon-Fri, 4.30-5.50pm; Sat-Sun, 5-5.50pm.*

NORTH WOOLWICH OLD STATION MUSEUM ☺ 🇫 ☀ ◔

ADDRESS Pier Road, E16
PHONE 0171 474 7244

Set in the restored North Woolwich Old Station, this delightful little museum charts the history of the Great Eastern Railway and the Docklands rail system. There is a reconstructed Victorian ticket office, display cases with easy-to-understand illustrations showing how steam is made and what it is used for, and lots of model trains. Outside on the station platform (which you can arrive on if you take the train) stands the 'Coffee Pot' engine, the oldest GER engine, as well as old carriages, signs and signalling devices. Engines are put in steam on Easter Sunday and the first Sunday of the month in summer. Young children enjoy arriving by train, as the station is part of the museum. Alternatively, if you are coming by car, try and take the free Woolwich ferry. Gardens opposite in which to picnic if fine. Shop. Very clean loos.

TRAVEL *North Woolwich rail, or Woolwich rail, then ferry or foot tunnel; bus 69, 101 or 473* • **OPEN** *Apr-Sep: Mon-Wed, 1pm-5pm, Fri 2pm-5pm, Sat 10am-5pm, Sun 2pm-5pm; closed after end of school holidays in Sep until April* • **PRICE** *Free*

OLD OPERATING THEATRE MUSEUM AND HERB GARRET ☔☀🌓

ADDRESS 9a St Thomas Street, SE1
PHONE 0171 955 4791

Up a steep, spiral staircase you can see the only surviving example of an early-19th-century operating theatre. The herb garret has a fascinating collection of objects revealing the horrors of medicine before the age of science, displayed alongside pickled bits of 19th-century bodies. In the operating theatre, patients would be propped up on the wooden table so they could watch the surgeon – if they could stand the pain. Ask the kids to shut their eyes and imagine the screams of the unanaesthetised amputees (alcohol was used to dull the patient's senses but surgeons relied on swift techniques – one minute or less for an amputation). Look out for the box of sawdust, which the surgeon would move round with his foot to catch the blood. There is a display devoted to Florence Nightingale (it was upon her advice that the hospital relocated to its present site in Lambeth). Dramatic re-enactment of an operation, with plenty of participation from children (minimum 10 children to be booked in advance). Toilets with area for baby-changing. No wheelchair access.

TRAVEL ⊖ *London Bridge* • **OPEN** *Daily, 10am-4pm; summer events every Thurs noon-1pm, phone for details regarding events* • **PRICES** *Adults £2.90, children £1.50 (under-8s free), concs £2, family ticket £7.25*

OLD ROYAL OBSERVATORY ☀🌓

ADDRESS Greenwich Park, SE10
PHONE 0181 858 4422

Renovations of the home of Greenwich Mean Time and Longitude Zero, Prime Meridian of the World, have transformed the once gloomy, specialist museum into a compelling and accessible display area with hands-on science stations for children, a light-and-sound show in the Telescope Dome (reached via a spiral staircase), exhibits illustrating the story of timekeeping and astronomy, and the apartments of the Astronomers Royal, not to mention the Millennium Clock. There is plenty more for children to enjoy, too, including some of the bizarre solutions offered over the years to the problem of measuring time across the world. One involved several unfortunate dogs, stabbed with the same knife then taken off to points around the world where, it was hoped, they would bark simultaneously voodoo-style when the knife was thrust into the 'powder of sympathy'. On the roof of the observatory is the red Timeball, which rises to the top of its mast and drops at exactly 1pm every day, controlled by the 24-hour clock on the wall below (once used as a time signal for ships on the Thames). Toilets for the disabled and baby-changing facilities.

TRAVEL *Greenwich or Maze Hill rail; DLR Bank to Island Gardens or DLR Stratford to Island Gardens, then walk through foot tunnel; boat from Westminster, Charing Cross or Tower Pier to Greenwich Pier* • **OPEN** *Daily, 10am-5pm, last admission 4.30pm, please call for times of shows; closed 24-26 Dec* • **PRICES** *Adults £5, children £2.50 (under-5s free but not allowed in the Planetarium), concs £4, family ticket (2+3) £15, group reductions for 10 or more. Tickets also give entry to the* **National**

Maritime Museum and the *Queen's House* and are valid for a
second visit within one year of the first.

POLLOCK'S TOY MUSEUM

ADDRESS 1 Scala Street, W1
PHONE 0171 636 3452

This charming museum, named after the toy-theatre designer Benjamin
Pollock, is like a child-size doll's house. Occupying two small, adjoining
18th-century houses connected by narrow winding staircases, the tiny, red-
painted rooms with their low ceilings are jam packed with toys from all
over the world. There are collections of lead miniatures, construction and tin
toys, mechanical toys, 19th-century toy theatres and games. Look out for the
tiny Egyptian clay mouse with moving jaw and tail, which is over 4,000
years old. There are also folk toys from Russia, Poland and the Balkans,
and a fascinating display showing how composition dolls were made, plus
a wonderful collection of doll's houses. Although many of the exhibits are
high up in glass cases, which means small children have to be lifted in the
confined space, toddlers can crawl around at ground level to see the farm
animals and the fort, and they will enjoy spotting the teddy bears that pop
up in unexpected places. Everything is meticulously labelled. There is also a
games room where you can try out old-fashioned board games. The
delightful, well-stocked shop sells all you need to stage your own production
of Aladdin, Cinderella or Ali Baba, and budding directors can buy toy
theatres, scripts, scenery and characters. Small toilet with narrow shelf for
emergency baby-changing. No wheelchair or buggy access.
TRAVEL ⊖ *Goodge Street* • **OPEN** *Mon-Sat, 10am-5.30pm (last admission,
4.30pm)* • **PRICES** *Adults £2.50, under-18s £1*

PUPPET CENTRE TRUST

ADDRESS Battersea Arts Centre, Lavender Hill, SW11
PHONE 0171 228 5335

A registered charity set up to promote and develop the art of puppetry
in Britain, the Puppet Centre provides information and resources covering
all aspects of puppetry, together with training workshops and an exhibition
of puppets from around the world. The exhibition is suitable for all children
with an interest in puppets, while older children who wish to take their
interest further will find the centre invaluable. Café. Book shop. Baby-
changing facilities.
TRAVEL ⊖ *South Kensington, then bus 45A, or Clapham Junction rail* • **OPEN**
Mon-Fri, 2-6pm • **PRICE** *Free*

QUEEN'S HOUSE

ADDRESS Romney Road, SE10
PHONE 0181 858 4422, phone for info regarding latest exhibitions

Originally designed by Inigo Jones in 1616 as a small royal palace for
King James I's wife, Anne of Denmark, and completed in 1635 in accord
with the more lavish tastes of Henrietta Maria, wife of Charles I, the
Queen's House has good collections of silk tapestries and 17th-century
paintings, and some sumptuous furniture. Regular programme of children's
holiday activities and workshops.
TRAVEL *Greenwich or Maze Hill rail; DLR Bank to Island Gardens or DLR
Stratford to Island Gardens, then walk through the foot tunnel; boat from
Westminster, Charing Cross or Tower Pier to Greenwich Pier* • **OPEN** *Daily,
10am-5pm, last admission 4.30pm; closed 24-26 Dec* • **PRICES** *Adults £5,*

*children £2.50 (under-5's free), concs £4, family (2+3) £15, reductions available for groups of 10 or more. Tickets also give entry to the **National Maritime Museum** and the **Old Royal Observatory** and are valid for a second visit within one year of the first. Free after 4.30pm.*

RAGGED SCHOOL MUSEUM ▣ ☂ ◔

ADDRESS 46-50 Copperfield Road, E3
PHONE 0181 980 6405

This canalside warehouse once housed Dr Barnardo's Ragged Day School, set up in the 1880s in response to the terrible living conditions in London's East End. Dress up and attend a typical lesson in the recreated classroom and see how it compares to lessons in today's schools, or join one of the regular art and craft workshops making Victorian sweets or cards. Café. Shop. Toilets (no disabled or baby-changing facilities).

TRAVEL ⊖ *Mile End* • **OPEN** *Wed and Thurs, 10am-5pm; 1st Sun of month, 2-5pm* • **PRICE** *Free (donations appreciated)*

ROCK CIRCUS ☺ ☂ ◔

ADDRESS London Pavilion, Piccadilly Circus, W1
PHONE 0171 734 7203

The rock version of **Madame Tussaud's** is hugely popular with children and teenagers, who can see electronically controlled moving, speaking, singing versions of their favourite pop stars from The Beatles, Elvis and Madonna to the nine-day wonders of the moment. You wander round the wax figures with your own set of headphones, which pick up infra-red signals from whichever display you happen to be looking at, including Prince, Status Quo, Jim Morrison, Bruce Springsteen and Janis Joplin. Snack bar. Shop has souvenirs, books and T-shirts. Toilets for the disabled and baby-changing facilities. Wheelchair and buggy access.

TRAVEL ⊖ *Piccadilly Circus* • **OPEN** *Mon, Wed-Thurs, Sun, 11am-9pm; Tues, 12-9pm; Fri-Sat, 11am-10pm (extended hours in summer)* • **PRICES** *Adults £7.95, under-16's £6 (under-5s free), concs £6.95 (disabled free) group discounts available but bookings must be made by phone.*

ROYAL AIRFORCE MUSEUM ☺ ☀ ◑

ADDRESS Grahame Park Way, NW9
PHONE 0181 205 2266

Standing on the site of the old Hendon Aerodrome, this impressive collection (which includes the Battle of Britain Hall and Bomber Command Hall) features a display of 70 full-size aircraft and will turn any child into a plane spotter. You can walk round and underneath the planes and sit in the cockpits. Have a go in the Tornado flight simulator (preferably before your lunch – it's stomach-churningly realistic) or the Jet Provost trainer. The Aircraft Hall, made from two huge First World War hangars, and the Battle of Britain Hall house original Spitfires, a Vulcan bomber and the Hawker Hurricane, and you can watch a 20-minute video showing the complete story (which will interest older children only). While the young children liked sitting in the cockpit best, the older ones were intrigued by the espionage gear and survival kits on display – maps hidden in boot heels or pens, and a dinghy with sea-water de-salting apparatus and fire-making tablets. In the RAF 2000 section, you can sit in on a fighter-pilot defence briefing in the concrete-reinforced briefing room before taking a simulated flight in the new Eurofighter plane. The museum runs children's workshops and in summer there is a Flight Activities Week, with various demonstrations, model- and kite-flying, computer simulations and so on. Restaurant and shop. Disabled and baby-changing facilities. Wheelchair and buggy access.

TRAVEL ⊖ *Colindale or Mill Hill; bus 303 from Edgware, Mill Hill or Colindale; free on-site parking •* **OPEN** *Daily, 10am-6pm (closed 24-26 Dec, 1 Jan) •* **PRICES** *Adult £6.50, children £3.25 (under-5s free), concs £3.25 (disabled and carer free), family ticket (2+2) £16.60, OAP £4.90*

ST PAUL'S CATHEDRAL 🄴 ♣ 🕒

ADDRESS The Chapter House, St Pauls Churchyard, EC4M 8AD
PHONE 0171 236 4128

However much one might like to think otherwise, the only real interest for children in Christopher Wren's masterpiece is in the dome itself – how high up it they can climb and how quietly they can whisper and still be heard. Catch a quick glimpse of Wren's epitaph in the centre of the floor – 'If you seek his monument, look around you' – before heading for the South Transept stairs leading to a series of galleries in the dome. The first, after 250 steps, is the Whispering Gallery, a balcony running round the inside of the dome, so called because a whisper directed along the wall on one side can be very clearly heard over a hundred feet away on the other. Up another 118 steps is the Stone Gallery, which has a wonderful view of London. Finally you can ascend the last 153 rather narrow steps to the Golden Gallery – but this is not for the faint hearted or very young. Shop. Toilet for the disabled and baby-changing facilities.

TRAVEL ⊖ *St Paul's •* **OPEN** *Daily, 8.30am-4.30pm, last 4pm; galleries, crypt and ambulatory: daily, 8.45am-4.30pm, last admission 4pm •* **PRICES** *Adults: cathedral and crypt £4 plus £3.50 for galleries; children (6-16): £2 plus £1.50 for galleries (under-6s free); concs £3.50 plus £3 for galleries; family ticket (2+2): cathedral and crypt £9 + £7.50 for galleries, each additional child £1; groups of 10 or more: adults, cathedral and crypt £3.50 + £3 for galleries, children)6-16) £1.50 + £1 for galleries, concs £3 + £2.50 for galleries*

SCIENCE FOR LIFE 🄴 ♣ 🕒

ADDRESS Wellcome Trust, The Wellcome Building, 183 Euston Road, NW1
PHONE 0171 611 7211

Award-winning permanent exhibition that makes biomedics accessible, telling the story of life through interactive exhibits, holograms, models, computers and microscopes. The exhibition explores the nature of scientific discovery and the mysteries of the human body. Children can walk through a cell magnified 1 million times, reverse the world with inverting goggles, and see the science behind *Jurassic Park*. Frequent workshops, demonstrations and performances for ages 10 and over.

TRAVEL ⊖ *Euston, Euston Square or Warren Street, Kings Cross or Euston rail •* **OPEN** *Mon-Fri, 9.45am-5pm, and Sat, 9.45am-2pm (closed Bank Holiday Mondays) •* **PRICE** *Free*

SCIENCE MUSEUM ☺ ♣ ●

ADDRESS Exhibition Road, SW7
PHONE 0171 938 8080

This is by far the most popular museum for children in Britain, although the queues to get into the Natural History Museum are usually longer. Five floors of interactive galleries and marvellous displays of scientific invention allow children to explore basic scientific principles as well as grapple with complex ideas in easy-to-understand form. As one of the first 'push-button' museums, it has always kept one step ahead of hands-on, interactive museum technology, standing as a monument to scientific achievement. Head for Launch Pad first before it gets crowded; this is a brilliant children's gallery full of do-it-yourself experiments, exploring basic scientific principles, including how to build a bridge and become a human battery. In Science of Sport you can pit yourself against the pros, play virtual volleyball, challenge a world-class sprinter on an audio-visual racetrack and get an instant dietary analysis. Food for Thought in the Sainsbury Gallery explains to older children the effect of science and technology on what we eat, while younger ones can busy themselves loading up mini-trolleys with packages and tins and ringing up their shopping at the check-out. All children love Flight Lab, where 24 hands-on exhibits demonstrate the principles of flight. Here you can climb up onto the Cessna light aircraft while listening to a pre-flight check on tape, and there is a full-size replica of the *Apollo II* Lunar Lander. Don't miss the basement rooms, which allow children to explore basic scientific principles while playing with water; construction play for ages 3-6 in the museum garden; Things, with experiments for ages 7-11; and The Network, for ages 8-12. Science Nights offer children of 8-11 years and accompanying adults a chance to camp overnight in the museum, take part in workshops, go on spooky torchlit museum tours and listen to late-night storytelling as they snuggle up in sleeping bags (booking on 0171 938 9785). Dramatised gallery talks and family lectures in school holidays. Café. Dillons book store. Toilets and baby-changing facilities. Wheelchair and buggy access.

TRAVEL ⊖ *South Kensington* • **OPEN** *Daily, 10am-6pm* • **PRICES** *Adults £6.50, children and concs £3.50 (under-5s and disabled free). Free admission after 4.30pm. Season ticket available.*

SHAKESPEARE'S GLOBE MUSEUM ☀ ◑

ADDRESS New Globe Walk, Bankside, SE1
PHONE 0171 902 1500

Destroyed by fire in 1613 when, during a performance of *Henry VIII*, the thatch caught fire, the original Globe Theatre premiered many of Shakespeare's plays. It has now been reconstructed as a living, working theatre dedicated to performing Shakespeare's plays in the open air to audiences standing in front of the stage or seated on wooden benches. The multimedia Globe exhibition charts the history of the theatre and shows the 17th-century techniques craftsmen used to rebuild it. You can learn about Elizabethan audiences, bear baiting and the stews, discover the rivalries between the Bankside theatres, and find out what penny stinkards and bodgers were. Guided tours. Toilets. Limited wheelchair and buggy access.

TRAVEL ⊖ *Mansion House or London Bridge* • **OPEN** *May-Sep: daily, 9am-12.15pm; Oct-Apr: daily, 10am-5pm* • **PRICES** *Adults £5, children £3 (under-5s free), concs £4, family ticket (2+3) £14*

TATE GALLERY ☺ **E** ❀ ◑

ADDRESS Millbank, SW1
PHONE 0171 887 8000

You will see mothers with newborns and children of all ages here – the toddlers love the animals depicted in the first four galleries, while older children can spend ages sorting out the images in the cubist paintings or finding their own in the abstract works. Exhibits date from the 16th century to the present day, with the national collection of British art permanently displayed. Stubbs's horses are very popular with young children, as are the Pre-Raphaelites. Look out for Millais's famous *Ophelia* – the model who posed for the picture submerged in a bath caught a chill, which prompted the threat of a lawsuit from her father. The popular roving Art Trolley provides an excellent focus for children, who can choose from a constantly changing range of trails and activities based on the paintings and sculptures on display. Although children must be accompanied, the trolley staff are there to help and the activities are suitable for ages 3-11. Art Trolley: every Sunday and some holidays (book a place on 0171 887 8765). Trails and special children's tours. Coffee shop. Shop with good selection of posters and postcards. Toilets for the disabled and baby-changing facilities. Wheelchair and buggy access.

TRAVEL ⊖ *Pimlico or Vauxhall* • **OPEN** *Daily, 10am-5.50pm (closed 24-26 Dec, 1 Jan, Good Friday, May Bank Holiday)* • **PRICES** *Free (charge for special exhibitions)*

THAMES BARRIER AND VISITORS' CENTRE
☺ ☀ ◑ ●

ADDRESS Unity Way, SE18
PHONE 0181 854 1373

A short boat trip takes you from Greenwich Pier past the least scenic part of the Thames to the enormous shining fins of the Thames Barrier, one of the most remarkable feats of engineering this century, to say nothing of its architectural beauty. The ten movable steel gates, each the height of a five-storey house when raised, form London's flood defence. The Visitors' Centre has a foyer exhibition and multimedia show, telling the story of the construction of the Thames Barrier. Take a picnic and sit on the grassy bank overlooking the Barrier while the kids play in the playground. The Barrier is raised for tests once a month, which you can watch from the bank, but on these days you cannot go through the barrier by boat. Cafeteria, souvenir shop, riverside walk, picnic and outdoor play area, toilets for the disabled and baby-changing facility. Wheelchair and buggy access.

TRAVEL *Charlton rail, bus 177 or 180, or boat from Greenwich or Westminster Piers* • **OPEN** *Visitors' Centre: Mon-Fri, 10am-5pm; Sat-Sun, 10.30am-5.30pm (closed 24-26 Dec)* • **PRICES** *Adults: £3.40, children and concs £2, family ticket (for 5 people) £7.50. Car park £1, refundable on admission to centre*

THEATRE MUSEUM ☺ ❧ ◑

ADDRESS 1e Tavistock Street, WC2
PHONE 0171 836 7891

A permanent exhibition of memorabilia from all major performing arts, illustrated by stage models, costumes, prints and drawings, puppets, props and posters. Popular exhibits include John Lennon's black Beatles suit and the rather more flamboyant costumes worn by Mick Jagger and Elton John. The museum also covers stage magic, from an ancient version of Find the Lady to prop umbrellas and flowers from Tommy Cooper's collection. Look out for the wheelbarrow of the legendary tightrope walker Charles Blondin, with which he crossed Niagara Falls in 1859, and display cases featuring Grimaldi, the father of all clowns, and Phineas T Barnum, showman extraordinaire, who coined the phrase 'There's a sucker born every minute.' Among the many pull-out panels of letters, photographs and engravings in the study room, see if you can find the telegram from Sarah Bernhardt cheerily announcing the forthcoming amputation of her leg! There is usually a make-up artist on hand to give you a hideous scar or bloody flesh wound, together with family workshops related to the current exhibition and led by professional actors. Café. Shop sells a huge range of postcards, posters and other theatrical paraphernalia. Toilets for the disabled and baby-changing facilities. Wheelchair and buggy access.

TRAVEL ⊖ *Covent Garden (entrance on Russell Street)* • **OPEN** *Tues-Sun, 11am-7pm, last admission 6.30pm* • **PRICES** *Adults £3.50, children & concs £2 (under-5s free)*

TOWER BRIDGE EXPERIENCE ☺ ✻ ◖

PHONE 0171 378 1928

In 1952, a double-decker London bus jumped a 3-ft gap over the open bridge after the traffic lights had failed to switch to red: 'I had to keep going,' said the driver, 'otherwise we should have been in the water.' A famous piece of Victoriana, London Bridge is brought to life in an imaginative multimedia permanent exhibition inside the bridge itself. Visitors are transported back in time to the 1890s, from where Harry, the animatronic bridge-worker, takes over, acting as guide and commentator, telling the story of the most famous drawbridge in the world. He doesn't mention that the climax of the tour is a Victorian theatre in the bridge's engine rooms, where the 1894 royal opening is recreated. There is plenty to capture the imagination of toddlers as well as teenagers. While the little ones let off steam along the high-level glass walkways spanning the Thames, older children can identify landmarks with the help of interactive computers. Try to time your visit to catch a 'bridge lift' (when the bridge opens to let large vessels through – for times and dates, call 0171 378 7700). Toilets, buggy and wheelchair access via lifts.

TRAVEL ⊖ *Tower Hill or London Bridge, or bus 15 to Tower Hill* • **OPEN** *Daily, Apr-Oct, 10am-6.30pm, last admission 5.15pm; Nov-Mar 9.30am-6pm, last admission 4.45pm (closed Good Friday, 24-26 Dec, 1 Jan) closed for maintenance until 27 Jan 1999* • **PRICES** *Adults £5.70, children and OAPs £3.90 (under-5s free), family ticket (2+2) £14*

TOWER OF LONDON ☺ ✻ ●

ADDRESS Tower Hill, EC3
PHONE 0171 709 0765

The best time to see the Tower if you live in London is on a clear autumn or winter day when there are no queues and few tourists. Try to fill children in on the background, especially the gory bits, embellishing the facts if you have to, as it does make it more fun for them, whatever their age (phone for a free leaflet in advance – it has some historic information). Older children will enjoy the guided tours given by the wonderfully friendly Yeoman Warders, who regale their audience with tales of executions, murder most foul, assignations, incarcerations, treachery, torture and plots. The family trail is fun for younger children, guiding you to all the best bits, with the added incentive of a prize on completion. There's the Bloody Tower, so called after the two young princes were murdered there at the behest of their uncle Richard III; the White Tower, in which Guy Fawkes was tortured on the rack before finally confessing to his part in the Gunpowder Plot; and Tower Green, where Lady Jane Grey was beheaded at the instigation of Queen Mary I. This last was particularly popular with our friend's daughter Sally, who expressed a wish to become a queen, looking murderously at her sister, who was whinging because she could not buy a raven as a pet. Tower Green is also where the Changing of the Guard takes place daily in summer and on alternate days in winter, usually at 11.30am. Edward I's medieval palace above Traitors' Gate has been restored to show what life was like in the Tower in 1280, with costumed guides on hand to lend authenticity as well as demonstrating 13th-century activities such as quill-making. The Crown Jewels are now housed in a separate Jewel House, round which visitors are conveyed on an airport-style moving walkway. Queues are still long but you could always take heart from the words of the Tower's resident governor, quoted as saying 'We like to think that what we are offering is not a queue but a line of anticipation.' Café and picnic area on wharf nearby. Toilet for the disabled and baby-changing facilities. Wheelchair and buggy access.

TRAVEL ⊖ *Tower Hill or Tower Gateway DLR; Fenchurch Street rail* • **OPEN** *Summer: Mon-Sat 9am-5pm, Sun 10am-5pm; winter (Nov-Feb): Tues-Sat 9.00am-4pm, Sun-Mon 10am-4pm (closed 24-26 Dec, 1 Jan)* • **PRICES** *Adult £9.50, children £6.25 (under-5s free), concs & OAPs £7.15, family ticket (2+3) £28.40. Visitors can buy a ticket from any tube station (except one which is connected to a railway station such as Kings Cross) to avoid ticket queues.*

VICTORIA & ALBERT MUSEUM ☺ ❀ ◐
ADDRESS Cromwell Road, SW7
PHONE 0171 938 8500
Across the road from the Science Museum, this museum of decorative arts and design is, perhaps surprisingly, popular with children. The dress collection provides a fascinating insight into social history. Note the ways the human (usually female) body has been shaped in accordance with changing fashions – the waist narrowed by corsets, the backside emphasised with bustles. Imagine trying to fit through a door wearing side-hoops or trying to sit comfortably in a crinoline. Don't miss Tipoo's Tiger (just outside the restaurant), a painted wooden figure of a tiger mauling a British soldier. Inside it, there is a pipe organ and bellows that produce roars and groans as the tiger attacks. Other things to locate are the Bed of Ware, the largest four-poster bed in England, and the Cabinet of Mirrors, an oval room with mirrored walls and a star-patterned floor. The V&A collects objects mainly for their aesthetic quality – ask your children which objects they would collect and which they would leave out. *The Young Visitor's Guide* is sold in the shop and has suggestions for a treasure trail and nine things to look out for. Free guided tours for children (and accompanying adults) last 45 minutes and are aimed at 6-11 year olds. Holiday workshops. Restaurant (tel: 0171 938 8358). Good café. Shop sells an excellent selection of postcards. Toilets for the disabled and baby-changing facilities. Wheelchair and buggy access.

TRAVEL ⊖ *South Kensington* • **OPEN** *Mon, 12-5.50pm; Tues-Sun, 10am-5.45pm* • **PRICES** *Adults £5, concs £3 (under-18s free; all free after 4.30pm)*

WESTMINSTER ABBEY ◼ ❀ ◕
ADDRESS Broad Sanctuary, SW1
PHONE 0171 222 5152
Westminster Abbey has been the scene of every royal coronation since William the Conqueror was crowned on Christmas Day in 1066. Nine English kings and queens are buried in St Edward's Chapel and there are more in Henry VII's beautiful chapel, including Elizabeth I. Here, too, are buried the bones found hidden in the Tower of London, which are probably those of the princes murdered there at the behest of their uncle,

Richard III. Near the entrance is the Tomb of the Unknown Warrior, which contains the body of an unknown British soldier from the First World War, who died on the battlefields of France. The first person to occupy Poets' Corner was Geoffrey Chaucer, who was buried here in 1400, since when the transept has been filled with tributes to all manner of writers (although many like Shakespeare, Byron, TS Eliot and Tennyson are not actually buried here). Ben Jonson was buried standing up to save space. The thing that caught 10-year-old Shay's lurid imagination was the scraps of skin preserved on the door of St Faith's Chapel – the remains of someone who attempted to rob the abbey in the 1500s and was subsequently flayed to death. The Museum of Abbey Treasures has models of the crown jewels, used for coronation rehearsals, and effigies of famous historic figures, including Elizabeth of York (whose face was used for the queens on traditional playing cards), Charles II and William III and Mary II.

TRAVEL ⊖ *Westminster or St James's Park* • **OPEN** *Mon-Fri, 9.15am-3.45pm; Sat, 9am-1.45pm and 3.45-5pm (closed Sun; services only)* • **PRICES** *Adults £5, students & concs £3, children (11-18) £2, under-11's free, reductions available for student groups who pre-book. Museum open daily 10am-4pm. Best time to go is weekday mornings (and on Wed evenings, 6pm-7.45 pm, when photography is allowed)*

WILLIAM MORRIS GALLERY 🄴 ☼ ◖

ADDRESS Lloyd Park, Forest Road, E17
PHONE 0181 527 3782 or 0181 527 5544 ext 4390
Although it welcomes children of all ages, this museum is best for over-5s, or for toddlers happy to remain in their buggies, as it has open display areas. I went with another adult so we could take turns enjoying the exhibits with the older children while the younger ones ran around in the beautifully landscaped Lloyd Park, which has lots to appeal to toddlers, including an aviary, a moat with black swans, geese and ducks, and play areas. For children 'doing' the Victorians, the gallery is an excellent place to start. The life and work of William Morris – poet, writer, textile and furniture designer, conservationist, socialist, printer and manuscript illuminator – touches on all aspects of the period. Take a picnic. Shop (mail-order service). Wheelchair and buggy access.

TRAVEL ⊖ *Walthamstow Central; bus 34, 97, 123, 215, 257 or 275* • **OPEN** *Tues-Sat, 10am-1pm and 2-5pm; 1st Sun of month, 10am-1pm and 2-5pm* • **PRICE** *Free*

WIMBLEDON WINDMILL MUSEUM ☼ ◗

ADDRESS Windmill Road, SW19
PHONE 0181 947 2825
Lord Baden-Powell, founder of the Boy Scout movement, lived in the mill house; the mill itself was built in 1817.

TRAVEL ⊖ *Wimbledon or East Putney then 93 bus; large car park* • **OPEN** *Easter-31 Oct, Sat-Sun, 2-5pm (then school visits and groups only)* • **PRICES** *Adults £1, children 50p; school visits and group bookings available during the week all year round – call to pre book*

STAGE AND SCREEN

Whether it's drama, comedy, circus, film or music, London is full of entertainment aimed at and suitable for children of all ages. For details, call Kidsline (tel: 0171 222 8070) Monday to Friday 4-6pm during term-time, or Monday to Friday 9am-4pm during school holidays.

CINEMA CLUBS

Kids' clubs offer a bit more for both parents and children than the usual cinema trip. Depending on the venue, there is generally some type of additional entertainment, colouring books, free sweets or competitions, and even seasonal parties. Most charge an annual membership fee.

CLAPHAM PICTURE HOUSE

ADDRESS 76 Venn Street, SW4
PHONE 0171 498 2242/3323
Kids' film club with competitions, prizes and movies. If one child takes out membership, brothers and sisters are entitled to join at reduced rates.
TRAVEL ⊖ *Clapham Common* • **HOURS** *Sat, 11.15am; film, 11.45am* • **PRICES** *Annual membership £3, then members £2.50, non-members £3, accompanying adults £4*

JUNIOR NFT

ADDRESS National Film Theatre, South Bank, SE1
PHONE 0171 928 3232
For monthly programme, send SAE to the Junior NFT.
TRAVEL ⊖ *Waterloo or Embankment* • **WHEN** *Sat-Sun afternoon* • **PRICES** *Children £3.35, accompanying adults £4.75*

PEPSI IMAX 3D CINEMA

ADDRESS Pepsi Trocadero, Piccadilly Circus, W1
PHONE 0171 434 0190; booking hotline 0805 6000505
Children love watching 2D and 3D films on this massive, five-storey-high screen, the first in Britain. There are 11 screenings daily.
TRAVEL ⊖ *Piccadilly Circus* • **HOURS** *Daily, 10am-midnight* • **PRICES** *3D films before 6pm: adults £6.95, children and concs £5.50; 3D films after 6pm: adults £7.95, children and concs £6.50; 2D films: adults £5.95, children and concs £4.50*

PHOENIX ☺

ADDRESS 52 High Road, N2
PHONE 0181 444 6789 or 0171 883 2233
Saturday Kids' Club as well as Saturday-afternoon and holiday programmes.
TRAVEL ⊖ *East Finchley* • **HOURS** *11am; film, 11.45am* • **PRICES** *Children £2, accompanying adults £3*

RIO CINEMA ☺
ADDRESS 107 Kingsland High Street, E8
PHONE 0171 249 2722 or 0171 254 6677
Saturday-morning children's picture club. Children under 5 must be
accompanied by an adult but you can drop off over-5s, do your shopping
and pick them up at the end of the film. Also play-centre matinees.
TRAVEL *Dalston Kingsland rail* • **HOURS** *Sat, 10.30am; film, 11am* • **PRICES**
Children £1.50, accompanying adults £2.50

RITZY CINEMA ☺
ADDRESS Brixton Oval, Coldharbour Lane, SW2
PHONE 0171 737 2121
There are two separate screenings, one for over-7s and one for under-7s.
Free tea and coffee for parents waiting in the bar.
TRAVEL ⊖ *Brixton* • **HOURS** *Sat, 10.30am* • **PRICES** *Children £1,
accompanying adults £2*

SPLODGE CLUB
ADDRESS Barbican Centre, Silk Street, EC2
PHONE 0171 638 8891
Shows a wide range of films and cartoons suitable for 5- to 12-year-olds
every Saturday. Restaurant, cafés, shops in Barbican Centre, car park.
Toilets for the disabled. Wheelchair and buggy access.
TRAVEL ⊖ *Moorgate or Barbican* • **HOURS** *Sat, 2.30pm* • **PRICES** *Annual
membership £4, then children £2.50, accompanying adults £3. Members
can take up to 2 guests.*

STRATFORD PICTURE HOUSE
ADDRESS Gerry Raffles Square, Falway Road, E15
PHONE 0181 522 0043
TRAVEL ⊖ *Stratford* • **HOURS** *Sat, 11am; film, 11.30am* • **PRICES** *Annual
membership £3 for 1 child, £5 for 2 siblings, £10 for 4, then all tickets £2*

THE TICK TOCK CLUB ☺
ADDRESS Croydon Clock Tower, Katherine Street, Croydon, Surrey
PHONE 0181 253 1030
The Tick Tock Club is for ages 3-11, with films in the David Lean Cinema,
live shows in the Braithwaite Hall and craft events in Lifetimes, the Clock
Tower's interactive museum. Also runs a small crèche.
TRAVEL *East Croydon or West Croydon rail* • **HOURS** *Sat, 11am* • **PRICES**
Children £1.50, accompanying adults £2.50

VIRGIN CINEMA HAMMERSMITH
ADDRESS 207 King Street, W6
PHONE 0181 748 2388
Saturday Morning Kids' Club.
TRAVEL ⊖ *Hammersmith* • **HOURS** *Sat, phone for details* • **PRICES** *Tickets
£1.50*

CIRCUS

The big cats and performing seals have gone, and Nelly the Elephant has
said her goodbyes, but the travelling circus is back in vogue and it's
bigger, brighter and better than ever.

BILLY SMART'S BIG TOP ☺

PHONE 01903 721200

Now completely animal-free, Billy Smart's circus has an international cast of performers displaying spectacular skills, including clowns, trapeze artists, flying acrobats and gymnasts. The brand-new, centrally heated big top has no restricted viewing, improved facilities and clean, baby- and child-friendly toilets.

CHINESE STATE CIRCUS ☺

PHONE 01260 297589 or 01260 276627

Rope dancers, foot jugglers, hoop divers and others perform an array of breathtaking skills, and the new three-woman contortion pyramid supporting lit candelabras is mind-boggling. Presentation is fresh, simple and free from slapstick, ringmasters, over-loud music and animals. Traditional Chinese musicians. Highly recommended for even very young children.

GERRY COTTLE'S CIRCUS ☺

PHONE 01932 828888

One of the biggest traditional family circuses in Britain, with an international line-up of street acrobats, jugglers, gymnasts, the illusionist Mina Novikova (whose grandfather was Coco the clown), and six Arabian stallions.

ZIPPO'S CIRCUS ☺

PHONE 01962 868092 or mobile 0836 641277

A delightful animal-free circus with virtuoso balancing acts, death-defying aerial stunts, exhilarating acrobatics, bizarre contortionists and many of the traditional circus tricks and treats. And, of course, the ever-popular clown Martin 'Zippo' Burton himself. Particularly suitable for under-8s.

DANCE

BROADGATE ARENA ⬛ ☀

ADDRESS Liverpool Street and Eldon Street, EC2
PHONE 0171 588 6565

Although this outdoor amphitheatre is used mainly for concerts, it often has visiting dance companies, martial-arts displays, race days and Giant Games which are suitable for children.

TRAVEL ⊖ *Liverpool Street* • **WHEN** *May-Sept*

CHISENHALE DANCE SPACE ☺

ADDRESS 64-84 Chisenhale Road, E3
PHONE 0181 981 6617 or 0171 980 8115

This venue does four shows a year specially designed for young children, with plenty of music, movement and audience participation.

TRAVEL ⊖ *Mile End* • **PRICE** *Tickets £2*

ROYAL FESTIVAL HALL

ADDRESS South Bank, SE1
PHONE 0171 960 4242

The Royal Ballet's annual Christmas ballet – usually *The Nutcracker*, *Cinderella* or *Tales of Beatrix Potter* – opens on Boxing Day and runs for a month.

TRAVEL ⊖ *Waterloo or Embankment* • **PRICES** *Tickets from £15* • **WHEN** *Opens 26 Dec*

THEATRES

Of the many touring theatre companies aimed particularly at children, look out for Pekko's Puppets, Theatre Centre, Tiebreak Theatre, Moving Hands, Kazzum Arts and Shakespeare 4 Kidz at a theatre near you.

ALBANY EMPIRE

ADDRESS Douglas Way, SE8
PHONE 0181 692 0231
As well as many excellent children's shows, the Albany usually does a very up-beat, streetwise panto with the London Bubble (suited to cynical children rather than wide-eyed innocents who still believe in fairies and Tinkerbell).
TRAVEL ⊖ *New Cross or Deptford rail*

BATTERSEA ARTS CENTRE ☺

ADDRESS Old Town Hall, Lavender Hill, SW11
PHONE 0171 223 2223
Excellent range of visiting theatre companies. Also home to the **Puppet Centre Trust** and lots of holiday and term-time courses and workshops.
TRAVEL ⊖ *Clapham South or Clapham Junction rail; bus 45, 77 or 156*
• **HOURS** *Sat, 2.30pm* • **PRICES** *Adults £5, children £4, concs £3*

THE BULL

ADDRESS 68 High Street, Barnet, Herts
PHONE 0181 449 0048
Exciting range of shows from some of the best children's touring theatre companies, plus various holiday programmes.
TRAVEL ⊖ *High Barnet or New Barnet rail* • **WHEN** *Sat afternoon* • **PRICES** *Tickets £3.95 in advance, £4.25 on the door*

CHICKEN SHED THEATRE

ADDRESS Chase Side, N14
PHONE 0181 292 9222
Saturday children's shows morning and afternoon. Also some workshops.
TRAVEL ⊖ *Southgate* • **PRICES** *Tickets from £3*

JACKSONS LANE COMMUNITY CENTRE ☺

ADDRESS 269a Archway Road, N6
PHONE 0181 341 4421
As well as hosting Saturday shows by touring companies, this very child-friendly centre is overflowing with drama, circus and craft workshops, after-school and holiday activities, plus term-time drama clubs.
TRAVEL ⊖ *Highgate* • **HOURS** *Sat, 11am and 2pm* • **PRICE** *Tickets £3*

LAUDERDALE HOUSE ☺

ADDRESS Waterlow Park, Highgate Hill, N6
PHONE 0181 348 8716
A family venue with shows, workshops, fairs and a restaurant (see Eating Out). Theatre shows for under-10s.
TRAVEL ⊖ *Archway* • **HOURS** *Venue open Tues-Fri, 11am-4pm; children's shows: Sat, 10am and 11.30am* • **PRICES** *Adults £3.50, children and concs £2.50*

LITTLE ANGEL MARIONETTE THEATRE ☺

ADDRESS 14 Dagmar Passage, off Cross Street, N1
PHONE 0171 226 1787
Hidden away in Islington, this delightful venue is one of London's few permanent puppet theatres, with Saturday and Sunday shows and holiday programmes. Specialising in dramatisations of traditional and folk tales using all kinds of puppetry, including beautifully carved marionettes, the Little Angel Theatre Company produces its own shows; when it is on tour, the venue hosts visiting puppet companies. Suitable for ages 3 and over (when phoning for details, note minimum age for performance – those under age may be turned away).
TRAVEL ⊖ Angel or Highbury & Islington • **HOURS** Sat, 11am and 3pm • **PRICES** Adults £5.50-£6, under-17s £4.50-£5

LONDON BUBBLE

ADDRESS 5 Elephant Lane, SE16
PHONE 0171 237 4434
A mobile arts company whose summer-tent tour travels through London's parks from May to September each year. In spring they do a community tour. The musicals, plays and promenade performances are of a high standard, and there is a large range of participatory theatre projects for under-5s and under-11s.

LYRIC HAMMERSMITH ☺

ADDRESS King Street, W6
PHONE 0181 741 2311
Hosts touring shows for children aged 3 and over. Café has children's portions.
TRAVEL ⊖ Hammersmith • **HOURS** Sat, 11am and 1pm • **PRICES** Tickets £4 (concs £3.50)

NOMAD PUPPET STUDIO ☺

ADDRESS 37 Upper Tooting Road, SW17
PHONE 0181 767 4005
A triple bill of popular folk and fairytales, specially adapted for this delightful little studio theatre, followed by a sing-along with Jo Jo Scruffy and Friends.
TRAVEL ⊖ Tooting Bec • **HOURS** Sun, 11.30am and 2pm • **PRICES** Adults £3, children £2.50. Also private parties by arrangement.

THE POLKA THEATRE FOR CHILDREN ☺

ADDRESS 240 The Broadway, SW19
PHONE 0181 543 4888/0363
As well as hosting top visiting companies, this splendid, purpose-built complex stages colourful, imaginative, specially commissioned children's plays in the main theatre, geared to different ages (phone to check details and suitability before booking). There are four shows a day in the school holidays and two a day in term-time. The facilities include an adventure theatre for under-5s and free, show-related exhibitions. Very popular Christmas shows. Good term-time clubs, Saturday and holiday workshops and courses. Café and playground. Induction loop for the hard of hearing, with signed performances available on request. Wheelchair access.

TRAVEL ⊖ Wimbledon or South Wimbledon • **HOURS** Box office: Tues-Fri, 9.30am-4.30pm; Sat, 11am-5.30pm • **PRICES** Tickets £4.20-£9

PUPPET THEATRE BARGE ☺

ADDRESS Blomfield Road, W9

PHONE 0171 249 6876 or mobile phone 0836 202745

The Movingstage Marionettes company gives performances throughout
the year on an old Thames barge converted into a delightful miniature
auditorium complete with proscenium arch and raked seating. The venue is
almost as much of a treat for children as the imaginative marionette and
shadow-puppet shows themselves. The barge is moored in Little Venice on
the Regent's Canal from October to May. It sails up the Thames between
June and September, giving performances at various moorings, including
Kingston and Richmond. Not all shows are for children.

TRAVEL ⊖ *Warwick Avenue* • **HOURS** *Times vary; phone for details* • **PRICES**
Adults £5.50, children £5

QUESTORS THEATRE

ADDRESS Mattock Lane, W5

PHONE 0181 567 5184

Family shows at Christmas and drama groups for children throughout the
year.

TRAVEL ⊖ *Ealing Broadway*

SOUTH BANK CENTRE

ADDRESS South Bank, SE1

PHONE 0171 928 8800

Various theatre programmes, clubs and events for children throughout the
year. Phone for full details. The Big Night Out Club is a chance for young
adults (14-21 years old) to dip into dance, music, jazz, theatre, visual arts,
literature and crafts, with workshops, tours and talks at a fraction of the
usual cost. Application forms from the South Bank Centre, Education
Department, Royal Festival Hall, Belvedere Road, SE1 8XX.

TRAVEL ⊖ *Waterloo or Embankment*

TRICYCLE THEATRE ☺

ADDRESS 269 Kilburn High Road, NW6

PHONE 0171 328 1000

Excellent children's shows on offer, as well as after-school and holiday
workshops. Children under 7 must be accompanied by a paying adult.
Wheelchair access and induction loop for deaf children. Children's menu
in the café on Saturdays.

TRAVEL ⊖ *Kilburn* • **HOURS** *Sat, 11.30am and 2pm (extra matinees summer
and Christmas holidays)* • **PRICE** *Tickets £3*

UNICORN THEATRE

ADDRESS Great Newport Street, WC1

PHONE 0171 836 3334

This is London's oldest professional children's theatre with an adventurous
programme of specially commissioned plays and performances as well as
lots of drama-based workshops, special birthday-party workshops and
Performance Specials. Term-time drama clubs for ages 8-12 and 12-16.
Café.

TRAVEL ⊖ *Leicester Square* • **HOURS** *Public performances: Sat, 11am and
2.30pm; Sun and weekdays during school holidays, 2.30pm* • **PRICE**
Tickets £5-£9.50

WAREHOUSE THEATRE

ADDRESS Dingwall Road, Croydon, Surrey
PHONE 0181 680 4060
Strawberry the Clown and Jacito Puppets are regular guests at this popular Saturday spot.
TRAVEL *East Croydon rail* • **HOURS** *Sat, 11am* • **PRICES** *Adults £3, children £2*

WATERMAN'S ARTS CENTRE ☺

ADDRESS 40 High Street, Brentford, Middx
PHONE 0181 568 1176
Children's theatre every Saturday, aimed at 3-10-year-olds. Pantomime season every December.
TRAVEL *Brentford rail* • **HOURS** *Sat, 2.30pm* • **PRICE** *Tickets £4 (concs £3)*

YOUNG VIC

ADDRESS 66 The Cut, SE1
PHONE 0171 928 6363
The Young Vic commissions plays for children that parents and teachers will also enjoy. They usually do at least one play from the GCSE syllabus and excellent Shakespeare productions. Café.
TRAVEL ⊖ *Waterloo*

MUSIC

ARTHUR DAVISON FAMILY CONCERTS

ADDRESS Fairfield Halls, Croydon, Surrey
PHONE 0181 688 9291
Season tickets are available for these orchestral concerts for children. The pieces chosen are short, use a wide range of instruments and are a very good introduction to music. Book well in advance.
TRAVEL *East Croydon rail* • **WHEN** *Seven concerts a year starting in Oct, on Sat, 11am* • **PRICES** *Tickets from £5*

ERNEST READ CONCERTS FOR CHILDREN

ADDRESS Royal Festival Hall, South Bank, SE1
PHONE Ernest Read Music Association 0181 336 0777 or
Royal Festival Hall 0171 960 4242
Ernest Read concerts introduce children to classical music and concert-going in a relaxed but very professional way. There is some audience participation, short 'fidget' breaks between pieces and the magazine-style concert programme is full of cartoons, quizzes and competitions for restless children. Suitable for ages 7-12. Season tickets available.
TRAVEL ⊖ *Waterloo or Embankment* • **WHEN** *Six concerts held between Oct and May* • **PRICES** *Tickets £4.50-£10*

KENWOOD CONCERTS ☺

ADDRESS Kenwood Lakeside, Hampstead Lane, NW3
PHONE English Heritage box office 0171 413 1443 or 0181 348 1286
Parents with very young children can enjoy these classical concerts for free on a grassy area outside the enclosure but English Heritage actively encourage even small children to attend. Fireworks on last night.
TRAVEL ⊖ *Hampstead* • **WHEN** *Jun-Sep* • **PRICES** *phone for prices*

MORLEY COLLEGE FAMILY CONCERTS

ADDRESS 61 Westminster Bridge Road, SE1
PHONE 0171 928 8501
Season of informal music-and-dance concerts for all the family, from classical to pop, folk and electronic.
TRAVEL ⊖ *Westminster* • **WHEN** *Monthly concerts Oct-Jun, Sat 10.30am* • **PRICES** *Adults £2, children £1*

MUSIC FOR YOUTH

ADDRESS 4 Blade Mews, Deodar Road, SW15
PHONE 0181 870 9624
Every November, three public concerts are held at the Royal Albert Hall, featuring over 1,200 young performers chosen from the National Festival of Music for Youth. Phone for details.
TRAVEL ⊖ *High Street Kensington or South Kensington*

YOUTH AND MUSIC

ADDRESS 28 Charing Cross Road, WC2
PHONE 0171 379 6722
A good source of information on music events for young adults, offering a membership scheme and discount tickets for classical, jazz and folk music and some West End musicals. For over-13s only.

PANTOMIMES FAX-BACK

Pantomimes and Christmas shows run from November to February, with the majority in December and January. For information on shows throughout Britain, call one of the following numbers from a fax machine and you will receive fax-back details: London and the Southeast 0660 600592; rest of England 0660 600593; Scotland, Wales and Northern Ireland 0660 600594.

STREET ENTERTAINMENT

Covent Garden is the best place to watch free street entertainment – jugglers, stilt walkers, clowns, fire-eaters and, on summer weekends, Punch and Judy shows. Many of the London parks have free puppet and magic shows at their bandstands in summer. Information from local libraries.

TELEVISION AND RADIO SHOWS

Join the throng of boppers on *Top of the Pops*, watch your favourite television show being made, and see how a radio programme is broadcast, all for free. Children under 14 are not usually admitted unless the show is aimed at a younger age group. Write with SAE and show preference to: BBC Radio and Television, Ticket Unit, Broadcasting House, Portland Place, W1. Older children can go along to Capital Radio's Extravaganza on the May Bank Holiday at Earl's Court. Admission £2. (tel: 0171 766 6000). Try phoning the London TV Centre on 0171 620 1620 to see which shows you can watch being made. Tickets for SMTV Live can be obtained by calling Powerhouse on 0171 287 0045.

BEHIND THE SCENES

If you are nosy by nature, this is the chapter for you. Wherever your interests lie, there are plenty of secrets just waiting to be uncovered... This chapter also includes details of walking and sightseeing tours suitable for children.

CHELSEA FC ☀ ◐

ADDRESS Stamford Bridge, Fulham Road, SW6
PHONE 0171 385 0710
Tours around the home of this Premier League football club take place on Mondays and Fridays. Booking essential.
TRAVEL ⊖ *Fulham Broadway* • **HOURS** *Mon and Fri, 11am* • **PRICES** *Adults £4, children £2*

THE GLASSHOUSE 🗐 ❀ ◐

ADDRESS St Alban's Place, N1
PHONE 0171 359 8162
Visitors can watch four artists at work from the gallery at this glass-blowing workshop. Glass is for sale in the shop and in the gallery.
TRAVEL ⊖ *Angel* • **HOURS** *Tues-Fri, 10am-1pm, 2-5pm*

LONDON PALLADIUM ❀ ◐

ADDRESS Argyll Street, W1
PHONE 0171 494 5091
See the auditorium from Oliver's point of view and stand on the same spot where Duke Ellington, Fats Waller, Louis Armstrong and Bing Crosby struck a chord. The Palladium, now synonymous with British variety, has had a colourful history since its beginnings as a home for touring circuses.
TRAVEL ⊖ *Oxford Circus* • **HOURS** *Mon-Tues and Thurs-Fri, 12.30pm and 4.30pm; Wed and Sat, 12.30pm* • **PRICES** *Adults £4, children £3*

LORD'S CRICKET GROUND ☀ ◐

ADDRESS St John's Wood, NW8
PHONE 0171 266 3825 or 0171 432 1033
Tour the home of world cricket and visit the Long Room, where MCC members watch matches; the art gallery full of famous cricketing faces; and the museum which, among its many treasures, holds the Ashes in a terracotta urn. You can also visit the Real Tennis court, where you can see how tennis was played in Henry VIII's day. Advance booking essential.
TRAVEL ⊖ *St John's Wood; bus 13, 74, 82 or 113; tours start from the Grace Gates* • **HOURS** *Daily, 12pm and 2pm (10am only during test matches, cup finals and preparation days)* • **PRICES** *Adults £5.80, children and OAPs £4.20. Minimum age 7 years.*

ROYAL COURTS OF JUSTICE (THE LAW COURTS) 🗐 ❀

ADDRESS Strand, WC2
PHONE 0171 936 6000

More like a fairytale castle complete with Gothic turrets than the home of English civil law, the Law Courts can be visited when in session. Children must be aged 14 and over and accompanied by an adult.

TRAVEL ⊖ *Temple* • **HOURS** *Mon-Fri, 10am-4.30pm (closed during summer recess in Aug and Sep)*

ROYAL NATIONAL THEATRE 🍂 🌙

ADDRESS South Bank, SE1
PHONE 0171 633 0880
See the prop room, costume room, wardrobe and workshops and discover just how much effort goes into a production. Tours, which last about one hour, must be booked in advance and children must be accompanied.
TRAVEL ⊖ *Waterloo* • **HOURS** *Mon-Sat, 10.15am, 12.45pm and 5.30pm*
• **PRICES** *Adults £3.50, children £3*

ROYAL SHAKESPEARE COMPANY 🍂 🌙

ADDRESS Barbican, EC2
PHONE Backstage Tours on 0171 628 3351
Tours include visits to the scenery, props and costume departments.
TRAVEL ⊖ *Barbican* • **HOURS** *Mon-Sat, 12pm and 5.15pm. Advance booking essential (min. 6 people)* • **PRICES** *Adults £4, under-18s £3*

THEATRE ROYAL 🍂 🌙

ADDRESS Drury Lane, WC2
PHONE 0171 494 5091
If, like Mrs Worthington, you don't want your daughters on the stage, then do not bring them here – voted the most popular of the 'arty' tours by our kids. We went backstage, under the stage, into the Royal Box, the Royal Retiring Room, the Grand Saloon and the boardroom. Booking essential.
TRAVEL ⊖ *Covent Garden* • **HOURS** *Daily (times vary)* • **PRICES** *Adults £4, children £3*

TWICKENHAM RUGBY FOOTBALL GROUND ☀ 🌙

ADDRESS Whitton Road, Twickenham, Middx
PHONE 0181 892 2000
The home of English rugby since 1909 has been impressively developed and enlarged in recent years. You can see the English dressing room and the players' tunnel on the Twickenham Experience Tour before immersing yourself in rugby history and memorabilia in the museum, which has interactive displays and a continuous-highlights film show.
TRAVEL *Twickenham rail* • **HOURS** *Tues-Sun, 10.30am, 12pm, 1.30pm and 3pm* • **PRICES** *Tour and museum combined ticket: adults £4, children £2.50 (less for museum or tour only). Minimum age 7 years.*

WEMBLEY STADIUM ☀ 🌙

ADDRESS Empire Way, Wembley, Middx
PHONE 0181 902 8833
This might be your only chance ever to climb the famous steps and collect the 'Cup', go through the players' tunnel and see the pitch close up, check security at Event Control, see the players' changing rooms, and watch the special cinema presentations of Wembley's greatest moments. Party packages available.

TRAVEL ⊖ *Wembley Park* • **HOURS** *Apr-Sep: daily, 10am-4pm; Oct-Mar: daily, 10am-3pm (except when there is a stadium event)* • **PRICES** *Adults £6.95, children £4.95 (under-5s free), concs £5.75, family ticket (2+2) £21. Duration 90 mins.*

WEST HAM UNITED FC ☀ ◐

ADDRESS Upton Park, Green Street, E13
PHONE 0181 548 2748 ext 210
Wally Morris will take you on a fascinating tour of the home of the Hammers. Booking essential.
TRAVEL ⊖ *Upton Park* • **HOURS** *Daily during school holidays; days and times vary*

WALKING TOURS

CANAL WALKS 🄴 ☀ ◐

PHONE Inland Waterways Association 0171 586 2556
Before the 1830s and the introduction of better roads and a decent railway network, heavy cargo came in and out of London via dozens of canals. The boats were pulled by horses walking along the tow-path and you can still walk for miles in the same way across London. For full details, phone the Inland Waterways Association. The best walks for children are from Camden Town to Little Venice (about $2^{1}/_{2}$ miles) and Little Venice to Willesden Junction (just over 3 miles).
TRAVEL ⊖ *Camden Town or Warwick Avenue* • **HOURS** *Daily, dawn to dusk* • **PRICE** *Free*

DOCKLANDS TOURS ☀ ◐

ADDRESS 60 Bradley House, Aspinden Road, SE16
PHONE 0171 252 0742
See where pirates were executed and where smugglers hid their goods on these guided coach, mini-bus or walking tours of Docklands. The guides are local people and the friendly service is tailored to the individual needs of families or groups. Recommended for children aged 8 and over. Booking essential.
PRICES *90-min walking tour: adults £5.50, children £3.50; prices vary according to tour*

GALLOWS, GARDENS AND GOBLINS ☀ ◐

PHONE 0171 435 4782
Grim tales of gruesome executions at the site of Tyburn Gallows get this exciting walk off to a great start before you are taken in search of the 'real' Peter Pan. Walk ends at the **London Toy and Model Museum** (entrance to which is an optional extra – see Museums and Galleries for details). Children really enjoy this walk, especially the horses stabled on the Bayswater Road. Booking essential.
TRAVEL ⊖ *Marble Arch; meet by Marble Arch itself* • **HOURS** *Phone for dates and times* • **PRICES** *Adults from £4, children from £2*

LONDON SILVER JUBILEE WALKWAY 🄴 ☀

ADDRESS Tourist Information Centre, Victoria Station, SW1
This 10-mile circular walk, created to celebrate the Queen's Silver Jubilee in 1977, is divided into seven sections. Each is guided with markers set in

the pavement and the route is easy to follow. It starts at Leicester Square, then goes through Westminster and over Lambeth Bridge, along the South Bank to Tower Bridge then back through the City, Fleet Street, Holborn and Covent Garden. Each section ends near a tube or rail station so you can choose to do any part of the walk. A leaflet is available from the Tourist Information Centre.

LONDON WALKS ☀ ◓

PHONE 0171 624 3978

London's oldest walking-tour agency organises over forty different walks through London, starting from various tube stations. Walks include The London of Shakespeare and Dickens, Jack the Ripper Haunts, The Beatles Magical Mystery Tour and Sherlock Holmes and the Baker Street Beat. **PRICES** *Adults £4.50, concs £3.50 (under-15s go free when accompanied by an adult). Discount Walkabout Ticket available*

SIGHTSEEING TOURS

ORIGINAL LONDON SIGHTSEEING TOURS ☙ ◓

PHONE 0181 877 1722

There are four routes to choose from on these 90-minute tours round the capital in the now-familiar red and cream double-decker buses, some of which are open-topped.

HOURS *Summer: daily, 9am-7pm; winter: daily, 9.30am-5.30pm* • **PRICES** *Adults £12, children £6. Combined tickets with Madame Tussaud's or the Tower of London also available, giving you express entry to sites.*

STAR SAFARI ☙ ◑

PHONE 01932 854721

Half-day tours of the haunts and homes of London's rich and famous, from Prince Charles and Michael Caine to the Spice Girls and Oasis. Plenty of gossip about who's in town at the time and a full commentary. Phone for dates and times.

WHEN *Apr-Sep* • **PRICES** *Adults £15, children £10*

DIY SIGHTSEEING TOURS ☺ 🄴 ☙

Children of all ages love exploring the capital at the top of a double-decker bus, and this is one of the cheapest ways of taking in the sights. A day's travel pass allows you to get on and off the buses as and when you wish. Try one of the following:

BUS 4 *from Waterloo via Aldwych, Fleet Street, St Paul's, Barbican, Islington and Finsbury Park to Archway.*

BUS 11 *from Liverpool Street Station via Bank, St Paul's, Fleet Street, Aldwych, Strand, Trafalgar Square, Whitehall, Westminster, Victoria, Sloane Square, Chelsea and Fulham to Hammersmith.*

BUS 38 *from Victoria via Hyde Park Corner, Piccadilly, Shaftesbury Avenue, Bloomsbury and Islington to Clapton.*

BIRD'S EYE VIEWS

Up a tower, on top of a hill, in a roof garden, under a hot-air balloon or above a bridge – if you've got a head for heights and want to put London in perspective, then head for a high spot.

ALAN MANN HELICOPTERS

ADDRESS Fairoaks Airport, Chobham, Surrey
PHONE 01276 857471
An expensive but rather amazing view of the capital. Alan Mann Helicopters will take up to four passengers for a spectacular ride, following the route of the River Thames, in a single-engine helicopter. Under-8s must be accompanied by an adult.
PRICES From £450 per hour

ALEXANDRA PALACE

ADDRESS Muswell Hill, N22
PHONE 0181 365 2121
Excellent views over north London, Kent, Surrey, Essex and Hertfordshire from the 250-ft-high terrace round Ally Pally, the Palace at the top of this steep park. See also The Great Outdoors.
TRAVEL ⊖ Wood Green, then bus W3 • **OPEN** Daily, 24 hours • **PRICE** Free

BALLOON SAFARIS

ADDRESS 27 Rosefield Road, Staines, Middx
PHONE 01784 451007
For a real bird's-eye view you can't beat a hot-air balloon flight round London and southeast England, although at £115 per person, you might want to try. The flight takes one hour but the whole experience takes three to four hours, including preparation, recovery by Land Rover and presentation of first-flight certificate. Venues in Kent and Surrey. Not suitable for under-10s.
PRICE £115 per person

GREENWICH HILL

ADDRESS Greenwich Park, Charlton Way, SE3
PHONE 0181 858 2608
Blackheath railway station is the best place to arrive if you want to start at the top of the park, where the view from the Wolfe Monument to Wren's naval college and the Thames as it loops around the Isle of Dogs is breathtaking. From here you can walk down to Greenwich and make your return journey from Greenwich or Maze Hill stations. See also The Great Outdoors.
TRAVEL Greenwich, Blackheath or Maze Hill rail; boat to Greenwich Pier (phone 0171 930 2062/4721 for details) • **HOURS** Daily, 5am to dusk

HAMPSTEAD HEATH ☺ 🄴 ☀

The views from here of London, as painted by Constable, are so wonderful they have special legal protection. Best views are from the high ground by Jack Straw's Castle, Whitestone Pond and **Parliament Hill**.

OPEN *Daily, 24 hours*

KENSINGTON ROOF GARDENS 🄴 ☀ ◐

ADDRESS 99 Kensington High Street (entrance Derry Street), W8
PHONE 0171 937 7994

High above the bustle of Kensington High Street, this secret garden in the sky – 1½ acres of lush greenery with a waterfall, wisteria and roses – is open to the public when not being used for private functions. Two pink flamingos live in the English Woodland pond, and from a small hole in the high brick wall you get a great view of west London.

TRAVEL ⊖ *High Street Kensington* • **HOURS** *Phone for details* • **PRICE** *Free*

THE LONDON BALLOON ☺ ☀ ◐

ADDRESS Spring Gardens, Kennington Lane, SE11
PHONE 0171 587 1111

Big Bob, as it is affectionately known, is the largest tethered passenger helium balloon in the world. As it hovers gracefully over Vauxhall, 400 ft in the air (half the height of Canary Wharf), you can see most of London and, on a clear day, a bit beyond. What is so thrilling about being suspended beneath this giant beach ball containing enough helium to fill 500,000 children's balloons, is that you can see the ground directly below your feet in a way that is not possible from a tall building, a high hill or even an aeroplane. This is no white-knuckle ride, but it is exhilarating nonetheless and, if there is a sudden gust of wind, just a tiny bit nerve-racking. Younger children enjoy the immediacy of seeing the ducks and horses at **Vauxhall City Farm** or following the progress of the trains as they glide in and out of the station. Older children can pick out landmarks – Big Ben, Canary Wharf, MI6, the Oval, Crystal Palace mast – and actually see how the River Thames snakes out its course. The gondola is completely caged and is suitable for all ages, including babies. Phone ahead to check that it is flying.

TRAVEL ⊖ *Vauxhall* • **HOURS** *Daily from 10am to dusk, weather permitting* • **PRICE** *Adults £12, children aged 12 and under £7.50 (under-2s free), family ticket (2+2) £35*

THE MONUMENT ☀ ◐

ADDRESS Monument Street, EC2
PHONE 0171 626 2717

The Monument was commissioned by King Charles II in 1666 to commemorate the Great Fire of London. When it was completed in 1677 it was the world's highest free-standing column at 202 ft, this measurement being equal to the distance due east to the site of the bakery in Pudding Lane where the five-day fire began. Ironically, almost as many lives have been lost due to people jumping from the top of the Monument as during the Great Fire itself. (To prevent further suicides, an iron cage has been erected.) Although the view is slightly obscured by modern high-rise office blocks, it is worth the clamber up the narrow, 311-step spiral staircase, but only if you have older children (don't try carrying toddlers or heavy babies unless you are hyper-fit).

TRAVEL ⊖ *Monument* • **OPEN** *Apr-Sep: Mon-Fri, 9am-5.40pm; Sat-Sun, 2-5.40pm; Oct-Mar: Mon-Sat, 9am-3.30pm (closed Sun)•* **PRICES** *Adults £1.50, children 50p (under-5s free)*

PARLIAMENT HILL ☺ 🄴 ☀

ADDRESS Hampstead Heath, NW3

PHONE 0171 485 4491

At the south end of Hampstead Heath, this kite-flyer's heaven affords a spectacular view right across central London. You can even see Crystal Palace on a clear day. Helpful information notices point out landmarks. Café. Toilets.

TRAVEL ⊖ *Kentish Town, then bus C2, or Hampstead Heath or Gospel Oak rail* • **OPEN** *Daily, 24 hours*

ST PAUL'S CATHEDRAL ☀ 🄲

ADDRESS Ludgate Hill, EC4

PHONE 0171 248 2705

The Golden Gallery was used to spot fires all over the city during the Blitz. This is not a good place to discover that your kids have vertigo, as the 627 steps are usually crowded. From the top you get a glorious view of the Tower, London Pool and the other 50 churches built by Wren. See also Museums and Galleries.

TRAVEL ⊖ *St Paul's* • **HOURS** *Daily, 7am-6pm; galleries, crypt and ambulatory: Mon-Fri, 10am-4.15pm, and Sat, 11am-4.15pm* • **PRICES** *Adults: cathedral and crypt £4 plus £1.50 for galleries, children £2 plus £1.50 (under-6s free), concs £3 plus £3.50*

TOWER BRIDGE ☺ 🕷 🄲

PHONE 0171 407 0922

There are stunning views over London and up and down the Thames from the high, glazed walkways, reached by lift, which kids can run along safely. The interactive computers tell you all you want to know about all you can see, and the museum and displays are good value for money. (See Museums and Galleries.)

TRAVEL ⊖ *Tower Hill or London Bridge, or bus 15 to Tower Hill* • **OPEN** *Daily in summer, 10am-6.15pm; winter to 5.15pm (closed Good Friday, 24-26 Dec, 1 Jan; last tickets sold 1 hour before closing)* • **PRICES** *Adults £5.70, children and OAPs £3.90 (under-5s free), family ticket (2+2) £14*

WESTMINSTER CATHEDRAL 🄴 🄲

ADDRESS Victoria Street, SW1

PHONE 0171 798 9055

The 280-ft-high viewing platform of St Edward's Tower can be reached by lift. From the top there is a splendid view of Westminster and the Thames, and you can even see into the gardens of Buckingham Palace. Much of the West End is obscured by modern office blocks but the views south over the Thames and west towards Kensington are impressive.

TRAVEL ⊖ *St James's Park or Victoria* • **HOURS** *Daily, 7am-8pm (lift open 9am-5pm; times vary in winter)* • **PRICES** *Adults £2, children and concs £1, family ticket £5*

THE GREAT OUTDOORS

From the wild expanses of Richmond Park to the ordered formality of St James's, from royal hunting grounds to common grazing land, there are literally hundreds of parks in London. There is also a surprising amount of heath land, nature reserves and woodland where kids can discover Roman remains and ancient burial sites and follow nature trails.

Most parks have sports facilities, playgrounds and special children's events, especially in the summer. For information on events in the Royal Parks, phone 0171 298 2000 or send an SAE (A5) to Old Police House, Hyde Park, London W2 2UH, asking for a copy of *Summer Entertainment Programmes*.

PARKS

ALEXANDRA PARK ☺ 🅴 ☀

ADDRESS Muswell Hill, N22
PHONE 0181 365 2121
The glorious setting for Alexandra Palace, this large, steep park with stunning views over London was the scene of Britain's first television transmission in 1936. There are children's activities daily from June to September and a popular free fireworks display around 5 November. The playground is well equipped and the sandpits clean, and there is a large boating lake with a small area for younger children to boat in safety on their own. There is also a café, a pitch-and-putt golf course, a small animal sanctuary and a dry ski slope. If it starts to rain you can take shelter in the ice rink. See also Ten Days Out and Bird's-eye Views.
TRAVEL ⊖ *Wood Green, then bus W3* • **OPEN** *Daily, 24 hours*

AVERY HILL PARK ☺ 🅴 ☀

ADDRESS Bexley Road, SE9
PHONE 0181 850 2666
The Winter Garden is full of tropical and sub-tropical Asian and Australasian plants to delight budding botanists. Tennis courts. Wonderful Victorian greenhouses. Small playground.
TRAVEL *New Eltham rail* • **HOURS** *Park: Mon-Sun, 7am-9pm (or dusk). Greenhouses: Mon-Thurs, 1-4pm; Fri, 1-3pm; Sat-Sun, 10am-6.30pm (to 4pm in winter)*

BATTERSEA PARK ☺ 🅴 ☀

ADDRESS Albert Bridge Road, SW11
PHONE 0181 871 7530/1; adventure playground 0181 871 7539
This very pretty, extremely well-equipped riverside park is famous for its Festival Gardens, Grand Vista fountains, the London Peace Pagoda and the annual Easter Parade. There is an exceptionally good free adventure playground for 5- to 15-year-olds, with helpers on hand at weekends, after school and during school holidays. The boating lake in the southeast corner is by far the best and most reasonably priced in London. There is

a garden for the disabled and excellent sporting facilities. There are also theatre shows and pony rides for kids in summer. The zoo has meerkats, pygmy goats and a pot-bellied pig as well as an aviary with flamingos, and a new reptiles-and-amphibians house. There is a café at the lakeside and toilets. The One O'clock Club is friendly and the dog-free play area has lots of equipment. The Easter Sunday Parade, with its exuberant, colourful floats, goes around the park and usually starts at 3pm.

TRAVEL ⊖ *Sloane Square or Battersea Park or Queenstown Road rail; bus 44, 137* • **HOURS** *Park: daily, dawn to dusk. Boating lake: summer weekends only, noon-7pm; daily during summer holidays. Zoo: Easter-Oct, daily, 10am-5pm; winter, Sat-Sun only, 11am-3pm* • **PRICES** *Zoo: adults £1.20, children 60p (under-2s free)*

BISHOP'S PARK ☺ 🄴 ☀

ADDRESS Bishop's Park Road, SW6

Paddling pool, children's small lake with nine two-child pedal boats (under-12s only; free). One O'clock Club, Rainbow Playhouse, sandpit. Access to Fulham Palace Gardens for picnics.

TRAVEL ⊖ *Putney Bridge* • **HOURS** *Park: 8am-10pm. Paddling pool: daily, noon-5pm, if staff available* • **PRICE** *Paddling pool: Free*

BLACKHEATH ☺ 🄴 ☀

PHONE 0181 854 8888

The start of the London Marathon held every spring, Blackheath is a large open common which is popular with kite-flyers (annual conventions held here on Easter Bank Holiday Monday and in June). Funfairs here on most bank holidays and at Easter. Model-boat sailing on Prince of Wales Pond.

TRAVEL *Blackheath rail* • **OPEN** *Daily, 24 hours*

BUSHY PARK ☺ 🄴 ☀

ADDRESS Hampton Court Road, Hampton, Middx
PHONE 0181 979 1586

Across the road from **Hampton Court Palace**, Bushy Park has two large ponds where fishing is allowed, dozens of swans (on Heron Pond) and the most accessible herd of red deer in London (usually congregate between Cobblers Walk and Leg o' Mutton Pond). There is children's entertainment throughout the summer.

TRAVEL *Hampton Court rail; car park near Diana Fountain* • **HOURS** *Daily, 24 hours for pedestrians, 7am-midnight for cars*

CHELSEA PHYSIC GARDEN ☀ ◐

ADDRESS Royal Hospital Road (Swan Walk), SW3
PHONE 0171 352 5646

Europe's oldest botanical gardens is, despite its formal appearance, very welcoming to children, for whom there are special summer events.

TRAVEL ⊖ *Sloane Square, then bus 11, 19, 22, 319* • **OPEN** *Apr 25-Oct, Sun 2-6pm, Wed noon-5pm* • **PRICES** *Adults £3.50, children and concs £1.80*

CLAPHAM COMMON 🄴 ☀

ADDRESS Clapham Common West Side (top of Broomwood Road), SW4
PHONE 0171 926 0105

The common has two dog-free playgrounds, both with rubber matting. Windmill Drive is an enclosed area with slides, swings, seesaw and sandpit, with public toilets and a pub nearby. It gets busy in summer, but the One O'clock Club held here Monday to Thursday is a good place to make friends. There is a café near the bandstand with a dog-free picnic area nearby. There are also tennis courts, a bowling green and another café near the Nightingale Road end of West Side. There is a smaller playground near Grandison Road and a good paddling pool opposite The Pavement. The Long Pond has model-boat yachting regattas during the summer.

TRAVEL ⊖ *Clapham Common* • **OPEN** *Daily, 24 hours*

CLISSOLD PARK ☺ 🄴 ☀

ADDRESS Green Lanes, N16

Two lakes, a large, well-furnished playground, a butterfly tunnel, deer, swans, chickens and goats. Large, well-maintained paddling pool and plenty of dog-free zones. The café is in a Grade-II listed building and is very popular with families. The cakes are delicious, the coffee good, the vegetarian food inexpensive and the Indian ice-cream excellent. Very friendly One O'clock Club.

TRAVEL *Stoke Newington rail* • **OPEN** *Daily, dawn to dusk*

CORAM FIELDS CHILDREN'S PLAYGROUND ☺ 🄴 ☀

ADDRESS 93 Guildford Street, WC1

PHONE 0171 837 6138

A shady, 7-acre playground with paddling pool, play equipment, sports area, pets corner and duck pond. Adults and over-16s are not admitted unless accompanied by a child.

TRAVEL ⊖ *Russell Square* • **HOURS** *Daily, 9am-8pm or dusk* • **PRICE** *Free*

CRYSTAL PALACE PARK ☺ 🄴 ☀

ADDRESS Thicket Road, SE20 and Crystal Palace Park Road, SE26

PHONE 0181 778 7148; Crystal Palace Eventsline 0181 778 9496

This is one of the best family parks in London. See Ten Days Out for full details.

TRAVEL *Crystal Palace rail* • **HOURS** *Daily, 7.30am to 30 mins before dusk* • **PRICE** *Farm: adults £1.10, children 55p (under-3s free), family ticket (2+2) £2.75. Land train: adults £1, children 60p*

DULWICH PARK ☺ 🄴 ☀

ADDRESS College Road, SE21

PHONE 0181 693 5737

Set close to the well-preserved Dulwich Village and to the Dulwich Picture Gallery. Small but well-equipped children's playground, tennis courts, small lake with boats for hire during summer, and a friendly café, serving breakfasts, lunches and teas at reasonable prices. Also sand horse track (riding lessons available locally). Speed-controlled road running round park makes a good place for cycling, roller skating and so on. For a good day out, have a picnic in the park combined with a visit to the gallery; alternatively, take a walk in the park after a big expensive lunch at the best restaurant in Dulwich, Belair House (tel: 0181 299 9788). You can walk from here up to Dulwich Woods (P4 bus, or North Dulwich or West Dulwich rail).

TRAVEL *North Dulwich rail* • **OPEN** *Summer: daily, 8am-9pm; winter: daily, 8am-4.30pm*

FINSBURY PARK ☺ 🄴 ☀

ADDRESS Seven Sisters Road, N4
PHONE 0171 263 5001

The park has a running track, bowls, tennis, a children's playground, summer boating and bank-holiday funfairs. The Parkland Walk, a beautiful rural corridor linking Alexandra Palace and Finsbury Park, follows the old railway line on a 4-mile nature trail with detours through Queen's and **Highgate Wood** (phone 0181 348 6005 for free booklet and map). Also a two-hour orienteering trail (maps £1 at athletics track). If it rains, head for Rowan's Ten Pin Bowling Centre, 10 Stroud Green Road, N4 (tel: 0181 800 1950).

TRAVEL ⊖ *Finsbury Park* • **HOURS** *Daily, 6am to dusk*

GREEN PARK 🄴 ☀

ADDRESS Piccadilly, W1 and The Mall, SW1
PHONE 0171 930 1793

Popular with 18th-century duellists, Green Park is now simply that – a green expanse with no water, no statues and no facilities. But it is pretty in spring when the daffodils are out.

TRAVEL ⊖ *Green Park* • **OPEN** *Daily, dawn to dusk*

GREENWICH PARK ☺ 🄴 ☀

ADDRESS Charlton Way, SE3
PHONE 0181 858 2608

This is my favourite park for its avenues lined with chestnut trees, its view across the Thames from the Wolfe Monument, its beautiful flower gardens and its ancient oaks. At the top of the park near the duck pond and inside the dog-free zone is a deer enclosure kept in memory of royal hunts. Here you can see the Accurist Millennium Countdown Clock, which is counting down the last days to the new millennium. It is a good place to set your watches as it is accurate to the nearest millionth of a second and sits on the Prime Meridian Line. The **Old Royal Observatory** is worth a visit, and if you are here at lunchtime you can watch the famous Greenwich Timeball on the roof, which is raised and dropped at 1pm. The cafeteria opposite has good food but expect to pay tourist prices for ice-creams at the kiosks. There is a bandstand with concerts in the summer and, at the bottom of the hill, a tiny boating pond and a good playground with sandpit (closes earlier than park), grassy dog-free slopes and picnic tables. See Ten Days Out for full details of Greenwich.

TRAVEL *Greenwich, Blackheath or Maze Hill rail; bus 177, 180 or 286; boat to Greenwich Pier from Westminster Pier (river-boat information, tel: 0171 930 2062/4721)* • **OPEN** *Summer: daily, dawn to dusk; winter: daily, 7am-6pm*

GUNNERSBURY PARK ☺ 🄴 ☀

ADDRESS Popes Lane, W3

You will find two playgrounds, a boating lake, miniature golf, a fishing lake and a café in this park. The house is a local- history museum (see Museums and Galleries) open every afternoon (summer 1-6pm, winter 1-4pm).

TRAVEL ⊖ *Chiswick Park* • **OPEN** *Daily, dawn to dusk*

HAMPSTEAD HEATH ☺ 🄴 ☀

PHONE Parliament Hill 0171 485 4491; Golders Hill 0181 455 5183

Once the stamping ground of poets Keats and Shelley, London's most natural park has 800 acres of rolling hills and fields, so buy a local map to avoid getting lost. There's a marvellous view of London from Parliament Hill (near South End Green at the south end of the park), so named after the 1605 Gunpowder plotter Guy Fawkes, whose accomplices planned to light fires here to signal that parliament had been successfully blown up (which, of course, it was not). Constable painted his famous view of the city from this spot, which is now popular for kite-flying. Nearby there is a play park, paddling pool, Olympic track, orienteering, cricket, football, rugby, rounders, and a One O'clock Club. At the north end of the park by the lake, near **Kenwood House**, there are open-air concerts on Saturday evenings in summer, some with fireworks (June to September; tel: 0171 413 1443). Funfairs are held at Easter and on May and August bank holidays at the upper and lower ends of the heath, and there are free brass-band and jazz concerts and children's shows from the bandstands at Golders Hill and Parliament Hill throughout the summer. There is also a delightful café, the Golders Hill Park Cafeteria (tel: 0181 455 8010), run by an Italian family. Children (and adults) can swim in Parliament Hill Lido (tel: 0171 485 3873; ⊖ Gospel Oak) from May to late September. There are toilets, and a fishing pond for the disabled.

TRAVEL ⊖ Belsize Park or Hampstead; Gospel Oak or Hampstead rail • **OPEN** Daily, 24 hours

HIGHBURY FIELDS ☺ 🄴 ☀

ADDRESS Highbury Crescent, N5

PHONE 0171 700 7720

The two well-equipped playgrounds are well supervised and the under-5s equipment is all in an enormous sandpit. There is a small paddling pool and some toilets.

TRAVEL ⊖ Highbury & Islington • **HOURS** Mon-Fri, 8am to dusk; Sat, 9am to dusk; Sun, 10am to dusk

HIGHGATE CEMETERY ☀

ADDRESS Swain's Lane, N6

PHONE 0181 340 1834

Highgate Cemetery is a Victorian Valhalla of gravestones, funereal follies, memorials and monuments. In the middle is the magnificent cedar tree around which winds the Circle of Lebanon, a circular passageway lined with catacombs. Here you can see the cemetery's largest monument, to the newspaper proprietor Julius Beer, who died in 1880. Search through the undergrowth for the sleeping stone lion on the tomb of a menagerie owner called George Wombwell, and the large stone dog on the tomb of Tom Sayers, the last and most popular of the bare-fist prizefighters, who died in 1865. The most famous resident is Karl Marx, whose large bust towers above the grave with its inscription 'Workers of the world unite'. Wheelchair and buggy access but paths are steep.

TRAVEL ⊖ Archway • **HOURS** West Cemetery: daily, 10am-4pm. Tours: Mon-Fri, 12pm, 2pm and 4pm; Sat-Sun, hourly from 11am • **PRICES** £1; tour £3

HOLLAND PARK ☺ 🄴 ☀

ADDRESS Kensington High Street, W8

PHONE 0171 602 2226

Excellent multi-level adventure playground with ever-changing tree walks, rope swings, an area for under-8s and a One O'clock Club. Peacocks and pheasants strut on the Yucca Lawn and squirrels dart across the woodland paths of The Wilderness. There is also a Japanese garden, a lovely orangery and a café.

TRAVEL ⊖ *Holland Park or High Street Kensington* • **OPEN** *Daily, dawn to dusk. Adventure playground: daily, 10am-6pm*

HORNIMAN GARDENS ☺ 🅴 🐝

ADDRESS London Road, SE23
PHONE 0181 699 8924

There are three different walks to do here (trail leaflets available from Park Manager's office for nominal fee) – the Dutch Barn Trail, the Coach Trail and the Railway Trail (taking you along the tracks of the old Crystal Palace line), all of which are suitable for children. See also **Horniman Museum**.

TRAVEL *Forest Hill rail* • **OPEN** *Daily, dawn to dusk* • **PRICE** *Free*

HYDE PARK ☺ 🅴 ☼

PHONE 0171 298 2100

Try to plan your visit on a **Gun Salute** day for the exciting, if noisy, free spectacle of the splendidly uniformed King's Troops of the Royal Horse Artillery galloping down the park to fire the big guns on the stroke of noon. Other special events include the Riding Horse Parade on Rotten Row on the first Sunday in August and the **London to Brighton Veteran Car Run**, which starts at Hyde Park Corner, on the first Sunday in November. Rowing and pedal boats for hire on the Serpentine Lake (open 9am-7pm daily). You can swim in the Serpentine Lido, which is chlorinated (May to end of September). There is also a small paddling pool, sandpit and slide. Speakers' Corner, in the northeast corner of the park below a bower of London plane trees, is the historic home of the soapbox orator. Sunday mornings are best for this colourful event, but be warned – your kids are likely to pick up every four-letter word under the sun as well as some pretty cranky views. There are military bands in the park every Sunday during summer. Underground car park on Park Lane. Toilets for the disabled.

TRAVEL ⊖ *Hyde Park Corner, Knightsbridge, Lancaster Gate, Marble Arch or Queensway* • **HOURS** *Daily, 5-12am (not very safe after dark). Gun Salute (tel: 0171 414 2357): held on Queen's Birthday (21 Apr), Coronation Day (2 Jun), Prince Philip's Birthday (10 Jun), Queen Mother's Birthday (4 Aug) on Park Lane side of park near Dorchester Hotel (arrive 11.30am for midday salute).*

KENSINGTON GARDENS ☺ 🅴 ☼

Adjoining **Hyde Park** are the royal gardens of Kensington Palace. The most famous attraction for children is Sir George Frampton's statue of Peter Pan, which stands on the spot where Peter's boat is supposed to have landed in the 'Never, Never Land of the child's mind'. The statue, commissioned by Peter's creator, Sir James (JM) Barrie, was erected unofficially overnight in the park as a 'magical' surprise for children. Barrie lived at 100 Bayswater Road from 1902-9, next to the Gardens, and it was in this house that he wrote *Peter Pan*. Just outside the playground is the Elfin Oak, with its carvings of fairies and animals. The playground has puppet shows in August (Monday to Saturday at 11am and 3pm), as well as workshops, all of which are free and suitable for under-11s. You can watch model-boat enthusiasts sail their vessels on the Round Pond on Sunday mornings and visit the Pet's Cemetery by Victoria Gate.

TRAVEL ⊖ *Bayswater, Lancaster Gate, Queensway or High Street Kensington*
• **HOURS** *Daily, 5am to 30 mins before dusk*

KEW GARDENS ☺ ❀

ADDRESS Kew Road, Richmond, Surrey
PHONE 0181 332 5000

Gape at the ten-storey Pagoda, which was built in 1761, or stand dwarfed beside the Chilean Wine Palm, raised here in 1846 from seed and now over 60 ft tall. Kew Gardens is the greatest botanical garden and seed bank in the world. It is also home to the world's largest collection of orchids. The Princess of Wales Conservatory has ten different habitats from desert to tropical pools, and houses orchids, palms, ferns, cacti, and giant water lilies which grow up to 6 ft in diameter in one week. The impressive Palm House holds banana, cocoa, papaya and rubber plants; beneath its curved glass roof is the Marine Display, with flowering marine plants and coral reef. The conservatory also houses the ever-popular carnivorous plants (particularly admired by our 3-year-old, who offered his Bacon Frazzles to every passing plant). The conservatories, tropical-palm and water-lily houses make it a great day out even in winter when it's raining. If the weather is fine, bring a picnic. No dogs. Toilets for the disabled. Wheelchair hire (free), wheelchair access.

TRAVEL ⊖ *Kew Gardens or Kew Bridge rail; bus 65, 391, 237 or 267; 1½-hour ride by river boat from Westminster Pier (river-boat information, tel: 0171 930 2062/4721)* • **HOURS** *Daily, 9.30am to dusk (closed Christmas Day and New Year's Day)* • **PRICES** *Adults £5, children £2 (under-5s free), concs £3.50*

LLOYD PARK ⛐ ☼

ADDRESS Forest Road, E17
PHONE 0181 521 7111

The park has an aviary, a moat with black swans, geese and ducks, six tennis courts, safe-surface play areas for under-12s, under-7s and under-5s (the last of which has little equipment) and a kick-about area with goal and netball posts. Toilets outside park near **William Morris Gallery**. Under-12s centre for local residents only.

TRAVEL ⊖ *Walthamstow Central; bus 34, 97, 215 or 257* • **HOURS** *dawn to dusk; William Morris Gallery Tues-Sat, 1st Sun of month, 10am-1pm, 2pm-5pm; Changing Room Art Gallery, Sundays in the summer only dawn to dusk.*

POSTMAN'S PARK ⛐ ☼

ADDRESS off King Edward Street, EC1

A small open space with probably the most sentimental memorial in London – a wall of ceramic tiles dedicated to ordinary people who died in acts of heroic self-sacrifice. The tiles briefly relate the deeds of these heroes, the youngest of whom was 'William Fisher [who], aged nine, lost his life on Rodney Road, Walworth, while trying to save his little brother from being run over, July 12, 1886.' Others include: 'Thomas Simpson [who] died of exhaustion after saving many lives from the breaking ice at Highgate Ponds, January 25, 1885'; 'Harry Sisley of Kilburn, aged 10, [who] drowned in attempting to save his brother after he himself had just been rescued, May 24, 1878'; and 'Daniel Pemberton, aged 61, Forman LSWR, surprised by a train when gauging the line, [who] hurled his mate out of the track, saving his life at the cost of his own, January 17, 1903.'

TRAVEL ⊖ *St Paul's* • **OPEN** *Daily*

RAVENSCOURT PARK ☺ 🖪 ☀

ADDRESS Paddenswick Road, W6
PHONE 0181 741 5378
Adventure playground, tennis courts, pitch-and-putt golf, bowling green, One
O'clock Club, sandpit, paddling pool, children's playground and a duck pond.
Ravenscourt Park Tea House has a good wholefood menu and high chairs.
TRAVEL ⊖ Ravenscourt Park • **OPEN** Daily, hours 10am-6pm

REGENT'S PARK ☺ 🖪 ☀

PHONE 0171 486 7905 or 0171 298 2000
This beautiful park has a large boating lake; a mosque (for details of
guided tours, tel: 0171 724 3363); tennis courts; four playgrounds (open
daily from 10.30am); cricket, baseball and football pitches; and a child-
friendly café. In the Inner Circle is Queen Mary's Rose Garden, which has
puppet shows in August (Monday to Saturday, 11am and 3pm) and
bandstand music. The Open Air Theatre's annual Shakespeare productions
are one of the best ways to introduce young children to Shakespeare in a
beautiful setting (May to September; bookings 0171 486 2431/1933).
You can take a picnic or eat there. The north end of the park houses
London Zoo. There is a boating lake and a shallow children's lake with
pedal boats for hire. At the top end of the park, near the canal, is the
Prince Albert Pub (11 Princess Road, NW1, tel: 0171 722 1886), which
welcomes children and on fine days has barbecues in the garden. Also
nearby is the popular **Sea Shell** Fish Restaurant and Take-away, 49-51
Lisson Grove, NW1 (0171 723 8703). Car park. Toilets for the disabled.
TRAVEL ⊖ Baker Street, Camden Town, Great Portland Street or Regent's
Park • **HOURS** Daily, 5am to dusk • **PRICE** Pedal boats: £1.60 per 20 mins

RICHMOND PARK 🖪 ☀

PHONE 0181 940 0654
Richmond Park is a great place for cycle rides, long walks, even a drive.
The herds of wild red and fallow deer that roam between beach and
chestnut trees are popular with the kids but can be quite dangerous in the
autumn rutting season or after the birth of their young (they particularly
dislike dogs). There are two public golf courses by Roehampton Gate
(tel: 0181 878 1795). Near Richmond Gate is Pembroke Lodge, which
does snacks and afternoon teas and has a lovely open terrace with
extensive views.
TRAVEL ⊖ Richmond • **OPEN** Mar-Sept: daily, 7am to 30 mins before dusk;
Oct-Feb: daily, 7.30am to 30 mins before dusk

ST JAMES'S PARK 🖪 ☀

ADDRESS The Mall, SW1
PHONE 0171 930 1793
A pretty, cultivated park popular with children despite the lack of amenities
for them. St James's Park houses several pelicans, whose ancestors were
given to Charles II in 1665 by a Russian ambassador. Their unsavoury
habit of eating the park pigeons led to their banishment to **London Zoo**
but now they are back and you can watch them being fed most days
around 3pm (not on pigeons). Duck Island also has flocks of water birds
and mandarin ducks. There are brass- and military-band concerts summer
lunchtimes, and a playground with a sandpit. In the 17th century a herd of
cows was kept in the park and milked on the spot to provide refreshment

for the public at 1d a shot. Now you have to make do with the Cake House teashop. Toilets for the disabled at Marlborough Gate.

TRAVEL ⊖ *St James's Park* • **OPEN** *Daily, dawn to midnight*

SYON PARK GARDENS ☺ ✿

ADDRESS London Road, Brentford, Middx
PHONE 0181 560 0881

England's first botanical gardens were laid out here in the 16th century and two of the original fruit-bearing mulberry trees still exist. The Great Conservatory of Syon House is now home to an aquarium and aviary. There is also a large garden centre, 6 acres of rose gardens, an arts centre, a wholefood shop, an aquatic centre, and the Syon Craft Show, which is held the first weekend in August. A $10\frac{1}{4}$-in gauge railway (daily, April to October, then weekends and bank holidays only) runs from the entrance to Flora's Lawn, where there is a picnic area. Also here is the **London Butterfly House**, home to hundreds of free-flying exotic butterflies; it also has tarantulas, scorpions and leaf-cutter ants in the insect rooms, which are always popular with the kids. Also Snakes and Ladders children's indoor adventure playground, open daily, 10am-8pm.

TRAVEL ⊖ *Gunnersbury, then bus 237 or 267 to Brent Lee, or Syon Lane rail then walk; car park* • **HOURS** *Gardens: Daily, 10am-6pm or dusk (closed 25-26 Dec). House: Apr-Sep, Sat-Sun and bank holidays, 11am-5pm (and Sun in Oct)* • **PRICES** *House: Adults £2.50, children £2. Combined ticket for house and gardens, adults £5.50, children £4. Picnic area: adults £1, children 50p*

VICTORIA PARK ☺ 🅴 ☀

ADDRESS Old Ford Road, E3

This beautiful, very well-maintained East End park is a real oasis in the middle of an urban jungle. It has two large lakes where the Victorian Model Boat Club meets most Sunday mornings, huge dog-free areas and a deer herd. The Pools playground is supervised and the squeaky-clean café in a conservatory opposite a lake has *Thomas the Tank Engine* and *Postman Pat* videos to keep the under-5s amused.

TRAVEL ⊖ *Mile End or Cambridge Heath rail* • **HOURS** *Daily 8am to dusk*

WANDSWORTH COMMON ☺ 🅴 ☀

PHONE 0181 871 6391

The common has a duck pond, an adventure playground and a highly recommended One O'clock Club.

TRAVEL *Wandsworth Common rail* • **OPEN** *Daily, 24 hours*

WIMBLEDON COMMON 🅴 ☀

PHONE 0181 788 7655

A vast open space for walking and riding, which also has a 19th-century windmill, now the **Wimbledon Windmill Museum**.

TRAVEL ⊖ *Wimbledon, then bus 93* • **OPEN** *Daily, 24 hours*

WIMBLEDON PARK ☺ 🅴 ☀

ADDRESS Wimbledon Park Road, SW19
PHONE 0181 946 6046

There is a huge lake in the middle of this popular local park, and two play areas with paddling pool and sandpit.

TRAVEL ⊖ *Wimbledon Park* • **HOURS** *Daily, dawn to dusk*

WOODS AND OPEN SPACES

Learn about forestry, play cowboys and Indians among the trees, go frog hunting and pond dipping, and learn how to survive in the wild. London's woods and nature reserves even have routes suitable for buggies and wheelchairs. The London Wildlife Trust (tel: 0171 261 0447) publishes a guide with details of free activities, workdays and children's events.

BARN ELMS RESERVOIR ▣ ☼

ADDRESS Merthyr Terrace, off Castelnau, SW13
PHONE 01734 593363
Hundreds of different birds can be spotted in this birdwatchers' paradise.
TRAVEL ⊖ Hammersmith; bus 9, 9a, 33 or 72 • **HOURS** Daily, 7.30am to sunset

BAYHURST WOOD COUNTRY PARK ▣ ☼

ADDRESS Breakspear Road North, Harefield, Middx
PHONE 01895 250651
Ancient woodland with variety of fungi, plus nature trails, guided walks by prior arrangement (suitable for over-4s), picnic and barbecue sites, toilets. Summer activities for children include pond dipping, nature quizzes, den-making, etc. Occasional displays of forestry equipment.
TRAVEL By car A4180 to Breakspear Road then right at Fine Bush Lane; car park • **OPEN** Daily, dawn to dusk

BECKENHAM PLACE PARK ☺ ▣ ☼

ADDRESS Beckenham Hill Road, SE6
If you live in the area or on the Ravensbourne line, then this delightful wood and meadow land is an ideal spot for children of any age – there are excellent trees to climb (even toddlers can have a go); open meadows for picnics in which you feel as if you are in the heart of the country. There is also a public golf course, putting green and tennis courts.
TRAVEL Ravensbourne or Beckenham Hill rail • **OPEN** Daily, dawn to dusk

BOX HILL ▣ ☼

ADDRESS The Old Fort, Box Hill Road, Jadworth (1 mile north of Dorking on A24)
Good, healthy climb for wonderful views, and there's also a restaurant at the top with a play area for children.
TRAVEL Box Hill or Westhumble rail (½ mile); car park £1.50

CAMLEY STREET NATURAL PARK ☺ ▣ ☼

ADDRESS 12 Camley Street, NW1
PHONE 0171 833 2311
Originally a coal drop on the Grand Union Canal, this tiny wildlife park has a pond, a wood and a marsh, all crammed into 2 acres. You can hire pond-dipping nets, join the summer play scheme or take part in the various Wildlife Watch events throughout the year.
TRAVEL ⊖ King's Cross • **HOURS** Mon-Fri, 10am-5pm; Sat-Sun, 11am-5pm
• **PRICE** Free (donations welcome)

DAWSON'S HILL WORKDAY 🟦 ☀

ADDRESS Dunstan's Road, SE22

PHONE 0181 693 8200

Children enjoy putting something back into the countryside, and here they can help with tasks like hand mowing, coppicing and planting on this grassland reserve. All ages welcome. Meet at the signpost to Dunstan's Road.

TRAVEL *East Dulwich rail* • **HOURS** *1st Sat of month, 11am-4pm* • **PRICE** *Free*

DULWICH WOOD 🟦 ☀

ADDRESS Low Cross Wood Lane, SE19

The 6-acre site includes a patch of ancient woodland and the neglected gardens of a Victorian house bombed during the war. There are over 200 species of plants, 230 different types of fungi and some exotic plants from the original gardens.

TRAVEL ⊖ Sydenham Hill rail

EAST HAM NATURE RESERVE ☺ 🟦 ☀

ADDRESS Norman Road, E6

PHONE 0181 470 4525

East London's largest churchyard is now a nature reserve – if you follow the nature trails (one of which is suitable for wheelchairs and buggies) you will spot anything from butterflies to pheasants. School-holiday activities include paper-making, making Roman armour and creating natural dyes. There are quiz sheets, a birdwatching hide (by appointment), natural-history displays, a Victorian school room and a wartime kitchen. Braille guide. Gift shop with pocket-money toys. Toilets for the disabled.

TRAVEL ⊖ *East Ham, then bus 101, 104 or 300; Beckton DLR* • **OPEN** *Summer: Tues-Fri, 9am-5pm, Sat-Sun, 2-5pm; winter: Tues-Fri, 10am-5pm, Sat-Sun, 1-4pm* • **PRICE** *Free*

EPPING FOREST ☺ 🟦 ☀

PHONE 0181 508 0028; Epping Forest Field Centre 0181 508 7714

Epping Forest is a vast crescent of land with everything from ancient woodland, grassland and heath to rivers, bogs and ponds, making it an ideal place to get lost while picking blackberries or mushrooms (maps available from the Epping Forest Field Centre, High Beach, Loughton, Essex IG10 4AF, priced £1.50). The area has been wooded since the end of the last Ice Age (about 8000 BC) and local legend has it that Queen Boadicea fought her last battle here at Ambresbury Banks. The Field Centre runs children's safaris and summer-holiday activities for would-be David Attenboroughs, with events including pond dipping, environmental games, nature trails and forest survival. It also runs environmental children's parties with pond dipping, treasure hunt and survival days (from £30 for up to 12 children, including use of room and tutor). Plenty of paths for wheelchairs and buggies.

TRAVEL ⊖ *Epping, Theydon Bois and Loughton or Debden rail* • **OPEN** *Mon-Sat, 10am-5pm; Sun, 11am-5pm* • **PRICES** *Field Centre activities: children £2.50, accompanying adults free*

FAIRLOP COUNTRY PARK ☺ ☀

ADDRESS Forest Road, Ilford, Essex

PHONE 0181 500 9911 (Al's Adventure World 0181 500 9922)

Large lake with watersports, conservation area and Al's Adventure World for kids. Picnic site, refreshments, toilets.

TRAVEL ⊖ *Fairlop; car park* • **HOURS** *Country park: Daily, dawn to dusk. Al's Adventure World: Mon-Thurs, 10am-7pm; Fri-Sun, 10am-8pm* • **PRICES** *Al's Adventure World: under-4s £2.75, over-4s £3.95*

FRYENT COUNTRY PARK ☺ 🅴 ☀

ADDRESS Fryent Way (A4140), NW9
PHONE 0181 206 0492

For a bit of real countryside in town, head for this lovely unspoilt country park, with woodland, meadows and ancient hedgerows accessible via a good network of paths (easy for wheelchairs and buggies). Various holiday activities for children and monthly birdwatching walks. Circular walk, nature trail. No toilets (this is real countryside). Phone for leaflets and maps.
TRAVEL ⊖ *Kingsbury or Wembley Park; car park* • **OPEN** *Daily, 24 hours*

GREEN CHAIN WALK 🅴 ☀

PHONE 0181 854 888 ext 3711

This is a 40-mile network of footpaths linking green open spaces. Popular walks for children include woods like **Oxleas** and Elmstead, and **Lesnes Abbey** with its ruined monastery. Maryon Wilson Park has a small children's zoo, and there is boating and angling at Southmere Lake. Thamesmead to Oxleas Wood is approximately 6 miles (takes about five hours with children over 6). Phone for an information leaflet with route map, or write to Green Chain Working Party, John Humphries House, Stockwell Street, London SE10 9JN.

GUNNERSBURY TRIANGLE ☺ 🅴 ☀

ADDRESS Bollo Lane, W4
PHONE 0181 747 3881

Set between the District and Northern tube lines, this nature reserve covers 6 acres of woodland and grassland and also has a large pond. Bird life includes tawny owls and green spotted woodpeckers. Leave buggies at the entrance. Catering facilities and toilets.
TRAVEL ⊖ *Chiswick Park* • **HOURS** *Sun, 2-4.30pm*

HIGHGATE WOOD ☺ 🅴 ☀

ADDRESS Muswell Hill Road, N6
PHONE 0181 444 6129

A stone's throw from the Archway Road and you are in the heart an ancient woodland bursting with birds, butterflies and other wildlife. There is a good playground, a sports ground, woodland trails, a nature hut and a very popular vegetarian café, Oshobasho (tel: 0181 444 1505). On the other side of the Muswell Hill Road is the slightly smaller, wilder Queen's Wood.
TRAVEL ⊖ *Highgate* • **HOURS** *Daily, 7.30am to 30 mins before dusk*

LEE VALLEY PARK 🅴 ☀

ADDRESS Abbey Gardens, Waltham Abbey, Essex
PHONE Information centre 01992 713838

Lee Valley Park follows the River Lee from Ware in Hertfordshire to London's East End. Large areas of water offer sailing, rowing, fishing and boat trips. There are guided walks, children's activities, quizzes, nature trails, and riding and swimming facilities. Leisurebus takes a circular route round the park and on Sundays links up with Liverpool Street Station. Phone for leaflets and events diary for indoor and outdoor activities.

TRAVEL ✆ *Tottenham Hale or various stations on Liverpool Street to Cambridge rail line* • **HOURS** *Daily, 9.30am-5pm*

ESNES ABBEY WOODS ▣ ☀

ADDRESS Lesnes Abbey Road, Belvedere, Kent
PHONE 0181 312 9717

The name comes from the 12th-century abbey whose remains still stand in this 200-acre wood, which is a riot of colour in the spring with daffodils, bluebells and wood anemones. Popular with children is the fossil bed, where you can search for prehistoric remains. Best for older children and good walkers as the woods are very hilly.

TRAVEL *Abbey Wood rail*

MORDEN HALL PARK ▣ ☀

ADDRESS Morden Hall Road, Morden, Surrey
PHONE 0181 648 1845

Originally laid out as a deer park, this park is now a wildlife and ecology centre owned by the National Trust. There is a complex system of waterways coming off the River Wandle, which was designed to power the snuff mill. Visit the craft workshops (closed Tuesdays) to see local artists making stained glass, wood turning, sculpting and repairing furniture. The environmental study centre runs day sessions for children in the holidays (phone Gillian on 0181 542 4239) with games and projects. Garden and aquatic centre. National Trust shop, tearoom, toilets for the disabled, picnic area (no tables). Half-mile walk from the main car park along the river corridor is Dean City Farm (tel: 0181 543 5300) for the usual farm animals and a spot of horse riding.

TRAVEL ✆ *Morden* • **OPEN** *Daily, dawn to dusk*

OXLEAS WOOD ▣ ☀

ADDRESS off Shooters Hill (A207), SE10

One of London's last remaining ancient woodlands, Oxleas Wood is approximately 8,000 years old and was recently saved from the road builders' bulldozers. Part of the **Green Chain Walk**. Annual Bluebell Walk in May (phone David Goodfellow on 0181 855 2868).

TRAVEL *Falcon Wood rail; free parking in woods*

RAILWAY FIELDS ▣ ☀

ADDRESS Green Lanes, N4
PHONE 0181 348 6005

This former British Rail goods yard has been turned into a conservation park designed to teach primary-school children about nature. There is a visitors' centre, woodland, meadow and pond. Don't miss the unique hybrid plant, the Haringey Knotweed.

TRAVEL ✆ *Manor House or Haringey or Green Lanes rail* • **HOURS** *Mon-Fri, 10am-5pm (phone to confirm)*

RUISLIP WOODS ☺ ▣ ☀

ADDRESS Ruislip, Middx

Head for Bayhurst Wood Country Park for a barbecue site – there is a charge to book barbecues, but you don't have to pay if you are prepared to take what's left. Also picnic sites. See leaflets available in local libraries or write to Recreation Unit, Local Service Civic Centre, Uxbridge, Middx UB8 1UW.

TRAVEL ✆ *Ruislip, then bus H13 or 114*

RUSSIA DOCK WOODLAND AND STAVE HILL ECOLOGICAL PARK ☐ ☀

ADDRESS off Redriff Road, near Onega Gate, SE16

PHONE 0171 237 9165 or Ranger Service Information 0171 525 1050

Britain's largest man-made ecological park adjoins these woodlands. To find out about the local history, visit the nearby Pumphouse Educational Museum (tel: 0171 231 2976). **NEARBY: Surrey Docks Farm** (see Animal Attractions).

TRAVEL ⊖ Rotherhithe; bus P11 or 225 • **HOURS** Daily, dawn to 9pm

SEVENOAKS WILDFOWL RESERVE ☐ ☀

ADDRESS Bradbourne Vale Road, Sevenoaks, Kent

PHONE 01732 456407

One-mile nature trail with hides and fully illustrated guide. Natural-history exhibition, café, shop and toilets in visitors' centre. Picnic area.

TRAVEL Sevenoaks rail • **HOURS** Wed, Sat-Sun and bank holidays, 10am-5pm (or dusk if earlier) • **PRICES** Adults £3, children 50p, OAPs £2

STREATHAM COMMON, NORWOOD GROVE AND ROOKERY GARDENS ☺ ☐ ☀

ADDRESS Streatham Common South, SE1

The grassy hill is good for kite-flying, while at the eastern end of the common, up the hill, is the Rookery Garden, which sometimes has jazz at the seasonal open-air theatre. Large safe picnic area in the orchard and rambling woodland paths to explore. Pond full of frogs. Tennis court. Great views across south London. Good café near toilets. The Greyhound Pub has its own brewery and does pub grub all day; it also has barbecues in its large garden and a conservatory where the kids can sit.

TRAVEL Streatham Common or Norbury rail • **OPEN** Daily, dawn to dusk

SYDENHAM HILL WOOD (FAMILY WALK) ☐ ☀

PHONE David Lloyd 0181 699 5698

Family Woodland Walk on the second Sunday in the month. Meet at The Bridge, Sydenham Hill, at 2pm.

TRAVEL Sydenham or Forest Hill rail • **PRICE** Free

THAMES PATH ☐ ☀

PHONE Thames Barrier Visitors' Centre 0181 854 1373 for leaflets

The Thames Path, a designated National Trail, follows the river for 180 miles from its source at Kemble in the Cotswolds to the Thames Barrier. Join the path at any point.

TRENT COUNTRY PARK ☺ ☐ ☀

ADDRESS Cockfosters Road, Barnet, Herts

PHONE Visitors' Centre 0181 449 8706

In addition to the Pets' Corner, water garden and two lakes, there is a very popular nature trail that you can do on your own or with a ranger guide. The Visitors' Centre can also draw up a programme of events for children, a slide show a week before the trail and a question-and-answer session on the day. There is also a Wildlife Club (meets twice a month) and a woodland trail for the blind. Good bluebells and daffodils in spring. Horse riding. Picnic and barbecue sites and café. Toilets.

TRAVEL ⊖ Cockfosters or Oakwood; car park • **HOURS** Daily, 7.30am to dusk • **PRICE** Free (car-park charges weekends and bank holidays)

THEME PARKS AND INDOOR FUN PARKS

Fun, fun, fun – whether you want to visit the pyramids of Egypt or ride the Rocky Mountain Railway, test your courage on the ultimate white-knuckle rides or relax on a boat through fantasy land; whether you are a tiny tot or a tearaway teenager, you will find something to thrill and delight in Britain's theme parks. And if you are looking for a couple of hours' distraction on a rainy day there are plenty of indoor fun parks in the centre of London from which to choose.

ONE- AND TWO-DAY TRIPS

ALTON TOWERS ✱ ●
ADDRESS Alton, Staffordshire
PHONE 01538 703344; hotel reservations 0990 001100
For white-knuckle aficionados the new SW4 (Secret Weapon 4) ride is the latest in terror technology, promising riders 'the most physically and psychologically challenging experience of their lives'. You will have to take their word for it as we were either too short or too cowardly to brave it. Other white-knuckle rides for adrenaline junkies include Nemesis (where you'll experience four seconds of weightlessness), the Corkscrew (with two 360-degree turns), Ripsaw and the Black Hole. Height restrictions apply to these rides, so those with younger and shorter children should head for the water-based rides such as the Log Flume and Congo River Rapids. And the real cowards (like me) should take an infant in tow and confine themselves to the joys of T Cups, the Vintage Cars, Doodle Doo Derby, Squirrel Nutty and Toyland Tours. Food has always been a bit of a let-down here. New to Alton Towers this year are McDonald's, Pizza Hut and KFC restaurants which offer high-street standards at high-street prices. A better – and cheaper – bet is to bring your own picnic and sit in the beautiful landscaped gardens. To do justice to Alton Towers, you need two days, especially if you are coming from London. A short monorail ride away is the new Alton Towers Hotel (tel: 0990 001100), a family oriented, well-equipped four-star hotel full of weird and wonderful surprises – talking trees, singing lifts and a secret drawer of goodies in every room. There are several specially themed suites – the Coca-Cola Fizzy Drinks Factory, with Coca-Cola on tap; the Cadbury's Chocolate Room, with a constant supply of chocolate; the Arabian Night or Princess Suite; the Nemesis Room, which sleeps six; two Peter Rabbit burrows; and SW4 for those wanting to relive the nightmare. There is also a Pirate Lagoon with swimming pool, bubble pool and, for exhausted parents, a sauna. Package prices start at £100 per night, including one day in the park and continental breakfast, based on two children sharing with two adults.

TRAVEL *Stoke-on-Trent rail, then service bus; by car: M6 to junction 15*
• **HOURS** *Daily, 9am-8pm (with some rides opening and closing 1 hour either side)* • **PRICES** *Adults £19, under-14s £15 (under-4s free), OAPs £6.50 (peak prices 50p more). Family tickets now available on the gate £57-£59 (1+3 or 2+2). Second day £9*

BUTLIN'S SOUTH COAST WORLD ☺ 🐛 ●

ADDRESS Bognor Regis, W Sussex
PHONE 01243 822445

Butlin's provides the traditional holiday-camp environment. Aquasplash Sub-tropical Water World (which is regulated into sessions) is popular with all the family, and there is a large funfair and a junior funfair as well as shows, bowls, darts and sports facilities. Wheelchair access to most of the complex. Cafés, restaurants, picnic areas, shops, toilets, baby-changing facilities. You could combine this trip with something completely different and head for the nearby **Weald and Downland Open Air Museum**.
TRAVEL *Bognor Regis rail; by car: 60 miles south of London off Gloucester Road, reached by either A259 or A27* • **OPEN** *Apr-Oct: daily, 10am-11pm; winter opening times and dates vary* • **PRICES** *Adults £7.50, OAPs and children £6.50 (under-4s free)*

CADBURY WORLD

ADDRESS Linden Road, Bournville, S Birmingham
PHONE Recorded information 0121 451 4180; booking 0121 451 4159

Visitors can take Cadabra, a journey aboard a four-seater Beanmobile, experiencing the sights, sounds and, more to the point, the tastes and smells of chocolate. Walk through a tropical rainforest, where the Aztecs traded cocoa beans, and sample the spicy drink 'chocolatl', favoured by Emperor Montezuma. Then follow the story of chocolate across Europe to a cobbled street in Georgian England, home to the Cadbury family. See the Packing Plant and watch products being wrapped and packed, and find out how Cadbury creates its television advertisements. New this year is the chocolate film set for Cadbury's sponsorship of *Coronation Street*, and the Planet Astro. **NEARBY: Drayton Manor Park.**
TRAVEL *Bournville rail; by car: off A38* • **HOURS** *Opening times vary*
• **PRICES** *Adults £6.25, children £4.50 (under-4s free), family ticket (2+2) £18.60*

CHESSINGTON WORLD OF ADVENTURES ☀ ●

ADDRESS Leatherhead Road, Chessington, Surrey
PHONE 01372 727227

Chessington has nine theme lands, including the Mystic East, where the Dragon River Water Ride takes you through bamboo jungles and rocky crevices only to plunge you alarmingly towards solid granite, and the Forbidden Kingdom, which houses the venomous vaults of Terrortomb and the infamous Rameses' Revenge, which does appalling things to those who brave it, including spinning, dropping and drenching them. Queues for the thrill-rides such as Rameses' Revenge and Rattlesnake ('the ride that bites back') can be up to two hours long but the children said it was 'all part of the fun'. Sixteen-year-old Gemma and her younger brother had spent most of the day on, or waiting to get on, Rameses' Revenge (total queuing time, three hours and 10 minutes, for four rides the combined duration of which was 12 minutes). Height restrictions vary on different rides, but if you want to avoid all the stomach churners, go armed with someone under 5 and head for Toytown, with its Truckers ride, roundabout, Weather House and

Cadbury Castle for chocoholics. There are plenty of other amusements and shows, and wild and exotic creatures in Animal Lands, including big cats and primates. There is also a Safari Skyway monorail, which takes you on a sky-high safari adventure above the animals. The restaurants are expensive but the themes extend to the food areas so you can sample food from around the world. Save queuing time and money by taking a picnic. There are plenty of toilets with good baby-changing facilities. Toilets for the disabled. Wheelchair and buggy access.

TRAVEL *Chessington South rail, then 10-min walk; Flightline bus 777 from Victoria; by car: M25 to junction 9, then A243* • **OPEN** *Mid-Mar to end-Oct: daily, 10am-6pm (to 9.30pm in summer holidays; last admission 3pm or 7pm in summer)* • **PRICES** *Adults £19, under-14s £15 (under-4s free), OAPs £8.50, disabled £7.50. Children under 10 must be supervised on all rides; children under 12 not admitted without an adult.*

DRAYTON MANOR PARK ☺ ❊ ●

ADDRESS Tamworth, Staffordshire
PHONE 01827 287979 (24-hour hotline)

To add to delights such as Shockwave, Europe's only stand-up rollercoaster, and the white-water Splash Canyon and Klondike Old Mine, Drayton Manor has come up with seven attractions new this year. The Magnificent Seven include the Super Dragon rollercoaster, a white-knuckle training ground for beginners, Flying Jumbos, Raft Ride and the twins' favourite, Mini Balloons. Of the theme areas, Cowboy Town and Pirate Cove are still the most popular with our kids, especially the Pirate Adventure. There is an impressive zoo with big cats, sea lions and, in the Small Mammal House, the delightful cotton-top tamarins, the smallest monkeys in the world. There is also a rare-breeds farm, museums, garden centre and a nature trail.

As part of the £5 million expansion, which began this year, there is a top-secret water ride planned for 1999, which promises to be 'like no other' and, for the year 2000, Drayton Manor Park Hotel will open its doors. Until then visitors can stay at The Belfry Resort (tel: 01675 470033 for reservations). **NEARBY: Cadbury World**.

TRAVEL *By car on the A4091, 10 miles north of Birmingham (signposted on the M42, junctions 9 or 10)* • **OPEN** *End Mar – end Oct: daily, from 10.30am, closing times vary between 5-7pm* • **PRICES** *Adults £3, children and OAPs £2 (unlimited rides: £10/£7.50)*

NEW DREAMLAND FUN PARK ❊ ●

ADDRESS Marine Terrace, Margate, Kent
PHONE 01843 227011

Home to Britain's oldest wooden rollercoaster and largest big wheel. Other attractions include a two-drop log flume, Stowaway (a dark ride) and a new coaster ride. Although Dreamland has mainly white-knuckle rides for strong-stomached children seeking ultimate thrills, there are plenty of attractions for smaller children. **NEARBY:** Coco's, Marine Terrace (tel: 01843 227011; daily, 11am-5pm), an indoor play centre with swings and ball ponds.

TRAVEL *Margate rail; by car: A2, M2 and A28 to Margate* • **OPEN** *Jun-Aug: daily, 10.30am-6pm; Easter to May and Sep: Sat-Sun, 10.30am-6pm* • **PRICES** *All-day wristband £14, allowing unlimited access to all rides except the go-karts. Children under 1.35 metres, wristband £9 (less if booked in advance)*

LEGOLAND WINDSOR ☺ ✿ ●

PHONE 01753 626111; information and booking hotline 0990 040404
Far more than just a very impressive model village, Legoland is one of the few genuinely interactive theme parks. The most popular rides are those powered or activated by children, and the witty walk-through attractions fuel their imagination. There are giant-size Duplo helicopters to be piloted, a driving school where children earn driving licences, and a boating school. You can pan for real 'gold', nuggets which can be exchanged for a gold medal (extra £1). Duplo Gardens is ideal for toddlers, with its Fairy Tale boat ride, puppet theatre and, best of all, Waterworks. Here children can make water flow uphill, play music by bouncing on stepping stones, fire water cannon and make frogs jump. Older children can run off steam in the Wild Woods labyrinth of tree-top walkways, and scramble down nets and chutes before trying their skills on the Muscle Maker, Breath Taker or Bone Shaker. Those over 1.1 metres tall can thrill to the excitement of the Dragon Ride without being terrified out of their wits (or bringing up their lunch), or take the Pirate Falls, a deceptively gentle meander along a pirate-peopled river, culminating in a thrilling, soaking end. There are several free-style building areas, where tall towers can be tested on earthquake tables against a Richter-scale reading, and models can be animated by computer programming. Great care has been taken to ensure that both adults and children have a thoroughly enjoyable time. And, remarkably for a theme park, it is all very calm and relaxed. There is no aggressive merchandising, and once you have paid the admission price there is no pressure to spend more. There are also plenty of reasonably priced pizza, hamburger and rib outlets, with a healthier but equally good-value menu in the Marché restaurant. In addition, there are stalls serving coffee, muffins and ice-creams. Wonderful fireworks and laser show on the last day of the season at the beginning of November. Toilets for the disabled and baby-changing facilities. Wheelchair and buggy access around the park.
TRAVEL *Windsor & Eton Riverside rail, then bus; by car on the B3022 Windsor to Ascot road, signposted from the M3 (junction 3), M4 (junction 6) and all approach roads* • **OPEN** *Mid-Mar to Nov: daily, 10am-6pm (or dusk if earlier); mid-Jul to Aug: daily, 10am-8pm* • **PRICES** *Adults £16, under-16s £13, OAPs £10. Booking advisable as park will close when and if capacity is reached.*

NAMCO STATION ✿ ◑

ADDRESS County Hall, Riverside Building, Westminster Bridge Road, SE1
PHONE 0171 967 1066
Namco Station offers two floors of electronic entertainment, including Turbo Bumper Cars and Techno Bowling. Older children and teenagers swear by (and, in several cases, *at*) the state-of-the-art arcade games. Popular for those with money to burn.
TRAVEL ⊖ *Waterloo or Westminster* • **HOURS** *Daily, 10am to midnight* • **PRICES** *Admission free; games from 10p to £2*

PAULTONS PARK ☺ 🅴 ●

ADDRESS Ower, nr Romsey, Hants
PHONE 01703 814455
The park is designed with 4- to 14-year-olds in mind, with no white-knuckle rides but plenty of fun for all the family. A ride on the Rio Grande train around the park will give you an idea of where everything is before you

follow the eerie marshland trail through the Land of the Dinosaurs or make your way through the Hedge Maze. The Krazi-Karts, whose steering will lead you all over the place, are enormously popular with older children. Try playing crazy snooker or crazy golf, take a ride on a pirate ship, whiz down the Astroglide or take a leap on Percy's Bouncer before getting splashed on the Bumper Boats. Kids' Kingdom is a popular adventure play area with a huge 130-ft-long structure where ages 7-13 can slip down the giant tube slide, scramble over the Super Spiral Spiders Web, and haul themselves along the cableways. Meanwhile, ages 3-7 will enjoy frolicking in the play village. Young ones will also enjoy a visit to the Magic Forest, where nursery rhymes come to life at the push of a button, and to the Farmyard, where they can pet the animals. Plenty of secluded picnic spots, extensive and very beautiful gardens, a huge wildfowl lake and a working 19th-century watermill make this an enjoyable place for adults as well. Plenty of kiosks, cafés and refreshment stalls. Full buggy access. Good value for money and much prettier than most theme parks.

TRAVEL *By car on M27, just off junction 2 •* **OPEN** *Mid-Mar to Oct: daily, 10am-6pm (last admission, 4pm) •* **PRICES** *Adults £8, children £7 (children under 1 metre free), disabled £4.50, various family tickets. All rides included in price except go-karts, £2 extra. Some rides have height restrictions. Allow at least 5-6 hours.*

PEPSI TROCADERO 🐾 ●

ADDRESS 1 Piccadilly Circus, W1

PHONE 0171 439 1791; information hotline 0990 100456

Seven floors of bright lights, techno-sounds and frenetic activity to ensure your senses are well and truly assaulted. There are games, rides, shops, themed restaurants, a 3D cinema and the type of mind-blowing virtual-reality adventures popular with older children whose pockets are well-lined. In the Emaginator, a ride-cinema with moving seats and tailor-made action films, you can travel to the outer limits of the universe in Space Race, or become the ball in Cosmic Pinball. In Funland and Lazerbowl you can play virtual bowling with laser pins and try out the latest computer games and virtual-reality simulators. For those with strong stomachs there is the Giant Drop, the only indoor free-fall ride in the world, where you are taken up to a height of 125 ft and then 'dropped' to the ground. Up one of Europe's longest escalators you enter Segaworld, six floors of ride attractions, including 3D Terrors of the Deep, which will put you off swimming for good, and the Magic of the Carnival Ride, which offers all the fun of the fair without the candy floss. In the **Pepsi IMAX 3D Cinema**, the audience wear special headsets with Surround Sound to make the experience of watching 3D films on the giant screen even more 'real'. There is more virtual reality to be experienced in the form of a Brazilian rainforest at the **Rainforest Café**. The food here is at least real, though the names of the dishes – African Wind and Mojo Bones to name two – are anything but, and the simple act of going for a meal is now called 'an adventure'.

TRAVEL ⊖ *Piccadilly Circus •* **HOURS** *Mon-Thurs and Sun, 10am-midnight; Fri-Sat, 10-1am •* **PRICES** *Free entrance; pay for rides as you use them. Pepsi IMAX 3D Cinema (0171 494 4153): adults from £5.95, children from £4.50*

GREAT THORPE PARK ☺ 🐛 ●

ADDRESS Staines Road, Chertsey, Surrey
PHONE 01932 562633

Thorpe Park is particularly good for families with young children. There are height restrictions on some rides but there is plenty for even very little ones to do while their older siblings join the inevitable queues for Logger's Leap, Thunder River, the Flying Fish rollercoaster, Depth Charge water slide and the infamous X:\No Way Out, the only backwards plummeting ride in the world in total darkness. Depth Charge, on the other hand, is fantastic fun and leaves you wet rather than queasy. You fly down a giant water slide in an inflatable boat which, on windy days, feels as if it will take off at any moment, adding to the thrill. Getting wet is par for the course here, and bringing all-in-one waterproofs is one of those excellent ideas usually remembered too late. New rides this year include the Dino Bumper Ride experience, featuring bumper boats in a giant swimming pool and indoor bumper cars. Children can get even wetter on Wet, Wet, Wet, a twirly water slide in the Fantasy Reef pool by the sandy beach area, for which you need swimming costumes. You can take the boat or train to the 1930s working farm, where there are plenty of animals to stroke and feed. To avoid queues, go either at the start of the season or when rain is forecast – you'll get wet on the rides anyway. The park is extremely family friendly, with baby-changing facilities, a mother-and-baby room, helpful staff, and total buggy access. On the down side, there are too many tacky side stalls encouraging you to part with your money, and the food in the restaurants is dull and expensive. There are, however, plenty of outdoor and under-cover picnic areas.

TRAVEL Staines rail; bus 718 from Victoria; by car on M25 (junctions 11 or 13) • **HOURS** Daily throughout holidays, 10am-6pm • **PRICES** Adults £16.50, under-14s £13 (children under 1 metre free; most height restrictions only apply to children under 90 cm). Plan-ahead Super Save ticket £12.50 per person for 4 or more people (purchase up to 24 hours in advance on 0990 880880)

LONGER STAYS

CENTER PARCS ☺ 🐛 ●

PHONE 01272 244744; reservations 0990 200300

This is quite possibly the most relaxing break with children available in the UK. Center Parcs has holiday villages at Elveden Forest in Suffolk, Longleat in Wiltshire and Sherwood Forest in Nottinghamshire, where even in mid-winter you can shoot the rapids of Jungle River or wander among lemon trees. In the huge glass domes, which make the weather redundant, the temperature is always tropical, the surroundings are rural, and the individual villas are dotted among the trees in a traffic-free environment. There are kids' clubs and activities for all ages. But the greatest pleasure is derived from villa life in the forest – biking through pines with not a car in site; walks round the lake; superb chalets and excellent facilities. Even the most boisterous little devils turn into angels here, and a good night's sleep for parents is guaranteed by the kids' sheer exhaustion. A family could easily spend days in the poolside paradise of well-run shallow ends and spine-tingling flume rides, if it weren't for the many other activities available. You can do almost anything from archery to aromatherapy, and there is a full children's programme, a kindergarten

and discos. Children can go off on bikes on their own without parents constantly worrying about their safety. There are also fully trained nannies and babysitters should you want to pamper yourselves in the sauna or have a round of golf. For those wanting a night out but not wishing to venture beyond the boundaries of the park, an evening in the superb La Caprice revolving restaurant (Elveden Forest only) is highly recommended – the food, which is exquisite, can hold its own with the best in Soho. The dome-area food is not so good – mostly unambitious, stodgy and expensive. But the chalets are well equipped for self-catering and there is a competitively priced supermarket. Book as many activities as possible as soon as you arrive, as they get booked out very quickly (they all cost extra except the pool).
OPEN *All year round* • **PRICES** *One week in a 2-bedroom villa sleeping 4 from £282-£719 (excluding food and most activities), depending on season. Short breaks available weekends or mid-week. Phone for details of different holiday villages.*

ƆISNEYLAND PARIS ☺ ✹ ●
ADDRESS BP 100, 777777 Marne-la-Vallée Cedex 4, France; Disney Travel Centre, 140 Regent Street, London W1
PHONE information 0990 030303
A Russian journalist once remarked that Disneyland Paris fondly reminded him of Moscow, because you have to queue for everything. However, for the ultimate theme-park experience with enough white-knuckle rides, dark rides, gentle rides, walk-through experiences, shows and other attractions to amuse and entertain the whole family, Disney cannot be beaten. And if you head for the major rides – Space Mountain, Big Thunder Mountain, Indiana Jones and the Temple of Peril – at the beginning or very end of the day you can fill the rest of your time with some of the quieter attractions. In fact, these ones are the most beguiling – the Small World and Fairytale rides, both taking you on little boats through narrative treats, are amongst the best entertainment experiences for young children anywhere in the world. The bigger rides have minimum age and height restrictions, and even adults may find them more terrifying than pleasurable. On-site shows such as Mickey and His Friends provide lots more fun and the well-known street parades are another dependable attraction. The park is divided into five areas, the centre of which is Main Street USA, with arcades of Victorian shops, vintage cars and street parades. While in Fantasyland, we spent most of our time exploring Sleeping Beauty's Castle, topsy-turvy cottages, a flying Dumbos ride, and the Small World canal cruise. The boys and I preferred Adventureland, Frontierland and Discoveryland, worlds of film-set adventure with rocky mountains, deserts, croc-infested swamps, pirate ships and space stations. There are plenty of themed restaurants, with the emphasis on self-service, as well as snacks and ice-creams from food carts. The kids enjoyed the food (burgers, chips, hot dogs, pizzas and other doughy delights), but by the end of three days, even they were begging for fruit and vegetables. The highlight of the trip was the Buffalo Bill Wild West Show, a stunning evening of cowboys and Indians, horses, stagecoaches, wagons, stampeding buffalo, longhorn cattle and delicious finger-lickin' western-style food eaten at ringside tables.
HOTELS: On our first trip we stayed in the wonderful pink and white, fairytale Disneyland Hotel, a real luxury hotel right over the park's main entrance. Second time around we chose the cheaper (but not that much cheaper) Newport Bay Club, which is a lovely New England-style hotel overlooking the lake, 10 minutes' walk from the park – sadly, a false

economy, as we ended up having to queue for everything at the hotel as well as in the park. The Sequoia Lodge (10 minutes' walk from park) is Rocky Mountain rustic in style, with rocking chairs, patchwork quilts, Rocky River swimming pool and health club. The Hotel Cheyenne (15 minutes' walk from park) has western-style bunkhouses, a log fort and staff dressed as cowboys. The self-catering David Crockett Ranch cabins are suitable for longer stays in summer; each has a living room, outdoor BBQ and a kitchenette with microwave and dishwasher (15 minutes' shuttle ride from park). There is also the Hotel Santa Fe (15 minutes' walk from park), which is decorated Pueblo style, with Tex Mex restaurant bar. The following prices are per adult (based on two adults) and include one night's accommodation, breakfast, and two days in the theme park. Most rooms sleep up to four people; children under 3 are free, as are ages 3-11 sharing a room with one adult. Disneyland Hotel from £115, Hotel New York from £83, Newport Bay Club from £79, Sequoia Lodge from £69, Hotel Cheyenne from £61, Hotel Santa Fe from £56. Disney prides itself on its ability to get you anything you want – bottle warmer, cots, nappies, and a kettle in the room in our case – and if they don't have it on site, they will send a cast member to Paris to find it!

GETTING THERE: Getting to Disneyland could not be easier now that Eurostar (tel: 0345 881881 – calls charged at local rate) takes you from London Waterloo to Disney's own station at Marne Les Valles, right by the entrance to the Park. The train is very convenient, quicker and far less hassle than flying, and the children love it. Prices, if booked in advance, start at £99 for adults and £65 for children under 12 (under-4s free if a seat is not reserved). The Eurostar runs daily throughout the summer and school holidays, and at weekends in the winter. The high-speed Inter-city passenger service from Waterloo to Marne-la-Vallée takes three hours and is extremely comfortable. There are family areas with space for carrycots or for infants to play, children's packs for sale, and face painting at weekends. Toilets for the disabled, baby-changing and bottle-warming facilities, and wheelchair and buggy access.

HOURS *Open daily but times vary* • **PRICES** *Adults £16.50-£22, under-12s £13-£18. Prices vary according to season; 1- and 2-day passes available, (Adults, ranging from £32-£41; children, £20-£34) as well as reduced-price passports for those staying longer. Average queuing time 15 mins, but in high season expect to queue for up to 2 hours for some of the attractions. Average length of stay 2-3 days.*

INDOOR FUN PARKS

It's raining and the kids are climbing the walls, so what do you do? Let them – at one of London's growing number of indoor adventure centres. These giant padded obstacle courses, often on several levels, with slides, ball ponds, climbing nets, rope bridges, aerial glides and biff-bash bags, enable children to let off steam in a fun, safe, fully supervised environment.

ACTION STATIONS ☺ ♣ ◖

ADDRESS Lakeside Shopping Centre, Unit 601 Pavilion Building, Thurrock, Essex
PHONE 01708 868222

With four of the highest indoor slides in Britain and five themed sections, this is one of the best children's indoor play areas around. While little ones enjoy Mini-Minor, with giant floor and wall puzzles, bridges, crawl-throughs and an ultra-violet room, 5- to 8-year-olds can join Dennis, Gnasher, Softie Walter and the gang in the interactive Beano Menace Maze.

Streetwise over-8s can explore Trash Can Alley, the ultimate urban jungle of graffiti-strewn tube slides and rope swings, before braving The Swamp, which has four giant slides. The adventure centre is also open to mums and dads on Sundays. Children's parties can be held in a Party Pod, a spacecraft suspended in mid-air seating up to 12 children around a table, in the middle of which is a video camera recording the celebrations.

TRAVEL *Chalford Hundred rail; By car A13, signs to Lakeside* • **HOURS** *Babies and toddlers only: term-time, Mon-Fri, 11am-2.30pm; all ages: Mon-Thurs 4-8pm, Fri 4-9pm, Sat 10am-7.30pm, Sun 11am-6pm* • **PRICES** *£2.50 per child per 30 mins, £3.50 per child per 90 mins, Family Day Adult Play £2.50, family ticket for 3 children £9.99*

BRAMLEY'S BIG ADVENTURE ☺ 🐾 ◗

ADDRESS 136 Bramley Road, W10
PHONE 0181 960 1515

Excellent three-storey play structure for ages 5 and over, with good climbing equipment replete with sound effects. Under-5s can play safely in a separate area with scaled-down equipment and a pulley slide. Café serves good coffee. Holiday activities include dance and computer days and summer Stay and Play days.

TRAVEL ⊖ *Ladbroke Grove or Latimer Road* • **HOURS** *Daily, 10am-5pm* • **PRICES** *Over-5s £2.95-£3.95, under-5s £1.95-£2.95 (babies and toddlers free with siblings); children's parties from £6.95 per child; Stay and Play day £20 including food and drink*

DISCOVERY PLANET ☺ 🐾 ◗

ADDRESS Surrey Quays Shopping Centre, Redriff Road, SE16
PHONE 0171 237 2388

Huge indoor fun centre designed by fitness experts for children up to 12 years old. Free drinks for parents and toddlers attending Totspots.

TRAVEL ⊖ *Surrey Quays* • **OPEN** *Totspots: term-time, Mon-Fri 10am-noon and 1-3pm; after-school 4 O'clock Club: Sat-Sun and holidays 10am-6pm* • **PRICES** *Children £1.99-£3.99 (adults and babes in arms free); birthdays in the party room from £4.99-£9.99 per child*

DISCOVERY ZONE ☺ 🐾 ●

ADDRESS First Floor, The Junction Shopping Centre, SW11
PHONE 0171 223 1717

The lack of natural light, the bright colours and the music are guaranteed to give carers a headache but the kids love this large, American owned, efficiently run and fully supervised indoor fun centre. There are Mini-zones, Multi-zones, bouncy castles, ball ponds, slides, tunnels, swings, pulleys and other obstacle courses. There is also a good, scaled-down version of slides and moon walks for toddlers. Burger King, TV room for parents and Skill Zone slot-machine area (extra charge).

TRAVEL *Clapham Junction rail* • **HOURS** *Mon-Fri, 10am-6pm; Sat-Sun and school holidays, 10am-7pm* • **PRICES** *Under-13s £3.99 (weekends £4.99), under-2s £2.99 (weekends £3.99), babes in arms and accompanying adults free (no time limit to sessions). Weekday toddler-group limited sessions (under-5s only) £1.99 per child; term-time after-school club from £1.99 per child (including hamburger and fries)*

FANTASY ISLAND PLAYCENTRE ☺❄●

ADDRESS Vale Farm, Watford Road, Wembley, Middx
PHONE 0181 904 9044

Based on a jungle theme, the 30-ft-high assault course is full of bish-bash equipment that talks back, together with slides, rope bridge, climbing nets, ball pond, witch doctor's den and monster serpent slide. Under-5s have their own Fantasy Adventure Island with talking animals and scaled-down equipment. Carers can escape to the relative safety of the Island Café, which offers a welcome change from the usual burgers and chips.
TRAVEL ⊖ *North Wembley* • **HOURS** *Daily, 10am-7pm* • **PRICES** *Under-14s £3.95 per 90 mins (5-ft height restriction), under-5s £2.50*

HOUSE OF FUN ☺❄◐

ADDRESS The Bridge Leisure Centre, Kangley Bridge Road, SE26
PHONE 0181 778 7158

Very small, informal play area with soft play equipment, ball pond, not very high rope bridge and slides. Good for parties because for £45 you have exclusive use of the playroom for two hours and up to 15 children.
TRAVEL *Lower Sydenham rail* • **HOURS** *Daily, 10am-6pm (times vary, check first)* • **PRICE** *Under-10s £2 per hour*

KIDS' CORNER INDOOR PLAYCENTRE ☺❄◑

ADDRESS 232 Hither Green Lane, SE13
PHONE 0181 852 3322

Housed in an old cinema, this three-level play centre is hugely popular with local children up to the age of 12, with its ball pools, dizzy discs, drop slides, nets, swinging bridges, spook room and toddler area.
TRAVEL *Hither Green rail* • **HOURS** *Daily, 10am-7pm (last admission, 5.30pm)* • **PRICES** *Under-4s £2.50, over-4s £3.50. Parties £5.95 per child (including food)*

KIDS' KINGDOM ☺❄◑

ADDRESS Wood Lane Sports Centre, Wood Lane, Dagenham, Essex
PHONE 0181 984 8828

Twister slide, ghost house, jelly mountain and plenty of ropes and things to climb. Soft play area. Height restriction of 4ft 10in.
TRAVEL ⊖ *Dagenham East, then bus 103* • **HOURS** *Daily, 10am-6pm* • **PRICES** *Under-5s £3 per 90 mins, over-5s £3.95. Weekday pre-school term-time sessions for under-5s: £3 for up to 5 hours*

MONKEY BUSINESS ☺❄◑

ADDRESS 222 Green Lanes (entrance in Lodge Drive), Palmers Green, N13
PHONE 0181 886 7520

Monkey tree house, twizzle maze, biff-bash bags, tube slides, spooky room, roller challenge. Toddler area with toddler mornings in term-time. Height restriction of 4ft 10in. Café.
TRAVEL *Palmers Green rail* • **HOURS** *Daily, 10am-7pm* • **PRICES** *Under-5s £2.50, under-14s £2.75 per 1-hour session*

PIRATES' PLAYHOUSE ☺❄◑

ADDRESS Sobell Leisure Centre, Hornsey Road, N7
PHONE 0171 609 2166

Pirate theme on three levels with slides, swings, punch bags and bridges. Adults can join in with their children on quiet days. Large, separate, soft play area for under-5s. Maximum height for children 1.39 metres.
TRAVEL ⊖ *Finsbury Park or Holloway Road* • **HOURS** *Mon-Fri, 9am-6pm; Sat-Sun, 9.30am-7pm* • **PRICES** *Under 1 metre £2, over 1 metre £2.90*

PLAY DOME ☺ ❀ ◐

ADDRESS Woodside Leisure Park, Kingsway, Garston, Watford, Herts
PHONE 01923 894801
Includes a 4-metre free-fall slide, twisting tube slides, tunnels, nets, bridges, ball pools and aerial runways. Separate under-5s' play frame and activity room. Organised parent and toddler sessions, children and toddler parties.
TRAVEL ⊖ *Watford, then free bus service* • **HOURS** *Mon-Fri, 9.30am-6.30pm; Sat-Sun and school holidays, 10am-7pm* • **PRICES** *Under-5s £2.75 per 90 mins, over-5s £3.50. Term-time until 2pm: under-5s £2.25 (siblings £1.75 with under-5s)*

RASCALS ADVENTURE CENTRE ☺ ❀ ◐

ADDRESS Waterfront Leisure Centre, High Street, SE18
PHONE 0181 317 5000
Brightly coloured indoor play centre for under-9s, with a two-tiered adventure area of climbing frames, bash bags, hanging snakes, rope bridges and ball ponds, plus a separate well-padded, scaled-down version for under-5s. Children's video corner, children's toilets, baby-changing facilities and high chairs. Electronic security-tagging system. Picnic at the tables or buy meals from the diner to eat here. Drop and Shop service available soon. Excellent facilities throughout the centre (including crèche).
TRAVEL *Woolwich Arsenal rail; bus 53, 51, 96 or 54* • **HOURS** *Daily, 10am-6pm* • **PRICES** *Two-hour sessions: first child £4, sibling £3 (members £3/£1.50); parking: 40p for up to 4 hours*

SNAKES AND LADDERS ☺ ❀ ◐

ADDRESS Syon Park, Brentford, Middx
PHONE 0181 847 0946
Slides, ropes, ball pond, climbing frame; also go-karting (extra charge). Height restriction of 4ft 8in.
TRAVEL ⊖ *Gunnersbury, then bus 237 or 267; Kew Bridge rail* • **HOURS** *Daily, 10am-6pm* • **PRICE** *Under-5s from £2.65, under-12s from £3.65*

SPIKE'S MAD HOUSE ☺ ❀ ◐

ADDRESS Crystal Palace National Sports Centre, Anerley Hill, SE19
PHONE 0181 778 9876
This play centre for ages 2-12 also acts as a crèche for parents wishing to use the sports centre.
TRAVEL *Crystal Palace rail* • **HOURS** *Mon-Fri, 10am-2pm and 4-8pm; Sat-Sun, 10am-6pm* • **PRICES** *Non-members £2.50 per hour, members £2 per hour, annual membership £7. Party package available from £6-£8 per child*

ANIMAL ATTRACTIONS

Have you ever wanted to adopt an aardvark, pet a pig, ride a camel, milk a cow or see a snake? In London's zoos, farms and animal sanctuaries not only can you see all kinds of animals, often at very close range, but you can also watch sheep-shearing, cheese-making or lambing, and clamber over old tractors and adventure playgrounds.

NOTE: All farms now have washing facilities and it is very important to ensure that, during and after farm visits, children wash their hands before handling and eating food. Pregnant women should avoid sheep and goat pens during the lambing season, as enzotic abortion can be transmitted to humans.

BATTERSEA DOGS' HOME ☺ 🐛 ◑

ADDRESS 4 Battersea Park Road, SW8
PHONE 0171 622 3626

Since Britain's largest sanctuary for lost or unwanted dogs opened in 1860, nearly 3 million dogs have found shelter here. The ever-shifting canine population stands at around 400 but during the Christmas and summer holidays it can swell to over 700. Human visitors fall into three categories – those searching for a lost companion, those wishing to find a new addition to their household and those just looking around. Prospective owners are carefully screened for suitability and compatibility with the dog of their choice and are required to fill out a long form. You can expect to pay between £25 and £70 for a dog, but customers returning animals within seven days get their money back. A card is attached to each cage identifying the occupant and its origins, with veterinary notes and keeper comments. Some simply say 'Leave alone' or 'Bullies smaller dogs', while others are more descriptive. We encountered Sonny, an 'Escape artist – [who] needs high-walled garden', but also 'begs and does tricks'. Don't expect to find puppies – they are kept at Bell Mead, the 'country annexe' in Windsor, which is also a canine nursery and maternity home. Toilets (no disabled or baby-changing facilities). Wheelchair and buggy access.
TRAVEL *Battersea Park or Queenstown Road rail; bus 44* • **HOURS** *Mon-Fri, 10.30am-4.15pm; Sat-Sun, 10.30am-3.30pm (strays and unwanted dogs accepted any time)* • **PRICES** *Adults 50p, children 20p*

BATTERSEA PARK CHILDREN'S ZOO ☺ ☀ ◑

ADDRESS Albert Bridge Road, SW11
PHONE 0181 871 7540

Yum Yum the pot-bellied pig has quite a fan club at this small zoo, which boasts a reptile house, meerkat and mongoose enclosures, monkeys, flamingos, ponies, deer and wallabies. Pygmy goats and sheep wander freely and can be safely handled by children of all ages. Thomas the Tank Engine ride round the park in summer leaves from here (50p). Toilets and baby-changing facilities in zoo Easter to October only, otherwise outside park gates. Buggy and wheelchair access. See also The Great Outdoors.

TRAVEL ⊖ *Sloane Square, then bus 44 or 137; Battersea Park or Queenstown Road rail* • OPEN *Easter-Oct: daily, 10am-5pm; winter: Sat-Sun only, 11am-3pm (closed for 2 weeks in Feb)* • PRICES *Adults £1, children 50p, OAPs 25p (under-2s and disabled free)*

BROOKS FARM ☺ 🄴 ☀ ◖

ADDRESS Skeltons Lane Park, E10
PHONE 0181 539 4278

There are a couple of lovely Vietnamese pot-bellied pigs here, as well as sheep, chickens, cows, donkeys, rabbits and doves, and some mention of emus in the near future. There is also a play area for under-6s and vending machines for refreshments.

TRAVEL ⊖ *Leyton, then bus 69 or Leyton Midland Road rail* • HOURS *Tues-Sun, 10.30am-5.30pm* • PRICE *Free*

CLISSOLD PARK ☺ 🄴 ☀ ◖

ADDRESS Green Lanes, N16
PHONE 0181 800 1021

The park has a small animal enclosure with waterfowl, chickens, peacocks and fallow deer, an aviary with tropical birds and a new butterfly garden and butterfly tunnel. The Nature Room is staffed in summer. Playground and outdoor paddling pool (filled mid-May to mid-September). Toilets in playground (toilets for the disabled near bandstand). See also The Great Outdoors.

TRAVEL ⊖ *Finsbury Park or Manor House* • HOURS *Daily 7.30am – 9pm*
• PRICE *Free*

CORAM FIELDS ☺ 🄴 ☀ ◑

ADDRESS 93 Guildford Street, WC1
PHONE 0171 837 6138

This is a much-loved children's play park which adults can visit only if accompanied by a child. In addition to a playground with large paddling pool, sports facilities and children's nursery, it has a small animal enclosure with sheep, goats, a pig, chickens, budgies, geese, ducks and some long-suffering, cuddly rabbits and guinea pigs. Café.

TRAVEL ⊖ *Russell Square* • OPEN *Summer: daily, 9am-8pm; winter: 9am to dusk* • PRICE *Free*

GOLDERS HILL PARK ☺ 🄴 ☀ ◖

ADDRESS North End Way, NW3
PHONE 0181 455 5183

Pygmy goats, wallabies, black buck and fallow deer, pheasants, cranes, flamingos and rheas in pens at the bottom of the park near the children's play area (where there are inflatables and children's entertainment during summer holidays). Toilets (with disabled and baby-changing facilities) by café at top of the park, although it's a bit of a trek.

TRAVEL ⊖ *Golders Green* • HOURS *Daily, 7.30am to 30 mins before sunset*
• PRICE *Free*

LONDON AQUARIUM ☺ 🐟 ◖

ADDRESS County Hall, Riverside Buildings, Westminster Bridge, SE1
PHONE 0171 967 8000

Dominated by two huge tanks of fish from the Atlantic and Pacific, which span three floors, this vast new aquarium has fish and marine life from the Mediterranean and Indian Oceans was well as corals from the Barrier

Reef, a touch pool and a beach pier where visitors can stroke rays. Spoilt by the wonderful, if smaller, sea-life centres in Brighton and Hastings, and by Nausicaa in Boulogne (see Out of Town), my children were not very impressed with the London Aquarium, although they did appreciate the fact that it was at least in London. Much more could be done with the vast spaces between the tanks. Benja was disappointed there were not more interactive displays, and Jake said, 'There isn't enough to read and find out all about the fish you see.' When we visited, the touch pool was not being monitored and several young children were lifting the sea life out of the water, despite notices asking them not to. There is a café and gift shop.

TRAVEL ⊖ *Waterloo or Westminster* • **HOURS** *Mon-Fri, 10am-6pm; Sat-Sun, 9.30am-6pm; bank holidays, 9.30am-7.30pm* • **PRICES** *Adults £6.50, children £4.50, concs £5.50, family ticket £20 (under-2s and wheelchair users free)*

LONDON BUTTERFLY HOUSE ☺ ❀ ◑

ADDRESS Syon Park, Brentford, Middx
PHONE 0181 847 0946

The huge collection of free-flying butterflies in tropical greenhouse gardens and ponds does not excite children nearly as much as the spiders, stick insects, snakes and locusts in the Insect House. Toilets for the disabled and baby-changing facilities. Also **Snakes and Ladders** indoor adventure playground.

TRAVEL ⊖ *Gunnersbury or Kew Bridge rail, then bus 237 or 267 to Brentlea Gate* • **HOURS** *Daily, 10am-6.30pm (last admission, 5pm)* • **PRICES** *Adults £2.75, children and OAPs £1.75, family ticket (2+4) £6.95*

LONDON ZOO ☺ ❀ ●

ADDRESS Regent's Park, NW1
PHONE 0171 722 3333; Zoo-line 0891 505767

If it's animals you want, nothing beats London Zoo. Chinese alligators, Sumatran tigers, Nile crocodiles, African eagles, Asiatic lions – there are over 12,000 mammals, birds, reptiles, fish and insects living here, with recent additions including sloth bears on the redesigned Mappin Terraces and pygmy hippos. Children can watch the elephants being weighed, have camel and pony rides, see the crocodiles, piranhas and sharks at feeding time or watch the pelicans catching fish in their beaks. Penguin feeding time is popular with all ages and it's fun to see them waddling up and down Lubetkin's masterpiece of architectural engineering. If it is raining you can take shelter in the famous aquarium or the eerie Moonlight World, with its nocturnal animals, including the Leadbeater possum, once thought to be extinct. There are regular Meet the Animals sessions and plenty of exciting, educational activity boards and exhibits dotted around the zoo. The children's zoo has sheep and goats to pet, a cow that is milked daily and some more unusual babies, depending on who's just been born. Children can find out how it feels to hear like an elephant and see like a giraffe, and make their own badge and brass rubbings in the Discovery Centre (daily, 2-4pm). There are also summer workshops for children aged 6 and over (booking essential, tel: 0171 722 3333). The self-service restaurant is very child friendly, and also has baby food, nappies, reduced-price children's meals and toddler portions, high chairs, baby-changing facilities and a feeding room. The grass area for picnics is near Barclays Court. Shop. Playground. Toilets for the disabled. Pushchair and wheelchair hire at the gate. Double buggy and wheelchair access.

TRAVEL ⊖ Camden Town or Baker Street, then bus 274; London Waterbus Company river bus along Regent's Canal; car park and meter parking near zoo entrance • **HOURS** Mar-Oct: daily, 10am-5.30pm; Nov-Apr: daily, 10am-4pm (closed Christmas Day) • **PRICES** Adults £8, children and concs £6 (under-4s free), OAPs and students £7, family ticket £24

CITY FARMS

These genuine working farms give children of all ages a chance to see a wide variety of farm animals and to get involved in day-to-day tasks such as milking, feeding and mucking out. Most also offer other activities like sheep-shearing demonstrations, riding, milking and craft sessions. Don't forget your wellies, even in summer.

COLLEGE FARM ☺ 🄴 ☀ ◐

ADDRESS 45 Fitzalan Road, N3
PHONE 0181 349 0690

Originally the main farm for Express Dairies, supplying milk to Londoners, this city farm now has Highland cattle, donkeys, pigs, sheep and rabbits. There is a special Open Day on the first Sunday of each month (1-6pm) with craft fair, donkey rides, puppet shows, cream teas in the lovely café, and a brass band. Visitors' centre, picture gallery and shop selling animal feed and pet food. Toilets with baby-changing area. No toilets for the disabled.
TRAVEL ⊖ Finchley Central; bus 13, 26, 82, 143 or 260 • **HOURS** Tues-Sun, 10am-6pm • **PRICES** Adults £1.50, children 75p (open days £2 and £1)

CRYSTAL PALACE PARK FARM ☺ 🄴 ☀ ◐

ADDRESS Crystal Palace Park Road, SE20
PHONE 0181 778 7148

Farm with pigs, cows, goats, rabbits, chickens, donkeys, horses, otters, flamingos and sheep. The animals roam free so there is limited buggy access on busy days. Two picnic tables, but as the roaming goats eat anything in sight, we have never seen anyone brave enough to use them. The shop sells food to feed some of the animals. Shire-horse cart rides around the park from here. Toilets for the disabled. Wheelchair access. Baby-changing facilities. See also Ten Days Out and The Great Outdoors.
TRAVEL Crystal Palace rail • **HOURS** Daily, 11am-5pm • **PRICES** Adults £1.10, children 55p, family ticket (2+2) £2.75

DEAN CITY FARM ☺ 🄴 ☀ ◐

ADDRESS 39 Windsor Ave, SW19
PHONE 0181 543 5300

On a fine day visitors can walk from Colliers Wood tube station along the riverside, past Merton Abbey Mills, to see this well-kept farm with its variety of animals, its riding school for able-bodied and disabled children, and its organic horticulture. In August there is a Discovery Week for 11- to 15-year-olds. Toilets for the disabled. No baby-changing facilities.
TRAVEL ⊖ Colliers Wood or Mitcham rail; bus 200 • **HOURS** Tues-Sun, 9.30am-5.30pm • **PRICE** Free (donation appreciated)

FREIGHTLINERS FARM ☺ 🄴 ☀ ◔

ADDRESS Sheringham Road, N7
PHONE 0171 609 0467
Plenty of opportunity to get involved with the care of animals on this small, busy farm with its sheep, cows, pigs, goats, ducks, geese and chickens. There is a friendly playgroup for under-5s on Wednesday and Saturday mornings, a sensory garden, café and farm shop selling honey and eggs. Toilets for the disabled and baby-changing facilities.
TRAVEL ⊖ *Highbury & Islington or Holloway; bus 43, 271, 4, 19 or 17* • **HOURS** *Tues-Sun, 9am-1pm and 2-5pm* • **PRICE** *Free (donations invited)*

HACKNEY CITY FARM ☺ 🄴 ☀ ◔

ADDRESS 1a Goldsmiths Row, E2
PHONE 0171 729 6381
There are bees, pigs, sheep, goats, ducks and rabbits at this lovely converted brewery with a cobbled yard in the centre. It also has a small orchard, ecological pond, butterfly tunnel and wild-flower area. Regular children's events and activities include pottery, spinning and weaving workshops, and you can watch sheep-shearing in May. Toilets for the disabled. Baby-changing surface.
TRAVEL *Cambridge Heath rail or bus 26, 48 or 55* • **HOURS** *Daily, 10am-4.30pm* • **PRICE** *Free*

KENTISH TOWN CITY FARM ☺ 🄴 ☀ ◔

ADDRESS 1 Cressfield Close, NW5
PHONE 0171 916 5421
Friendly farm with horses, chickens, ducks, cows, geese and rabbits as well as a children's garden, a pensioners' garden and a nature area. Horse riding for Camden residents. Farm shop with duck eggs and manure for sale. Toilets for the disabled. Baby-changing can be arranged.
TRAVEL ⊖ *Chalk Farm or Kentish Town or Gospel Oak rail* • **HOURS** *Tues-Sun, 9.30am-5.30pm* • **PRICE** *Free*

MUDCHUTE FARM ☺ 🄴 ☀ ◔

ADDRESS Pier Street (off Manchester Road), Isle of Dogs, E14
PHONE 0171 515 5901
The largest of the city farms, Mudchute Farm also includes a wildlife area, woodland and parkland. Children can meet Mary the Aberdeen Angus cow, Perky the rare-breed pig, and Larry the llama. There's a lot of walking involved if you want to see it all. Good riding facilities (for lessons, phone 0171 515 0749). Café (good, but prices are higher than other city farms). Agricultural show mid-August. Wheelchair access and toilets for the disabled. No baby-changing facilities.
TRAVEL *Mudchute DLR* • **HOURS** *Daily, 9am-5pm* • **PRICE** *Free*

NEWHAM CITY FARM ☺ 🄴 ☀ ◔

ADDRESS Stansfeld Road, E6
PHONE 0171 476 1170
A beautifully kept farm with popular Farm Club, where children can muck in and help look after the livestock, which includes cows, pigs, horses, ducks, geese and even a llama. Café, summer barbecues, picnic area, pony rides, craft sessions.
TRAVEL *Royal Albert DLR* • **HOURS** *Tues-Sun, 10am-5pm* • **PRICE** *Free*

PLUMRIDGE FARM ☺ 🄴 ☼ ●

ADDRESS Stagg Hill, Barnet, Herts
PHONE 0181 449 0695
A wonderful, friendly goat farm where you can see the different stages involved in goat-cheese production and then sample the different cheeses, which are also sold in the shop.
TRAVEL By car on M25 to junction 24; car park • **HOURS** Daily, 8am-5pm • **PRICE** Free

SPITALFIELDS FARM ASSOCIATION ☺ 🄴 ☼ ◑

ADDRESS Weaver Street, E1
PHONE 0171 247 8762
Learn to feed, muck out, milk and bed down the animals, which include pigs, goats, sheep, cows, rabbits, donkeys and poultry. Local-history tours in a horse-drawn cart and pony rides available. Also free pottery and dairy workshops.
TRAVEL ⊖ Whitechapel or Bethnal Green • **HOURS** Tues-Sun, 9am-6pm (winter to 5pm) • **PRICE** Free (voluntary donations welcome)

STEPNEY STEPPING STONES FARM ☺ 🄴 ☼ ◑

ADDRESS Stepney Way, E1
PHONE 0171 790 8204
Pigs, goats, cows, sheep, geese, ducks, rabbits and donkeys, plus a wildlife pond and a nice picnic garden. Café and shop sell farm produce. Toilets for the disabled (baby-changing can be arranged).
TRAVEL ⊖ Stepney Green or Limehouse DLR • **HOURS** Tues-Sun, 9.30am-5pm (later in summer) • **PRICE** Free (donations invited)

SURREY DOCKS FARM ☺ 🄴 ☼ ◑

ADDRESS Rotherhithe Street, SE16
PHONE 0171 231 1010
This is our favourite city farm, despite the fact the kid goats tried to eat Benjamin's shorts (while he was wearing them). It is very small but has a lovely atmosphere and very friendly staff, and the café sells drinks and biscuits at amazingly low prices. Children can roam free among the goats and sheep in the yard, while more timid tots can watch from the safety of the raised wooden gallery running along one side. There is a genuine working forge and plenty of holiday activities, including felt-making, egg painting and farm work. Small orchard, wild area, riverside walk and duck pond. Café. Farm shop. Toilets for the disabled (no baby changing-facilities).
TRAVEL Surrey Quays DLR; parking outside gates • **HOURS** Tues-Thurs and Sat-Sun, 10am-1pm and 2-5pm • **PRICE** Free

VAUXHALL CITY FARM ☺ 🄴 ☼ ◑

ADDRESS Tyers Street (off Kennington Lane), SE11
PHONE 0171 582 4204
Plenty of opportunity for hands-on work with the resident goats, sheep, pigs and rabbits. Good riding facilities at reasonable rates, plus pony and donkey rides for the very young. Spinning Club and holiday play scheme. No café but reasonable picnic area. Toilets for the disabled. Baby-changing facilities. Next door is the **London Balloon**.
TRAVEL ⊖ Vauxhall • **HOURS** Tues-Thurs and Sat-Sun, 10.30am-5pm • **PRICE** Free (except tours; donations welcome)

YOUNG'S BREWERY ☺☼◑

ADDRESS Wandsworth High Street (entrance in Ram Street), SW18
PHONE 0181 875 7005

Visitors can join a tour of the stables to see the team of Young's heavy horses, used to deliver beer to local pubs. The team includes black and white shires, dappled grey Percherons, Clydesdales and Suffolk punches, sharing their stables with a ram, goats, a pony, donkeys, geese and ducks. A farrier makes all the horses' shoes in the smithy behind the stables.
TRAVEL *Wandsworth Town rail* • **HOURS** *Mon-Sat, 10am, noon, 2pm and 4pm* • **PRICES** *Full brewery tour (including stable tour), adults £5.50, children (5-18) £3, concs £4.50 (includes soft drink or a pint of beer) or stable tour only, adults £3.50, under-5's free, children (5-18) £2, but phone ahead since advance booking is recommended.*

HORSES AND WHERE TO FIND THEM

A hundred years ago there were more than 50,000 working horses on the streets of London. Today there are fewer than 1,500 employed in the capital, mostly by the Army, police, brewers, riding stables and the Royal Family. Over the past few years the number of horses employed by the Metropolitan Police has been on the increase, and since 1985, Harrods has also employed eight Dutch stallions for deliveries. Show horses and their riders dressed in full show regalia or hacking gear assemble at the west end of Rotten Row on the first Sunday in August (for details, phone 0181 761 5651). The Horse of the Year Show is held annually at the end of September in Wembley Arena (tickets: 0181 900 1234/1919), and **Trooping of the Colour** every June in Horse Guards Parade, Whitehall (for tickets write with SAE between 1 January and 28 February to the Ticket Office, Headquarters, Household Division, Chelsea Barracks, SW19 5AE). The **London Harness Horse Parade** is held on Easter Mondays in Regent's Park, NW1 (details on 0171 486 7905). **Horseman's Sunday**, at the Church of St John and St Michael, Hyde Park Crescent, W2, usually takes place in the second or third week in September (details on 0171 262 1732). The vicar, on horseback, rides to the front of the church to bless more than 100 horses and riders, after which the congregation trot across the road for an afternoon of showjumping in Kensington Gardens. Young's 20 drays, the only working drays in London, can be seen delivering beer from their Wandsworth brewery to 40 pubs in south London. The Royal Mews, Buckingham Palace, is open in July, Tues-Thurs, 12pm-4pm, last admission 3.30pm and in August and September, Mon-Thurs, 10.30am-3.30pm, last admission 3pm, is home to the Queen's 30 carriage horses. At Horse Guards Parade, Whitehall, SW1, two mounted troopers of the Household Cavalry are posted outside until July 1st, daily from 10am-4pm, changing every hour and after July 1st 11am-4pm when the guards are posted outside on every even date in Jul, every odd date in Aug and every even date in Sep. The **Changing of the Guard** also takes place at Buckingham Palace and Windsor Castle Phone Buckingham Palace on 0171 930 4832 for details and Windsor Castle on 0891 505 452. For riding lessons, see Sports and Leisure.

WATERWAYS

Messing about in boats – whether you are cruising along Regent's Canal in a traditional narrow boat, rowing round the Serpentine or taking a pleasure boat along old Father Thames – is always a hit with the kids and not necessarily reliant on the weather, although you will see more from the boat if it is not actually raining.

RIVER AND CANAL TRIPS AND VISITS

You can take trips up and down the Thames throughout the year, from Westminster and Charing Cross Piers. Day and half-day trips include Historic Greenwich, Tower of London, Thames Flood Barrier, Richmond Pier to Hampton Court, Disco Cruises and Lunch Cruises. Prices from £3 (children half-price). For full details, phone the London Tourist Board's Special River-boat Information Service on 0839 123432 (calls cost 39p/49p per minute); Catamaran Cruises on 0171 987 1185; Tower Hill Cruises on 0171 930 3373; and City Cruises on 0171 237 5134.

HMS BELFAST ☺ ☀ ◖

ADDRESS Morgans Lane, Tooley Street, SE1
PHONE 0171 407 6434
Launched in 1938, this Royal Navy cruiser played an important role in the Battle of Northcape in December 1943. Little has changed in this permanent museum since it was in active service. Not suitable for the very young or those who do not like climbing lots of steps. See also Museums and Galleries.
TRAVEL ⊖ London Bridge or Tower Hill; Tower Gate DLR; ferry from Tower Pier • **OPEN** Mar-Oct: daily, 10am-6pm; Nov-Feb: daily, 10am-5pm (closed Christmas Day) • **PRICES** Adults £4.70, children £2.40 (under-5s free), concs £3.30

CANAL-BOAT TRIPS AND OVERNIGHT STAYS ☀

PHONE 0181 810 9126
Boat hire, one-day and overnight trips on a narrow boat cruising up the Grand Union Canal. Phone for details and prices.

CATAMARAN CRUISERS ☺ ☀

ADDRESS Charing Cross Pier, Victoria Embankment, WC2
PHONE 0171 987 1185
A great, hassle-free way for children to see the sights and get a real feel for London (as long as they're not sea-sick). Trips run to the **Tower of London** and **Greenwich**.
TRAVEL ⊖ Charing Cross • **HOURS** Daily every 30 mins from 10.30am to 4pm • **PRICE** Adults from £3, children from £1.50

CUTTY SARK ☺ 🐛 ◖

ADDRESS King William Walk, Greenwich Pier, SE10
PHONE 0181 858 3445

The *Cutty Sark* was built as a tea clipper in 1869 and now stands in dry dock. Children love exploring the deck and can see where the sailors worked, slept and ate. In the summer you can also go aboard the ***Gypsy Moth IV***, the boat in which Sir Francis Chichester sailed round the world single-handed in 1966. See also Ten Days Out and Museums and Galleries.

TRAVEL *Greenwich or Maze Hill rail; Island Gardens DLR, then foot tunnel* • **OPEN** *Summer: Mon-Sat 10am-6pm, Sun noon-6pm; winter: Mon-Sat 10am-5pm, Sun noon-5pm* • **PRICES** *Adults £3.50, children and concs £2.50 (under-7s free), family ticket £8.50*

GREAT RIVER RACE ☺ ☀ ◖

PHONE 0181 398 9057

Over 200 traditional craft, including cutters, whalers and gigs, race 22 miles from Richmond to Island Gardens, opposite Greenwich Pier. See also London by Season.

WHEN *Early Sep*

JASON'S CANAL-BOAT TRIP 🐛 ◖

ADDRESS opp 60 Bloomfield Road, W9
PHONE 0171 286 3428

A one-and-a-half-hour round trip by narrow boat (with commentary) from Little Venice, through the Maida Hill Tunnel, under Blow-up Bridge, past **London Zoo**, Primrose Hill and the Cumberland Basin, to Camden Lock Market. Lunches and teas available on board if booked before 10.30am that day (otherwise limited range of sandwiches available). Children's birthday parties can be arranged. There is covered seating on board, and a canalside restaurant.

TRAVEL ⊖ *Warwick Avenue; bus 6 or 46* • **WHEN** *Apr-May: 10.30am, 12.30pm, 2.30pm; Jun-Aug: 10.30am, 12.30pm, 2.30pm, 4.30pm; Sep: 10.30am, 12.30pm, 2.30pm; Oct: 12.30pm, 2.30pm* • **PRICES** *Adults £5.95 (single £4.95), children £4.50 (single £3.75, under-4s free), family ticket (2+3) £17.50*

JENNY WREN 🐛 ◖

ADDRESS 250 Camden High Street, NW1
PHONE 0171 485 4433/6210

The cruise is a one-and-a-half-hour round trip from Camden Lock to Little Venice and back, which is rather long for young children, and there are no one-way tickets. You can also book privately to travel eastwards through the Islington Tunnel. Advanced booking is advisable. There is covered seating in case of rain.

TRAVEL ⊖ *Camden Town* • **WHEN** *Mar-Oct: daily, 11.30am, 2pm, 3.30pm; Nov-Feb: weekend cruises subject to weather conditions* • **PRICES** *Adults £5, children £2.75 (children on laps go free)*

LONDON CANAL MUSEUM 🐛 ◖

ADDRESS 12-13 New Wharf Road, N1
PHONE 0171 713 0836

Learn about the cargoes and canal crafts, about the people who strove to make a living from the canals, and the horses that pulled their boats. Housed in a warehouse built in the 1850s by the ice-cream manufacturer

Carlo Gatti, the museum traces the story of London's canals from the early days as important trade routes to today's more leisurely activities. See also Museums and Galleries.

TRAVEL ⊖ *King's Cross* • **HOURS** *Tues-Sun, 10am-4.30pm (last admission, 3.45pm; times vary in winter)* • **HOURS** *Adults £2.50, children £1.25*

LONDON WATERBUS COMPANY ☺ ☂ ◑

ADDRESS Blomfield Road, W9 (entrance at corner of Westbourne Terrace road bridge) and Camden Lock Place, NW1 (off Chalk Farm Road)
PHONE 0171 482 2660; bookings and enquiries 0171 482 2550
Covered seating if it rains. If you want to get off to visit the zoo, tell the ticket master and you get a reduction on the price of admission. Also boat hire for children's parties.

TRAVEL ⊖ *Warwick Avenue (for Little Venice) or Camden Town (for Camden Lock)* • **WHEN** *Apr-Oct: daily service; Nov-Mar: weekends only. Three boats run hourly between Camden Lock and Little Venice (every 2 hours in winter)* • **PRICES** *Adults single £3.70 (return £4.80), children £2.30 (return £2.90, under-3s free)*

POOL OF LONDON ☺ ☂ ◑

PHONE City Cruises 0171 488 0344
Hop-on-hop-off ferry service connecting Tower Pier, HMS *Belfast*, St Katharine's Docks, London Bridge Pier and Butler's Wharf, which also offers discounts on attractions in the area.

WHEN *Mid-Mar to mid-May: daily, 11am-5pm, every 30 mins (Jun-Sep, every 15 mins)* • **PRICES** *Adults £2, children £1*

PUPPET THEATRE BARGE ☺ ☂

ADDRESS Blomfield Road, W9
PHONE 0171 249 6876 or mobile phone 0836 202745
Movingstage Marionettes company gives performances throughout the year on an old Thames barge converted into a delightful miniature auditorium complete with proscenium arch and raked seating. On Regent's Canal in Little Venice from November to June and sailing up the Thames with performances at Kingston and Richmond from June to September.

TRAVEL ⊖ *Warwick Avenue* • **WHEN** *Times vary; phone for details* • **PRICES** *Adults £5.50, children £5*

RICHMOND BRIDGE MOTOR- AND ROWING-BOAT HIRE ☼

PHONE 0181 948 8270
PRICES *Rowing boats £2.50 per person per hour (under-14s free). Fully equipped holiday boats start at £80 per person for a weekend.*

THAMES BARRIER AND VISITORS' CENTRE ☺ ☼ ◑

ADDRESS Unity Way, SE18
PHONE 0181 854 1373
Learn about the history of the river and why the barrier was built. Cafeteria, picnic area, souvenir shop, play area and riverside walk with view of the barrier. To get a closer look at this remarkable piece of 20th-century engineering, take a Barrier Cruise from Barrier Pier next to the Visitors' Centre (cruise lasts approx. 25 mins). See also Museums and Galleries.

TRAVEL *Charlton rail; buses 177 or 180; boat from Greenwich or Westminster Piers* • **HOURS** *Visitors' centre: Mon-Fri, 10am-5pm; Sat-Sun,*

10.30am-5.30pm (closed 25-26 Dec and 1 Jan) • **PRICES** *Adults £3.40, children and concs £2, family ticket (for 5 people) £7.50. Car park 50p*

TOWER BRIDGE EXPERIENCE ☺ 🌓 ◑

ADDRESS Tower Bridge, E1
PHONE 0171 378 1928

There is an imaginative multimedia permanent exhibition inside the Bridge itself (see Museums and Galleries) and wonderful views of the Thames from the high-level glass walkways. Try to time your visit with a 'bridge lift', when the bridge opens to let large vessels through (for times and dates, phone 0171 378 7700).

TRAVEL ⊖ *Tower Hill or London Bridge, or bus 15 to Tower Hill* • **OPEN** *Summer: daily, 10am-6.15pm; winter: daily, 10am-5.15pm (closed Good Friday, 24-26 Dec, 1 Jan; last admission 1 hour before closing)* • **PRICES** *Adults £5.70, children and OAPs £3.90, family ticket (2+2) £14*

SUMMER BOATING IN LONDON PARKS

ALEXANDRA PARK ☺ ☀

ADDRESS Muswell Hill, N22
PHONE Boating 0181 889 9089; general information 0181 365 2121

Large boating lake with an island and small area for young children to boat on their own. Life jackets must be worn by under-12s, who must also be accompanied by an adult.

TRAVEL ⊖ *Wood Green tube, then bus W3* • **HOURS** *Daily, 10am-8pm (summer only)* • **PRICES** *5-seater rowing boats £3.50, 6-seater £5.50, 3-seater pedal boat £4, all for 45 mins*

BATTERSEA PARK ☺ ☀

ADDRESS Albert Bridge Road, SW11
PHONE 0181 871 7530/1

Large tree-bordered lake in southeast corner of this well-equipped riverside park offers excellent-value boating. You cannot land on the two islands in the middle but you can get up close for plenty of bird-spotting opportunities, and it's fun trying to circumnavigate the islands in one of the 35 fibre-glass rowing boats.

TRAVEL *Battersea Park or Queenstown Road rail* • **HOURS** *Sat-Sun, noon-6pm (Apr-Sep or when weather breaks)* • **PRICES** *£4 per hour per boat (max. 5 people). Under-10s must be accompanied by an adult.*

BISHOP'S PARK ☺ ☀

ADDRESS Bishop's Park Road, SW6
PHONE 0171 731 5215

Small, shallow lake with a few four-seater pedal boats and a couple of rowing boats (max. one adult, two children).

TRAVEL ⊖ *Putney Bridge* • **HOURS** *Daily, 11am-7pm until end Sep* • **PRICE** *Free 10-minute sessions (expect long queues on sunny days)*

CRYSTAL PALACE PARK ☺ ☀

ADDRESS Thicket Road, SE20 and Crystal Palace Park Road, SE26
PHONE 0181 778 7148; Crystal Palace Eventsline 0181 778 9496

Although you cannot get a good view of the prehistoric monsters lurking on Dinosaur Island from the boats, you can still thrill small children with the idea that one of the monsters they have spotted lurking in the water on their way to the boating area might come alive and chase them. Under-13s must wear life jacket and be accompanied by someone aged 16 or over.

TRAVEL *Crystal Palace rail* • **HOURS** *Sat-Sun, 11am-4.30pm (weather permitting)* • **PRICE** *Pedal boats (max. 4 people) £3.25 per half-hour*

FINSBURY PARK ☺ ☀

ADDRESS Seven Sisters Road, N4
PHONE 0171 263 5001

There are 20 rowing boats for hire. Under-11s must wear life jacket and be accompanied by an adult, although younger children are sometimes allowed to go without an adult if they keep in site of the boat house. Life jackets are also available for nervous adults.

TRAVEL ⊖ *Finsbury Park* • **HOURS** *Daily, noon-7pm (weather permitting)* • **PRICE** *Rowing boats (max. 4 people) £2.50 per half hour, £3.50 per hour*

GREENWICH PARK ☺ ☀

ADDRESS Carlton Way, SE10
PHONE 0171 262 3751; park information 0181 858 2608

Tiny but very popular boating pond right next to the well-equipped playground and sandpit.

TRAVEL *Greenwich or Maze Hill rail* • **HOURS** *Daily, 9am-6pm, until end Sep* • **PRICE** *One-person pedal boats £1.50 per 20 minutes. Rowing boats for 1 adult and up to 2 children £3 for 20 minutes (longer on quiet days)*

HYDE PARK ☺ ☀

PHONE 0171 262 3751

No children under 5. This park was once a favourite haunt of highwaymen and duellists, but popular activities are now of a more aquatic bent, although children aged 5 and over can take riding lessons at the Hyde Park Riding Stables. There are nearly 100 rowing boats and pedal boats for hire on the enormous Serpentine lake, but still expect to queue at weekends. You can also take a 10-minute motor-boat trip around the lake or go swimming in Serpentine Lido (until end September). There is a small children's paddling pool, sandpit, slide and grassy picnic area.

TRAVEL ⊖ *Hyde Park or Knightsbridge* • **HOURS** *Daily, 9am-6.30pm* • **PRICES** *Rowing boats £6.50 per hour (max. 4 people) plus £5 deposit*

REGENT'S PARK ☀

PHONE 0171 262 3751

Life jackets must be worn. Parents can go boating in peace on the large lake while their offspring paddle about in their own separate, shallow children's pond. Child-friendly café, four playgrounds and **London Zoo** all nearby. You could arrive by boat along Regent's Canal from Camden Lock or Little Venice with the **London Waterbus Company**.

TRAVEL ⊖ *Baker Street* • **HOURS** *Daily, 9am-7pm, until 30 Sep* • **PRICES** *Rowing boats (max 4 people) £6.50 per hour (plus £5 deposit). No children under 5. Separate under-12s lake with rowing boats (max. 4 people) £4 and 1-person pedal boats £1.60 per half-hour*

STEAM ENGINES

A puff of smoke, a whistle and you enter the bygone days of steam. No child can resist the excitement of steam travel, whether it is the funny face of Thomas the Tank Engine or the romantic charm of a Victorian paddle steamer. But it is not just railways and boats that are powered by steam. Impressive, huge stationary engines, which once powered heavy industry, textile mills and pumping stations, are also put 'in steam' at many of Britain's steam and industrial museums and sites.

LONDON

KEW BRIDGE STEAM MUSEUM ☺ ❀ ◖

ADDRESS Green Dragon Lane, Brentford, Middx
PHONE 0181 568 4757
This 19th-century pumping station supplied London's water for over 100 years, powered by five enormous beam engines (three of which have been restored and are put in steam at weekends and on Bank Holiday Mondays). Miniature steam railway, other engines, working forge, etc.
TRAVEL ⊖ Gunnersbury or Kew Gardens, then bus 27, 237 or 267; Kew Bridge rail; car park • **HOURS** Daily, 11am-5pm. Engines in steam at weekends and bank holidays • **PRICES** Weekends: adults £3.80, children £2, concs £2.50, family ticket (2+3) £10.50; weekdays: adults £2.80, children aged 5-15 £1 and concs £1.50, family ticket £7

NORTH WOOLWICH OLD STATION MUSEUM ☺ ❀ ◖

ADDRESS Pier Road, E16
PHONE 0171 474 7244
The engines at this delightful little museum are put in steam on Easter Sunday and the first Sunday of the month in summer.
TRAVEL North Woolwich rail or Woolwich rail, then foot tunnel or ferry; bus 69, 101, 276 • **HOURS** Mon-Wed and Sat, 10am-5pm; Sun and bank holidays, 2-5pm • **PRICE** Free

OUT OF TOWN

BLUEBELL RAILWAY ☺ ❀ ●

ADDRESS Sheffield Park Station, nr Uckfield, East Sussex
PHONE 01825 723777; 24-hour talking timetable 01825 722370
The Bluebell Railway makes a memorable day's outing for anyone of any age. The locomotive sheds are at Sheffield Park and the station has been restored in the late-Victorian style, with signals, signal boxes and vintage enamel advertisements. The small museum on platform 2 is crammed with models, tickets, photographs and signs. The highlight of the visit, however, is the train journey, which takes you along a 5-mile stretch of the old branch line between Sheffield Park and Horsted Keynes in historic

coaches, meticulously restored in the elegant 1930s style of the Southern Railway. If you are feeling flush you can have lunch or a cream tea on the 1920s Golden Arrow Pullman (runs at weekends), or less expensively in the 1882 station buffet at Horsted Keynes. The Bluebell Railway gets very crowded at weekends, especially in May when the bluebells blossom in the woods through which the line passes (and from which it gets its name). Round trip takes about an hour and a half. Café and picnic area at both stations. Restaurant and well-stocked gift shop. Toilets. Wheelchair access (phone in advance). **NEARBY:** Alongside the Bluebell Railway is Capability Brown's majestically landscaped Sheffield Park (tel: 01825 790231; open Apr-Nov, Tues-Sat 11am-6pm, Sun 1-6pm or sunset; admission £4 adults, £2 children).

TRAVEL *Haywards Heath or East Grinstead rail; 46 miles south of London – car park* • **HOURS** *Daily, first train 11am, last train Mon-Fri 3.40pm, Sat and Sun 4pm. During school summer vacation (27th Jul-6th Sep) trains run from 11am-4pm and leave on the hour from Sheffield Park* • **PRICE** *All Day Rover: adult £7.40, children £3.70, (under-3s free), family ticket (2+3), £19.90, OAP £6. Prices include train ride, admission to museum, station and locomotive sheds. Single or return tickets can be bought at either station but if you only want a single, start at Horsted Keynes because the museum and locomotive sheds are at Sheffield Park Station.*

CHUFFA TRAINS MUSEUM ☺ ☀ ◑

ADDRESS 82 High Street, Whitstable, Kent
PHONE 01227 277339

A museum and model-train shop that recalls the days of the Crab and Winkle Railway, opened in 1830. Children's activity area. Under-10s must be accompanied. No wheelchair or buggy access. Combine this with a visit to Whitstable beach and a pub lunch in the Neptune on the beach, or sample the local catches at the wonderful Royal Oyster Factory fish restaurant. Tourist Information, tel: 01227 275482.

TRAVEL *Whitstable rail* • **HOURS** *Mon-Fri, 10am-3pm (5pm during school holidays and bank holidays); Sat, 10am-5pm* • **PRICES** *Adults £1.50, children 75p, OAPs £1, family ticket (2+3) £3.75*

DIDCOT RAILWAY CENTRE ☺ ☀ ●

PHONE 01235 817200

Once a major maintenance post for Brunel's idiosyncratic broad-gauge Great Western Railway, Didcot is now a Mecca for railway enthusiasts. The engine shed houses steam locomotives, some of which are still being restored, carriages and freight wagons. You can take train rides on the first and last Sunday of the month and Bank Holiday Mondays until the end of May, then every Sunday until end August. Special events include Thomas the Tank Engine weekends (phone for details). Admission price depends on the event, but includes all rides and entertainment.

TRAVEL *Didcot rail; car park* • **OPEN** *Sat-Sun all year, 11am-5pm (4pm winter); Easter-25 Sep and 22-30 Oct: Mon-Fri, 11am-5pm;* • **PRICES** *Adults from £4, children from £3 (under-5s usually free)*

EAST ANGLIA RAILWAY MUSEUM ☺ ☕ ◑

ADDRESS Chapel Station, Colchester, Essex
PHONE 01206 242524

A working museum where visitors can watch the locomotives and coaches being restored, as well as taking steam passenger rides. There is wheelchair access but no toilets for the disabled.

TRAVEL *Chapel rail* • **HOURS** *Daily, 10am-5pm (closed Christmas Day)* • **PRICES** *Adults £2.50, children £1.50 (under-4s free), OAPs £2, family ticket (2+4) £7; when engines are in steam: £4.50, £2.50, £3, £13 respectively*

FRENCH BROTHERS BOAT TRIPS ☺ ☼ ◑

ADDRESS The Runnymede Boathouse, Windsor Road, Old Windsor, Berks
PHONE 01753 851900 or 01753 862933

Regular 45-minute trips from Runnymede to Hampton Court, Windsor and several stops in between aboard the *Lucy Fisher*, a replica paddle steamer. Tearooms. Souvenirs.

TRAVEL *Windsor rail* • **HOURS** *Easter-Nov: daily on the hour from 11am-5pm* • **PRICES** *Adults £3, children £2, babes in arms free*

HOLLYCOMBE STEAM COLLECTION AND GARDENS ☺ ☼ ●

ADDRESS Iron Hill, Liphook, Hants
PHONE 01428 724900

This delightful, story-book fairground, set in a beautiful woodland garden, is ideal for children of any age. The very reasonable entrance fee covers everything, and you can have an unlimited number of rides on traditional steam-powered fairground attractions: the Orton and Spooner Steam Roundabout (ideal for the smallest of children), the Big Wheel, Ghost House, Steam Yacht, Swingboats and Razzle-Dazzle. Traction engine rides take you to a steam-powered farm to meet Simon the llama, Smoky the miniature donkey and a host of other friendly animals. Also miniature railway and station, bioscope travelling cinema with fairground organ, working paddle-steamer engine, a quarry railway and more. Woodland walk and gardens, steam farm, sawmill, ghost house, tearoom. Staff are very friendly and helpful, and even if you are here on your own with lots of small children it is easy to keep track of them. Special school-holiday events such as Santa's Special, Children's Fayre Day and the Festival of Working Steam. Café and picnic area. Limited wheelchair access. Highly recommended.

TRAVEL *Liphook rail; by car: A3 to Portsmouth, follow signs 2 miles beyond Liphook turn-off; car park* • **OPEN** *Easter to mid-Oct: Sun and bank holidays 1-6pm, rides from 2pm; Jul and Aug (phone for dates): daily 1-6pm* • **PRICES** *Adults £5.50, children and OAPs £4.50 (under-2s free), family ticket (2+2) £17*

KENT AND EAST SUSSEX RAILWAY ☺ ☼ ◑

ADDRESS Tenterden, Kent
PHONE 01580 765155; talking timetable 01580 762943

The first of the rural lines, opened in 1898, steams through the Wealden countryside from the refurbished Edwardian Tenterden Town Station to Northiam in Sussex. This is a delightful way to see the countryside, from the hops and oast houses of the Tenterden farmland to the reeds, lily ponds and coastal waterways beyond Rolvenden. This 7-mile stretch of railway was the inspiration for one of the Thomas the Tank Engine stories. There is

also a museum, buffet, railway shop and children's playground. Special events in the summer. Toilets with baby-changing facilities at Northiam. Buggy and wheelchair access. Good venue for birthday parties (phone for details). **NEARBY:** Sissinghurst Castle (5 miles). Steam river boats run from Northiam to Bodiam (tel: 01797 280363). See also **Bodiam Castle**.
TRAVEL *M20 to junction 9, then A28 to Tenterden; Ashford or Hastings rail, then bus* • **OPEN** *Mar: Sun only; Apr-Oct: weekends only; Jun and Sep: Sat-Sun, Tues-Thurs; Jul-Aug: daily. Phone talking timetable. Santa Specials weekends in Dec.* • **PRICES** *Adults £6, children £3, family ticket (2+3) £16*

NEW ROMNEY, HYTHE AND DYMCHURCH RAILWAY ☺ ☀ ●

ADDRESS Hythe, Kent
PHONE 01797 362353
The 15-inch-gauge line, which runs for 14 miles from Hythe to Dungeness, is – depending on how you look at it – the world's largest toy railway or smallest public train service. The steam locomotives are one-third scale models of those used in the 1920s when the line was built. Originally a tourist attraction linking the resorts along the coast, it is perfect for toddlers, who love the tiny carriages that rattle alongside fields of cows and sheep so close you could almost reach out and touch them (as our toddler almost proved). All visitors should stop off at New Romney Station (three stops from Hythe) to see the model-train and toy exhibition before continuing on to Dungeness, a bleak, shingled expanse of wasteland where you can take a free guided tour round Dungeness Nuclear Power Station (tel: 01797 321815; afternoons daily in summer, Thurs, Fri and Sun in winter; safety helmets provided; wear sensible shoes and phone in advance) or climb the 168 steps up the Old Dungeness Lighthouse (tel: 01797 321300; daily Mar-30 Sep, 10.30am-5pm and other times by arrangement) for some splendid views and an insight into how the lantern was worked and cleaned. Picnic site at Dymchurch. Gift and souvenir shops at Hythe and New Romney; café at New Romney.
TRAVEL *Hythe rail* • **OPEN** *Trains run up to 12 times daily from Easter-30 Sep and at weekends in Mar and Oct* • **PRICES** *Adults from £4.92 return, children half-fare*

PADDLE STEAMER ☺ ☀ ◐

ADDRESS Kingswear Castle, AQHM's House, The Historic Dockyard, Chatham, Kent
PHONE 01634 827648
Trips from Chatham Historic Dockyard to Strood Pier on vintage river paddle steamer, built in 1924 complete with panelled saloons.
TRAVEL *Chatham rail* • **OPEN** *May-Jun and Sep: Wed and Sun, 2.30-5pm; Jul-Aug: Wed-Fri and Sun, 2.30-5pm (all subject to change, phone first)* • **PRICES** *2½-hour cruises: Adults £7.95, children £3.95 (under-3s free), concs £6.95 (less for shorter cruises)*

VOLKS ELECTRIC RAILWAY ☺ ☀ ◐

ADDRESS Madeira Drive, Brighton, E Sussex
PHONE 01273 681061; Brighton Tourist Information 01273 323755
Britain's first public electric railway, opened in 1883, will be of interest to railway enthusiasts despite the fact that it is not steam powered. Nearly 2 miles of 2-ft 8-in gauge runs along Brighton's sea front from the Pier to the Marina. Phone for times and prices.
TRAVEL *Brighton rail*

SHOPPING AND SERVICES

Whether buying clothes, comics and toys, or indulging your child's new-found interest, this section provides all the information you need.

ARTS, CRAFT, HOBBY AND MODEL-MAKING SHOPS

BEAD SHOP

ADDRESS 43 Neal Street, WC2
PHONE 0171 240 0931
Beads of every imaginable shape, size and colour (often hand carved or hand painted) for making earrings, necklaces and bracelets, plus string, clasps and earring hooks. Prices start at 3p each.
TRAVEL ⊖ *Covent Garden* • **HOURS** *Mon, 1-6pm; Tues-Fri, 10.30am-6pm; Sat, 11.30am-5pm*

BEATTIES

ADDRESS 202 High Holborn, WC1 (and branches)
PHONE 0171 405 6285/8592
Hornby, Lima and Marklin models, train sets, railway landscapes and other components can all be found here, as well as a good range of radio-controlled toys, die-cast cars, games and general toys. There are plenty of good old-fashioned, politically incorrect plastic guns and swords for those children who just won't be told.
TRAVEL ⊖ *Holborn* • **HOURS** *Mon, 10am-6pm; Tues-Fri, 9am-6pm; Sat, 9am-5.50pm*

COMET MINIATURES

ADDRESS 46-8 Lavender Hill, SW11
PHONE 0171 228 3702
Specialists in rare and obsolete aircraft kits. Also stocks other kits, such as space rockets, Batmobile, Thunderbirds and Martian war machines.
TRAVEL *Clapham Junction rail* • **HOURS** *Mon-Sat, 9.30am-5.30pm*

COVENT GARDEN CANDLE SHOP

ADDRESS 30 The Market, WC2
PHONE 0171 836 9815
Huge variety of candles, plus candle-making demonstrations and kits.
TRAVEL ⊖ *Covent Garden* • **HOURS** *Mon-Sat, 10am-8pm; Sun, 10.30am-6pm*

HOBBY STORE

ADDRESS 39 Parkway, NW1
PHONE 0171 485 1818
You can buy almost any type of model aircraft kit here, from simple balsawood gliders to giant jumbos.

TRAVEL ⊖ *Camden Town* • **HOURS** *Mon-Sat, 9.30am-5.30pm*

POTTERYCRAFT
ADDRESS 8-10 Ingate Place, SW8
PHONE 0171 720 0050
Everything a potter could possibly need – even kilns.
TRAVEL ⊖ *Sloane Square, then bus 137 or 137a; Queenstown Road rail*
• **HOURS** *Mon-Sat, 9am-5pm*

REEVES DRYAD
ADDRESS 178 Kensington High Street, W8
PHONE 0171 937 5370
One of the best places for art materials of all kinds, plus a huge selection of hobby and craft materials.
TRAVEL ⊖ *High Street Kensington* • **HOURS** *Mon-Fri, 9am-5.30pm; Sat, 9.30am-5.30pm*

BABYSITTING

CHILDMINDERS
PHONE 0171 935 2049; 24-hour information 0171 935 5040
Respectable, reliable agency that covers Belgravia, Pimlico, Clapham, Battersea and south London.
PRICES *Annual membership £38 (plus VAT), then sliding scale of fees depending on number of hours and day of the week. Daytime sitters £4.65 per hour*

CINDERELLA HOME SERVICES AND NANNY AGENCY
PHONE 0181 676 0917
Babysitting service in southeast London. Also day sitters, cleaning, ironing, party helpers and gardening. Minimum childcare session three hours.
PRICES *Annual membership £100 (plus VAT). Babysitters £3-£3.50 per hour, £4 after midnight*

NIPPABOUT ACTIVE CHILDCARE
PHONE 01296 712658
Active mobile childcare and entertainment for exhibitions, conferences, sports events, shoppers' crèches, weddings, private parties. Can provide childcare for between 15 and 5,000 children, from babies to 16-year-olds.

SOUTH OF THE RIVER
PHONE 0171 228 5086
Babysitting service that also arranges domestic help and gardening.
PRICES *Annual membership fee £42, booking fee £1.80-£3.50, babysitters from £3.50-£4 per hour (more after midnight)*

UNIVERSAL AUNTS
PHONE 0171 386 5900
Universal Aunts boasts an ability to deal with any domestic crisis – providing babysitters, minders to meet children from trains, nannies to take them out for the day, etc. Mimimum childcare session four hours.
PRICES *From £3.50 per hour*

BOOKS AND COMICS

BOOKS ETC

ADDRESS First Floor, Whiteleys, W2 (and branches)
PHONE 0171 229 3865

New premises and an enlarged children's section, which often hosts storytelling, performance poetry, signings and other children's events, make shopping here a relaxing business.

TRAVEL ⊖ *Bayswater* • **HOURS** *Mon-Sat, 10am-10pm (Tues from 10.30am); Sun, noon-6pm*

BOOKS FOR CHILDREN

ADDRESS 97 Wandsworth Bridge Road, SW6
PHONE 0171 384 1821

A wide range of children's fiction, non-fiction and tapes in a charming atmosphere with endlessly patient, knowledgeable staff.

TRAVEL ⊖ *Parson's Green* • **HOURS** *Mon, 10am-6pm; Tues-Fri, 9.30am-6pm; Sat, 9.30am-5.30pm*

BOOKSPREAD

ADDRESS 58 Tooting Bec Road, SW17
PHONE 0181 767 6377/4551

Reading advisory service and activities centre with daily activities, including storytelling, rhymes, singing, baby craft, drama, and reading and writing clubs. The bookshop has a good selection of self-help books (on divorce, etc). Send an SAE for the monthly news sheet, listing times of activities. Catalogue, mail order and activity sheets.

TRAVEL ⊖ *Tooting Bec* • **HOURS** *Mon-Fri, 10am-5pm (Tues and Thurs to 7pm); Sat, 10am-3pm*

THE BOOK TRUST

ADDRESS Book House, 45 East Hill, SW18
PHONE 0181 516 2977

An educational charity with a section for younger readers which promotes the reading of, and gives information on, children's books. There is a children's library with copies of every children's book published in the last two years (open to the public). Send an SAE for one of the Trust's book lists, suitable for different ages (babies to 11 years old – state age of child).

TRAVEL *Wandsworth Town rail* • **HOURS** *By appointment*

CHILDREN'S BOOK CENTRE

ADDRESS 237 Kensington High Street, W8
PHONE 0171 937 7497

A huge and appealing children's book shop with thousands of titles for babies to teenagers, and helpful staff on hand to offer advice and ideas. Also games, puzzles, videos, cassettes, CD-ROMs and some toys. Storytelling, competitions and signing sessions in the holidays.

TRAVEL ⊖ *High Street Kensington* • **HOURS** *Mon, Wed and Fri-Sat, 9.30am-6.30pm; Tues, 9.30am-6pm; Thurs, 9.30am-7pm; Sun, noon-6pm*

CHILDREN'S BOOKSHOP

ADDRESS 29 Fortis Green Road, N10
PHONE 0181 444 5500

There are over 20,000 titles in this small, busy, specialist book shop, together with helpful, well-informed staff who will point you in the right direction for pre-school books or those on the National Curriculum. Summer storytelling sessions and other events throughout the year.

TRAVEL ⊖ *East Finchley or Highgate* • **HOURS** *Mon-Sat, 9.15am-5.45pm*

COMIC SHOWCASE

ADDRESS 76 Neal Street, WC2

PHONE 0171 240 3664

Comics and comic novels for adults and children. Also comic-related T-shirts and toys.

TRAVEL ⊖ *Covent Garden* • **HOURS** *Mon-Wed, 10am-6pm; Thurs-Sun, 10am-7pm*

DILLONS THE BOOKSTORE

ADDRESS 82 Gower Street, WC1 (and branches)

PHONE 0171 636 1577

Dillons main store has a well-stocked children's section.

TRAVEL ⊖ *Goodge Street* • **HOURS** *Mon-Fri, 9am-7pm (Tues from 9.30am); Sat, 9.30am-6pm; Sun, noon-6pm*

FORBIDDEN PLANET

ADDRESS 71 New Oxford Street, WC1

PHONE 0171 836 4179

Science-fiction fans' heaven, stuffed full of comics, sci-fi, fantasy and horror.

TRAVEL ⊖ *Tottenham Court Road* • **HOURS** *Mon-Sat, 10am-6pm (Thurs and Fri to 7pm)*

FOYLES

ADDRESS 113-19 Charing Cross Road, WC2

PHONE 0171 437 5660

This enormous, impressive bookshop, the largest in London, has a good children's section. Foyles has, at last, modernised its sales system so you no longer have to queue up twice to buy your chosen book.

TRAVEL ⊖ *Leicester Square* • **HOURS** *Mon-Sat, 9am-6pm (Thurs to 7pm)*

GOSH! COMICS

ADDRESS 39 Great Russell Street, WC1

PHONE 0171 636 1011

Wham, whiz, bang, boff – comics galore, from all over the world, and a huge selection of newspaper strip-cartoon compilations.

TRAVEL ⊖ *Holborn or Tottenham Court Road* • **HOURS** *Daily, 10am-6pm (Thurs and Fri to 7pm)*

HATCHARDS

ADDRESS 187 Piccadilly, W1

PHONE 0171 439 9921

Good children's section and useful search department.

TRAVEL ⊖ *Green Park or Piccadilly Circus* • **HOURS** *Mon and Wed-Fri, 9am-6pm; Tues and Sat, 9.30am-6pm; Sun, 11am-5pm*

SPORTSPAGE

ADDRESS 94-6 Charing Cross Road, WC2

PHONE 0171 240 9604

All you could ever want to know about sport and fitness is covered in this well-stocked book shop, which also has sports magazines and videos.
TRAVEL ⊖ *Leicester Square* • **HOURS** *Mon-Sat, 9.30am-7pm*

THE TINTIN SHOP
ADDRESS 34 Floral Street, WC2; 62a Sloane Avenue, SW3
PHONE 0171 836 1131 (WC2); 0171 838 0901 (SW3)
Tintin books as well as Tintin postcards, T-shirts, key rings and slippers, together with clothes from the quite expensive to the outrageous.
TRAVEL ⊖ *Covent Garden (WC2);* ⊖ *South Kensington (SW3)* • **HOURS** *Mon-Sat, 10am-6pm; Sun, noon-5pm*

WATERSTONES
ADDRESS 121-5 Charing Cross Road, WC2; 193 Kensington High Street, W8 (and branches)
PHONE 0171 434 4291 (WC2); 0171 973 8432 (W8)
Well-stocked children's book sections throughout this chain.
TRAVEL ⊖ *Tottenham Court Road (WC2);* ⊖ *High Street Kensington (W8)* • **HOURS** *Mon-Sat, 9.30am-8pm; Sun, noon-6pm*

CLOTHES
ADAMS
ADDRESS Unit 11, Redriff Road, SE16 (and branches)
PHONE 0171 252 3208
The mix-and-match clothes are amazingly good value for money and wash and wear through several hand-me-downs. The range is mainly tough-wearing, cool shirts, simple pinafore dresses, brightly coloured leggings and denim jackets. Also good for pyjamas, hats, coats, belts, socks and tights. Good-quality shoes from the Birthday range.
TRAVEL ⊖ *Surrey Quays* • **HOURS** *Mon-Fri, 9.30am-7pm (Thurs to 8pm); Sat, 9.30am-6.30pm*

ANTHEA MOORE EDE
ADDRESS 16 Victoria Grove, W8
PHONE 0171 584 8826
Classic children's clothes. The shop specialises in made-to-measure smocked dresses, coats and party clothes, and has a layette department for the traditional baby. Also informal wear for children from birth to 14 years.
TRAVEL ⊖ *Gloucester Road* • **HOURS** *Mon-Fri, 9am-5pm; Sat, 10am-1pm*

BABY GAP
ADDRESS Gap Kids, 144-6 Regent Street, W1
PHONE 0171 287 5095
Children from toddlers upwards look gorgeous in Gap's trendy, hard-wearing, good value American sweatshirts, denims, dresses and jumpers. The newborn and baby range is delightful, practical, and survives several hand-me-downs. Look out for the sale rail.
TRAVEL ⊖ *Oxford Circus* • **HOURS** *Mon-Fri, 9am-7pm (Thurs to 8pm); Sat, 9.30am-6.30pm*

BANANAS
ADDRESS 128 Northcote Road, SW11
PHONE 0171 228 2384

A good selection of clothes for the under-9s, as well as a range of gifts.
TRAVEL *Clapham Junction rail* • **HOURS** *Mon-Sat, 9.30am-5.30pm*

ARNEY'S

ADDRESS 6 Church Road, SW19
PHONE 0181 944 2915
Cacharel, Cantimini and other coveted labels can be found here, with cute
clothes for newborns, bright, fun clothes for under-10s, lovely customised
gift baskets, and some cards and books.
TRAVEL ⊖ *Wimbledon Park or Wimbledon* • **HOURS** *Mon-Sat, 10am-6pm;
Sun, noon-5pm*

0-12 BENETTON

ADDRESS 131 Kensington High Street, W8 (and branches)
PHONE 0171 937 2960
Italian store that sells expensive but bright and attractive separates for
children up to 12 years. Especially good value for jumpers, sweatshirts
and leggings, which are as popular with children as they are with parents.
TRAVEL ⊖ *High Street Kensington* • **HOURS** *Mon-Wed and Fri, 10am-7pm;
Thurs and Sat, 10am-8pm*

CHILDREN'S WORLD

ADDRESS Trafalgar Way, Croydon, Surrey (branches in Islington and Richmond)
PHONE 0181 760 0484
Large warehouse with rows and rows of children's clothes, as well as toys,
games and nursery equipment. Also has shoe department. Children like
the giant slide, down which they enter the 'world' (parents can use the
more conventional doorway if they so wish). Catalogue.
TRAVEL *Waddon Marsh rail* • **HOURS** *Mon-Fri, 10am-8pm; Sat, 9am-6pm;
Sun, 11am-5pm*

LA CIGOGNA ROMA

ADDRESS 6a Sloane Street, SW1
PHONE 0171 235 3845
Price tags read like bar codes on these chic, mainly Italian designer
children's clothes from Armani, Young Versace and Cacharel. Fortunate
tots do look gorgeous in lawn cotton and fine linen dresses, but for most
of us, one Lottery scratch card just isn't enough.
TRAVEL ⊖ *Knightsbridge* • **HOURS** *Mon-Sat, 9.30am-6pm (Wed to 7pm)*

HENNES

ADDRESS Oxford Circus, W1
PHONE 0171 493 4004
Huge range of fashionable and fun clothes in natural fibres at budget
prices (many jeans and shirts under £9), from birth onwards. Sizes very
generous. Best place for sensible, no-frills girls' clothes.
TRAVEL ⊖ *Oxford Circus* • **HOURS** *Mon-Fri, 10am-6.30pm (Thurs to 8pm);
Sat, 9.30am-6pm; Sun, noon-6pm*

HUMLA

ADDRESS 23 St Christopher's Place, W1; 9 Flask Walk, NW3
PHONE 0171 224 1773 (W1); 0171 794 8449 (NW3)
Original, jolly knitwear in wool and cotton for ages 0-12, which can
be made to order, plus a colourful range of mix-and-match clothes at
reasonable prices. Also traditional wooden toys and mobiles. Play area.

TRAVEL ⊖ *Bond Street (W1);* ⊖ *Hampstead (NW3)* • **HOURS** *Mon-Sat, 10.30am-6pm*

JOANNA'S TENT

ADDRESS 289b King's Road, SW3
PHONE 0171 352 1151

With prices starting at £16 for a No No T-shirt and rising into three figures for Junior Armani, Paul Smith and Blu Kids, you won't be feeding the little darlings carrot and tomato purée.

TRAVEL ⊖ *Sloane Square; bus 19 or 22* • **HOURS** *Mon-Sat, 9.45am-6pm*

LAURA ASHLEY

ADDRESS 256-8 Regent Street, W1 (and branches)
PHONE 0171 437 9760

Sailor suits, pretty pinafores, pastoral printed skirts and shirts, and fancy party dresses are all a bit old fashioned, but granny will love the little perishers in them.

TRAVEL ⊖ *Oxford Circus* • **HOURS** *Mon-Tues, 10am-6.30pm; Wed and Fri, 10am-7pm; Thurs, 10am-8pm; Sat, 9.30pm-7pm; Sun, noon-6pm*

THE LITTLE FOLK STORE

ADDRESS Stoke Newington Church Street, N16
PHONE 0171 249 6438

Funky clothes, hats, soft suede shoes, sheepskin booties and pixie slippers. The corduroy and moleskin Cornish fisherman-style clothes for boys are charming, and the staff are delightful.

TRAVEL *Bus 73* • **HOURS** *Tues-Fri, 10am-5pm; Sat, 10am-6pm; Sun, 11am-4pm*

MARKS & SPENCER

ADDRESS 458 Oxford Street, W1 (and branches)
PHONE 0171 935 7954

Excellent-value children's clothes and shoes, with a good range of trousers and dresses that teenagers will actually wear. Essential for underwear.

TRAVEL ⊖ *Marble Arch* • **HOURS** *Mon-Sat, 9am-7pm (Thurs and Fri to 8pm); Sun, noon-6pm*

MOTHERCARE

ADDRESS 461 Oxford Street, W1 (and branches)
PHONE 0171 629 6621

As a parent you cannot avoid going to Mothercare at some point, and for basics it is great value. Good-quality, hard-wearing, co-ordinated tops, bottoms and accessories, as well as wellies, jellies, overalls and aprons. A good selection of co-ordinated nursery equipment. Good for basic maternity wear, bras, disposable pants and breast pads. Mail order available. Nappy-delivery service. Mother-and-baby room.

TRAVEL ⊖ *Marble Arch* • **HOURS** *Mon-Sat, 9am-7pm (Thurs and Fri to 8pm); Sun, noon-6pm*

NEXT

ADDRESS 54-60 Kensington High Street, W8 (and branches)
PHONE 0171 938 4211

Trendy kids' clothes, some good shoes, beautiful but expensive duffel coats, reasonably priced shirts and accessories, and lovely pyjamas. Best value are the wool-mix jumpers and thick cotton tracksuits. Mail order.

TRAVEL ⊖ *High Street Kensington* • **HOURS** *Mon-Sat, 10am-6.30pm (Thurs to 8pm); Sun, noon-6pm*

OSH KOSH B'GOSH

ADDRESS 17-19 King's Road, SW3
PHONE 0171 730 1341
Pinstriped dungarees and other Osh Kosh basics, including jeans and jackets, for children up to 12 years. Patterned printed dresses for under-6s. Clothes last and last.
TRAVEL ⊖ *Sloane Square or bus C, 11, 19, 22 or 211* • **HOURS** *Mon-Tues and Thurs-Sat, 9.30am-6pm; Wed 10am-7pm*

PLEASE MUM

ADDRESS 69 New Bond Street, W1
PHONE 0171 493 5880
Designer clothes at designer prices, from newborns upwards.
TRAVEL ⊖ *Bond Street* • **HOURS** *Mon-Sat, 9.45am-6.30pm (Thurs to 7.30pm)*

TROTTERS

ADDRESS 34 King's Road, SW3; 127 Kensington High Street, W8
PHONE 0171 259 9620 (SW3); 0171 937 9373 (W8)
A lovely shop for browsing, Trotters is full of beautiful clothes, imaginative toys and good books. Clothes are expensive, with baby wear from Petit Bateau and Galipete, and Paul Smith and Ralph Lauren servicing older children, but Trotters' own duck-appliquéed pinafore dresses are a must for any little girl's wardrobe (£31.99).
TRAVEL ⊖ *Sloane Square (SW3)*; ⊖ *Kensington High Street (W8)* • **HOURS** *Mon-Sat, 9am-6.30pm (Wed to 7pm)*

YOUNG ENGLAND

ADDRESS 47 Elizabeth Street, SW1
PHONE 0171 259 9003
Very traditional clothes and nursery items all made in the UK.
TRAVEL ⊖ *Sloane Square or Victoria; bus C1 or 11* • **HOURS** *Mon-Fri, 9.30am-5.30pm*

CONSUMER GUIDE

BABY PRODUCTS ASSOCIATION

ADDRESS The Coach House, Erlegh Manor, Vicarage Road, Leighton Buzzard, Beds LU7 9EY
Send an SAE for a leaflet on buying new and second-hand equipment for babies.

BRITISH TOY AND HOBBY MANUFACTURER'S ASSOCIATION

ADDRESS 80 Camberwell Road, SE5 0EG
PHONE 0171 701 7271
Send an SAE for a free booklet on choosing toys, including toys for the handicapped. The Association also operates a toy- information service.

BRITISH TOY MAKERS' GUILD
ADDRESS 124 Walcot Street, Bath BA1 5BG
PHONE 01225 442440
Can supply names of toy-makers in your area if you are looking for
particular items such as rocking horses, doll's houses, china dolls.

CHILD ACCIDENT PREVENTION TRUST
ADDRESS 18 Farringdon Lane, EC1R 3AU
PHONE 0171 608 3828
Send an SAE for leaflets on children's safety equipment and advice on
what to buy and why you might need it.

CITIZENS' ADVICE BUREAU
Offers advice if you cannot get your money back on faulty goods. See
phone directory for your nearest branch.

OFFICE OF FAIR TRADING
ADDRESS Field House, 15-25 Bream's Buildings, EC4A 1PR
PHONE 0171 242 2858
Has a detailed guide on consumer rights.

DEPARTMENT STORES

DAISY & TOM'S
ADDRESS 81 King's Road, SW3
PHONE 0171 352 5000
A soda bar serving knickerbocker glories, a fairground carousel, puppet
shows and a giant toy cupboard are some of the attractions at Britain's
'first luxury department store for children'. The shop was the brainchild of
Tim Waterstone, the bookshop chain founder, so books feature large. The
store also sells top-of-the-range children's clothes, shoes, games, toys. First
haircut with photo and certificate £12.
TRAVEL ⊖ *Sloane Square* • **HOURS** *Mon-Fri, 10am-6pm (Wed to 7pm);
Sat, 9.30am-6.30pm; Sun, noon-6pm*

HARRODS
ADDRESS Knightsbridge, SW1
PHONE 0171 730 1234
Harrods used to sell everything from hairgrips to a baby elephant, the
latter having been bought in 1975 as a present for the then Governor of
California, Ronald Reagan. Now Harrods will provide 'anything within
reason', at a price. Teenagers are well catered for, and not all the children's
clothes are expensive. The Harrods sale is excellent (we've bought a child's
jumper down from £35 to £7 and trousers from £40 to £10.99). Children's
first haircuts £14 (includes framed diploma and First Lock of Hair).
TRAVEL ⊖ *Knightsbridge* • **HOURS** *Mon-Sat, 10am-6pm (Wed and Fri to 7pm)*

PETER JONES/JOHN LEWIS
ADDRESS Sloane Square, SW1 (Peter Jones); Oxford Street, W1 (John Lewis)
PHONE 0171 730 3434 (Peter Jones); 0171 629 7711 (John Lewis)
A good range of top-quality children's clothing at competitive prices,
especially the John Lewis own brand, as well as some wonderful French
and Italian imports for impulse buys. Equipment from bottle warmers and
breast pads to carrycots and high chairs, a huge school uniform department

and excellent shoe-fitting service. Staff are helpful and knowledgeable.
Maternity dresses. Home delivery. Mother-and-baby room.

TRAVEL ⊖ *Sloane Square (Peter Jones);* ⊖ *Oxford Circus (John Lewis)* •
HOURS *Peter Jones: Mon-Sat 9.30am-6pm (Wed to 7pm); John Lewis:*
Mon-Wed and Fri 9.30am-6pm, Thurs 10am-8pm, Sat 9am-6pm

ENTERTAINMENT

KIDSLINE

PHONE 0171 222 8070

Telephone information service giving details of shows and films, famous
attractions, galleries, museums, holiday courses and workshops for children.

HOURS *Holidays: Mon-Fri, 9am-4pm; term-time: Mon-Fri, 4-6pm*

EQUIPMENT HIRE

G JOLLIFF & CO

ADDRESS 48-54 Chapel Street, Marlow, Bucks
PHONE 01628 475757

Fancy-dress and formal-wear hire service, with page-boy and bridesmaids'
clothes, period fancy dress for adults and children, and ladies' formal wear
at very reasonable prices. Also accessories such as page-boy buckle shoes.

NAPPY EXPRESS

ADDRESS 128 High Road, N11
PHONE 0181 361 4040

Long- and short-term hire of everything you might need for a baby (travel
cot for two weeks £20.50, double buggy for six months £76.50). Will
deliver and collect in central and southwest London. Members of the Baby
Equipment Hirers' Association. Phone for free price list.

HAIRCUTS

Ask around in your area for people who do home visits – it's often the
same price and a lot less hassle. Barber's shops offer the cheapest and
often quickest cuts, but it is best to visit one that has been recommended –
Jake looked like a balding eagle after a visit to our local barber. If you
wish to record the event, the following salons all issue a certificate for first
haircuts.

CHILDREN'S WORLD

ADDRESS Trafalgar Way, Croydon, Surrey
PHONE 0181 760 0484
TRAVEL *Waddon Marsh rail* • **HOURS** *Mon-Fri, 10am-8pm; Sat, 9am-6pm;*
Sun, 11am-5pm • **PRICES** *Under-3s £4.95, under-11s £6.25, under-15s*
£7.95

CHEEKY MONKEYS

ADDRESS 202 Kensington Park Road, W11; 24 Abbeville Road, SW4
PHONE 0171 792 9022 (W11); 0181 673 5215 (SW4)
No-nonsense hairdresser (appointment necessary).
TRAVEL ⊖ *Notting Hill Gate (W11);* ⊖ *Clapham South (SW4)* • **HOURS**
Mon-Fri, 9.30am-5.30pm; Sat, 10am-5.30pm

DAISY & TOM'S
ADDRESS 81 King's Road, SW3
PHONE 0171 352 5000
First haircut with photo and certificate £12.
TRAVEL ⊖ *Sloane Square* • **HOURS** *Mon-Fri, 10am-6pm (Wed to 7pm); Sat, 9.30am-6.30pm; Sun, noon-6pm* • **PRICES** *£10 (trim)*

HARRODS
ADDRESS Knightsbridge, SW1
PHONE 0171 730 1234
Located in the children's clothes section. Certificate and lock of hair for child's first haircut.
TRAVEL ⊖ *Knightsbridge* • **HOURS** *Mon-Sat, 10am-6pm (Wed and Fri to 7pm)* • **PRICE** *£14*

THE LITTLE TRADING COMPANY
ADDRESS 7 Bedford Corner, The Avenue, W4
PHONE 0181 742 3152
TRAVEL ⊖ *Turnham Green* • **HOURS** *Mon-Fri, 9am-5pm; Sat, 9am-4.30pm* • **PRICE** *£6.50, including certificate*

SWALLOWS & AMAZONS
ADDRESS 91 Nightingale Lane, SW12
PHONE 0181 673 0275
Open most afternoons; phone for appointment.
TRAVEL ⊖ *Clapham South or Wandsworth Common rail* • **PRICES** *£5 plus £1.50 for certificate*

TROTTERS
ADDRESS 34 King's Road, SW3
PHONE 0171 259 9620
TRAVEL ⊖ *Sloane Square* • **PRICES** *Under-3s £8.50 (includes first-haircut certificate), over-3s £9.50*

HOTELS FOR CHILDREN

HOPES AND DREAMS
ADDRESS 339-41 City Road, EC1
PHONE 0171 833 9388
As well as a nursery, Monica Whalley and her ex-nanny Susan Bingham run an attractive alternative to agency babysitters, in the form of a five-star hotel for children. Guests are fêted, entertained and fed organic food by the resident chef. Staff references are scrupulously checked and all have NNEB or Montessori qualifications.
TRAVEL ⊖ *Angel* • **PRICE** *£100 for a 24-hour stay*

PIPPA POP-INS
ADDRESS 430 Fulham Road, SW6
PHONE 0171 385 2458
Children's nursery school and overnight nursery, plus school runs with afternoon teas, a babysitting service and holiday activities and excursions (see Workshops). Located in a lovely, child-friendly, bright-yellow Georgian house. Pippa's staff specialise in looking after children aged 2-12, 24

hours a day, seven days a week. Guests book in after 6pm on Mondays to Thursdays, after 5pm on Fridays, Saturdays and Sundays. Children can look for fairies in the garden, or enjoy a midnight feast at 8pm.
TRAVEL ⊖ *Parson's Green* • **PRICES** *Mon-Thurs £40 per night, Fri-Sun £50 per night*

KITES

THE KITE STORE
ADDRESS 48 Neal Street, WC2
PHONE 0171 836 1666
A kite that swims through the air like a shark, or a seagull that flaps its wings in the wind – you name it and they probably have a design for it (and if not, they do a range of kite-making books). Prices from under £10 to over £200. Also frisbees and boomerangs. Mail-order service.
TRAVEL ⊖ *Covent Garden* • **HOURS** *Mon-Fri, 10am-6pm (Thurs to 7pm); Sat, 10.30am-6pm*

MAIL ORDER

Gone are the days of down-market, dowdy mail-order catalogues where everything was Tuppaware and Crimplene. Now even the most exclusive of shops are offering this easy, hassle-free form of shopping. However, with the growing popularity of shopping by post, some companies are having trouble fulfilling their 28-day delivery goal, especially around Christmas. To avoid disappointment, order early (for Christmas, aim to order by 15 November to be safe).

ACTIVE TOY COMPANY
ADDRESS Langley Farm, World's End, Newbury, Berks RG20 85D
PHONE 01635 248683
Everything children could possibly want in garden toys – sandpits, seesaws, playhouses, climbing frames in wood and metal, slides, trampolines and more. Comes flat packed for self-assembly.

BABY STATIONERY
ADDRESS 36 Perry Hill, Chelmsford, Essex CM1 5RD
PHONE 01245 359865
Wide range of personalised stationery for babies and children, including pregnancy and birth announcement cards, special invitation and birthday-party cards, colour-your-own Christmas cards, and party bags.

COTTON MOON
PHONE 0181 305 0012 (free catalogue)
Pure-cotton boys' and girls' separates for 0- to 12-year-olds. Sweatshirts from £12.95, dresses from £18.95. Good sunhats and protective beach wear, especially all-in-one, zip-up Fishskins from £23.50 (sizes come up small).

FINGERS AND TOES

ADDRESS 5 Potters Lane, Kiln Farm, Milton Keynes, Bucks MK11 3HE
PHONE 01908 260165
Supplies DIY kits to make a life-cast of your baby's hands and feet, including moulding material, synthetic stone powder for casting, and telephone advice (£19.99 plus p&p).

GALT

ADDRESS Brookfield Road, Cheadle, Cheshire SK8 2PN
PHONE 0161 627 5086
Extensive glossy catalogue with good wooden indoor and outdoor toys, brightly painted, pleasant to hold, and especially good for small children. Also educational toys, games, dressing up, puppets and storage systems.

HAWKINS & CO

ADDRESS St Margaret Street, Harleston, Norfolk IP20 0KS
PHONE 01986 782536
Even if you don't plan to buy anything mail order, this hilarious catalogue makes great bedtime reading. Take the Eleven-blade Knife entry: 'A Chinese copy of the Swiss Army pocket knife at a quite remarkable price. Of course you would expect it to be cheaper than the real thing, but this one is the result of a rather exceptional deal. (Not absolutely 'Fell off the back of a rickshaw, guv', but that sort of thing.)' The knife in question is £2.95! By far the best mail order for stocking presents and unusual gifts, from clockwork tin toys to funny faces, and lots of things for under 10p.

HILL TOY COMPANY

ADDRESS PO Box 100, Ripon, North Yorkshire HG4 4XY
PHONE 01765 689955
Good-quality toys and popular fancy-dress outfits.

LETTERBOX

ADDRESS PO Box 114, Truro, Cornwall TR1 1F2
PHONE 01872 580885
Imaginative and unusual personalised presents, plus bright, attractive wooden toys and stocking fillers from under £5.

MINI BODEN

ADDRESS Midland Terrace, Victoria Road, NW10 6DB
PHONE 0181 453 1535 (Mon-Fri, 9am-6.30pm; Sat, 10am-6.30pm)
Good, hard-wearing, logo-free clothes. Excellent for plain sweatshirts, cardigans and traditional pinafore dresses.

PARTY PIECES

ADDRESS Unit 1, Childs Court Farm, Ashampstead, Berks RG8 8QT
PHONE 01635 201844
A wide range of children's party goods – gift bags, gifts, masks, hats, party boxes, musical candles, sweatshirts and lots of personalised items.

TRIDIAS

PHONE 01225 314730
A lovely catalogue with a wide range of toys from party bag novelties to collector's items. Shop in South Kensington (see also Toys, Games and Magic, below). Unusual, attractive, fun toys from a glow-in-the-dark dinosaur for 39p to a hand-carved wooden rocking horse at £545.

MARKETS

Markets can be great fun for children of all ages but they can get very crowded, so you need to keep a tight rein on younger ones.

BILLINGSGATE

ADDRESS North Quay, West India Docks Road, E14

The wholesale fish market has been in operation since Saxon times (though not always at this location). It is an amazing place, with tons of fish changing hands each week. Look out for the porters, some of whom still wear bobbing hats, made from leather and wood, with flat tops on which to carry the crates.

TRAVEL *West India Quay DLR* • **HOURS** *Mon-Sat, 5-8am*

BRICK LANE MARKET

ADDRESS Brick Lane, E1

Wonderful East End market full of everything you could possibly want, and a whole lot more you wouldn't. Second-hand bargains to be had in the indoor warehouse up Cheshire Street. The guttural cries of stallholders can be heard round Cygnet Street where the fruit and veg is.

TRAVEL ⊖ *Aldgate East, Shoreditch or Liverpool Street* • **HOURS** *Sun, 6am-1pm*

BRIXTON MARKET

ADDRESS Brixton Station Road and Electric Avenue, SW9

A lively market where stalls are full of every kind of fruit, veg, meat and fish. Especially interesting are the exotic selections of Afro-Caribbean food, such as yams, plantain and breadfruit. Second-hand clothes stalls are good and there are plenty of cafés.

TRAVEL ⊖ *Brixton* • **HOURS** *Mon-Tues and Thurs-Sat, 8.30am-5.30pm; Wed, 8am-1pm*

CAMDEN LOCK

ADDRESS Chalk Farm Road (at crossing of Regent's Canal), NW1

Sprawling beyond its canalside site, this colourful market sells a hotch-potch of items from antiques to ethnic clothing. Good food stalls. Gets very crowded by 1pm. You can pick up a boat from here to Little Venice via **London Zoo** (see Waterways).

TRAVEL ⊖ *Camden Town* • **HOURS** *Sat-Sun, 9.30am-6pm*

COVENT GARDEN MARKET

ADDRESS The Piazza, WC2

The 30 or so stalls within the Piazza sell toys, hats, hand-knitted jumpers, jewellery, mobiles and games to catch the eye.

TRAVEL ⊖ *Covent Garden* • **HOURS** *Daily, 9am-5pm*

DEPTFORD MARKET

ADDRESS Douglas Way, SE8

A few stalls with cheap new children's clothes and piles of second-hand clothes, toys, bric-a-brac and junk. Chris is well known to local mums and has reams of second-hand children's clothes all for 50p (bargains have included a Tintin T-shirt, never-worn Osh Kosh dungarees, Baby Gap vests and a good smattering of Next, Oilily, Marks & Spencer and Petit Bateau). Alison and her husband run a fabric stall selling designer seconds for £1.50 a yard, which in perfect condition would cost over £30 a yard.

TRAVEL *Deptford rail* • **HOURS** *Best on Wed, Fri and Sat morning*

EAST STREET MARKET

ADDRESS East Street, SE17
One of London's best fruit and vegetable markets, but there are also plenty of good stalls selling clothes, toys, material and household items.
TRAVEL ⊖ *Elephant & Castle; bus 12, 35, 40, 45, 68, 171 or 176*
● **HOURS** *Tues-Thurs and Sun, 8am-3pm; Fri-Sat, 8am-5pm*

GREENWICH ARTS AND CRAFT MARKET

ADDRESS Covered Market Square, SE10
General arts and crafts and good wooden toys to be found here. Prices are reasonable compared to Covent Garden and standards are just as high. Découpage loo seats, printed T-shirts, cot quilts, jewellery, and even a stall selling flavoured ground coffee (anything from vanilla or double chocolate fudge to lemon and orange).
TRAVEL *Greenwich rail* ● **HOURS** *Sat-Sun, 10am-5pm*

PETTICOAT LANE MARKET

ADDRESS Middlesex Street, E1
London's most famous Sunday market is best for fashion – teenagers love it here.
TRAVEL ⊖ *Aldgate, Aldgate East or Liverpool Street* ● **HOURS** *Sun, 9am-2pm*

PORTOBELLO MARKET

ADDRESS Portobello Road, W11
Fruit, antiques and some second-hand goods. We found bargain second-hand children's clothes on a Friday (Gap jeans 15p, Osh Kosh trousers £2) but apparently we were just lucky.
TRAVEL ⊖ *Ladbroke Grove or Notting Hill Gate* ● **HOURS** *Fri, 8am-3pm; Sat, 8am-5pm*

OLD SPITALFIELDS MARKET

ADDRESS Brushfield Street, E1
PHONE 0171 247 6590
England's first and largest organic-food market as well as a general market with jewellery, wooden toys and crafts.
TRAVEL ⊖ *Liverpool Street* ● **HOURS** *Fri, 11am-3pm; Sun, 9am-3pm*

MATERNITY WEAR

BLOOMING MARVELLOUS

ADDRESS 6 Mount Parade, Mount Pleasant, Cockfosters, Barnet, Herts
PHONE 0181 441 5582; mail order 0181 391 4822/0338
Excellent mail-order catalogue with good-quality, non-frumpy maternity clothes suitable for smart or casual wear. Best buy: long-cut shirts roomy enough to wear while pregnant (and long enough to hide pregnant bottoms), with false pockets for breast-feeding. Leggings cost £17.99.
TRAVEL ⊖ *Cockfosters* ● **HOURS** *Mon-Sat, 10am-5pm*

BUMPSADAISY

ADDRESS 43 The Piazza, WC2
PHONE 0171 379 9831
Flattering leggings, Italian-design shirts for smart and casual wear, separates and posh frocks for special occasions. Also has clothes for hire, including ball gowns and wedding dresses.

TRAVEL ⊖ *Covent Garden* • **HOURS** *Mon-Fri, 10am-6pm (Thurs to 7.30pm);*
Sat, 10am-7pm

FORMES
ADDRESS 313 Brompton Road, SW3; 33 Brook Street, W1;
28 Henrietta Street, WC2
PHONE 0171 584 3337 (SW3); 0171 493 2783 (W1);
0171 240 4777 (WC2)
Smart designer maternity clothes and business wear. Range includes
Empire-line dresses, mini skirts and jackets with adjustable sides, flattering
trousers and smart skirts and suits.
TRAVEL ⊖ *Knightsbridge (SW3);* ⊖ *Bond Street (W1);* ⊖ *Covent Garden
(WC2)* • **HOURS** *Mon-Sat, 10am-6pm*

GREAT EXPECTATIONS
ADDRESS 78 Fulham Road, SW3
PHONE 0171 584 2451
Suits and dresses for work, plus lingerie and casual clothes, ranging from
stretch jeans for £55 to Neuf Lune's posh frocks with high three-figure price
tags. Mail-order service (phone for catalogue).
TRAVEL ⊖ *South Kensington* • **HOURS** *Mon-Sat, 10am-6pm*

MISCELLANEOUS
ANYTHING LEFT HANDED
ADDRESS 57 Brewer Street, W1
PHONE 0171 437 3910
Specialist shop for the sinistrally challenged, selling anything from scissors
and corkscrews to left-handed boomerangs. But be warned – if your left-
handed children are used to using right-handed implements, they might not
grasp the joys of this shop immediately. Jake got to grips with the scissors
with ease but Benja, also left-handed, found the pencil sharpener difficult
because 'You have to twist the other way.' The rulers are particularly
useful, apparently. Mail-order service available.
TRAVEL ⊖ *Piccadilly Circus* • **HOURS** *Mon-Fri, 9.30am-5pm; Sat, 10am-5pm*

THE BACK SHOP
ADDRESS 14 New Cavendish Street, W1
PHONE 0171 935 9120
Sells children's chairs and desks designed to encourage good posture.
TRAVEL ⊖ *Bond Street* • **HOURS** *Mon-Fri, 10am-5.45pm; Sat, 10am-2pm*

NAME MAKER
ADDRESS 7 Friston Street, SW6
PHONE 0171 371 5231
Washable, iron-on name-tapes, available in six different styles, three different
colours and up to 24 letters, numbers or spaces. Mail-order prices from £6.50
for 100 tapes and £9.95 for 200. Phone for free brochure and order form.

SAFE & SOUND
ADDRESS 8 Porchester Place, W2
PHONE 0171 402 5943
A shop selling and fitting child car-safety products, with a back-up advice
service. Founder John Handman was so shocked by the lack of available
information when he tried to buy a car seat for his own baby that he set

up Safe & Sound. He will advise you on the make of seat most suitable for your car, and give safety tips – for example, a rear-facing baby seat should not be used in the front seat if your car is fitted with a passenger airbag.
TRAVEL ⊖ *Marble Arch* • **HOURS** *By appointment, Mon-Fri, 8am-6pm*

NAPPY DELIVERY

BOOTS

PHONE 0800 622525
Boots will deliver their own and other brands.
PRICE *Free*

EEZY PEEZY

ADDRESS West Hill House, Orpington, Kent
PHONE 01959 534207
For those wishing to make the break from disposables without the chore of washing cotton nappies, Eezy Peezy will deliver environmentally friendly (and parent friendly – no pins required) nappies, liners and deodorising bins, and collect for laundering. Areas south of the river only.
PRICE *£8.50 per week*

JOHN LEWIS PARTNERSHIP

PHONE 0171 629 7711
If you have an account or live within the quite large delivery area of any shop in the group you can order nappies (and almost anything else) by phone.
PRICE *Free*

NAPPY EXPRESS

ADDRESS 128 High Road, N11
PHONE 0181 361 4040
Delivers the usual disposable brands of nappy to north, west and southwest London (pay on delivery). Also a hire service for cots, high chairs, pushchairs and nannies.
PRICE *No delivery charge*

NURSERY FURNISHINGS

DRAGONS OF WALTON STREET

ADDRESS 23 Walton Street, SW3
PHONE 0171 589 3795
Traditional, nostalgic, classic, expensive – a Rosie Fisher nursery is a status symbol. Her hand-made and painted furniture and co-ordinating fabrics are all on view in her shop. Prices for individual pieces start from around £60 for a hand-painted chair to a hefty £2,600 for a child's double four-poster bed. A complete room costs from £3,000 to upwards of £20,000 for one like that of King Hussein's twin granddaughters.
TRAVEL ⊖ *South Kensington* • **HOURS** *Mon-Fri, 9.30am-5.30pm; Sat, 10am-5pm*

IKEA

ADDRESS Purley Way, Croydon, Surrey (and branches)
PHONE 0181 208 5601

Imaginative, practical and amazingly good-value nursery items from matching wallpaper and fabrics, to beds, desks, lamps and toys. Cots for as little as £49 and nappy-changing mats at £4.50 make this an ideal stop for those on a tight budget. (It's not easy getting even a second-hand cot for under £50).

TRAVEL *Waddon Marsh rail* • **HOURS** *Mon-Fri, 10am-8pm; Sat and bank holidays, 10am-6pm; Sun, 11am-5pm*

LITTLE BRIDGE

ADDRESS 56 Battersea Bridge Road, SW11
PHONE 0171 978 5522

The emphasis is on fun, with bold patterns and bright colours adorning pint-size wardrobes, beds and chairs, as well as the very popular large toy boxes. Items are customised and hand-painted, but prices are reasonable. Also nursery-design service.

TRAVEL *Clapham Junction rail* • **HOURS** *Mon-Fri, 9.30am-5.30pm; Sat, 10am-5pm*

NURSERY WINDOW

ADDRESS 83 Walton Street, SW3
PHONE 0171 581 3358

Small but good range of fabric and wallpaper designs from bright but tasteful trains, boats and planes, or pastel bunnies, to tartan prints and interesting stripes. Also matching accessories from a basinette and cover (£350) to a bathcap (£11.75). Not for the budget conscious.

TRAVEL ⊖ *South Kensington* • **HOURS** *Mon-Sat, 10am-5.30pm*

SECOND-HAND CLOTHES AND EQUIPMENT

Look in your local paper or charity shops, in the free-ads paper *Loot* or at car-boot sales for second-hand items. You can pick up anything, from lovingly hand-knitted jumpers to designer kids' clothes that have never been worn, for just a few pence, plus buggies, cots and high chairs that look brand new for a fraction of the original price. Don't forget – you can always sell what you no longer need in the same way.

Car-boot sales are excellent for toys, especially larger items like trikes and bikes. To hire toys at a nominal charge, join your local toy library (especially good for bulky outdoor play equipment like toddler slides, seesaws and tractors, as well as puzzles and games). Call the National Toy Libraries Association (0171 387 9592) for your nearest branch.

CHANGE OF HABIT

ADDRESS 25 Abbeville Road, SW4
PHONE 0181 675 9475

Second-hand children's and women's clothes in top-quality condition.

TRAVEL ⊖ *Clapham South* • **HOURS** *Mon-Sat, 10am-5.30pm (Wed to 7pm)*

CHEEKY MONKEYS

ADDRESS 202 Kensington Park Road, W11; 24 Abbeville Road, SW4
PHONE 0171 792 9022 (W11); 0181 673 5215 (SW4)

As well as toys and some lovely nursery accessories, these shops also sell a good selection of second-hand clothes and dressing-up clothes.

TRAVEL ⊖ *Notting Hill (W11);* ⊖ *Clapham South (SW4)* • **HOURS** *Mon-Fri, 9.30am-5.30pm; Sat, 10am-5.30pm*

ENCORE

ADDRESS 53 Stoke Newington Church Street, N16
PHONE 0171 254 5329

If it is designer labels you are after, then regular trips to Encore will kit your little darlings out in Osh Kosh, Oilily, Chipie and Gap at a fraction of the original price, and no one would guess the clothes were not new. Popular shop with a fast turn-over.

TRAVEL *Bus 73* • **HOURS** *Mon-Sat 10am-5pm (soon to extend hours and open on Sunday)*

HEY DIDDLE DIDDLE

ADDRESS 106 Lordship Lane, SE22
PHONE 0181 693 5575

Busy, friendly shop with knowledgeable staff selling plenty of good quality, nearly-new children's clothes (0-10 years) and equipment. Good range of new, unusual and very appealing knitwear. Also gifts, cards, books and craft ideas. Locals hire party tables and chairs, and there is a reasonable range of tableware, hats, balloons and party-bag items. Upstairs, the Family Natural Health Centre has homoeopaths, osteopaths and herbalists, all working towards the holistic health of your family. Notice board with local news and adverts for nanny shares and babysitters.

TRAVEL *East Dulwich rail* • **HOURS** *Mon-Sat, 9.30am-6pm*

THE LITTLE TRADING COMPANY

ADDRESS 7 Bedford Corner, The Avenue, W4
PHONE 0181 742 3152

The quality is reflected in the price, with good-condition cast-offs including Osh Kosh, Babar, Oilily, Baby Mini and Gloverall. Also nursery equipment, maternity wear and a school rail. Haircuts £6.50.

TRAVEL ⊖ *Turnham Green* • **HOURS** *Mon-Fri, 9am-5pm; Sat, 9am-4.30pm*

PIXIES

ADDRESS 14 Fauconberg Road, W4
PHONE 0181 995 1568

On my visit, half the second-hand clothes looked as if they had never been worn, and there were plenty of designer labels at very reasonable prices, as well as equipment, toys and books. If you are looking for a particular second-hand item, there is an efficient phone ordering service.

TRAVEL ⊖ *Chiswick Park* • **HOURS** *Mon-Fri, 10am-4.30pm (Wed to 2pm); Sat, 10am-3pm*

SCARECROW

ADDRESS 131 Waltham Green Court, Moore Park, SW6
PHONE 0171 381 1023

A must for those in search of second-hand nursery equipment, cots, playpens, buggies, high chairs and those wonderful Silver Cross carriage prams. The large clothes section is very popular with fashion-conscious local parents, who snap up good-quality cast-offs, including Gap, Jacardi, Chipie, Oilily and Tatin au Chocolat labels at less than half the original price. Excellent selection of sailing, riding and ski wear for toddlers to teenagers.

TRAVEL ⊖ *Fulham Broadway* • **HOURS** *Tues-Fri, 10am-5pm; Sat, 9.30am-1pm*

SWALLOWS & AMAZONS

ADDRESS 91 Nightingale Lane, SW12

PHONE 0181 673 0275

While the second-hand toys, books and equipment were in good condition, the second-hand clothes looked rather scruffy on two of our visits, and quality was not reflected in the price. However, I have friends who swear by the constantly changing stock, and I must admit their children are always well dressed. Children's hairdresser.

TRAVEL ⊖ *Clapham South or Wandsworth Common rail* • **HOURS** *Mon-Sat, 10am-5.30pm*

SHOES

Experts say you should not buy shoes until your child has been walking at least six weeks (some recommend leaving it until three months). Mothercare, Woolworth's and Shoe Express sell less expensive children's shoes but usually only in one-width fittings and no half-sizes. Shops with trained staff stocking shoes in whole and half-sizes and four different width fittings include: **The Clarks Shop**, **Harrods**, **John Lewis**, **Peter Jones**, Russell & Bromley, **Trotters** and Start-Rite.

BUCKLE MY SHOE

ADDRESS 19 St Christopher's Place, W1

PHONE 0171 935 5589

Fashionable and fun shoes for 0- to 8-year-olds are fitted by expert staff who take their job seriously. Buckle My Shoe Italian shoes are made of soft leather and all have arch supports. Although the shoes are expensive, your children's feet will not get a better start in life anywhere else.

TRAVEL ⊖ *Bond Street* • **HOURS** *Mon-Sat, 10am-6pm (Thurs to 7pm)*

THE CLARKS SHOP

ADDRESS 476 Oxford Street, W1 (and branches)

PHONE 0171 629 9609

One of the best places for proper foot measurement and for shoes to fit narrow and extra-wide feet. Shoes come in four width fittings and half-sizes from pre-walkers to adults. Members of TAMBA, the twins club, get a 10 per cent discount. The Clarks Factory Shop sells end-of-range shoes and seconds often up to half-price. If you know what you want and the exact size you want it in, they will send shoes direct to you. The Clarks Factory Shop, Unit 13, Clarks Village, Street, Somerset BA16 0YA (tel: 01458 442131).

TRAVEL ⊖ *Oxford Circus* • **HOURS** *Mon, Wed and Sat, 9.30am-6.30pm; Thurs, 9.30am-8pm; Fri, 9.30am-7pm; Sun, noon-6pm*

INSTEP

ADDRESS 45 St John's Wood High Street, NW8 (and branches)

PHONE 0171 722 7634

Very good shoe shop where staff take care to fit the shoe to the foot rather than the other way round. Stocks all kinds of shoes for toddlers to teenagers (up to size 8), including school shoes, ballet pumps, wellies, sandals and the Start-Rite range, plus imported continental shoes. Video cartoons and play area.

TRAVEL ⊖ *St John's Wood* • **HOURS** *Mon-Sat, 9.30am-5.30pm*

SHOE STATION

ADDRESS 3 Station Approach, Kew Gardens, Richmond, Surrey
PHONE 0181 940 9905

This is such a well-stocked shop it is worth a trip in itself. Ideally, however, combine kitting out the family's feet with a visit to **Kew Gardens**. Everything from Start-Rite to Dr Martens, with French, Italian and American imports, wellies, slippers, trainers, gym shoes and padders.

TRAVEL ⊖ *Kew Gardens* • **HOURS** *Mon-Sat, 10am-1pm and 2-5.30pm*

SPORTS EQUIPMENT AND CLOTHING

HAMLEY'S

ADDRESS 188-96 Regent Street, W1
PHONE 0171 734 3161

The basement stocks all kinds of sports equipment and clothing.

TRAVEL ⊖ *Oxford Circus* • **HOURS** *Mon-Fri, 10am-7pm (Thurs to 8pm); Sat, 9.30am-7pm; Sun, noon-6pm*

LILLYWHITES

ADDRESS 24-36 Lower Regent Street, SW1
PHONE 0171 930 3181

The six floors of this large department store overflow with equipment for every kind of sport from skiing to skateboarding, climbing to canoeing, angling to abseiling.

TRAVEL ⊖ *Piccadilly Circus* • **HOURS** *Mon-Wed, Fri, 10am-8pm; Thurs, 10am-9pm; Sat, 9am-7pm; Sun, 11am-5pm*

WEARITE

ADDRESS 237 Royal College Street, NW1
PHONE 0171 485 9989

Tents, rucksacks, hiking boots and outdoor accessories at incredibly reasonable prices. Free catalogue.

TRAVEL ⊖ *Camden Town* • **HOURS** *Mon-Sat, 10.30am-6pm*

YHA ADVENTURE SHOPS

ADDRESS 14 Southampton Street, WC2
PHONE 0171 836 8541

Maps, guides, clothing and equipment for the outdoor enthusiast.

TRAVEL ⊖ *Covent Garden or Charing Cross* • **HOURS** *Mon-Wed, 10am-6pm; Thurs-Fri, 10am-7pm; Sat, 9.30am-6.30pm; Sun, 11am-6pm*

STAMP COLLECTING

THE STAMP CENTRE

ADDRESS 79 Strand, WC2
PHONE 0171 836 2579

British, Commonwealth, continental and worldwide stamp collections. Staff are keen to introduce beginners to the joys of philately.

TRAVEL ⊖ *Charing Cross* • **HOURS** *Mon-Fri, 10am-5.30pm; Sat, 10am-5pm*

STANLEY GIBBONS INTERNATIONAL

ADDRESS 399 Strand, WC2

PHONE 0171 836 8444

One of the oldest and largest stamp shops in the world, with a huge stock, a postal-history section, accessories and excellent catalogues. Prices start at under £1. Mail order.

TRAVEL ⊖ Charing Cross • **HOURS** Mon-Fri, 8.30am-6pm; Sat, 9.30am-5.30pm

TOYS, GAMES AND MAGIC

ARGOS

ADDRESS 80-110 New Oxford Street, WC1

PHONE 0171 637 1869; for your nearest local branch, call 0181 749 2572

Good value, cut-price standard range of brand-name toys and equipment. Free catalogue.

TRAVEL ⊖ Tottenham Court Road • **HOURS** Mon, Wed and Fri-Sat, 9.30am-6pm; Tues, 9.30am-10pm; Thurs, 9.30am-8pm; Sun, noon-6pm

BENJAMIN POLLOCK'S TOY SHOP

ADDRESS 44 Covent Garden Market, WC2

PHONE 0171 379 7866

Exquisite antique dolls for lucky children and collectors, as well as more affordable Victorian cut-out model theatres and some pocket-money toys.

TRAVEL ⊖ Covent Garden • **HOURS** Mon-Sat, 10.30am-6pm; Sun, noon-5pm

CHILDREN'S WORLD

ADDRESS Trafalgar Way, Croydon, Surrey (branches in Islington and Richmond)

PHONE 0181 760 0484

This store also sells children's clothes – extensive in terms of choice, limited in appeal (see Clothes and Shoes, above). However, you cannot fault the choice of toys, nursery basics and smaller essentials, including discount bulk-buy nappies. There is a play area, although children have to be supervised. Also hairdresser's, party shop, on-site McDonald's, children's toilets, father-and-baby room, mother-and-baby room, feeding facilities, ample parking and home- and nappy-delivery service. Conveniently near IKEA and Toys 'R' Us.

TRAVEL Waddon Marsh rail • **HOURS** Mon-Fri, 10am-8pm; Sat, 9am-6pm; Sun, 11am-5pm

DAVENPORT'S MAGIC SHOP

ADDRESS 7 Charing Cross Underground Concourse, Strand, WC2

PHONE 0171 836 0408

London's most famous magic shop celebrates its 100th birthday this year. It is an Aladdin's Cave of tricks, from the complex devices used by members of the Magic Circle to pocket-money jokes, tricks and puzzles. Whoopee cushions and joke sweets are always popular, and the magic-egg trick is a good one for beginners.

TRAVEL ⊖ Charing Cross • **HOURS** Mon-Fri, 9.30am-5.30pm; Sat, 10.15am-4pm

THE DISNEY STORE

ADDRESS 104 Regent Street, W1

PHONE 0171 287 6558

Toys, clothes and other merchandise relating to Disney's latest and favourite characters. Merchandise for toddlers is in the basement and there is no lift.

TRAVEL ⊖ *Piccadilly Circus* • **HOURS** *Mon-Sat, 9.30am-8pm; Sun, noon-6pm*

EARLY LEARNING CENTRE

ADDRESS 225 Kensington High Street, W8 (branches all over London, some with community notice board)

PHONE 0171 937 0419; mail order 01793 444844

You will find equipment, clothes and accessories as well as the well-known non-sexist, non-racist toys (and no guns). Toys are always safe, usually fun, often educational, mostly stimulating, of good quality and reasonably priced, with plenty for under £5. Children can try out most toys before purchase, and space is provided for them to play while you browse.

TRAVEL ⊖ *High Street Kensington* • **HOURS** *Mon-Sat, 9am-6pm*

HAMLEY'S

ADDRESS 188 Regent Street, W1

PHONE 0171 734 3161

The largest toy shop in the world stocks everything from traditional nursery toys to all the latest fads, squeezed into six floors. Try to avoid the chaos of Saturdays, or any festive countdown, especially the six weeks before Christmas. People do come here for a day out, and you can have lunch in the café. Hamley's stocks everything from the unimaginably expensive to the dirt cheap, but prices are often considerably higher than in other shops.

TRAVEL ⊖ *Oxford Circus or Piccadilly Circus* • **HOURS** *Mon-Wed and Fri, 10am-7pm; Thurs, 10am-8pm; Sat, 9.30am-7pm; Sun, noon-6pm*

HILL TOY COMPANY

ADDRESS 71 Abingdon Road, W8

PHONE 0171 937 8797

The high quality of the wonderful wooden toys, castles, train sets, farms, puppet theatres and doll's houses is reflected in the prices, but the merchandise is still good value. Lots of traditional games, craft kits and imaginative dressing-up clothes.

TRAVEL ⊖ *High Street Kensington* • **HOURS** *Mon-Fri, 9.30am-5.30pm; Sat, 10am-5pm*

JUST GAMES

ADDRESS 71 Brewer Street, W1

PHONE 0171 437 0761

Every imaginable board game, from Chess and Mahjong to Snakes and Ladders and Cluedo, as well as Snap, Mouse Trap, Jenga and other tried-and-tested favourites. The staff are happy to give advice.

TRAVEL ⊖ *Piccadilly Circus* • **HOURS** *Mon-Sat, 10am-6pm (Thurs to 7pm)*

LONDON DOLL'S HOUSE COMPANY

ADDRESS 29 Covent Garden Market, WC2

PHONE 0171 240 8681

Doll's houses in all architectural styles, from Victorian and Georgian to art deco and modern, either made up or in kit form. These can be furnished with inexpensive plastic furniture and fabric dolls, or with more expensive hand-made dolls and crafted wooden furniture and accessories. The catalogue is a good investment, as young enthusiasts will while away endless hours planning their next pocket-money purchase (£2 from the shop, £2.50 by post).

TRAVEL ⊖ *Covent Garden* • **HOURS** *Mon-Sat, 10am-7pm; Sun, noon-5pm*

ROUTE 73

ADDRESS 88 Stoke Newington Church Street, N16
PHONE 0171 923 7873

Wonderful, quite old-fashioned shop with lots of wooden toys, Galt toys and things parents like as much as children. Useful notice board, nappy-changing facilities and incredibly friendly staff who will happily track things down for you and order obscure items.

TRAVEL *Stoke Newington rail* • **HOURS** *Tues-Sat, 10am-5pm*

SINGING TREE

ADDRESS 69 New King's Road, SW6
PHONE 0171 736 4527

A magical shop, full of new and antique doll's houses and exclusive miniature accessories, including hallmarked silverware and porcelain, for the serious collector. Large intricate doll's houses can cost over £3,000; a simple Edwardian shop in kit form costs £190.

TRAVEL ⊖ *Fulham Broadway or bus 22* • **HOURS** *Mon-Sat, 10am-5.30pm*

SNAPDRAGON

ADDRESS 56 Turnham Green Terrace, W4
PHONE 0181 995 6618

Brightly coloured shop crammed with everything your children could want – good-quality wooden toys, all the top brand names, books, party novelties, kit doll's houses, traditional rocking horses, helium balloons, outdoor equipment, dressing-up clothes and craft kits.

TRAVEL ⊖ *Turnham Green* • **HOURS** *Mon-Sat, 9.30am-5.30pm*

TOYS 'R' US

ADDRESS Trojan Way, off Purley Way, Croydon, Surrey; also at Tilling Road, NW2, and 76-8 High Road, N22 (other branches on Old Kent Road and Hayes Road)
PHONE 0181 686 3133 (Croydon); 0181 209 0019 (NW2);
0181 881 6636 (N22)

The enormous warehouse is piled up from floor to ceiling with toys and games, which is fine if you know what you want, but my kids get frustrated because everything is packaged and even the outdoor slides and climbing frames can't be tried out. Whenever we ask for things, the staff never seem to know where anything is. However, the games and multimedia sections are excellent. Toilets, mother-and-baby room. Conveniently near IKEA and Children's World.

TRAVEL *Waddon Marsh rail (Croydon);* ⊖ *Brent Cross (NW2);* ⊖ *Wood Green (N22)* • **HOURS** *Phone for times*

TRIDIAS

ADDRESS 25 Bute Street, SW7
PHONE 0171 584 2330; mail order 01225 469455

Parents love the toys because they are wooden, and children love them because the wood is painted in bright, high-gloss colours. I love Tridias because you can buy everything mail order from an excellent catalogue with plenty of stocking-filler ideas (from 1p), as well as larger items, pictures of which you can thrust in front of generous godparents around birthday times.

TRAVEL ⊖ *South Kensington* • **HOURS** *Mon-Fri, 9.30am-6pm; Sat, 10am-6pm*

WARNER BROTHERS STUDIO STORE

ADDRESS 178-82 Regent Street, W1 (branches at Gatwick Airport and Kingston upon Thames)
PHONE 0171 434 3334

Two floors of Warner Bros merchandise and toys from all the animated and some live-action films, including favourite characters such as Bugs Bunny, Daffy Duck, Batman and Superman. Interactive paint station where children can computer-colour animated scenes. Original cartoon cels from the Animation Gallery.

TRAVEL ⊖ *Piccadilly Circus or Oxford Circus* • **HOURS** *Mon-Wed and Fri, 10am-7pm; Thurs and Sat, 10am-8pm; Sun, noon-6pm*

WOOLWORTHS

ADDRESS 168 Edgware Road, W2 (and branches)
PHONE 0171 723 2980

Every local high street has a Woolies and they can't be beaten for seasonal sales bargains. Cheap toys, party ware, school equipment (from uniforms to Disney rulers) and pocket-money toys and sweets. Also own, good-quality, practical, long-lasting Ladybird clothes range.

TRAVEL ⊖ *Edgware Road* • **HOURS** *Mon-Fri, 9am-8pm; Sat, 9am-7pm; Sun, 11am-5pm*

EATING OUT

This chapter aims to take the stress out of eating out with young children. There are child-friendly cafés; themed fast-food outlets; restaurants that entertain children; and those with children's menus, reduced-price children's portions, high chairs, booster seats and baby-changing facilities.

ENTERTAINMENT AND THEME RESTAURANTS

ART 4 FUN

ADDRESS The Creative Café, 444 Chiswick High Road, W4
PHONE 0181 994 4100

Workshop for the whole family in a relaxed café atmosphere where, over tea and cakes, you can paint on ceramics, glass or wood. Buy individually priced items to decorate, have fired and take home.

TRAVEL ⊖ *Chiswick Park* • **HOURS** *Phone for opening times* • **PRICES** *From £3 for paint and firing*

CAPITAL RADIO CAFE

ADDRESS Leicester Square, WC2
PHONE 0171 484 8888

Capital Radio DJs play live at central decks, round which you sit and eat, surprisingly, very good food. Children can meet the DJs, request their favourite songs and enter competitions. Chicken fingers, spaghetti, mini-clubs and pizzas on the children's menu come in huge portions, followed by a choice of ice-creams, sodas and milk shakes, while for the adults the choice is 'global'. High chairs and baby-changing facilities.

TRAVEL ⊖ *Leicester Square* • **HOURS** *Mon-Sat, 11.45-midnight; Sun, 11.45am-10.30pm* • **PRICES** *Adults main course £7-10, children's menu £3.99 (average)*

DEALS

ADDRESS Chelsea Harbour, SW3
PHONE 0171 352 5887

The eclectic menu offers anything from English bangers and mash to Tong's Yu Soup, a spicy Thai speciality, taking in a few American dishes along the way. Sunday is family day in this friendly restaurant. Magician and face painting from noon to 3pm. Booking essential. High chairs. Also at: Bradmore House, Hammersmith Broadway, W6 (tel: 0181 563 1001).

TRAVEL *Bus 11 or 22; car park* • **HOURS** *Mon-Wed, noon-11pm; Thurs-Sat, noon-11.30pm; Sun, noon-10pm* • **PRICES** *Children's menu with fish fingers £4.25, burgers and fries £4.95*

FASHION CAFE

ADDRESS 5-6 Coventry Street, W1
PHONE 0171 287 5888

Elle Macpherson, Naomi Campbell, Claudia Schiffer and Christy Turlington have combined their favourite foods with fashion memorabilia. Ideal for fashion-conscious teens but way over the heads of most under-10s. Unambitious children's menu.

TRAVEL ⊖ *Piccadilly Circus or Leicester Square* • **HOURS** *Daily, noon-midnight* • **PRICES** *Average meal £15*

FOOTBALL FOOTBALL
ADDRESS *57-60 Haymarket, SW1*
PHONE *0171 930 9970*

For a total football experience while eating anything from pizzas, pasta and potatoes to hamburgers, steaks and chicken dishes, you can't fault Football Football, and children will be for ever in your debt. They can watch all the magic moments from cup finals, matches and tournaments past and present, and take in all the football memorabilia.

TRAVEL ⊖ *Piccadilly Circus* • **HOURS** *Daily, noon-11.30pm (Sun to 10pm)*
• **PRICES** *Children's menu with main course, pudding and drink £4.95*

HAMLEY'S METROPOLIS AND MASSARELLA'S
ADDRESS *188-196 Regent Street, W1*
PHONE *0171 734 3161*

Over 100 Sega games in this basement restaurant will keep the children amused while the adults choose from a menu including salads, soups, burgers, fries and sandwiches. There is also a children's menu.

TRAVEL ⊖ *Oxford Circus or Piccadilly Circus* • **HOURS** *Mon-Sat, 10am-6.30pm (Thurs to 8pm); Sun, noon-6.30pm* • **PRICES** *Children's menu £2.25*

LUNA NUOVA
ADDRESS *22 Shorts Gardens, WC2*
PHONE *0171 836 4110*

Very friendly, popular pizzeria where one Sunday a month Spotty Dotty will entertain your children between 1pm and 3pm, while they eat pizza, pasta and ice-cream, leaving parents to choose from a more imaginative menu. At other times children can make their own pizzas (with a little guidance from the chef), play with dough and cookie cutters, and scribble on blackboards.

TRAVEL ⊖ *Covent Garden* • **HOURS** *Mon-Sat, noon-11.30pm, Sun, noon-10.30pm* • **PRICES** *Adults £17 (average), children's menu £4.75*

PJ'S GRILL
ADDRESS *30 Wellington Street, WC2*
PHONE *0171 240 7529*

Popular with families on Sundays (but not so child friendly during the rest of the week), PJ's has an additive-free children's menu with wholesome options like carrot and cucumber sticks and people-shaped peanut-butter sandwiches. The New York grill-style set menu for adults is imaginative and you can eat in relative peace while the children run amok in the play area or enjoy Uncle PJ's Sunday Funclub, with balloon bending and face painting. Food is generally good and prices reflect the area.

TRAVEL ⊖ *Covent Garden* • **HOURS** *Mon-Sat, noon to midnight; Sun, noon-4pm* • **PRICES** *Adults £17, children £5 (average)*

RAINFOREST CAFE
ADDRESS *20 Shaftesbury Avenue, W1*
PHONE *0171 434 3111*

Billing itself as 'a wild place to shop and eat', this huge space, filled with large trees, vines, foliage, thunder and lightning displays, and life-like animals that make alarming noises, is not conducive to a quiet meal out, but if you have noisy children at least no one will notice. You are allocated a safari guide to shepherd you through the 'experience', and on busy days your Rainforest passport is time stamped so you can browse around the shop instead of standing in a queue. The children thought it was great but with salads at £8, main courses around £12 and puddings a hefty £5, it is an expensive treat. The American-style food is fairly imaginative, and the cocktails, fruit and yoghurt drinks and smoothies are delicious.

TRAVEL ⊖ *Piccadilly Circus* • **HOURS** *Daily, 11-midnight*

MOLLENSKY'S BALLOON

ADDRESS 1 Dover Street, W1
PHONE 0171 491 1199

It is absolutely essential to book well in advance for this popular, American-style, child-friendly watering hole, especially for the weekend family lunches. The children's menu has burgers, junior steaks and outrageous desserts. To make your offspring feel really grown-up there are Kids' Koktails, too. There is also a puppet show from 2.30 to 3pm, balloons, and magic tricks at your table.

TRAVEL ⊖ *Green Park* • **HOURS** *Mon-Wed, noon-midnight; Thurs-Fri noon-1am; Sun, noon-4pm; family lunches Sat and Sun, noon-3pm* • **PRICES** *Adults £14, children £7 (based on an average 3 course lunch)*

MOLLENSKY'S ON THE STRAND

ADDRESS 105 The Strand, WC2
PHONE 0171 497 2101

This is an exceptional restaurant that bends over backwards to accommodate and entertain children at the weekend. There is a supervised play area, video games, balloons, a raffle, and a kids' magic show (2.30pm). There are plenty of high chairs, booster seats, a decent baby-changing area in the toilet. Nobody seems to mind how much mess the kids (or adults) make with the food, which pleases even fussy children. While the children enjoy bangers and mash, chicken nuggets, fish fingers, hamburgers, hot dogs or steak, adults can choose either the fixed-price menu of starter, steak and fries plus a drink, or the à la carte selection, which includes the varied and delicious steaks for which Smollensky's is famous. Booking advised.

TRAVEL ⊖ *Charing Cross* • **HOURS** *Family Affair (family lunch and children's entertainment): Sat-Sun and bank holidays, noon-3pm* • **PRICES** *Adults £14, children £7 (based on an average 3 course lunch)*

FAMILY RESTAURANTS

ABENO

ADDRESS First Floor, Yaoham Plaza, 399 Edgware Road, NW9
PHONE 0181 205 1131

Very popular with families and great novelty value if your kids haven't had Japanese food before (several dishes have been specially designed for children). The speciality is Okonomi-yaki (thick chewy pancakes), cooked at your table. Children's menu, high chairs, crayons, baby-changing facilities.

TRAVEL ⊖ *Colindale* • **HOURS** *Wed-Fri, noon-3pm; Mon-Fri, 6-11pm; Sat-Sun, noon-11pm* • **PRICES** *Set lunch from £7.80 to £15.80*

BENIHANA

ADDRESS 100 Avenue Road, NW3

PHONE 0171 586 7118

Sunday lunch is cheerful, though not necessarily cheap, at this impressive, American-style Japanese restaurant. Although it no longer has table-side magicians, you can still marvel at the magic of the chefs' knife-wielding feats. Branches at 37 Sackville Street, W1 (tel: 0171 494 2525) and 77 King's Road, SW3 (tel: 0171 376 7799).

TRAVEL ⊖ *Swiss Cottage* • **HOURS** *Lunch: daily, 12.30-3pm* • **PRICES** *Set lunch from £8.50 to £24*

BLUE ELEPHANT

ADDRESS 4-6 Fulham Broadway, SW6

PHONE 0171 385 6595

For a real treat, this very expensive, very good and wonderfully atmospheric Thai restaurant is great on Sundays, when they do a splendid brunch offering adults all-you-can-eat for £16.75. The children's menu has a pricing system by which kids under 4 ft tall are measured and charged per foot (£4-£6). Clowns entertain the children while you eat. Dress smart.

TRAVEL ⊖ *Fulham Broadway* • **HOURS** *Mon-Fri and Sun, noon-2.30pm and 7pm-12.30am (closed Sat lunch, Sun to 10.30pm)*

THE BLUE LEGUME

ADDRESS 101 Stoke Newington Church Street, N16

PHONE 0171 923 1303

Delicious, mainly vegetarian food, yummy breakfasts and endlessly patient staff make this a popular haunt for local families. While adults pig out on anything from organic mushrooms and crème fraîche on ciabatta to pistachio and courgette burger with sour cream, children are seduced by the fried breakfasts (served until 2pm) and a selection of superlative cakes. High chairs and reduced-price children's portions.

TRAVEL *Stoke Newington rail; bus 73* • **HOURS** *Tues-Wed, 9.30am-6.30pm; Thurs-Fri, 9.30am-11pm; Sat, 10.30am-11pm; Sun, 10.30am-6pm. No credit cards.*

CALABASH

ADDRESS Africa Centre, 38 King Street, WC2

PHONE 0171 836 1976

Babies and children are welcome at this large restaurant in the basement of the Africa Centre. It's a fun place to try dishes from every corner of Africa. Reduced-price children's portions available on request.

TRAVEL ⊖ *Covent Garden* • **HOURS** *lunch Mon-Fri, 12.30-3pm, dinner Mon-Sat, 6-10.30pm* • **PRICES** *Adults £15 (average)*

CHUEN CHENG KU

ADDRESS 17 Wardour Street, W1

PHONE 0171 437 1398

Lunchtime dim sum comes on a trolley loaded with small baskets of goodies from which to choose. This large, busy restaurant is very baby and child friendly, provides high chairs and boasts the longest menu in Chinatown.

TRAVEL ⊖ *Leicester Square or Piccadilly Circus* • **HOURS** *Mon-Sat, 11-midnight; Sun, 11am-11.15pm* • **PRICES** *About £10 per person*

INDIVICK

ADDRESS 201 Liverpool Road, N1
PHONE 0171 607 7710

Bright, light Australian restaurant adorned with colourful aboriginal art. Brunch is the thing here – from own-made muesli and fruit (£3.25) to The Full Monty fry-up (£6.50). It is amazingly child friendly at weekends (you can't move for buggies) and the food is delicious. Crayons, toys, high chairs and baby-changing facilities.

TRAVEL ⊖ *Angel* • **HOURS** *Brunch: Sat-Sun, 10.30am-3.30pm; lunch: Tues-Fri, noon-3pm; dinner: Mon-Sat, 6-10.45pm*

OANNA'S

ADDRESS 56 Westow Hill, SE19
PHONE 0181 670 4052

Joanna's stands out for its fast, friendly service, imaginative cooking and lively atmosphere. The speciality may be burgers, which you can have every-which-way, but this is no ordinary diner. The style is Californian with Thai, Mexican and Mediterranean dishes. Try the Thai Red Curry Mussels or the Supreme of Chicken with Ginger Mint Butter (£8.95). Fussy chip eaters have a choice of fat chips, French fries or aptly named shoe-string chips. Lunchtime and early-evening children's menu, high chairs, booster seats and crayons for tablecloth works of art.

TRAVEL *Gypsy Hill rail* • **HOURS** *Daily, 10am to late*

LEFTIKO

ADDRESS 293 Chiswick High Road, W4
PHONE 0181 994 0305

Locals will welcome back this popular Greek, bistro-style restaurant, which has relocated from Turnham Green. As before, children are given a warm welcome at lunchtimes and at weekends, and there is a children's buffet on Sundays (noon-3pm). There is a good variety of food from meze to Metaxa. The meze (which come in three different sizes) are an excellent way to get kids to try different foods. Reduced-price children's portions available on request. High chairs. Also at: 186 Holland Park Road, W14 (tel: 0171 603 0807).

TRAVEL ⊖ *Chiswick Park or Gunnersbury* • **HOURS** *Mon-Sat, 7am-2pm, 6-11.30pm* • **PRICES** *Set lunch £4.95, set dinner £10.50*

MARCHE

ADDRESS Portland House, Stag Place, SW1 (and branches)
PHONE 0171 630 1733

This Swiss chain of fresh fast-food restaurants is very popular with health-conscious parents whose children are fussy. The kids can choose exactly what they want (and how they want it done) from the colourful display of hot and cold food, and watch bread being made when they get bored. Reduced-price children's portions, high chair and baby-changing facilities.

TRAVEL ⊖ *Victoria* • **HOURS** *Mon-Sat, 11am-11pm; Sun, 11am-10pm*

AMERICAN-STYLE RESTAURANTS

THE CHICAGO RIB SHACK

ADDRESS 1 Raphael Street, SW7
PHONE 0171 581 5595

Usual Chicago fare, but the spicy barbecued salmon is delicious and the puddings are a treat (try the chocolate cheesecake). The children's menu is still £5.95, with colour-in menus, competitions and balloons. The staff are very friendly and do very good children's parties. Baby-changing facilities, bibs, high chairs and booster seats.

TRAVEL ⊖ *Knightsbridge* • **HOURS** *Mon-Sat, noon-11.45pm; Sun, noon-11pm*

HARD ROCK CAFE

ADDRESS 150 Old Park Lane, W1
PHONE 0171 629 0382

Called the Smithsonian of rock 'n' roll, this legendary burger bar has what it claims to be the world's greatest collection of pop-music memorabilia. Bookings not accepted so expect to join long queues. Food is better than most of its imitators but people come here for the myth, not the menu. High chairs, children's menu, toys.

TRAVEL ⊖ *Hyde Park Corner* • **HOURS** *Mon-Thurs, Sun, 11.30am-12.30pm; Fri, Sat, 11.30am-1am* • **PRICES** *Adults £17 (average), children's menu £5.50*

McDONALD'S

ADDRESS See phone directory for your nearest branch
PHONE 0171 937 3705

Let's face it, you can't fault McDonald's as far as children are concerned. It serves food they are guaranteed to eat, and the service is fast and friendly, with balloons and other bits and bobs, especially at weekends. You can drop your food all over the floor and they don't bat an eyelid; spill a drink and another one miraculously appears at no extra charge. High chairs, booster seats, uniform hamburgers and great milk shakes. For birthdays, children are entertained with games and activities by trained hostesses; there is a special present for the birthday child and party gifts for others. Invitations and birthday cake available.

HOURS *Most branches open daily, 7am-11pm*

PIZZA EXPRESS

ADDRESS See phone directory for your nearest branch
PHONE 0171 636 3232

Pizza Express serves consistently excellent, thin, crispy pizzas with a variety of good toppings (Jake and Benja's favourite is the Veneziana with sultanas, capers, pine kernels, onions and olives). Kids can 'share-a-pizza'. Very friendly attitude to children.

TRAVEL ⊖ *Holborn or Tottenham Court Road* • **HOURS** *Most branches open daily, phone for opening hours* • **PRICES** *pizzas from £5.85*

PLANET HARRODS

ADDRESS Harrods, Knightsbridge, SW1
PHONE 0171 730 1234

Chicken meteors, solar fries, satellite lasagne and other space-age food make up the 'mini-crew meals' for children, while the video wall shows

non-stop cartoons, ensuring your offspring don't have to talk to you at all.
High chairs, baby-changing facilities.

TRAVEL ✪ *Knightsbridge* • **HOURS** *Mon-Sat, 10am-6pm* • **PRICES** *Main course £6.95, children £4.95 (average)*

PLANET HOLLYWOOD

ADDRESS Trocadero, Piccadilly, W1
PHONE 0171 287 1000

Children and teenagers love the loud music, garish decor and fabulous
collection of film memorabilia in this very in-your-face restaurant. Food is
reliably good, if expensive, and the burgers and chips are the best we've
had. Sci-fi room, alien grotto and 75-seater preview theatre. Huge portions
are a big advantage. Children's menu, high chairs and baby-changing
facilities.

TRAVEL ✪ *Piccadilly Circus* • **HOURS** *Daily, 11am to late* • **PRICES** *Adults £20 (average), children's menu £8.95*

STICKY FINGERS

ADDRESS 1a Phillimore Gardens, W8
PHONE 0171 938 5338

The Rolling Stones' ex-bass player Bill Wyman's American-style restaurant
is popular with pop celebrities as well as the kids. Surrounded by rock 'n'
roll memorabilia, you can choose from a menu of burgers, sandwiches,
barbecue chicken wings, chilli dogs and a range of sticky puddings.
Children are given colouring books and crayons and invited to enter a
'draw your waiter' competition. On Sundays there is a magician on hand
to entertain from 1pm to 3pm. Children's menu, high chairs.

TRAVEL ✪ *High Street Kensington* • **HOURS** *Daily, noon-11.30pm* • **PRICES** *Set lunch £5.95, children's menu £7*

GI FRIDAY

ADDRESS 6 Bedford Street, W2 (and branches)
PHONE 0171 379 0585

Branches of this immensely popular American import have popped up
all over the place in recent years (see telephone directory). This noisy,
lively, very big diner is not to everyone's taste (and it's not cheap) but the
Tex-Mex food is good, the choice extensive and the portions enormous.
Children's hamburger menu or smaller portions of the regular menu
available. High chairs and booster seats. Children's entertainment Sundays.
Excellent for children's parties but you cannot book.

TRAVEL ✪ *Covent Garden or Charing Cross* • **HOURS** *Daily, noon-midnight*
• **PRICES** *Starters £4-£5, main courses from £8, children's menu from £5.95*

TEXAS EMBASSY CANTINA

ADDRESS 1 Cockspur Street, SW1
PHONE 0171 925 0077

Before joining the Union, Texas had its own embassy in London (further up
the road from here). Like everything Texan, the venue is huge, the meals
gigantic and the service very friendly. The usual Tex-Mex food is served
quite speedily and the free, multi-coloured tortilla chips are a blessing for
ravenous, impatient children. Children's menu, high chairs, crayons and
friendly, long-suffering staff.

TRAVEL ✪ *Piccadilly Circus or Charing Cross* • **HOURS** *Mon-Thurs, noon-late, Fri, Sat, 12.30pm-late, Sun 12.30-11pm* • **PRICES** *Adults £18 (average)*

FREE MEALS FOR KIDS

BABUR BRASSERIE **E**

ADDRESS 119 Brockley Rise, SE23
PHONE 0181 291 2400/4881

Sunday buffet lunch at this excellent Indian restaurant is free for under-7s and half-price for ages 7-10. Children must be accompanied by an adult. The staff are very welcoming. Plenty of high chairs.

TRAVEL *Honor Oak Park rail* • **HOURS** *Sun lunch: noon-2.30pm* • **PRICES** *Adults £18 (average), set Sun lunch £7.95, free for under-7s, half price for ages 7-10*

BIG EASY **E**

ADDRESS 332-4 King's Road, SW3
PHONE 0171 352 4071

Service is fast and friendly at this American crab-shack-style restaurant. There are plenty of burgers (from £4.95), ribs, sandwiches and chicken dishes, but the real specialities are the huge portions of wonderful prawn, crab and lobster. Children's menu, high chairs, crayons and, best of all, children under 10 eat free when accompanied by an adult.

TRAVEL ⊖ *Sloane Square* • **HOURS** *Mon-Sat, noon-11pm, Sun, noon-10.30pm* • **PRICES** *Adults £5 (average), 1st child under 10 eats free, additional children's meal, £3.95*

EL METRO **E**

ADDRESS 10-12 Effie Road, SW6
PHONE 0171 384 1264

Traditional Spanish dishes, tapas, soups, paella (£18 for two) as well as full English breakfast (£3.95) served until 5pm. Babies and children are welcome until 7pm and children under 7 eat free from the children's menu. High chairs, colouring books. Booking advisable at weekends.

TRAVEL ⊖ *Fulham Broadway* • **HOURS** *Daily, 9am-midnight*

MESON BILBAO **E**

ADDRESS 33 Malvern Road, NW6
PHONE 0171 328 1744

On Sundays in winter children under 7 eat free at this wonderful Spanish restaurant whose mussels are a local legend. Tapas go down well with children wishing to expand their culinary experiences, and the set menus are good value. High chairs, reduced-price children's portions.

TRAVEL ⊖ *Maida Vale* • **HOURS** *Mon-Sat, noon-3pm and 6-11.30pm (closed summer Sundays)* • **PRICES** *phone for prices*

SAHARA **E**

ADDRESS 1 Devonshire Street, W1
PHONE 0171 436 4547

Meze feature large on the menu of this Lebanese restaurant, which offers reduced-price children's portions as well as free meals for under-6s. High chairs. Dress quite smart.

TRAVEL ⊖ *Great Portland Street* • **HOURS** *Daily, noon-1am* • **PRICES** *Set lunch £14.95*

FISH 'N' CHIPS

GEALES FISH RESTAURANT

ADDRESS 2 Farmer Street, W8
PHONE 0171 727 7969

This is a delightful, homely, up-market chippie. The fish is wonderfully
fresh and the batter deliciously crispy, but prices are high. Reduced-price
children's portions. High chairs and booster seats.

TRAVEL ⊖ *Notting Hill Gate* • **HOURS** *Tues-Sat, noon-3pm and 6-11pm*
(closed Sun and Mon) • **PRICES** *Fish from £7.50-£9 plus £1.50 for chips*

ROCK AND SOLE PLAICE

ADDRESS 47 Endell Street, WC2
PHONE 0171 836 3785

Reasonably priced and generous portions of cod, plaice, haddock and
rock salmon. High chairs and reduced-price children's portions on request.

TRAVEL ⊖ *Covent Garden* • **HOURS** *Mon-Sat, 11.30am-10pm; Sun,*
11.30am-9pm • **PRICES** *Fish from £5-£6*

SEA SHELL

ADDRESS 49-51 Lisson Grove, NW1
PHONE 0171 723 8703

Highly regarded, and long-established. Delicious fish cakes (£2.50) and
seafood casserole (£3.50). High chairs and reduced-price children's portions.

TRAVEL ⊖ *Marylebone* • **HOURS** *Mon-Fri, noon-2pm and 5.15-10.30pm;*
Sat, noon-10.30pm; Sun, noon-2.30pm

TWO BROTHERS FISH RESTAURANT

ADDRESS 297-303 Regent's Park Road, N3
PHONE 0181 346 0469

Excellent fish and chips from about £6, as well as more unusual sauce-
based dishes. High chairs and reduced-price children's portions.

TRAVEL ⊖ *Finchley Central* • **HOURS** *Tues-Sat, noon-2.30pm and 5.30-*
10.15pm

CAFES AND CREPERIES

ALFREDO'S

ADDRESS 4-6 Essex Road, N1
PHONE 0171 226 3496

At this popular, friendly budget café with art deco décor, you would be
hard pushed to spend more than a fiver a head. Alfredo's has been in
business for nearly 80 years and has got breakfast, which is served all
day, down to a tea (hot, strong, sweet and in a mug).

TRAVEL ⊖ *Angel* • **HOURS** *Mon-Fri, 7am-2.30pm; Sat, 7am-noon*

BOILED EGG & SOLDIERS

ADDRESS 63 Northcote Road, SW11
PHONE 0171 223 4894

Plastic tablecloths, bare floors and cartoons on the walls make this an
ideal watering hole for children, especially for brunch or high tea. The
choice of simple meals – sausage and beans, baked potatoes – is popular
with the kids, leaving plenty of locally baked cakes for everyone else.
Children's menu, high chairs. Book at weekends.

TRAVEL *Clapham Junction rail* • **HOURS** *Mon-Sat, 9am-6pm; Sun, 10am-5pm*
• **PRICES** *All day breakfast £4.75*

CAFE IN THE CRYPT

ADDRESS St Martin-in-the-Fields, Duncannon Street, WC2
PHONE 0171 839 4342

Its central location, next to the **London Brass Rubbing Centre** off
Trafalgar Square, makes this an ideal place to refuel after a spot of
sightseeing. All the food is made on the premises, with a choice of hot
meats and vegetarian dishes, as well as salads, sandwiches and hot
puddings. Half-portions are half price. Soup and a roll is £1.95; more
substantial meals from £5.50. High chairs.

TRAVEL ⊖ *Charing Cross* • **HOURS** *Mon-Sat, 10am-8pm; Sun, noon-8pm*

CAFE LAVILLE

ADDRESS 453 Edgware Road, W2
PHONE 0171 706 2620

Straddling the canal at Maida Vale, this small, friendly café is a good pit
stop if you're taking a boat trip or canal walk. Recently rebuilt, it opens
onto a terrace at the back with a lovely waterway view. Breakfast and
brunch all day (eggs Benedict, scrambled eggs with toast or croissants), as
well as more substantial dishes, such as spag bol and bangers and mash,
and vegetarian meals. Advisable to book on Sundays. Also pavement
tables. Reduced-price children's portions.

TRAVEL ⊖ *Warwick Avenue or Edgware Road; bus 6* • **HOURS** *Daily,
10am-10.30pm*

CHELSEA BUN DINER

ADDRESS 9A Limerston Street, SW10
PHONE 0171 352 3635

You can get a really good three-course meal at this busy budget café for
under £10. With literally hundreds of mainly American dishes to choose
from, including pasta, burgers, pies, moussaka and sandwiches, there will
be something on the menu for all the family. Breakfast is served all day,
with an excellent-value fry-up (£3.35) and large eggs Benedict (£5.20), or
you can opt for one of the many snacks on offer. Reduced-price children's
portions, vegetarian dishes and a take-away service. There are tables on
the first-floor balcony for eating alfresco without losing toddlers to the traffic.

TRAVEL *Bus 11, 19 or 31* • **HOURS** *Mon-Sat, 7am-11.30pm; Sun, 9.30am-
11.30pm*

ESCAPED COFFEE HOUSE

ADDRESS 141-3 Greenwich South Street, SE10
PHONE 0181 692 5826

This delightful little craft shop doubles as a café, with generous portions of
vegetarian and vegan hot or cold dishes. Although the food is sometimes
hit and miss, when it is good it is really good, and the children's room
with entertainers makes it worth the gamble. The savoury crumble of
vegetable and Guinness stew topped with oats and wheat is delicious,
and the puddings are popular with even the fussiest children. If it's sunny,
aim for the tiny backyard patio. Gets crowded, so arrive early. Good
painted wooden toys and cards in the shop. Children's portions, high
chairs, toys and books available.

TRAVEL *Greenwich rail* • **HOURS** *Mon-Sat, 10am-10.30pm; Sun, 11am-8pm*
• **PRICES** *All main courses £5.50*

REE RANGE

ADDRESS 159 Lordship Lane, SE22
PHONE 0181 693 5008

On a warm summer day in the patio garden full of flowers, regulars at this charming café enjoy ample portions of bangers-and-mash-style food. We rarely waver from the superb breakfast, served all day (10.30am-4pm), which as well as the usual bacon, beans and sausages, often includes kedgeree and poached eggs done to perfection. Reduced-price children's portions. High chairs.

TRAVEL Bus 185 or 176 • **HOURS** Summer: daily; winter: Fri-Sun (opening times vary, phone in advance)

GOLDERS HILL PARK REFRESHMENT HOUSE

ADDRESS North End Way, NW3
PHONE 0181 455 8010

This wonderful park café is run by an Italian family, whose home-made food is heavenly. A main course will set you back £3.70, with children's portions at £2, and there are plenty of snack options, such as sandwiches and soups, as well as delicious puddings. Home-made Italian ice-creams can also be bought at a hut at the side of the café from 90p. Children are most welcome and high chairs are available. No smoking inside (there are tables on the terrace). Don't miss the flamingos in the park's mini-zoo.

TRAVEL ⊖ Golders Green • **HOURS** Apr-Sep: daily, 10.30am to sunset

HOLLAND PARK CAFE

ADDRESS Holland Park, W8
PHONE 0171 602 2216

Perfect setting with lots of outside seating and good home-made Italian food, including soups, pasta, pizza and ice-cream. Generous, reasonably priced child portions.

TRAVEL ⊖ Holland Park or High Street Kensington • **HOURS** Daily, 10am to 30 mins before sunset (closed Jan)

KENSINGTON GARDENS CAFE

ADDRESS Broadwalk, Kensington Gardens, W2
PHONE 0171 727 9578

Next to the Elfin Tree, this is a cut above most park cafés, serving delicious lamb burgers, lamb chops, toasted sandwiches (£2.50) and hot dogs. Also ice-creams and lollies. Children's menu and high chairs.

TRAVEL ⊖ Bayswater or Queensway • **HOURS** Summer: daily, 10am-8.30pm; winter: daily, 10am-7pm (closed Dec)

LAUDERDALE HOUSE

ADDRESS Waterlow Park, Highgate Hill, N6
PHONE 0181 341 4807

The café at the back of this community arts centre overlooks the beautiful park, and has its own terrace for summer lunches. Food is good, plain and family oriented (fish fingers, lasagne and salads all under £5). See also Stage and Screen.

TRAVEL ⊖ Archway • **HOURS** Tues-Sun, 9am-6pm

PHOTOGRAPHER'S GALLERY CAFE

ADDRESS 5-8 Great Newport Street, WC2

PHONE 0171 831 1772

Once you have found this spacious, airy and relaxing café, with budget-priced snacks, good cakes and a healthy, friendly attitude to children, you are bound to come back. Savoury filled croissants, sun-dried tomato and mozzarella ciabatta, and spinach tortilla are all delicious and under £2. Gallery has ever-changing photography exhibitions. Reduced-price children's portions, high chairs and baby-changing facilities.

TRAVEL ⊖ *Leicester Square* • **HOURS** *Tues-Sat, 11am-5.30pm*

LE SHOP/THE VERITABLE CREPERIE

ADDRESS 329 King's Road, SW3

PHONE 0171 352 3891

Deliciously light crêpes and lots of combinations to choose and mix. From noon to 5pm you can have a set lunch consisting of a savoury galette with any two fillings, salad and a glass of wine for £6. Otherwise a meal costs £10. Reduced-price children's portions. High chairs, toys and books for kids.

TRAVEL ⊖ *Sloane Square, then bus 11, 19 or 22* • **HOURS** *Daily, noon-midnight*

THE WELL

ADDRESS 2 Eccleston Place, SW1

PHONE 0171 730 7303

Hot budget meals of the home-made variety include quiches, casseroles and baked potatoes served weekdays only. The delicious cakes (all 95p), good coffee and selection of cold snacks make this a welcome weekend retreat, and the regularly changing art exhibitions are an added bonus. Reduced-price children's portions on request. High chairs.

TRAVEL ⊖ *Victoria* • **HOURS** *Daily, 9am-6pm (Sat to 5pm)*

AFTERNOON TEAS

DAISY & TOM SODA BAR

ADDRESS 181 King's Road, SW3

PHONE 0171 352 5000

Good range of sandwiches, including peanut butter and jam, and chocolate nut spread with M&Ms. Lots of sticky cakes, biscuits and other delectables, such as chocolate cake with fudge sauce, mixed fruit with melted Mars Bar dip, Daisy and Tom gingerbread children, ice-creams and sweets. Also Beechnut natural baby food available in jars.

TRAVEL ⊖ *Sloane Square* • **HOURS** *Mon, Tues, Thurs, Fri, 10am-5.30pm; Wed, 10am-6.30pm; Sat, 9.30am-6pm; Sun, noon-5.30pm* • **PRICES** *Sandwiches from £1.75 to £5.75*

FORTNUM & MASON FOUNTAIN ROOM

ADDRESS 181 Piccadilly, W1

PHONE 0171 734 8040

This elegant tearoom, with its uniformed waitresses and pretty décor, is best kept for celebration treats. Not really suitable for young, boisterous children, although they do have a babies-and-children-welcome policy and provide high chairs. The ice-creams, made specially for Fortnums, come in a dozen varieties and are also available as sorbets, sundaes, sodas and frappés. The list of high teas is extensive (there are seven different types of tea alone). Not cheap but very charming.

TRAVEL ✈ *Green Park or Piccadilly Circus* • **HOURS** *Mon-Sat, 7.30am-11pm*

MAIDS OF HONOUR

ADDRESS 288 Kew Road, Richmond, Surrey
PHONE 0181 940 2752

Named after the Maids of Honour curd tart in puff pastry, of which Henry VIII was so fond and which are still served here, this is a tea-time favourite for all the family. Teas come with a choice of delicious scones and cakes, as well as more substantial fare like home-made sausage rolls and chicken pies. Babies and children are welcome and high chairs available. Lunch bookings obligatory (two sittings). Get there early for tea to avoid queues.

TRAVEL ✈ *Kew Gardens* • **HOURS** *Tues-Sat: lunch served 12.30pm and 1.30pm; tea served 2.45-5.30pm* • **PRICES** *Afternoon tea £4.65*

ICE-CREAM PARLOURS

ADA'S ICE-CREAM PARLOUR

ADDRESS 118 Sydenham Road, SE26
PHONE 0181 776 6747

Formerly Criterion Ices, this wonderful old-fashioned gelateria, whose ice-cream is still made by Criterion, is hard to beat. There are about 20 different ice-creams, all made with Guernsey or Jersey cream and including such scrumptious flavours as lemon meringue, white chocolate and toffee nut crunch. Also tea, coffee and snacks. Reduced-price children's portions, high chairs, toys.

TRAVEL *Sydenham rail; bus 75, 108 or 194* • **HOURS** *Mon-Sat, 9.30am-6pm; Sun, 11am-6pm* • **PRICES** *Single cones £1, medium £2, large £2.80; take-away tubs £4 for 1 litre*

GOLDERS HILL PARK REFRESHMENT HOUSE/ARTE GELATO

ADDRESS North End Way, NW3
PHONE 0181 455 8010

The Italian owners of this exceptional park café make ice-cream every day. Inside you can have banana splits, gondolas and knickerbocker glories as well as a limited, but delicious and often-changing choice of individual flavours. At an almost unbelievable 85p per scoop, you can afford to pile high some wild and wacky combinations. High chairs.

TRAVEL ✈ *Golders Green* • **HOURS** *Mar-Oct: daily, 10.30am to sunset*

HAAGEN-DAZS ON THE SQUARE

ADDRESS 14 Leicester Square, WC2
PHONE 0171 287 9577

Incredibly expensive ice-cream, but once you've tried a Häagen-Dazs you won't care. The venues look a bit clinical, even after their refurbishment, but the tastes and textures of the various ices, shakes, sundaes, cakes and creams are unbelievable. My kids will do anything for a lick of Belgian chocolate or a bite of macadamia nut brittle, but £1.40 is a bit steep for a cappuccino. High chairs. Reduced-price children's portions. Branches include: Unit 6, The Piazza, Covent Garden, WC2 (tel: 0171 240 0436); 83 Gloucester Road, SW7 (tel: 0171 373 9988).

TRAVEL ✆ *Leicester Square* • **HOURS** *Mon-Thurs, Sun, 10am-midnight; Fri, Sat 10am-1am* • **PRICES** *Scoop of frozen yoghurt £1.95, 3 ice-cream scoops £3.25, toppings from 45p, praline basket £4.25*

HARRODS ICE-CREAM PARLOUR & CREPERIE

ADDRESS Fourth Floor, Harrods, Knightsbridge, SW1
PHONE 0171 225 6628/730 1234

Conveniently near the toy department, this parlour seats 100 in an Italo-English country garden with wrought-iron furniture, umbrellas, hedges and a mural, all of which looks rather odd. However, the home-made, American-style ice-cream in nine flavours makes up for the ambience. Flavours include mint and chocolate chip, macadamia nut brittle and maple walnut, and kumquat sorbet. Service, especially when we had the crêpes, was slow and the results were disappointing. Stick with the ice-cream. Reduced-price children's portions and high chairs.

TRAVEL ✆ *Knightsbridge* • **HOURS** *Mon-Tues and Sat, 9am-6pm; Wed-Fri, 10am-7pm* • **PRICES** *From £2.95 for 2 scoops; specialities from £4.95 to £9.95*

MARINE ICES

ADDRESS 8 Haverstock Hill, NW3
PHONE 0171 485 3132

The additive-free Italian ice-creams and sorbets are made on the premises by the Mansi family, who have run this gelateria since 1913. With 15 flavours of ice-cream and seven flavours of sorbet, it's not easy to choose, but at £1.10 per scoop you can always go back for more. Give in to the hedonistic delights of a blissful bombe or sumptuous sundae, which will make the eyes of even the jaded ice-cream junky pop out in wonder. The lemon, orange and melon sorbets are to die for. The venue also doubles up as an Italian restaurant, which is cheap and cheerful, if a little brusque.

TRAVEL ✆ *Chalk Farm* • **HOURS** *Ice-cream parlour: Mon-Sat, 10.30am-11pm; Sun, 11-10pm*

REGENT'S MILK BAR

ADDRESS 362 Edgware Road, W9
PHONE 0171 723 8669

Formica dominates this wonderful 1950s milk bar with original fittings, including ice-cream signs advertising the choice of sundaes, soda fountains and milk shakes. Choose from nearly two dozen ice-cream flavours, which cost 60p a scoop. Also snacks and sandwiches. Eat in or take away.

TRAVEL ✆ *Edgware Road* • **HOURS** *Daily, 9am-5.30pm*

WINTON'S SODA FOUNTAIN

ADDRESS Second Floor, Whiteleys, Queensway, W2
PHONE 0171 229 8489

A chocaholic's heaven of white-, dark- and milk-chocolate sundaes, children's sundaes (£2.50), waffles (from £2.80), imaginative milk shakes and floats (from £2), plus 16 ice-cream flavours (£1.20 per scoop) with scrummy toppings, including Dime Crunch and Kit Kat (30p a portion). If you have to bribe your children to shop with you, this is your answer.

TRAVEL ✆ *Bayswater or Queensway* • **HOURS** *Mon-Thurs, Sun, 11am-10pm; Fri-Sat, 11am-11pm*

CHILDREN'S PARTIES

From a traditional tea party for toddlers to an overnight stay in a museum, here is a host of ideas to ensure your child's birthday goes with a bang.

VENUES

Your local leisure or sports centre will usually hire out football or cricket pitches, netball or tennis courts as well as offering packages for swimming or trampoline parties. Football clubs can arrange birthday parties. McDonald's and Burger King provide a party leader, organised games, hats, balloons, badges and a gift for the birthday child. For other restaurants offering children's party facilities see Eating Out.

AMERICAN STRETCH LIMOUSINE

PHONE 0181 889 8889

Live like the stars and hire a white stretch limo to transport up to eight children in total luxury, complete with television, video, stereo, ice box, mini-bar and your very own uniformed chauffeur.

PRICE *From £35 per hour*

BATTERSEA PARK CHILDREN'S ZOO

ADDRESS Albert Bridge Road, SW11

PHONE 0181 871 7540

Anything from a self-catering package to an all-inclusive party with birthday tea, decoration, entertainers, zoo tour and pony rides.

TRAVEL *Battersea Park rail* • **PRICE** *From £110*

HMS *BELFAST*

ADDRESS Morgan's Lane, off Tooley Street, SE1

PHONE 0171 407 6434

HMS *Belfast* has recently introduced a party service which includes party food, decorations, a guided tour, quiz trail and games.

TRAVEL ⊖ *London Bridge or Tower Hill; Tower Gate DLR; ferry from Tower Pier*

CHELSEA FC

ADDRESS Stamford Bridge, Fulham Road, SW6

PHONE 0171 385 0710

Football coaching, food, tour of ground, signed football for birthday child and visit from surprise guest.

TRAVEL ⊖ *Fulham Broadway* • **PRICES** *£8, £10 or £13 per head*

DISCOVERY ZONE

ADDRESS First Floor, The Junction Shopping Centre, SW11

PHONE 0171 223 1717

Two hours of moon walking, ball ponds, giant mazes, climbing, bouncing, crawling, party games and activities, and parents don't have to lift a

finger. Parties at this indoor adventure playground are hugely popular.
TRAVEL *Clapham Junction rail* • **PRICES** *£5.99 per child or £8.95 with burger, chips, drink and a present for the birthday child*

EPPING FOREST FIELD CENTRE
ADDRESS High Beach, Loughton, Essex
PHONE 0181 508 7714
Environmental birthday parties with activities including pond dipping, treasure hunt, mini-beast search, forest survival and tree detectives.
TRAVEL ✪ *Loughton* • **PRICES** *Nov-Mar: £42 for mini-safari led by qualified tutor for up to 12 children; additional children £3.50 each. Apr-Oct: £48 for up to 12 children; additional children £4 each (max. 22 children)*

FANTASY ISLAND
ADDRESS Vale Farm, Watford Road, Wembley, Middx
PHONE 0181 904 9044
Children from seven months to 12 years can party for 90 minutes before sitting down to hot and cold food in the restaurant.
TRAVEL ✪ *North Wembley* • **HOURS** *Daily, 10am-6pm* • **PRICES** *£7.95 per child for 2-hour party (£8.95 Sat-Sun and school holidays)*

FULHAM FC
ADDRESS Craven Cottage, Stevenage Road, SW6 6HH
PHONE 0171 736 6561
As for **Chelsea FC**, above.
TRAVEL ✪ *Putney Bridge* • **HOURS** *£9 per head including food, £7.50 without*

GOLDEN HINDE

ADDRESS St Marie Overie Dock, Cathedral Street, SE1
PHONE 0171 403 0123
A shipboard adventure for wannabe pirates like no other. Up to 15 children have the run of this full-size replica of Sir Francis Drake's 16th-century flagship for one and a half hours. The authentic atmosphere is enhanced by the costumed crew, who lead the children on a fun guided tour, regaling them with tales of uncomfortable nights and storm-tossed days at sea. There is a treasure hunt and tug of war, plenty of games and sea shanties, and the children eat their birthday tea at the captain's table. Best 5-year-olds' party we have had.
TRAVEL ✪ *Monument or London Bridge* • **PRICES** *Pirate Party with food £150, without food £100. Ages 5-11*

GURNELL LEISURE CENTRE
ADDRESS Ruislip Road East, W13
PHONE 0181 998 3241
Pool parties in the baby pool or shallow pool include lifeguard, party host, inflatables and children's menus. Book two months in advance.
TRAVEL *West Ealing rail, then bus E2, E7 or E9* • **HOURS** *Sat-Sun, 5-7pm* • **PRICE** *£95 for 1 hour in the pool and 1 hour eating (max. 10 children)*

JUBILEE SPORTS CENTRE
ADDRESS Caird Street, W10
PHONE 0181 960 9629

Splash parties in your own section of the pool filled with rafts and other water toys, with a party host and lifeguard.

TRAVEL ⊖ *Queens Park* • **PRICE** *£40 per hour*

LONDON TOY AND MODEL MUSEUM

ADDRESS 21-3 Craven Hill, W2

PHONE 0171 402 5222 or 0171 706 8000

An excellent place to hold a children's dream birthday party. Children have free rides on the carousel and mini railway, which is put in steam on Sundays, and the run of the whole museum and garden. There are three set menus aimed at different age groups. Maximum 40 children.

TRAVEL ⊖ *Lancaster Gate, Bayswater, Queensway or Paddington* • **HOURS** *Daily, 9am-5.30pm* • **PRICES** *From £6.50 per head*

LONDON WATERBUS COMPANY

ADDRESS Blomfield Road, W9; Camden Lock Place, NW1

PHONE 0171 482 2550

Children's parties aboard one of the canal boats that go between Camden Lock and Little Venice; stop-off at **London Zoo** optional.

TRAVEL ⊖ *Warwick Avenue (W9) or Camden (NW1)* • **PRICE** *From £150*

PIPPA POP-INS

ADDRESS 430 Fulham Road, SW6

PHONE 0171 385 2458

This children's hotel can be the venue for any kind of party, from adventure parties, complete with camp fires and an assault course, to more traditional tea parties, dinner parties and theme weekends.

TRAVEL ⊖ *Parson's Green* • **HOURS** *Daily, 24 hours* • **PRICE** *From about £10 per head*

PLAYSCAPE PRO-RACING

ADDRESS Hester Road, SW11

PHONE Central booking 0171 801 0110

Up to 10 children can zoom round a safe track for an hour on 160cc Honda Biz Karts at a speed of 45 mph. The children have exclusive use of the track, which is protected by Formula One and lorry tyres, fully supervised and has an excellent safety record. The party pack for ages 8-16 includes exclusive use of the go-karting track, full tuition, overalls, crash helmets and gloves.

TRAVEL *Battersea Park or Queenstown Road rail, then walk; bus 49 or 345* • **HOURS** *Mon-Fri, before 5.30pm; Sat-Sun, before 2pm* • **PRICE** *£150*

THE POLKA THEATRE FOR CHILDREN

ADDRESS 240 The Broadway, SW19

PHONE 0181 543 4888/0363

See a show, then have a party in the café for up to 30 children. Price includes hats, balloons and novelty chocolates.

TRAVEL ⊖ *Wimbledon or South Wimbledon* • **PRICE** *Set menu £4.95 per child*

QUASAR IN ARCHWAY

ADDRESS 13 Junction Road, N19

PHONE 0171 281 5001

A technological version of hide and seek, with laser beams that kids just can't get enough of, followed by tea (pizzas, burgers, chips and so on).
TRAVEL ⊖ *Archway* • **PRICES** *£120 for exclusive use of centre (max. 20 children); otherwise £9.95 per head*

RAFFLES
ADDRESS 287 King's Road, SW3
PHONE 0171 352 1091
Children aged 6 and over can have a disco party with DJ in a real nightclub. The party tea in the private dining room includes such sophisticated fare as mini chicken satay, gourmet sausages and mini grape tarts. Also theme parties with magician for younger children.
TRAVEL ⊖ *Sloane Square* • **PRICES** *Venue hire from £176.25 for 2 hours. Menu for 10-20 children from £14.75-£27.50 per child*

SCIENCE NIGHTS
ADDRESS Science Museum, Exhibition Road, SW7
PHONE 0171 938 9785
Once a month, Science Nights offer children aged 8-11 the chance to camp overnight in the Science Museum, go on spooky torchlit tours and listen to late-night storytelling while snuggled up in sleeping bags. For six or more children accompanied by an adult. Book well in advance.
TRAVEL ⊖ *South Kensington* • **PRICE** *£20 per child, £18 per adult including breakfast*

STREATHAM MEGA BOWL
ADDRESS 142 Streatham High Road, SW2
PHONE 0181 678 6007
Bowling parties for children aged 6 and over (minimum six children). Price includes a game, Burger King meal with free gift.
TRAVEL *Streatham rail* • **PRICE** *£6.99 per child during the week, £7.99 at the weekend*

UNICORN THEATRE
ADDRESS 6 Great Newport Street, WC2
PHONE 0171 836 3334; bookings on 0171 379 3280
Up to 15 children can put on a short play in a real theatre rehearsal room. The two-hour workshop in theatre games and improvisation is based on the child's favourite story, film or show. Ages 5 and over.
TRAVEL ⊖ *Leicester Square* • **PRICE** *£100 including £25 annual membership*

WEMBLEY STADIUM
ADDRESS Empire Way, Wembley, Middx
PHONE 0181 902 8833
Go behind the scenes to the England changing rooms, the control rooms and television studio, then walk up the famous 39 steps, receive 'The Cup' to the roar of the crowd and sit in the Royal Box.
TRAVEL ⊖ *Wembley Park*

ENTERTAINERS AND PARTY PLANNERS

ACTIVITY PARTIES FOR CREATIVE KIDS

ADDRESS 17 Broadhurst Avenue, Edgware, Middx
PHONE Michelle on 0181 905 4104 or 0973 154093
Jewellery-making, slumber art, cookies, fancy dress, limbo, fashion. You name it, Michelle is bound to have a good party idea for it. Prices vary.

ALBERT AND FRIENDS

PHONE 0181 677 6871
The roar of the crowds, the smell of the greasepaint and the thrill of the big top, all in a circus workshop party in the venue of your choice.
PRICE From £150

ANNIE FRYER CATERING

ADDRESS 134 Lots Road, SW10
PHONE 0171 351 4333
Very popular up-market theme parties for small children to teenagers. Menus designed to children's taste, with shaped sandwiches, meringue mice, knickerbocker glories and so on. Adults catered for too.
PRICES Average £10 per head for standard tea for ages 3-5; complete parties £70-£100 upwards

BARNEY THE CLOWN

PHONE David Barnes 0181 452 9505
Clowning, magic, games, balloon modelling and competitions.
PRICE Average £65 for 1-hour show and party of up to 30 children (no food)

CAROLYN & CINDY'S PUPPETS

ADDRESS 12 York Road, Richmond, Surrey
PHONE 0181 940 8407
Carolyn James and Cindy Peters offer parties on any theme – from traditional fairytale puppets behind a booth, plus some magic, nursery rhymes and games (ages 2-8), to Camelot, Peter Pan or Star Wars (boys aged 5-7) and Cinderella or Aladdin (for girls). Or invite 'Queen Victoria' to your party, dress up and play Victorian games (6- to 10-year-olds).
PRICE From £90

CLICK'S PARTIES

PHONE 01453 836390 or 0410 462558
Good package for 9- to 16-year-olds. Choose from moments in history, fairytales or biblical stories. They bring the costumes and make-up so the children can put on a play for the adults. Also drama parties for under-9s.
PRICE £200 plus travel expenses for 3-hour party

COOKIE CRUMBLES COOKING PARTIES

ADDRESS 40 Tantallon Road, SW12
PHONE Jane or Venetia on 0181 675 2705
Cordon Bleu trained chefs teach boys and girls aged 7-12 to create, bake and eat their own Feast of Treats. Choose from pizza faces, jelly faces, marshmallow men, bunny puffs and cheesy feet. They bring all the ingredients, clear up everything afterwards and, for a small extra charge, will provide party-bag presents like aprons, wooden spoons or chefs' hats.

PRICES £180 per 12 children (extra children £15 each). Some of the proceeds go to the Great Ormond Street Hospital for Sick Children.

CRECHENDO PARTY

PHONE 0181 675 6611

This well-established party service will tailor the party to the age and needs of the child, with Chendo the clown, a 'lion hunt', mini-magic, bouncy castle, bubbles and party games.

PRICES From £90 per hour; theme parties (eg, Pirate Party including pirate entertainer) around £225 for 2 hours

DIANE'S PUPPETS

ADDRESS 9 Mercury Court, Southey Road, SW9

PHONE 0171 820 9466

Friendly and humorous with plenty of interaction. Diane and storyteller Tim offer the Bobby Bunny show for ages 2-5, and the scary Big Bad Wolf show or Punch and Judy for 5- to 9-year-olds. Parties include face painting or finger puppets, songs and a puppet show.

PRICES From £120 for 2 hours; £95 for 1 hour

FO-FUM PUPPET PRODUCTIONS

PHONE 0181 898 9247

Twickenham and southwest London area. Formerly Piccolo Puppet Company, Fo-Fum specialises in theatre-quality shows for ages 3-8, which need a large living room or hall. Choose between Boola Bear, a show about a polar bear who doesn't like the cold, and Jack and the Beanstalk.

PRICE £75 plus travel

JOHN PEEL PUPPETS

ADDRESS 52 High Street, Hampton Wick, Kingston upon Thames, Surrey

PHONE 0181 977 2976

Performed in a mobile theatre with imaginative puppets, these traditional stories are guaranteed to entertain (with money back if the children are not delighted!). Different programmes for ages 3-6 and 5-8, plus 10 shows to choose from, including The Three Billygoats Gruffl and Jack and the Beanstalk.

PRICE From £80 (depending on distance travelled)

KICK IT

PHONE 0171 737 5987

Run by Bexercise, who also run weekend football classes, Kick It will organise football birthday parties at a venue of your choice.

LYDIE'S CHILDREN'S ENTERTAINMENT

PHONE 0171 622 2540

Lydie the clown will set up a mini-theatre in your home, with plenty of props, balloons, music, tales and games. There are 20 themes to choose from, including Cowboys, Princes and Princesses and Fairyland.

PRICE From £70 per hour

MARMADUKE

PHONE 01992 446211

A very popular children's entertainer who uses live animals such as owls, chinchillas, snakes, spiders, bats and even a meerkat. While younger children have magic and animals, older children can have a show just

with the animals. Marmaduke is exceptionally good with shy children and popular with all ages. Book well in advance.
PRICES *£150 for 1 hour, £190 for 90 minutes*

NORMAN MYERS
PHONE 0181 371 9497
Norman Myers has been doing very traditional children's parties for over 30 years and will provide a little bit of everything – puppets, Punch and Judy, magic, party games and films for ages 3-13.
PRICE *£125 for 2 hours*

PATCHY PETER AND SNOWY THE DOG
PHONE 01442 261767
Two hours of traditional entertainment with a real white rabbit, a mischievous ventriloquist's dog, magic and balloon modelling for all ages.
PRICE *From £120 for 2 hours*

PEKKO'S PUPPETS
ADDRESS 28 Dorset Road, W5
PHONE 0181 579 7651
Traditional tales from all over the world using rod, glove or giant puppets. Shows last one hour and include songs and clowning. Book three months in advance for weekends and holidays.
PRICE *From £80*

PETER PINNER ENTERTAINMENT
ADDRESS 30 Manor Park Drive, North Harrow, Middx
PHONE 0181 863 1528
Phone for a detailed information pack from these versatile children's entertainers, who can cater for all events with games, clowns, magic shows, balloon modelling, Punch and Judy shows, ventriloquism and junior discos. Bouncy castles to hire.
PRICE *From £75*

POTTERY WORKSHOPS
PHONE 0171 209 0261
Mobile pottery workshop for up to 10 children.
PRICE *£150*

PROFESSOR ALEXANDER'S PUNCH AND JUDY
ADDRESS 59 Wilton Way, E8
PHONE 0171 254 0416
Traditional Punch and Judy show performed in theatres as well as at private parties. Also magic shows.

RAINBOW THE CLOWN
PHONE 0181 764 1626
Covers Sheen, Fulham and Oxted areas. For ages 3-6 Rainbow offers face painting, balloon modelling, circus skills, magic and some amazing juggling with anything from marshmallows to marmalade sandwiches. For ages 6 and over he runs circus workshops in juggling, plate spinning and balancing as well as magic tricks and games.
PRICES *£70 for 90 mins (max. 15 children); £80 for over 15 children*

RICHARD WARNER
PHONE 0171 481 4251

Best known for his songs for CBBC's *Spider* series, the singer-entertainer will compose a special song for the birthday child, perform on the guitar at the party and tape the song and other activities for the child to keep.
PRICE *From £125 for 2 hours*

SMARTIE ARTIE
PHONE 01582 461588

Magic, clowning and party games for ages 3-7. A full two-hour party, excluding a break for tea, includes comedy magic, clowning, games, balloon modelling and competitions (with prizes included), tailored to the age of the child. Also disco parties with DJ for older children. There are several Smartie Arties so make sure that if your kids have seen a particular one they like, you ask for the same one.
PRICES *From £100-£120*

TIDDLEYWINKS
ADDRESS 9a Brechin Place, SW7
PHONE 0171 736 1842

Drama-based party workshops for ages 2-12 with plenty of audience participation. Three- to 7-year-olds have a theme party with drama games, dressing up, storytelling and simple performances (2 hours). Eight- to 12-year-olds produce a play in their own home, helping to make the costumes and props and do the make-up (3-4 hours). Also storytelling sessions.
PRICE *From £155*

TWIZZLE ENTERTAINMENT
ADDRESS 31 Lillian Road, SW13
PHONE 0181 748 3138

Complete party agency with a wide range of performers on its books. Twizzle himself is very popular with children aged 2-8, with his games, magic, balloon modelling, stories and Punch and Judy. If you want Twizzle in person you will need to book at least 10 weeks in advance. Otherwise Mr Mustard, Wizzo the Wizzard and Custard are also popular. The agency can arrange stilt walkers, craft parties, magic shows, go-karting for older children or a pony in your garden. A very caring and personalised service (one boy had a cowboy party with the world gun-slinging champion in attendance).
PRICE *From £140 for 2 hours*

WONDERLAND PUPPET THEATRE
PHONE 01932 784467

Based in Middlesex and specialising in puppet theatre and magic shows, Wonderland Parties has over 30 years' experience of staging children's parties for ages 2-9. It will arrange games before tea, provide prizes and party bags, and organise a complete party or just a half-hour show.

ZOZO THE FRENCH CLOWN
ADDRESS Le Club Tricolor, 10 Ballingdon Road, SW11
PHONE 0171 924 4649

Magic tricks, games, songs, balloon modelling and plenty of mischievous antics from this talented French clown.

PARTY SHOPS, FANCY DRESS AND EQUIPMENT HIRE

AMERICAN PARTY STORE
ADDRESS 16 Woodstock Street, W1
PHONE 0171 493 2678
This excellent party shop can provide balloons, banners, bags, napkins, hats, tablewear, invitations etc, and what they don't stock they will get for you. Catalogue features an amazing choice of over 400 children's costumes, priced at anything from £15. Some of the costumes and accessories are based on films only just released here, so you can be first with the latest Disney craze, but you must allow 3-4 weeks for costumes to arrive. Also cake and balloon delivery services and a list of entertainers.
TRAVEL ⊖ *Bond Street or Oxford Circus* • **HOURS** *Mon-Sat, 10am-6pm (Wed to 7pm)*

BALLOON & KITE EMPORIUM
ADDRESS 613 Garratt Lane, SW18
PHONE 0181 946 5962
The Balloon & Kite Emporium will print balloons with a message of your choice (£32 for 100), decorate halls with them, and organise balloon releases.
TRAVEL *Earlsfield rail or* ⊖ *Tooting Broadway* • **HOURS** *Mon-Sat, 9am-5.30pm*

BARNUMS CARNIVAL NOVELTIES LTD
ADDRESS 67 Hammersmith Road, W14
PHONE 0171 602 1211
Large choice of masks from 69p as well as streamers, poppers, flags, balloons and party hats (no theme merchandise).
TRAVEL ⊖ *Olympia or West Kensington* • **HOURS** *Mon-Fri, 9am-5.30pm; Sat, 10am-5pm*

CHEQUERS
ADDRESS 318 and 320 Portobello Road, W10
PHONE 0181 969 4119
Balloons in all shapes, sizes, colours and finishes, plus plates, cups, napkins and decorations, and plenty of jokes, novelties and face-painting kits.
TRAVEL ⊖ *Notting Hill Gate* • **HOURS** *Mon-Sat, 9.30am-5.30pm*

CIRCUS CIRCUS
ADDRESS 176 Wandsworth Bridge Road, SW6
PHONE 0171 731 4128
This delightful little shop with its white picket fence has all manner of inexpensive novelties for party bags, as well as balloons, tableware and decorations. Also fancy dress for sale or hire.
TRAVEL ⊖ *Fulham Broadway* • **HOURS** *Mon-Sat, 9.30am-6pm*

CITY DRESS ARCADE
ADDRESS 437 Bethnal Green Road, E2
PHONE 0171 739 2645
Excellent-value costume hire for children – anything from Andy Pandy and

Clowns to Cavaliers and Cinderella.

TRAVEL ⊖ *Bethnal Green* • **HOURS** *Mon-Wed and Fri-Sat, 11am-4.30pm (closed Thurs)* • **PRICES** *Ages 2-4 around £5, ages 4 and over £10, plus £20 refundable deposit (identification required)*

ESCAPADE

ADDRESS 150 Camden High Street, NW1

PHONE 0171 485 7384

Everything you could want for a party – costumes, masks, wigs, hats, tricks, jokes and novelties. You can also hire children's costumes.

TRAVEL ⊖ *Camden Town* • **HOURS** *Mon-Fri, 10am-7pm; Sat, 10am-6pm; Sun, noon-5pm* • **PRICES** *Costume hire from £15-£20 plus £20 refundable deposit*

HEY DIDDLE DIDDLE

ADDRESS 106 Lordship Lane, SE22

PHONE 0181 693 5575

Plenty of theme cups, plates, party bags, novelties and other accessories to buy, as well as tables and chairs to hire.

TRAVEL *East Dulwich rail* • **HOURS** *Mon-Sat, 9.30am-6pm*

IT'S MY PARTY

ADDRESS 23 Webbs Road, SW11

PHONE 0171 350 2763

In addition to children's themed party plates, mats, masks, cutlery and napkins featuring anything from Batman to Thomas the Tank Engine and princesses to pirates, this shop has a hire service for tables, chairs, cake tins and bouncy castles, and a list of reliable entertainers. Also stocks a good range of novelties, cards, masks, balloons and cakes.

TRAVEL ⊖ *Clapham South* • **HOURS** *Mon-Sat, 9.30am-5pm (Wed to 4.30pm; closed some lunchtimes, 1-2pm)*

J&M TOYS

ADDRESS 46 Finsbury Drive, Wrose, Bradford, West Yorkshire BD2 1QA

PHONE 01274 599314

If it's fancy dress you're after, look no further. With prices ranging from £5 to £18 per outfit, this mail-order costume company offers unbeatable value. The costumes are imaginative, hard wearing and a huge hit with adults and children alike. Highly recommended. Phone for catalogue.

JUST BALLOONS

ADDRESS 127 Wilton Road, SW1

PHONE 0171 434 3039

All kinds of balloons for sale here – and if you can't find the design you want, they will make them for you. Balloons start at 15p. Specialists in novelty balloons such as cartoon animals, fish and fruit.

TRAVEL ⊖ *Victoria* • **HOURS** *Mon-Sat, 9.30am-6pm*

NON-STOP PARTY SHOP

ADDRESS 214-16 Kensington High Street, W8; 694 Fulham Road, SW6 (other branches in Surrey)

PHONE 0171 937 7200 (W8); 0171 384 1491 (SW6)

Ten party-ware ranges, plus fancy-dress accessories, hats, masks, balloons, decorations and a good selection of novelties for party bags and prizes. Fancy dress to buy. Bouncy-castle and cake-tin hire. Also has a party service.
TRAVEL ⊖ *High Street Kensington (W8);* ⊖ *Putney Bridge (SW6)* • **HOURS** *Mon-Sat, 9.30am-7pm*

OSCAR'S DEN
ADDRESS 127-9 Abbey Road, NW6
PHONE 0171 328 6683
As well as novelties, paper tableware, balloons, jokes, masks, toys, cakes and take-away party gift bags (to any value), Oscar's Den will find you entertainers, hire out bouncy castles, tables and chairs, and organise whole parties.
TRAVEL ⊖ *West Hampstead* • **HOURS** *Mon-Fri, 9.30am-5.30pm; Sun, 10am-2pm*

PARTY PARTY
ADDRESS 11 Southampton Road, NW5
PHONE 0171 267 9084
Best known for its customised novelty cakes. Also fancy dress, table and chair hire, novelties, masks, streamers and party bags.
TRAVEL ⊖ *Belsize Park* • **HOURS** *Mon-Sat 9.30am-5.30pm*

PARTY PROPS
ADDRESS 24 Melrose Avenue, SW19
PHONE 0181 946 8796
Hire service for tables (£1.50), chairs (50p), bouncy castles (£35), bubble machines and ball ponds.

YOUNG'S DISCO CENTRE
ADDRESS 20 Malden Road, NW5
PHONE 0171 485 1115
Supplies sound systems and DJs for children's parties from £100. Popcorn and candy-floss machines also for hire from £70.

CAKES

HARRODS
PHONE 0171 730 1234
Harrods will make sponge or fruit cakes to almost any design – clowns, cowboy forts, Disney characters, football pitches, trains, planes and automobiles – from around £40-£200. One week's notice.
TRAVEL ⊖ *Knightsbridge* • **HOURS** *Mon-Sat, 10am-6pm (Wed and Fri to 7pm)*

JANE ASHER PARTY CAKES
ADDRESS 24 Cale Street, SW3
PHONE 0171 584 6177
Range of delicious cakes hand made to any theme or design. You can sample the cakes in the café while leafing through the portfolios. Prices start at £45 but expect to pay an average of £90 for a child's special theme cake. One week's notice required. Delivery service available.
TRAVEL ⊖ *Sloane Square* • **HOURS** *Mon-Sat 9.30am-5.30pm*

OUT OF TOWN

Take a break from the city and spend the day in the country. Follow a woodland trail in Sevenoaks, lose the kids in a maze near Maidstone, climb a Norman keep in Kent, tickle a skate in Sussex, adopt a donkey at Lockwood or take a day trip to France. Castles, country houses, farms, zoos, wildlife parks, museums and monuments – whatever the weather, there is something to suit everyone.

If you are coming from the other side of London, or if you have children of different ages with different interests, you might wish to visit more than one site, so where possible we have indicated other attractions nearby. Please phone to check opening times and prices before setting off on a long journey.

ALDENHAM COUNTRY PARK ☺ 🄴 ☼ ◑

ADDRESS Dagger Lane, Elstree, Herts
PHONE 0181 953 9602
Lovely country park with the added attraction for children of a recreation of Winnie-the-Pooh's 100 Acre Wood, where you can see Christopher Robin's home, and those of Piglet, Owl and Pooh Bear laid out to resemble the famous map in the front of the books.
TRAVEL By car: A41 towards A1, take left turn at junction with A5183, take next left (which is Aldenham Road). Park is ¾ mile on left • **HOURS** Daily, 9am-6pm • **PRICE** Free (car park £2)

BADSELL PARK FARM ☺ ❀ ●

ADDRESS Crittenden Road, Matfield, Tonbridge, Kent
PHONE 01892 837228
A working fruit and arable farm which has turned the clock back, offering a glimpse of rural culture between the wars. Watch the daily farming activities; visit the pet area; see rare breeds of cow, goat, sheep, bantam and pig; pick your own fruit and visit the Butterfly House. Outdoor play area with a real fire engine and wooden fort (also large indoor play barn with ball pond, soft toys and bouncy castle for under-9s). Open-air and covered picnic areas. Café, farm and gift shop. Children's parties with tractor, pony and donkey rides. Two-mile nature trail through woods and meadows for older children (unsuitable for buggies). No dogs. Baby-changing facilities. Buggy access. **NEARBY: Whitbread Hop Farm**.
TRAVEL By car: 44 miles from central London on A228, off A21; Paddock Wood rail, then taxi 2 miles • **OPEN** Apr-Nov: daily, 10am-5.30pm • **PRICES** Adults £4, children and OAPs £2.50 (under-3s free)

BEAULIEU ☺ ❀ ●

ADDRESS Beaulieu, Brockenhurst, Hants
PHONE 01590 612345
Central to the vast site is the National Motor Museum, one of the finest and most comprehensive in the world, which includes the 1930 Supercharged Bentley, the Morris Minor, the 1950s Mercedes 300 SL, the Aston Martin DB5 once owned by Peter Sellers, and the much-loved Mini. In addition, there are motorbikes, fire engines, Grand Prix racing cars and a double-decker bus. There is also a large model train set, a high-level monorail that circuits the site, radio-controlled cars to race, and a miniature car and bike

track. The Palace House has a lovely, fully equipped Victorian kitchen. Information centre, restaurants, shops, toilets, baby-changing facilities. **TRAVEL** *By car: 85 miles south of London; M27 West, junction 2 then follow signs; Southampton rail then bus, or Brockenhurst rail then 6-mile taxi ride* ● **OPEN** *May-Sep: daily, 10am-6pm; Oct-Apr: daily, 10am-5pm (closed Christmas Day)* ● **PRICES** *Adults £8.75, children £6.25 (under-4s free), OAPs £7.50, family ticket (2+3) £28.50*

BEKONSCOT MODEL VILLAGE ☺ ☀ ●

ADDRESS Warwick Road, Beaconsfield, Bucks
PHONE 01494 672919

Built in the 1920s by a London accountant, this delightful miniature village has entranced generations of London children on day trips with their families. There is everything from a working model railway and a village green to a zoo, airport, racecourse, coal mine and fairground. The attention to detail is wonderful, which is a good thing as, in summer, it gets very crowded and progress along the narrow set route is slow. The quiz (10p) keeps older children busy spotting minute details, while younger ones enjoy scenes of daily life – thatchers busy at work and a policeman chasing a robber at the races. Not suitable for double buggies. Playground, picnic area, café, shop. Toilets for the disabled and baby-changing facilities. Narrow wheelchairs available on request. **NEARBY: Odds Farm Park**.
TRAVEL *Beaconsfield rail; by car: M40 to junction 2, then A40 to Beaconsfield and follow signs* ● **OPEN** *Mid-Feb to end Oct: daily, 10am-5pm (restricted opening times in winter)* ● **PRICES** *Adults £3.60, children £1.80, concs £2.50, family ticket (2+2) £10*

BENTLEY WILDFOWL AND MOTOR MUSEUM ☺ ☀ ●

ADDRESS Halland, nr Lewes, E Sussex
PHONE 01825 840573

The late Gerald Askew built up the largest private collection of rare wildfowl in the UK amidst the lakes, ponds, shrubs and trees that surround Bentley House. You can see every kind of swan in the world and over 115 species of waterfowl, all roaming freely in the parkland setting. Pick up an identification chart on your way in and follow one of three buggy-friendly routes, taking 30, 45 or 60 minutes, which allow you close access to the birds (especially if you have bought bird feed for 25p a bag at the entrance). The motor museum has an impressive, gleaming collection of veteran, Edwardian and vintage cars and bikes, some of which take part in the annual London to Brighton run in June (see London by Season), for which Bentley is used as a checkpoint. There is a hands-on woodland education area, a small animal section with tame farm animals, an adventure playground and, on summer Sundays, a miniature steam railway. There is also a woodland walk which is especially lovely when bluebells are out in mid-May. Events throughout the year include an Easter-egg quiz, a craft fair, falconry displays, and the annual vintage- transport rally. Education centre available for birthday parties. Tearoom. Picnic area. Restaurant with high chairs. Full facilities for the disabled; baby-changing facilities and buggy access. Nearby: Barham Manor Vineyard (tel: 01825 722103).
TRAVEL *By car: M25, then A22 towards Eastbourne (signposted after Uckfield), free on-site parking* ● **OPEN** *Apr-Oct: daily, 10.30am-4.30pm (house open from noon)* ● **PRICES** *Adults £3.80, children and concs £2.50 (under-4s free), family ticket (2+4) £12*

BIRDWORLD/UNDERWATER WORLD ☺ ❀ ●

ADDRESS Holt Pound, Farnham, Surrey
PHONE 01420 22140

Birdworld, with its enormous variety of birds, from the tiny wren to the giant ostrich, will turn the most reluctant child into a bird fan. The highlight for most children is feeding time (11.30am and 3.30pm) at Penguin Island, which has an underwater viewing area so you can see the birds swimming and diving below water level. You can feed the penguins yourself for £5 (which goes to charity) but you must book in advance. Children can also feed the parrots – macaw fruit feed is on sale from the gift shop. There is also the imaginative Seashore Trail, featuring a recreated seashore complete with waves, a boat wreck and sea birds; a rearing and incubation centre; and the Jenny Wren children's farm. Near the picnic area and tables there are two small play areas, one for under-8s, and there is also a fun-and-fitness trail for older children. Café. Birthday teas, pizza parties and barbecues can be arranged. Next door is Underwater World, a useful bolt hole if the heavens open. It has meat-eating piranhas, blind cave fish, giant pacu and other tropical fish. Restaurant with high chairs and baby-changing facilities. Unlimited wheelchair and buggy access.

TRAVEL *Aldershot rail, then 15-min bus ride; Green Line coach from Victoria (Apr-Sep, Sat-Sun only); by car: 35 miles from central London, 3 miles south of Farnham on A325; free on-site parking* • **OPEN** *Apr-Aug: daily, 9.30am-6pm; Sep: daily, 9.30am-5pm; Oct-Mar: daily, 9.30am-4.30pm (closed Christmas Day)* • **PRICES** *Combined ticket: adults £6.95, children £3.75 (under-3s free), concs £5.50, family ticket (2+2) £18.95. Birdworld only: adults £5.50, children £3.25, concs £4.50, family ticket £15.95*

BOCKETTS FARM ☺ ☀ ●

ADDRESS Young Street (off Fetcham Roundabout), Fetcham, Leatherhead, Surrey
PHONE 01372 363764

Even if it is raining you can easily spend a whole day at this excellent, family-run farm, as most of the animals – goats, sheep, calves, piglets and a drayhorse – are in enclosures within a giant open barn. Children can feed the animals (30p a bag) and there is a separate area for rabbits, chicks and guinea pigs which toddlers particularly appreciate. There are plenty of information panels and helpful staff on hand to answer the inevitable barrage of questions, plus agricultural equipment displays and demonstrations, farm walks and pony rides. Well-equipped adventure playground, huge sandpit and picnic area. The Old Barn tearooms do excellent home-made lunches, cakes and cream teas and provide a children's menu, high chairs and toys. Covered and outdoor picnic areas. Farm and gift shop. Toilets with baby-changing facilities. Access for the disabled. **NEARBY: Box Hill** for picnics and views.

TRAVEL *By car: 5 mins from M25 (junction 9), A3 to A24 Leatherhead by-pass* • **HOURS** *Daily, 10am-6pm* • **PRICES** *Adults £2.95, children 3-17 years £2.50, children 2-3 years £1.75 (under-2s free), concs £2.25 (weekdays slightly less)*

BODIAM CASTLE ☺ ☀ ●

ADDRESS Bodiam, Robertsbridge, E Sussex
PHONE 01580 830436

Children love Bodiam Castle. It looks just like a story-book castle, complete with a huge, water-filled moat and its very own breed of bat, the Bodiam bat. Children are free to scramble over the walls, climb up winding staircases to the top of spooky turrets, and let their imaginations run riot. While we stood back and wallowed in the beauty of it all, the kids spent an hour playing hide-and-seek and knights in shining armour, wearing paper crowns they had made that morning. Bodiam is amazingly well preserved and you really do get a feel for what life must have been like all those years ago. In the southeast tower there is a circular room with a fireplace and narrow windows on each of the four levels, as well as medieval loos, which would have emptied into the moat below. There is plenty of space for running around, flying kites and playing games, although I wouldn't recommend ball games, having seen one family lose theirs in the moat. There is a self-service café and an Egon Ronay-listed restaurant, Knolly's, as well as idyllic slopes on which to picnic on dry days. Events include the dragon-egg hunt (April), a medieval fair (May) and Family Day (July). Shop. Baby-changing facilities. Wheelchair and buggy access.

TRAVEL *Robertsbridge rail then taxi or Hastings rail then bus; by car: M20 to junction 6 (off A229)* • **OPEN** *1 Apr to 31 Oct: daily, 10am-6pm (last admission, 5.30pm); 1 Nov to 31 Mar: Tues-Sun, 10am to dusk* • **PRICES** *Adults £3.30, children £1.65 (under-5s free), family ticket £8.25, car park £1. National Trust property.*

BOULOGNE/NAUSICAA

This day trip to France cost less than £100 for a family of six, starting with a full tank of petrol. We left southeast London at 6.30am, caught the eight o'clock ferry from Dover to Calais (making use of the special ferry deals available throughout the year), changed our remaining cash into francs, bought three croissants, several teas and a coffee, and sat back while our children played in the soft play area. Leaving the ferry, Calais (and the map) behind us, we headed straight for Boulogne along the well-signposted coastal road, about 25 minutes' drive. You can't miss the signs to Nausicaa (Centre Nationale de la Mer), which you come to just before Boulogne. There is a car park that stretches along the seafront up to the sea-life centre. We parked at the other end and walked along the beach, watching the boats, windsurfers and a few very brave swimmers (this was not summer), and had a quick play on the slide, swing and climbing frame in the sand next to the centre itself. If you like the British sea-life centres, just wait till you see Nausicaa. It is one of the largest, newest and most high-tech ocean centres in the world. Quite apart from the astonishing array of sea creatures, the interior design and the clever use of ultra-violet light and weird, New Age music combine to create a marvellously eerie, underwater, other-worldly experience. There are plenty of buttons to push, telephones to listen to and a touch tank to amuse and delight the kids while you step back and enjoy the atmosphere. Everything is very well labelled in both French and English, with plenty of illustrations, explanations and demonstrations. We spent over two hours in here and went round twice. Jake and Benja didn't want to leave, but the twins and adults were getting hungry and wanted to see the town itself. Boulogne is one of the prettiest of the Channel ports, with its attractive medieval quarter, the Ville Haute, and its impressive fortress with grassy ramparts. In the lower, new town are some excellent pâtisseries and good fish restaurants (to which our budget sadly didn't stretch). We avoided this part of town on this particular trip, although newcomers shouldn't miss Philippe Olivier's famous cheese shop in the rue Thiers, which displays over 200 different cheeses lovingly gathered from all over Europe. And if you are here on a Wednesday or Saturday, the produce market in place Dalton is excellent (7am-1pm). If we hadn't forgotten that French shops shut between noon and 2pm we would have bought a picnic to eat on the grassy slopes by the cathedral (you can buy French bread, pâté, olives, cheese, fresh fruit and juice, and even a bottle of wine for less than £10 – just remember to bring a knife, bottle opener, tea towel and some plastic cutlery from home). As it was, we ate at a little café, just beyond the gateway (two *croques monsieur*, a large plate of French fries, hot chocolates all round and some French bread, and still we had some coins spare to buy lollipops from the next-door sweet shop). Then a quick wander along the 13th-century ramparts (lined with rose beds, buggy-friendly gravel paths, and plenty of benches) for a splendid view of the town and port below (you can see Dover on a clear day) before heading back for the 9pm ferry, where Jake, Benja and the girls had supper with our remaining cash, climbed into their pyjamas just before we got into the car and were soon dreaming of angel fish and sea anemones.

GETTING THERE *We travelled on P&O Ferries (tel: 01304 203388) on one of their special-offer day-returns for £15 per car and £1 per person over the age of 5. Ferry offers are usually advertised in the national press. Nausicaa, Boulogne (tel: 00 33 1 21 30 98 98); open all year round, daily, 10am-6pm (7pm at weekends). Adults 55f, under-13s 45f. Office de Tourisme, Pont Marguet (tel: 00 33 1 21 31 68 38); open daily, 10am-noon and 2-7pm.*

BOWMANS OPEN FARM ☺ ☀ ●

ADDRESS Coursers Road, London Colney, St Albans, Herts
PHONE 01462 424055

If you can persuade your children to venture beyond the well-equipped playground, this is a wonderful working dairy and pig farm. Milking demonstrations daily, 1.30-3pm. Bird-of-prey flying displays twice daily. Plenty of noisy squealing piglets, sleepy sows, newborn calves and a very impressive Friesian bull. The Touch Barn has rabbits, goats and kids, calves, lambs and piglets. High chairs in restaurant. Farm shop sells meat you can cook on the farm's barbecues (bring your own charcoal). Picnic area overlooking lake. Toilets with baby-changing facilities. Buggy and wheelchair access.

TRAVEL *By car: M25 to junction 22 for St Albans, then follow signs;* ⊖ *High Barnet, then taxi* • **HOURS** *Daily, 9am-5pm* • **PRICES** *Adults £3.75, children and OAPs £2.75 (under-3s free)*

BRAMBLES WILDLIFE AND RARE BREEDS ☺ ☀ ◑

ADDRESS Wealden Forest Park, Herne Common, Herne, Kent
PHONE 01227 712379

Follow the woodland trail to Rabbit World, see farmyard animals, wallabies, mara, guanaco, Scottish wild cats, deer, foxes and owls. Indoor garden with terrapins and toads. Adventure playground and under-5s' play area. Tearoom and picnic area. Gift shop. Toilets for the disabled and baby-changing facilities. Wheelchair and buggy access.

TRAVEL *By car: off A291* • **OPEN** *Mid-Apr to end Oct: daily, 10am-5pm (last admission, 4.15pm)* • **PRICES** *Adults £3, children £1.50*

BRIGHTON SEA LIFE CENTRE ☺ ☔ ◑

ADDRESS Marine Parade, Brighton, E Sussex
PHONE 01273 604233

The oldest public aquarium in England has four dozen tanks of sea- and freshwater fish, and a unique whale and dolphin exhibition. The floor-to-ceiling tanks and viewing platforms make it ideal for children of any age. There is a sandy-sea bed where children are given instruction on how to stroke the rays, and an old harbour area with huge crabs you can feed (special food on sale at the entrance). There is also a wonderful, rare Kingdom of the Seahorse display. The children's favourite is the underwater tunnel (approached through a shipwreck entrance) full of British sharks, stingrays and conger eels, which provides a suitably gory show at feeding time! Plenty of information panels and displays. Café where birthday parties can be booked in advance. Sea Life shop. Baby-changing facilities. Buggy access (leave through side entrance on seafront). **NEARBY:** Brighton is full of things for children to do – the Pier, the Pavilion, the beach, amusements, markets. Ask for an information pack to be sent to you from the Tourist Information Centre (tel: 01273 23755) or pick one up when you arrive.

TRAVEL *Brighton rail; by car: 45 miles south of London on M23 and A23* • **HOURS** *Daily, 10am-5pm (closed Christmas Day)* • **PRICES** *Adults £5.50, children £3.95 (under-4s free), concs £4.25*

CHATHAM HISTORIC DOCKYARD ☺ ❀ ●

ADDRESS Dock Road, Chatham, Kent
PHONE 01634 812551

The Chatham Naval Dockyard, which served the Royal Navy for over 400 years, has now been turned into an open-air museum, as a perfectly preserved example of an 18th-century river dockyard, with eight galleries and the largest concentration of ancient monuments in Britain. It has proved a huge hit with children of all ages. You can see rope-making in the traditional working ropery and guess the strength of a finished rope as it is stretched to breaking point. Try your hand at knot-tying or breaking out a flag, or find out about the on-going restoration of HMS *Gannet*. The award-winning Wooden Walls, a multimedia 'living history' attraction, shows how HMS *Valiant*, a wooden warship, was built here in 1758; it captured the imagination of our 5- and 7-year-olds. If you have time, jump in the car and visit the submarine *Ocelot* a mile down river; the guided tours can be booked in advance. Children love scrambling through the cramped quarters (not recommended for babies as there is no buggy access). Events throughout the year include model railway exhibitions, Dockyard in Steam days and an Easter Mad Hatter's Tea Party. At Chatham there is a café, teashop, open and covered picnic areas, children's play area and baby-changing facilities. Wheelchair access.

TRAVEL *Chatham rail then bus to dockyard's Alexandra Gate; by car off A25 (free on-site parking)* • **OPEN** *Easter to 31 Oct: Wed-Sun and bank holidays, 10am-6pm; 1 Nov to 31 Mar: Wed and Sat-Sun, 10am-4.30pm* • **PRICES** *Adults £5.60, children £3.60 (under-5s free), concs £4.60, family ticket (2+4) £15*

CHATLEY HEATH SEMAPHORE TOWER ☼ ◑

ADDRESS Old Lane, Cobham, Surrey
PHONE 01932 862762

Explore the tower, enjoy the rooftop views and see the semaphore arms working, then have a picnic and follow the marked trails through the woods to the latest acquisition – a mausoleum. From the car parks it is a 20-minute walk along a well-marked trail over sandy heath land (easy even with buggies, but the tower has stairs). Picnic site and refreshments;

toilets in car park. **NEARBY:** Cobham Bus Museum (tel: 01932 864078) is open most spring and summer weekends and bank holidays and houses a private collection of 40 vehicles dating from 1925 to 1960. Go on an Open Day in early April, when children can ride on vintage buses. Also **Painshill Park**.

TRAVEL *By car on M25/A3, then follow signs to Effingham and park in Old Lane car parks* • **OPEN** *School holidays: Sat-Sun, bank holidays and some Wed, noon-5pm; winter: 1st Sun of month, noon-5pm* • **PRICES** *Adults £2; children and concs £1 (under-8s free)*

CHILTERN OPEN AIR MUSEUM ☺ ☀ ●

ADDRESS Newland Park, Gorelands Lane, Chalfont St Giles, Bucks
PHONE 01494 871117

Buildings that would otherwise have been destroyed have been rescued and rebuilt here, including Iron Age and Saxon dwellings, a blacksmith's forge, a 1940s prefab, a toll house and even a Victorian furniture factory. There is a comprehensive programme of children's workshops and events throughout the holidays, including rug-making, storytelling round the fire, and a chance to meet an Iron Age family. There is also a parkland nature walk and a 25-seat sculpture trail. Café, shop, playground and toilets.

TRAVEL ⊖ *Chalfont & Latimer, then 2-mile walk or taxi* • **OPEN** *Apr-Oct: Wed-Sun and bank holidays, 2-6pm* • **PRICES** *Adults £5, children £3 (under-5s free), concs £4*

CHISLEHURST CAVES ✱ ◗

ADDRESS Old Hill, Chislehurst, Kent
PHONE 0181 467 3264

If you have sensible shoes and children who are not afraid of the dark, then this wonderfully eerie, lantern-lit tour through an amazing network of man-made caves, enhanced by chilling tales, amusing anecdotes and historical detail from the superb guide, is a must. Jake, who was allowed to hold a lantern, was intrigued by the loos, the pool and the stage, while Benja occupied himself searching for bats. Although the caves can be booked for private functions, you can no longer stay in them overnight because, so we were told, the last person to do so was never seen again. Café, picnic area, shop, surrounding woods to explore. No buggy or wheelchair access.

TRAVEL *Chislehurst rail; free parking* • **HOURS** *Wed-Sun, 11am-4.30pm (winter: 10am-3pm)* • **PRICES** *Adults £3, children £1.50 (under-5s free). Prices are for short trip only; longer tours of caves at 2.30pm on Sun and bank holidays, visiting parts not otherwise seen. Lantern tours of caves leave on the hour (45 mins).*

COLCHESTER ZOO ☺ ☀ ●

ADDRESS Maldon Road, Stanway, Colchester, Essex
PHONE 01206 330253

Popular, well-laid-out zoo, with elephants, rhinos, monkeys, reptiles, lions, leopards, domestic animals, sea lions and more. Summer pony rides (extra charge) and animal-petting area. Daily presentations include feeding the elephants, handling a snake, sea-lion and parrot displays, penguin parade and falconry. The new Chimp World enclosure is hugely popular with children, who love the interactive displays. There is an undercover soft play area, a road train, two adventure play areas, regular face painting and brass rubbing (all included in admission price). Special events include

Santa's Grotto, Easter-egg hunt and summer festival. Self-service restaurant, kiosks, gift shops. Nursing and baby-changing facilities (men's facilities opposite Kalahari Capers). Hilly terrain makes access a little difficult for wheelchairs and pushchairs. **NEARBY:** Colchester Castle Museum (tel: 01206 282931/2), where you can find out how Boadicea took her revenge on the Romans, hear the secrets of the castle prison or try on a toga. Adults £7.50, children (3-13) and concs £5.25

TRAVEL *By car: 50 miles northeast of central London, just off A12 south of Colchester* • **HOURS** *Daily, 9.30am-6pm (last admission, 5pm; Mar-Oct last admission, 4pm)* • **PRICES** *Adults £7, children and concs £3.50-£5*

COTSWOLD WILDLIFE PARK ☺ ☀ ●

ADDRESS Burford, Oxon
PHONE 01993 823006

Zebras, rhino, deer, red pandas and antelope roam in relative freedom across what used to be the lawns of this impressive Gothic mansion. You can get a really good look at these animals. Admittedly, our children were terrified by the rhinos in the rhino house, but it is a unique opportunity to see these large beasts at close quarters. The park has an excellent safety record and the kids cheered up when asked to help bottle feed the baby camel. There is also a zebra house, leopard house and some very handsome lions. Staff are friendly, patient and informative, and children can play with the pigs, goats, llamas, rabbits and lambs in the farmyard. In addition, there is an adventure playground for all age groups, pony rides and a narrow-gauge railway in summer. Special events such as car rallies and snake days during the year. Restaurant and brass-rubbing centre (phone for details). Excellent family facilities, including baby changing. Buggy and wheelchair access.

TRAVEL *By car: 75 miles west of London on M40, Oxford exit and then Oxford ring road north signposted A40 Cheltenham, then A40 to Burford and follow signs* • **HOURS** *Daily, 10am-5pm or dusk (closed Christmas Day)* • **PRICES** *Adults £5.50, children and concs £3.50*

DEAL CASTLE ☀ ◗

PHONE 01304 372762

The best way to see Deal Castle, which was built in 1540 in the shape of a Tudor Rose, is from the air. Sadly, most of us don't have access to a private aeroplane, but you can still get some sense of the rose-petal pattern from the battlements, and there are plenty of dark, spooky passages to explore. There is also an exhibition about Henry VIII's castles. Deal has no less than three worthwhile museums. The Maritime and Local History Museum in St George's Road (tel: 01304 372679; open May-Sep, daily, 2-5pm) has a collection of original boats, models, smugglers' paraphernalia and other items reflecting Deal's maritime history. The Timeball Tower Museum on Victoria Parade (tel: 01304 360897; open Spring Bank Holiday to mid-Sep, Tues-Sun, 10am-5pm) is dedicated to time, telegraphy and maritime communications, from the first bonfire signals to modern satellites. Finally, the Victoriana Museum in the High Street (tel: 01304 380546; open Jun-Oct, Tues-Sun, 10am-5pm) has a fully furnished parlour as well as everyday objects and works of art.

TRAVEL *Deal rail* • **HOURS** *Daily, 10am-6pm (Oct-Mar: Tues-Sun, 10am-1pm and 2-4pm)* • **PRICES** *Adults £3.00, children £1.50, concs £2.30*

DOVER CASTLE ☼ ◐

PHONE 01304 201628

Occupying a commanding position atop the famous White Cliffs, Dover Castle was in medieval times one of the most powerful fortresses in western Europe. The 12th-century keep presides over the fortress, which was used for various military purposes right up to 1958. There is also an inner bailey, curtain walls, medieval, Georgian and Victorian earthworks. Included in the admission price is a guided tour round Hellfire Corner, the network of tunnels beneath the castle. In the grounds, which host regular historic re-enactments and other events, you can see the 1900-year-old Roman lighthouse or Pharos, the tallest surviving Roman structure in Britain. For details of special events, call the Events Hotline on 01304 202754. Restaurant, shops. **NEARBY:** Crabble Corn Mill (tel: 01304 823292), also in Dover, is a restored watermill. In the Old Town Gaol (tel: 01304 242766) you can learn about the miseries of penal incarceration in Victorian times from the felons, some of whom were children, and their gaolers, who are brought to life through audio-visuals. The White Cliffs Experience (tel: 01304 214566) tells the story of Britain – of weird gods, savagery, battles fought, seas untamed; on summer weekends you can meet Romans, Vikings and a host of other invaders.

TRAVEL Dover rail; by car on the A258 • **HOURS** Daily, 10am-6pm (4pm in winter; closed Christmas Day) • **PRICES** Adults £6.60, children £3.30 (under-5s free), concs £5.00, family ticket (2+3) £16.60

DRUSILLAS ZOO PARK ☺ ☼ ●

ADDRESS Alfriston, E Sussex

PHONE 01323 870234

Arrive early and be prepared to spend the whole day at 'the best small zoo in the country'. Its raison d'être is to delight small children, especially those frightened by the larger animals in traditional zoos. Designed so that children get really close to the animals in their natural settings, the park is compact enough for even the very young to walk right round. Step into the Australian Outback to see wallabies, Cape Barren geese and emus; get an underwater view of the penguins, then enjoy the antics of the furry inhabitants in the eponymous Beaver Country, before making your way to the Butterfly House. 'Down on the Farm' children can have a go at milking a (plastic) cow and follow the journey of a pint of milk from farm to shop. Everything is accessible by wheelchair and buggy, with doors and windows at just the right height for tiny tots, who are also invited to touch many of the animals. The emphasis is on learning through play – there are quizzes, information points and the popular Zoolympics, a series of mental and physical exercises designed to make children laugh as they learn, introducing them to a series of animal antics. Exhausted adults might find some peace from the squeals of delighted children in the formal Japanese and Rose Gardens before venturing into the 'village' area, which is full of craft shops, or heading for the Thatched Barn, where cream teas and snacks are served. Even if it rains you can enjoy a day here, as half the zoo is under cover. The large adventure playground is very well equipped, as is the indoor play barn, so leave plenty of time to enjoy them. There are picnic areas and the excellent, extremely child friendly Toucans Restaurant (Egon Ronay's Family Restaurant of the Year, 1991) has a good children's menu, with 'kiddies cocktails', play area, baby food, bottle-warming facilities, high chairs, pleasant nursing and changing areas, and even room to accommodate buggies. Disabled and baby-changing facilities in toilets.

Wheelchair and buggy access. There are plenty of nearby attractions but I defy anyone to spend less than a day at Drusillas. Battle Abbey is 16 miles away, the **Bluebell Railway** 14 miles and Brighton 15 miles. In Alfriston itself is **The Living World** for insect lovers.

TRAVEL *Berwick rail, then taxi or walk; by car off the A27; free on-site parking* • **HOURS** *Daily 10am to dusk (4.30pm in winter, closed 25-26 Dec; some attractions closed in winter – phone for details)* • **PRICES** *Zoo, train and Play Land: adults £6.25, children £5.25 (under-3s free), concs £4.50. Phone for details of half-term and holiday special events.*

DUNGENESS RSPB NATURE RESERVE ☀ ◑

ADDRESS Boulderwall Farm, Dungeness Road, Lydd, Kent
PHONE 01797 320588

The shingle foreland, which stretches into the English Channel, is an important breeding colony for gulls and terns in summer, wildfowl in winter and migrating birds in spring and autumn. There is a visitors' centre, nature trail and six hides. Nearby is the Old Dungeness Lighthouse (tel: 01797 321300) which can be reached by car from Lydd and New Romney or by steam train at the end of the line on the **New Romney, Hythe and Dymchurch Railway**. The lighthouse is open from end of March to September daily, 10.30am to 5pm (phone for other times during the year); adults £1.60, children and concessions £1. You can climb the 168 steps for some wonderful views and see how the lantern was worked and cleaned when in use.

TRAVEL *Dungeness rail* • **HOURS** *Daily, 9am to sunset; visitors' centre: Mon and Wed-Sun, 9am-5pm* • **PRICES** *Adults £2.50, children 50p, concs £1.50, family ticket (2+4) £5*

FARM WORLD ☺ ☀ ●

ADDRESS Great Knelle, Beckley, nr Rye, E Sussex
PHONE 01797 260250

Included in the admission price at Farm World are lambs to feed twice a day in spring, milking to watch daily at 3pm, a tractor ride, an adventure playground, grass go-karting and a half-hour puppet show about the do's and don'ts of the countryside. There is also a trekking centre and various demonstrations throughout the year. Tearoom and picnic site. Shops sell toys, crafts, farm produce and even antiques. Disabled and baby-changing facilities. Wheelchair and buggy access.

TRAVEL *By car on M25, A21, A268 and then follow signs* • **OPEN** *Mar: Sat-Sun, noon-5.30pm; Apr-Sep: daily, 10.30am-5.30pm* • **PRICES** *Adults £4, children £3*

FISHERS FARM PARK ☺ ✿ ●

ADDRESS Newpound Lane, Wisborough Green, W Sussex
PHONE 01403 700063

If you're at a loss for something to do on a winter's day, head for Fishers Farm; it has a heated indoor playbarn with fort and sandpit, and lots of the animals are under cover. In summer, children are actively encouraged to go into the pens to stroke the animals. Look out for Casper, one of the biggest horses in the world, and Jacko, one of the smallest. Information on the animals is clearly set out and there are also woodland trails, trailer rides and home-made cakes at tea time. Camping in summer. Older children can try go-karting (£1 extra). Also an adventure playground (follow the trail through the woods) with old tractors, a combine harvester and the usual play equipment. Restaurant does family lunch. Baby-changing facilities in men's and women's toilets. Wheelchair access limited.

TRAVEL *Billingshurst rail* • **HOURS** *Daily, 10am-5pm (closed 25- 26 Dec)* • **PRICES** *Adults £4.75, children over 1 year £4.25*

GATWICK ZOO ☺ ☀ ◑

ADDRESS Russ Hill, Charlwood, Surrey
PHONE 01293 862312

Gatwick Zoo has a variety of birds and free-flying butterflies in the tropical garden, as well as providing a home for otters, penguins, wallabies, Vietnamese pigs, eagle owls and the ever-popular monkeys on Monkey Island. There is an excellent play area and a log-cabin adventure playground. Café, outdoor and under-cover picnic tables; burgers and chips stall summer only. Full facilities for the disabled, and wheelchair and buggy access. The zoo is small and takes no more than two hours to visit so could be combined with a visit to Gatwick Airport three miles away, especially on a wet day. You can ride the transit train from the North to the South Terminal and wander round the airport, then visit the viewing gallery, have a go on the flight simulator, walk through the Herald plane and visit the multimedia theatre. Lots of restaurants and shops, toilets for the disabled and nappy-changing facilities. Buggy and wheelchair access. (Viewing gallery, tel: 01293 503843, open summer 8am-7pm, winter 9am-4pm. Adults £1, children 60p, under-5s free.)

TRAVEL *By car off A23* • **OPEN** *Mar-Oct: daily, 10.30am-6pm; Jan-Feb and Nov-Dec: Sat-Sun and daily during school holidays, 10.30am-4pm or dusk (closed 25-26 Dec)* • **PRICES** *Adults £3.95, children £3.50 (under-3s free), concs £4.25.*

GODSTONE FARM ☺ ☀ ●

ADDRESS Tilburstow Hill Road, Godstone, Surrey
PHONE 01883 742546

For a perfect family outing on which kids can run off steam while parents sit back and relax, you cannot fault Godstone Farm. Children are positively encouraged to handle the farm animals and can climb into the pens with the sheep, lambs and calves, as well as petting the rabbits, guinea pigs, and hens. There are plenty of information panels and everything is meticulously labelled. Staff are friendly, helpful and well prepared – even for insect stings! There are several covered picnic areas, places to shelter, and a covered under-5s' play area so rain cannot spoil your day. However, the highlight of the visit is the adventure play area, spread over three enormous fields, which is still by far the best we have ever visited. There are ropes to climb, bridges to cross, several wooden forts, mazes, well-equipped sandpits, old tractors, climbing frames, bridges, slides, pulleys, tobogganing on Astroturf, and so on. It doesn't matter how many people there are, it never feels crowded, the toilets are always clean and never run out of loo paper, and there is plenty of room to spread out on the grass or tables for a picnic. Refreshment kiosks and shop. Baby-changing facilities. Wheelchair and buggy access.

TRAVEL *By car off A22 or M25 (junction 6), then go through Godstone and follow signs; free on-site parking* • **OPEN** *Mid- Feb to Oct: daily, 10am-6pm (5pm in winter); Oct-Feb: Sat-Sun only* • **PRICES** *Child accompanied by one adult £3.45, additional adults £3.45 each (under-2s free), OAPs £2.10*

HAM HOUSE ✿ ☽

ADDRESS Ham, Richmond, Surrey
PHONE 0181 940 1950
Although you can get to Ham House by car, following the road down from
Richmond Hill, it is more fun to summon the foot ferry, manned by one
man (and his dog) by ringing the bell on a post by the north bank of the
Thames or shouting loudly. This is one of the few houses in Britain that
has been restored, not to a specific period, but to reflect the tastes and
fashions of different periods during which it was occupied. Resident ghosts
include the Black Widow, a formidable woman who flirted with Cromwell
in order to secure the release from prison of her second husband, then
promptly rejoined the Royalists when the monarchy was restored. The
ghost of a small Cavalier King Charles spaniel has been seen to scuttle
along before disappearing through a wall. The formal gardens have been
restored to their 17th-century splendour and you can picnic in the Rose
Garden. Ghost Guide available. Children's quiz, and special events in
school holidays. Restaurant and tearoom with high chairs and outdoor
tables. Toilets for the disabled and baby-changing facilities. No buggies
in house but slings and reins available.
TRAVEL ⊖ Richmond, then bus 65 or 71 • **OPEN** End Mar to end Oct: Mon-
Wed and Sat-Sun, 1-5pm • **PRICES** Adults £5, children £2, family ticket
£12.50. National Trust property.

HAMPTON COURT PALACE ✿ ☽

ADDRESS East Molesey, Surrey
PHONE 0181 781 9500 or 0181 977 8441
Hampton Court was built in the 1500s by Henry VIII's chief minister,
Cardinal Wolsey, and was at the time the largest palace in Europe. Henry
moved in in 1525 and spent five of his six honeymoons at the Palace.
In the Haunted Gallery you might hear the screams of the ghost of
Catherine Howard, Henry's fifth wife, whom he accused of adultery and
had executed. Our children enjoyed the Tudor kitchens best – their eyes
stood out on stalks when they discovered the amount of food prepared
for feasts. The gardens, designed to rival those of Versailles, house the
famous maze, whose yew-hedge walls are over 7 ft high. Look out for the
complicated astronomical clock on Anne Boleyn's Gate, which gives not
only the time but the date, zodiac signs, moon phases and Thames high
tides. Take a picnic to eat in nearby **Bushy Park** with its deer herds,
ornamental ponds and horse chestnut trees (good supply of conkers in
autumn). Children's trails. Shop. Holiday events and storytelling sessions.
Toilets and access for disabled.
TRAVEL Hampton Court rail; 15 miles west of central London; on-site
parking • **OPEN** Mid-Mar to mid-Oct: Mon 10.15am-6pm, Tues-Sun
9.30am-6pm; mid-Oct to mid-Mar: closes at 4.15pm (closed 24-26 Dec,
1 Jan) • **PRICES** Adults £9.25, children £6.10 (under-5s free), OAPs £7,
family ticket (2+3) £27.65. Car park £1.75

HASTINGS SEA LIFE CENTRE ☺ ✿ ◑

ADDRESS Rock-a-Nore Road, Hastings
PHONE 01424 718776
The large glass tanks full of octopus, lobster, sharks, rays and hundreds
of other sea creatures from Britain's deep waters are easily visible to
even small children. The highlight is the underwater viewing tunnel with a
carpeted step running along one side. There are no reflections here, and

looking up can make you feel quite dizzy. There are outdoor pools where children can pick up crabs – if they dare – and picnic tables providing a good place for snacks (bring your own). If you don't have a picnic, there is the Breakers Restaurant. We took a double buggy round with ease, but there are 12 steps down to the tunnel. The alternative wheelchair route misses out the tunnel but stops by a huge floor-to-ceiling concave wall, making you feel as if you are standing inside the tank with the sharks, stingrays and other sea beasties. **NEARBY:** the Fisherman's Museum, the Shipwreck Heritage Centre, the East Hill Cliff Railway and Hastings Castle and the 1066 Story. Details from Hastings Tourist Information Centre (tel: 01424 781111).

TRAVEL *Hastings rail; National Express bus from Victoria* • **HOURS** *Daily, 10am-6pm (summer holidays to 9pm; closed Christmas Day)* • **PRICES** *Adults £3.95, children £2.75, concs £3*

HEVER CASTLE ☺ ☀ ●

ADDRESS Edenbridge, Kent
PHONE 01732 865224

You will need plenty of time to explore the beautiful grounds, discover the grotto, get lost in the maze, examine the strange and beautiful statues and sculptures in the formal Italian Garden, wander round the Rose Garden, and roll down the hill from which you can overlook the castle and maze. New this year is the 'splashing maze', a hilarious adventure that involves reaching the folly in the middle of the pond via a stepping stone path, while avoiding jets of water which try to hinder your progress. Inside the enchanting 13th-century double-moated castle, complete with huge gatehouse, arrow slits and portcullis drawbridge, stands the 15th-century manor house, childhood home of Anne Boleyn and scene of her courtship by Henry VIII. Hever has a restaurant but it's more fun to picnic on the sloping grass overlooking the maze and castle. The small but very popular adventure playground is near the exit. Gift shop. Toilets for the disabled. Baby-changing facilities in restaurant. Jousting tournaments held here in summer.

TRAVEL *Hever rail then 1-mile walk, or Edenbridge rail then 3-mile taxi ride; by car on M25 to junction 5, then B206; free car park* • **HOURS** *Castle: daily, noon-6pm (4pm in winter); gardens from 11am* • **PRICES** *Adults £6.50, children £3.30, family ticket (2+2) £16.30 (gardens only: adults £4.90, children £3, family ticket £12.80)*

HOBBS CROSS OPEN FARM ☺ ☀ ◑

ADDRESS Theydon Garnon, Epping, Essex
PHONE 01992 814862

Put on wellies and old clothes and find out what a working dairy and livestock farm is really all about. Watch the 400 Friesian cows being milked at 1.30pm each day and see the journey from cow to bottle of a pint of milk (there is a processing diary where milk is pasteurised and bottled). Also pig house, poultry house with newly hatched chicks, sheep, ponies, donkeys, goats, rabbits and a Friesian bull. Very good information plaques. Café. Picnic area. Gift and farm-produce shop. Toilets. Buggy and wheelchair access (except to milking-parlour gallery).

TRAVEL ⊖ *Theydon Bois then taxi or 1¹/₂-mile walk; free on-site car park* • **HOURS** *Mon-Fri, 8.30am-5pm; Sat-Sun, 8.30am-6pm* • **PRICES** *Adults £2.75, children and concs £2.25, under-2's free*

HORTON PARK CHILDREN'S FARM ☺ ❀ ●

ADDRESS Horton Lane, Epsom, Surrey

PHONE 01372 743984

A working farm with common and rare breeds of animals, including miniature ponies, angora goats and angora rabbits. You can stroke the goats or bottle feed the lambs and, depending on the time of year, you can see lambing, goat milking, sheep-shearing, spinning, weaving and ponies in harness. Horton is an ideal place to introduce small children to farm life, and there is plenty of activity to keep the older ones amused too. As it was raining, our children spent a good deal of time in the straw pit, the contents of which we are still finding in our car, but the whole experience got the thumbs up despite the weather, so it was a small price to pay. There is a farm walk, tractor rides (50p), playground, large sandpit, picnic area, shop and tearoom (closes 4.15pm).

TRAVEL *Epsom rail or bus 598* • **HOURS** *Daily, 10am-6pm (5pm in winter; closed 25-26 Dec)* • **PRICES** *Children £3.30, one accompanying adult free with each paying child (additional adults £3.30, under-2s free)*

HOWLETTS WILD ANIMAL PARK ☀ ●

ADDRESS Bekesbourne, nr Canterbury, Kent

PHONE 01303 264646/7

John Aspinall's park is dedicated to the breeding of rare species, and the animals enjoy conditions as close to those of the wild as is possible in captivity. This does mean that the animals are rather more difficult to see than in a conventional zoo, so you have to be patient and look carefully. As well as the largest collection of tigers in the world and a massive breeding colony of gorillas, there are deer, antelope, chimps, cheetahs, African elephants, wolves, bongos and bison. Plan your day carefully, especially if you have small children who tire easily. We had saved the gorilla house until last, ran out of time and had literally to drag our children away. There are small observation huts along the path to rest tired feet, breast-feed demanding babies, stop for a quick snack and watch the animals. Cafeteria, kiosks, picnic sites. Shop with animal-related toys and books from pocket-money prices up. Toilets. Baby-changing facilities in café. Children's birthday parties available.

TRAVEL *By car: off A2 south of Canterbury* • **OPEN** *Summer: daily, 10am-7pm (last admission, 5pm); winter: 10am-5pm (last admission, 4pm)* • **PRICES** *Adults £7.99, children and OAPs £5.99 (under-4s free), family ticket (2+2) £22*

KNEBWORTH HOUSE ☀ ◑

ADDRESS Knebworth, nr Stevenage, Herts

PHONE 01438 812661

This Gothic, gargoyle-covered house, whose origins date back to Norman times, is still home to the Lytton family and has a cosy, lived-in feel, with family photos on display. Explore the formal gardens and search for the sika and red deer that inhabit the 250 acres of parkland. Fort Knebworth Adventure Playground, near the entrance, is excellent for all ages and has a very popular Astroglide, a corkscrew slide for ages 6 and over, and a miniature rail for all. Special events include American Civil War re-enactment weekends. Nature trails. Café in tithe barn. No baby-changing facilities. No buggy access in house (wheelchair and buggy access on paths through the gardens).

TRAVEL *By car: A1(M) to junction 6 and follow signs; Knebworth or Stevenage rail then taxi* • **OPEN** *22 Mar to 7 Apr and 24 May to 2 Sep:*

Gardens, park and Fort Knebworth, daily 11am-5.30pm; house, Tues-Sun noon-5pm (Sat-Sun only rest of year) • **PRICES** *House and garden: adults £5, children £4.50; garden only: adults £4, children £3 (under-5s free), family ticket £14*

LEEDS CASTLE ☺ ☀ ●

ADDRESS Maidstone, Kent
PHONE 01622 765400

Leeds Castle is a real fairytale medieval castle, built spectacularly upon two islands in a lake. Dating from the 9th century, it is one of the oldest castles in the country. For scenic reasons the car park is a long way from the castle itself, so as you meander through the grounds you get a very good idea of why it was a favourite home of the medieval queens of England. The walk is as varied as it is beautiful; our children were much amused by the first section, the Duckery. Here the waterfowl and peacocks have right of way and visitors must keep to the set paths (an order studiously ignored by many people, nonetheless). From here you follow the path through the Woodland Gardens, which in early spring is a carpet of daffodils, and finally you reach the castle itself. Apart from Les Chambres de la Reine, two rooms recreated as they might have looked in the 15th century, and Henry VIII's magnificent Banqueting Hall, I thought the inside of the castle was rather disappointing. However, you can see everything in under 15 minutes which is, of course, a great relief to most children gagging to get back out into the spring sunshine. The Culpeper Garden is beautifully laid out and full of wonderful smells. The children loved the delightful underground fairy grotto, complete with tunnels, caves and falling water, and there was plenty of scope for them to get lost and frighten their parents in the classical maze. There are lovely woodland walks, more suitable for older children, and ancient vineyards which were recorded in the Domesday Book in 1086 and still provide the grapes for the castle's own wine. The Dog Collar Museum is a unique and quite bizarre collection of medieval and ornamental canine collars from all over the world. Special events at Leeds Castle include an International Hot Air Balloon Festival in June, a grand fireworks display in November (to be held on 7 November in 1998), and open-air concerts in summer. Restaurant, cream teas, barbecues. Picnic area by car park. Toilets. Wheelchair access to castle limited; leave buggies at entrance. **TRAVEL** *Bearsted rail, then 10-minute coach transfer; all-inclusive train, coach and admission tickets available on 0171 620 1032; by National Express coach from Victoria (phone 0171 730 0202); by car: 40 miles southeast of central London off M20 (junction 8); on-site parking* • **HOURS** *Daily, 11am-5pm (closed Christmas Day, 26 Jun, 3 Jul, 29 Aug and 6 Nov)* • **PRICES** *Adults £8.80, children £5.80 (under-5s free), concs £6.80, family ticket (2+2) £23; park and gardens only: adults £6.80, children £4.30, concs £5.30, family ticket £19*

LEE VALLEY PARK FARMS ☺ ☀ ●

ADDRESS Stubbins Hall Lane, Crooked Mile, Waltham Abbey, Essex
PHONE 01992 892781 or 01992 892291

Two farms for the price of one. Holyfield Hall is a large working farm, where visitors can watch the daily milking (2.45-4pm), and Hayes Hill Farm has a wide range of animals, including llamas and ponies, as well as a Tudor barn and plenty of space for play. Picnic areas, shop, farm trails and play area, toilets.

TRAVEL *Waltham Cross rail; Lee Valley Leisure bus (phone 0181 889 0404 for times)* • **HOURS** *Mon-Fri, 10am-4.30pm; Sat-Sun, 10am-6pm or dusk* • **PRICES** *Adults £2.75, children and concs £1.80*

LITTLEHAMPTON BEACH ☺ ☀ ●

PHONE Tourist information 01903 713480

The beaches either side of the River Arun are sandy, clean, safe for swimming, and at low tide do not feel too crowded (check papers for tidal times). Even at high tide there is plenty to do on and off the beach. The port itself is a hive of maritime activity, and boat trips from here either head out to sea and around the harbour or back up the river to Arundel, a journey that takes about an hour (Skylark Cruises, tel: 01903 717337). At high tide you can fish for crabs over the harbour wall (fishing lines available in seafront shops – we used cold sausages as bait but I'm told raw bacon is better). At the western end of the beach is a funfair, and there is also a train ride along the promenade, fish and chip restaurants and the usual seaside shops. At high tide it gets very crowded on the seafront, but you can take the road train to the eastern end which has a small play area, a putting green, café and far less people (unfortunately, the toilets are all at the western end). There is a ferry across to the West Beach Conservation Area and Nature Reserve, which is perfect for picnics. Younger children can let off steam by running about on the sand dunes and older children can follow the two-hour nature route (maps available on the ferry). Baby-changing facilities at the western end of the beach. **NEARBY:** Arundel Castle (tel: 01903 883136).

TRAVEL *Littlehampton rail; by car: A24 or A27/M27 along the coast*

LIVING WORLD ☺ ❀ ◐

ADDRESS Seven Sisters Country Park, Seaford, E Sussex
PHONE 01323 870100

Housed in two restored Sussex barns, this natural-history exhibition has living displays of insects and sea creatures from around the world. There are tropical butterflies, stick insects, moths, mantises and marine and fresh-water aquaria. Observation beehive and photographic displays. You can venture out to a forest, river or downland walk and picnic in several areas. Cafeteria. Toilets for the disabled and baby-changing facilities. Wheelchair and buggy access. Lovely place for a family walk with the exhibition as the treat at the end.

TRAVEL *by rail; change at Brighton for Seaford, then 5-minute taxi ride or bus 712 or 711; by car: M23, A23 and A259, then follow signs* • **OPEN** *Mid-Mar to Oct: daily, 10am-5pm; winter: Sat-Sun (and weekdays during school holidays), 10am-5pm* • **PRICES** *Adults £2.50, children and concs £1.70 (under-5s and disabled free)*

LOCKWOOD DONKEY SANCTUARY ☺ ☀ ◑

ADDRESS Farm Cottage, Sandhills, Wormley, Godalming, Surrey
PHONE 01428 682409

Old and sick donkeys from all over the world find their way here to this wonderful, privately run sanctuary. Children are made to feel very welcome. In addition to nearly 200 donkeys, the sanctuary houses 50 horses, 3 cows, 10 sheep, 15 goats, hundreds of cats, deer, wallabies, dogs, geese, ducks, cockerels and a white llama called Sultan of Arabia. If you forget to take carrots, biscuits or sugar lumps you can buy a bucket of food for the animals. Don't bring apples for donkeys – they cause colic which can be fatal. There is an Adoption Scheme by which, for as little as

£1 a year (£2 for adults), you can adopt a donkey or any other animal at the sanctuary. You receive a certificate and can visit as often as you like. Full facilities for the disabled.

TRAVEL *By car: off the A283 Godalming-Chiddingfold Road* • **HOURS** *Daily, 9am-5.30pm or dusk* • **PRICE** *Free*

MARWELL ZOOLOGICAL PARK ☺ ☀ ●

ADDRESS Colden Common, Winchester, Hants
PHONE 01962 777407; recorded information 01426 943163
Known for its conservation of endangered species, Marwell prides itself on offering animals the maximum amount of space, so spotting them is not always easy. The best way to get around with little ones is by the land train from which, if you are lucky, you can spot lions, tigers, rhinos, giraffes and monkeys. At the other end of the park from the entrance is the children's zoo, with face painting, a funny-bunny maze, several long-suffering rabbits and guinea pigs, and occasionally a more unusual visitor like a baby camel. The new penguin pool is very popular too. Treetops Restaurant, near the entrance, serves good food and there are also picnic areas. Adventure playground and play areas.

TRAVEL *By car: M3 (junction 11), then B2177 Bishops Waltham road* • **OPEN** *Summer: daily, 10am-6pm; winter: daily, 10am-4pm* • **PRICES** *Adults £7.50, children £5.50, OAPs £6.50, family ticket £24*

MICHELHAM PRIORY ❀ ●

ADDRESS Upper Dicker, Hailsham, E Sussex
PHONE 01323 844224
This magnificent 13th-century priory is approached by an imposing 14th-century gatehouse, spanning one of the longest moats in the country. The exhibits inside capture eight centuries of history, and the beautiful grounds are full of things to amuse and impress children – wagons, a Tudor barn, a physic garden, a blacksmiths and wheelwrights museum, a rope museum and a working watermill that grinds locally grown wheat into wholemeal flour. The flour can be bought in the shop along with craft items and books. Restaurant. Picnic site. Wheelchair access.

TRAVEL *By car: phone for directions depending on where you are coming from; free on-site parking* • **OPEN** *End Mar to end Oct: daily, 11am-5.30pm; Mar and Nov: Sun, 11am-4pm (closed Dec-Feb)* • **PRICES** *Adults £4, children £2.20, OAPs £3.40, concs £2, family ticket (2+2) £10.50*

MISTLEY PLACE PARK ANIMAL-RESCUE CENTRE ☺ ☀ ●

ADDRESS New Road, Mistley, Colchester, Essex
PHONE 01206 396483
Children raised on *Animal Arc*, James Herriot and *Animal Hospital* will find plenty of interest at this sanctuary, which is home to over 2,000 animals, from shire horses to rabbits.

TRAVEL *Mistley rail* • **HOURS** *Tues-Sun, 10am-5.30pm* • **PRICE** *£2*

MOUNTFITCHET CASTLE ☀ ●

ADDRESS Stansted, Essex
PHONE 01279 813237
This wonderful reconstruction of an 11th-century village, with its motte and bailey castle, really does bring history to life, warts and all. Wallow in the filth and grime of life 800 years ago, peer into the gloom of a charcoal

burner's hut, hear realistic-looking costumed characters talk about their experiences as peasants or barons, and secretly thank heaven you weren't born then. There is plenty to do and loads to see, including a giant catapult, a pottery kiln, blacksmiths and, inside the inner bailey, the Grand Hall ready for a banquet. Next to the Norman village is the Toy Museum, which provides a good shelter from the weather and houses a wealth of teddies, dolls, doll's houses and trains, dating from Victorian times to the present. Some of the toys are animated, and the glass cases reach down to ground level, which is much appreciated by toddlers. Café. Picnic area. Gift shop. **NEARBY:** Stansted Airport for plane spotting or Stansted village for tea.

TRAVEL *Stansted Mountfitchet – not Stansted – rail, then 2-min walk; by car: M11 (junction 8) then B1383* • **HOURS** *Castle: Mar-Nov, daily, 10am-5pm; Toy Museum: daily, 10am-5pm* • **PRICES** *Castle: adults £4, children £3; Toy Museum: adults £3, children £2.50*

NEPICAR FARM ☺ ☼ ◑

ADDRESS Wrotham Heath, Sevenoaks, Kent
PHONE 01732 883040
This is a marvellous place for children who think milk only comes from cows (or worse still, bottles). They can watch sheep being milked at close range, and in spring help bottle feed the lambs. Sheep-shearing and cheese-making demonstrations. Large, well-stocked children's play area with bicycles, footballs, rounders and cricket equipment. Tearoom. Toilets for the disabled and baby-changing facilities. Wheelchair and buggy access.
TRAVEL *By car: on A25 between Maidstone and Sevenoaks* • **OPEN** *Mar to end Sep: daily, 10am-5pm* • **PRICES** *Adults £2.75, children £1.75, concs £2.25, family ticket (2+2) £8*

ODDS FARM PARK RARE-BREEDS CENTRE ☺ ☼ ◑

ADDRESS Green Common Lane, Wooburn Common, High Wycombe, Bucks
PHONE 01628 520188
Check at the entrance for feeding and handling times at this small, friendly rare-breeds farm. The staff, easily recognisable in green sweatshirts, will encourage children to help with anything from collecting eggs to feeding pigs, depending on the time of year. You can adopt animals and buy rabbits. Babies and toddlers are not left out, as buggies can be taken into one of the petting enclosures. There is a grassy adventure play area with a separate section for under-5s. **NEARBY: Bekonscot Model Village.**
TRAVEL *By car: M40 to junction 2, A40 towards High Wycombe for nearly 2 miles, turn left in Broad Lane and go 1 mile further. Farm is second on left, just after pub.* • **HOURS** *Thurs-Sun, 10am-4pm (daily during school holidays; phone to check dates)* • **PRICES** *Adults £3.50, children £2.25 (under-3s free), concs £2.50*

PAINSHILL PARK ☺ ☼ ●

ADDRESS Portsmouth Road, Cobham, Surrey
PHONE 01932 868113
This delightful 18th-century landscape garden with lake, islands, a Gothic temple, Turkish tent, Chinese bridge and grotto was designed to express certain moods and inspire corresponding emotions, and really appeals to children's imaginations as well as adults'. Learn about water power from the 19th-century waterwheel and animal engine; conjure up the mysteries

of the East in the Turkish tent or explore the ruined abbey. There is a circular route that takes you past all the main features, and the path is buggy friendly. Painshill is a great venue for children's birthday parties; choose from themes such as Survival, Technology, Happy Earthday, Pirate, Costume, and Treasure Hunt (£80–£95 for up to three hours and 25 children; includes one Education Trust staff member; suitable for ages 6-12). Excellent holiday activities include survival days, treasure hunts, pond-dipping, cracker-making, Earthdays, and Easter-egg hunts. Picnic site, light refreshments, shop. Full facilities for the disabled. Wheelchair and buggy access. **NEARBY: Chatley Heath Semaphore Tower.**

TRAVEL By car: off the A245 • **OPEN** Summer: Tues-Fri, 10.30am-6pm; winter: Tues-Thurs, 11am-4pm • **PRICES** Adults £3.80, children £1.50 (under-5s free). No dogs

PARADISE WILDLIFE PARK ☺ ☀ ●

ADDRESS Broxbourne, Herts
PHONE 01992 468001
Zoo with lions, tigers, zebras and, bizarrely, the country's largest rabbit village. There are four themed playgrounds, tractor rides, go-karting, various other children's rides and crazy golf. Restaurant. Picnic area. Shop.
TRAVEL By car on M25 to junction 25 • **HOURS** Daily, 10am-6pm • **PRICES** Adults £5, children £4

PARSONAGE FARM RURAL HERITAGE CENTRE ☺ ☀ ●

ADDRESS North Elham, nr Canterbury, Kent
PHONE 01303 840766 or 01303 840356
This friendly family farm, with its traditional and rare breeds of farm animals, including sheep, cattle, pigs, chickens, ducks and geese, is immensely popular with children. Follow the farm trail with quiz sheets (there is a prize for those with the right answers); see the development of domestic animals from the Stone Age to the present day; and find out about the farm's history in the small museum which also houses displays of farm tools. The tearoom serves home-made goodies all day and there is a pleasant picnic site. Toilets for the disabled but no baby-changing facilities. Wheelchair and buggy access.

TRAVEL By car: A2 (Canterbury exit) or M20 (Folkestone exit); signposted off the Elham Valley Road • **OPEN** Easter to 30 Sep: Tues-Sun and bank holidays, 10.30am-5pm • **PRICES** Adults £3.10, children £1.90, OAPs and concs £2.30

PENSHURST PLACE AND GARDENS ☺ ☀ ●

ADDRESS Penshurst, nr Tonbridge, Kent
PHONE 01892 870307 or 01892 870255
The medieval manor house is full of wonderful furniture, tapestries and portraits for adults to marvel at, while older children might appreciate the splendours of the enormous Baron's Hall, dating back to 1341. Younger children can be persuaded round with the use of the activity sheets (finding evidence of porcupines, the family emblem, and other objects) and there is a small toy museum. But the real treat for all children, toddlers as well as teenagers, is the adventure playground, which is well thought out, great fun and safe. The interconnecting, walled Tudor gardens are fun to explore and there are nature and farm trails. Restaurant. Shop. Toilets for the disabled. Wheelchair and buggy access. Special events include a Balloon Fiesta (July) and a kite festival (August). **NEARBY:** Tonbridge Castle, Castle

Street, Tonbridge (tel: 01732 770929); open Mon-Sat 9am-4pm, Sun and
bank holidays 10.30am-4pm; adults £3.25, children £1.60, family ticket
(2+2) £7.75.

TRAVEL By car: M25 to junction 2, then A21 to Tonbridge and follow signs
• **OPEN** Apr-Sep: daily, house 12-5.30pm, grounds 11am-6pm (Mar and
Oct: Sat-Sun only) • **PRICES** Adults £5.70, children £3.20, concs £5.30,
family ticket £15 (grounds only: adults £4.20, children £2.80, concs £3.70)

POOH'S FOREST ADVENTURES ☺ ☀ ◑

ADDRESS Ashdown Forest, E Sussex
PHONE Maire McQueeny on 01273 607910

Explore the East Sussex village of Hartfield, inspiration and location of AA
Milne's Pooh stories. Chose a 2- or 3-mile walk to visit such Very Important
Places as 100 Acre Wood, Eeyore's Gloomy Place, Roo's Sandy Pit and
Poohsticks Bridge. You can buy a map and do the walk yourself or join
one of Maire's guided walks. For details of walks and events, call the
above number. For a copy of the map, send £2 to Maire McQueeny,
22 Warleigh Road, Brighton, BN1 4NT.

PORT LYMPNE WILD ANIMAL PARK ☺ ☀ ●

ADDRESS Lympne, nr Hythe, Kent
PHONE 01303 264646/7

In summer the best way to see the animals here is to take a Safari trailer
ride (pre-book as it is very popular). Alternatively you can make the 2-mile
trek around the park to see the rhinos, elephants, tigers, wolves, monkeys,
deer and antelope. There is a lot of walking to do but it is all accessible
by double buggy. Cafeteria, kiosks, picnic sites. Shop with animal-related
toys and books from pocket-money prices up. Toilets; baby-changing
facilities in café. Children's birthday parties available.

TRAVEL By car: M20 (exit 11), south of Ashford off the B2067 • **HOURS**
Daily, 10am-5pm or dusk (closed Christmas Day) • **PRICES** Adults £7.99,
children and concs £5.99 (under-4s free), family ticket (2+2) £22

ROALD DAHL CHILDREN'S GALLERY ☺ ✿ ●

ADDRESS Buckinghamshire County Museum, Church Street, Aylesbury
PHONE 01296 331441

A truly fantastic, award-winning museum, which is inspired by rather than
about Roald Dahl and is worth a visit how ever far you have to travel. The
displays encourage children to investigate history, science, technology, and
natural history through practical hands-on activities relating to real museum
objects. At the same time, the spirit of Dahl's writing weaves its magic
spell throughout the gallery, complemented by Quentin Blake's wonderfully
quirky drawings. Visitors can wander into the Giant Peach for a closer
look at James's mini-beast friends with the aid of video-microscopes, and
crawl through Fantastic Mr Fox's Tunnel for a glimpse of life underground
and buried treasures from the past. Try exploring sound with the BFG, play
his giant pipe organ and discover the secrets of the whispering world.
Upstairs, via the Great Glass Elevator, the Imagination Gallery will baffle
your brain and boggle your eyes with things that are not what they seem.
See the Twits' upside-down room, feel the things hidden in their wall or
turn your own world upside down with the camera obscura. Freeze your
own shadow or write a magic message on the shadow wall and watch
it fade. Step into one of Quentin Blake's illustrations or draw your own
backdrop with the videochromakey. The gallery has a capacity of only
85 people so at busy times your visit will be restricted to an hour. Phone

before making a special journey as tickets sell out early in the day and there is no pre-booking facility. While waiting for your entry time, there is plenty to do and see in the equally brilliant Buckinghamshire County Museum, of which the Roald Dahl Gallery is a part. Café, garden for picnics, shop, toilets for the disabled and baby-changing facilities. Eating: McDonald's and Deep Pan Pizza in the High Street in Aylesbury. **NEARBY:** Kidzone Adventure Playground, Gate House Close, Aylesbury (tel: 01296 330405).

TRAVEL *Aylesbury rail then short walk; by car: M1 or M25, then A41 to Aylesbury; town-centre parking* • **HOURS** *Mon-Sat, 10am-5pm; Sun and bank holidays, 2-5pm; term-time weekdays, 3-5pm (schools have exclusive use until 3pm)* • **PRICES** *Adults £1.75, children £1.50 (under-8s must be accompanied by an adult). Buggy park (no buggy access to Gallery)*

SEVEN SISTERS SHEEP CENTRE ☺ ☀ ●

ADDRESS Birling Manor Farm, East Dean, Nr Eastbourne
PHONE 01323 423302 or 01323 423207

If your toddler has just learnt to say 'Baa!' or your youngster wants to be a sheep farmer, then this is the place to come. Terry and June Wigmore have over 40 British breeds of sheep in all shapes, sizes and colours. You can see every aspect of farming sheep, from lambing, shearing and milking (according to season) to the spinning of wool. Children can help with daily bottle-feeding sessions during lambing in March and April. Watch sheep's milk being turned into yoghurt and cheese, which you can then buy in the shop, and learn about the history of sheep on the Downs through well-presented displays. Picnic site and Hayrack tearoom. **NEARBY:** Beachy Head (1 mile).

TRAVEL *By car: 3 miles west of Eastbourne off the A259* • **OPEN** *May to mid-Sep: daily, 2-5pm; mid-Mar to 30 Apr: Mon-Fri, 2-5pm, Sat-Sun, 10am-5pm* • **PRICES** *Adults £3, children £2, concs £2.50*

THE SHUTTLEWORTH COLLECTION ☺ ☀ ◑

ADDRESS Old Warden Aerodrome, Biggleswade, Beds
PHONE 01767 627288

Flying Days are held here during the summer in good weather only, but the collection is on permanent display undercover throughout the year. It charts the history of aviation, from a Bleriot 1909 aeroplane and the 1912 Blackburn monoplane, the oldest British plane still flying, to First World War fighters, the Gloster Gladiator and a Second World War Spitfire. In addition, there is a large collection of vehicles from steam cars to fire engines, horse-drawn carriages to tricycles, all in perfect working order. Look out for the 1898 Panhard Levassor in which Richard Ormonde Shuttleworth, the collection's founder, won the London to Brighton run in 1928. Adventure playground and restaurant with children's menu of Skyliners, Spitfire Sandwiches and Flying Hot Dogs. Facilities for the disabled.

TRAVEL *Biggleswade rail; by car: 45 miles north of London on A1 North to second Biggleswade roundabout and follow signs; on-site parking* • **OPEN** *Apr-Oct: daily, 10am-5pm (last admission, 4pm); Nov-Mar: daily, 10am-4pm (last admission, 3pm)* • **PRICES** *Adults £6, children £4 (under-5s free), family ticket (1+3 or 2+2) £15. Flying Display days extra*

SOUTH FORELANDS LIGHTHOUSE ☀ ◐

ADDRESS St Margaret's-at-Cliffe, Dover, Kent
PHONE 01304 852463

This clifftop Victorian lighthouse once lighted Goodwin Sands and was used by Marconi for the first successful trials in radio navigation. Access to the tower is by guided tour (45 minutes). You can see the original light mechanism, an exhibition and working model, and magnificent views.
TRAVEL Martin Mill rail, then bus (Stagecoach East Kent) 90, Folkestone-Deal (phone 0345 696996); by car: to Dover on M20 or A2, from Dover take A258 following signs to St Margaret's-at-Cliffe. Access on foot from St Margaret's-at-Cliffe or the National Trust car park at Langdon Cliffs (2 miles) only. • **OPEN** Apr-Oct: Sat-Sun and bank holidays, 2-5.30pm (last admission, 5pm)
• **PRICES** Adults £1.50, children 75p. National Trust property.

SOUTH OF ENGLAND RARE BREEDS CENTRE ☺ ☀ ●

ADDRESS Highlands Farm, Woodchurch, Ashford, Kent
PHONE 01233 861494

Apart from the 65 rare farm breeds to be seen on this working farm, there's a kids' corner, where children are encouraged to touch the pigs, sheep, goats, rabbits and cattle, and watch milking, grooming and shearing demonstrations, and a lovely woodland walk. Follow the nature trails or save your energy on a farm trailer ride. Good picnic area, tearoom and well-stocked farm and gift shop. Playground. Toilets for the disabled. Wheelchair and buggy access.
TRAVEL By car: M20 (junction 10), then A2070 to Hamstreet and B2067 for 3 miles • **HOURS** Daily, 10.30am-4.30pm (Mar-Oct to 5.30pm, closed 24-25 Dec) • **PRICES** Adults £3.25, children £1.50, OAPs £2.75

THE SWAN SANCTUARY

ADDRESS Thorpe, Surrey
PHONE 01784 431667

The Swan Santuary nurses sick and injured swans back to life. As of January 1999 you will be able to visit all year round at its new site, which backs onto Thorpe Park. Phone for further details.

WEALD AND DOWNLAND OPEN AIR MUSEUM ☺ ☀ ●

ADDRESS Singleton, Chichester, W Sussex
PHONE 01243 811348

There is plenty to see at this vast open-air museum, so arrive early and bring a picnic, the buggy and plenty of children. The museum has rescued, dismantled and rebuilt 30 derelict buildings indigenous to the southeast – you can enter a 16th-century farmhouse, run riot in a medieval timber-framed hall, and see the inside of a 19th-century schoolhouse, an 18th-century barn, and a 19th-century carpenter's shop. Special events and demonstrations such as heavy horses or vintage tractor ploughing. Mill pond, woodland walks. Restaurant, picnic areas, shop. Limited wheelchair access because of uneven paths; buggy access fair.
TRAVEL Singleton rail; by car: 60 miles southeast of London, A3 then A286 to Midhurst and Chichester. Signposted from Singleton village (halfway between Midhurst and Chichester); on-site parking • **OPEN** Mar-Oct: daily, 11am-5pm; Nov-Feb: Wed and Sat-Sun, 11am-4pm • **PRICES** Adults £5.20, children £2.50 (under-5s free), family ticket (2+2) £14

WHIPSNADE WILD ANIMAL PARK ☺ ☀ ●

ADDRESS Whipsnade, nr Dunstable, Beds
PHONE 01582 872171

You can drive round in your own car or ride on the train in this large, open-air conservation park which houses 3,000 animals, including cheetahs, lions, tigers, rhinos, elephants and reptiles and many endangered species. There are Animal Encounters sessions where you can meet the animals and talk to the keepers; Birds of Prey demonstrations; a Discovery Centre with hands-on displays; a miniature desert and a rainforest. The adventure play area is large. Café and picnic area. Baby-changing facilities. Pushchairs for hire. Don't forget to take binoculars (or use the telescopes provided).
TRAVEL *Luton rail, then bus 43 from Luton Bus Station; by car: 32 miles north of London off M1 (junctions 9 or 12)* • **OPEN** *May-Sep: daily, 10am-6pm (to 7pm on Sun and bank holidays); Oct-Apr: daily, 10am to sunset* • **PRICES** *Adults £8.50, children £6 (under-3s free), concs £7*

WHITBREAD HOP FARM ☺ ☀ ●

ADDRESS Beltring, Paddock Wood, Kent
PHONE 01622 872 068

A working farm that provides hops for the Whitbread Brewery and trains the Whitbread shire horses that pull the barrel-laden drays through the City of London (also retirement home for the older horses). It has the largest collection of Victorian oast houses in the world as well as two museums – one telling the story of hops from Roman days to the present, the other having displays of rural crafts and tools used by hedgers, blacksmiths, wagoners, wheelwrights and other tradesmen. Jake never really got past the horses, whose size and strength amazed him – he spent most of the day loitering around them with his father, watching the grooming, harnessing and driving demonstrations. Felix preferred the Animal Village, where he was presented with an Animal Activity Pack and thought the animals were more his size. None of our kids was much taken by the flying displays featuring owls and birds of prey, but they enjoyed playing I-spy round the farm trail, and cowboys and Indians in the adventure play area. Take a picnic and spend the day here, especially if your visit coincides with one of the event days held throughout the year. Nature trails, craft workshops, playground, picnic area, café, Roundels restaurant, Brookers Oast pub (with Charlie Chalk children's menu and outside play area). Toilets for the disabled and baby-changing facilities.
TRAVEL *Beltring or Paddock Wood rail then bus; free on-site parking* • **OPEN** *Mar-Oct: daily, 10am-6pm; Nov-Feb: Sat-Sun, 10am-4pm (also open daily at half-term)* • **PRICES** *Adults £5, children and concs £3 (less in winter)*

WHITSTABLE ☺ ☀ ●

PHONE Tourist Information Office 01227 275482

We used to come here when we wanted a relaxing day on the beach with toddlers whose movements couldn't be controlled on sandy beaches. Not only do the stones and shells provide hours of beachcombing fun, but they severely restrict the movement of roaming offspring once their jelly shoes or sandals have been removed. Now we are regular visitors because, as there are almost no facilities, you are guaranteed a people-free day and can claim one of the stretches of beach between the windbreakers as your own. There is an excellent pub, The Old Neptune, on the beach, which you can reach by seafront path with buggies, or by road. The main beach, Tankerton Slopes, is only 15 minutes from the train station so if you have brought a heavy picnic, lighten the load here. There are plenty of grassy slopes to spread out if you don't want a beach picnic but still want a view of the sea. At the harbour you can see the oyster trawlers, and there is a small Oyster Exhibition with a live shellfish display and a seashore touch pool. The town centre is full of bric-a-brac shops, twisting alleyways and fishermen's cottages, although it is not very buggy friendly. For a real treat, book lunch at the Royal Native Oyster Stores (tel: 01227 276856). Do not be deceived by the utilitarian appearance of the interior or the apparently limited choice. You will not eat better cooked, fresher fish in the Southeast and the management is very welcoming to families.

TRAVEL *Whitstable rail* • **OPEN** *Oyster Exhibition: May-Sep, Mon-Tues and Thurs-Sun, 10am-4pm. Chuffa Trains: Mon-Sat, 10am-3pm (to 5pm on Sat and during school holidays)* • **PRICES** *Oyster Exhibition: adults 50p, children 30p. Chuffa Trains: Adults £1, children 50p*

WINDSOR CASTLE ☺ ☀ ●
PHONE 01753 831118

Originally built by William the Conqueror, this is the oldest and largest inhabited castle in the world and, despite the terrible fire in 1992, it is a splendid royal residence. It is, however, rather formal. The highlight of the trip for many children is the enormous Queen Mary's Doll's House, an exquisite miniature palace complete with running water, real leather-bound books and a working Hoover. No buggies in State Apartments. The **Changing of the Guard** can be seen outside free of charge on most days at 11am. Toilets but no restaurant. If desperate, there is a McDonald's opposite the castle walls, which is popular in an otherwise expensive tourist town. Alternatively, picnic on either side of the river and watch the boats rowing by.

TRAVEL *Windsor & Eton Riverside rail; by car: 20 miles west of London, M4 junction 6 or M3 junction 3; town-centre car parks but parking is difficult* • **HOURS** *Grounds, State Apartments, St George's Chapel and Queen Mary's Doll's House open daily from 10.30am (closing times vary and State Apartments closed when Royal Family in residence)* • **PRICES** *Adults £9.50, children £5, concs £7, family ticket (2+2) £21.50 (less on Sundays). Prices due to increase. Doll's House £1 extra*

WOBURN SAFARI PARK ☺ ❀ ●
PHONE 01525 290407/8

Britain's largest drive-through wildlife park takes you on a safari trail past tigers, wolves, bears, rhinos and monkeys. It is an ideal place to visit when it's cold outside, as you have to stay in your car with the windows closed for the hour and a bit it takes to drive round. Children get very excited as the metal gates clang shut behind the car and you enter the special secure enclosure for the lions and tigers, although when we visited the large cats were looking very tame and sleepy. The monkeys are particularly popular with children; they hitch a lift on your car and you get plenty of time to study them up close, especially those with babies. If the weather is good there is plenty to do at the Wild World leisure area, including pedal-powered swans on the lake, indoor and outdoor adventure play areas (particularly well equipped for older children), pets corner, elephant and sea-lion shows and plenty more. New this year is a Tree Tops Action Trail. Café. Picnic area. Gift shop. Toilets.

TRAVEL *By car: M1 to junction 13* • **OPEN** *Mid-Mar to Oct: daily, 10am-5pm; Nov to mid-Mar: Sat-Sun, 11am-3pm* • **PRICES** *Adults £9, children £6.50 (under-3s free); winter: adults £6.50, children £5. No soft-top cars.*

SPORTS AND LEISURE

Sportsline (tel: 0171 222 8000) operates Monday to Friday, 10am-6pm, and gives information on sports clubs and venues in London. Most local councils lay on sports facilities for children during summer and other holidays which can be anything from riding, shooting, archery and fencing to nature days, golf, canoeing, football, tennis and sailing. Your local library and leisure services department will have details.

BRITISH SPORTS ASSOCIATION FOR THE DISABLED
ADDRESS Solecast House, 13-27 Brunswick Place, N1
PHONE 0171 490 4919
Information on sports clubs with special facilities and related advice.
HOURS Mon-Fri, 9am-5.30pm

THE ENGLISH SPORTS COUNCIL
ADDRESS 16 Upper Woburn Place, WC1
PHONE 0171 273 1500
Information on all sport in and around London and on the various sports governing bodies.

ADVENTURE PLAYGROUNDS

Although 'adventure playground' has become a loose term for all army-style, wood-and-rope assault courses designed for children, the official ones, which are run either by charities or by London boroughs, are areas fully supervised at all times by trained play workers. They are situated all over London, extremely successful and absolutely free, and children from 5-14 love them. For information on adventure playgrounds near you, phone 0171 820 3800. The following are the largest.

BATTERSEA PARK ADVENTURE PLAYGROUND 🇫
ADDRESS Albert Bridge Road, SW11
PHONE 0181 871 7539
Ages 5-16. On quiet days the playground is also open to under-5s if accompanied by an adult (there is an adjacent playground specially for under-5s). Indoor area for workshops such as ceramics, photography, drama and games. See also The Great Outdoors.
TRAVEL Battersea Park or Queenstown Road rail; ⊖ Sloane Square then bus • **HOURS** Term-time: Tues-Fri, 3.30pm-7pm; school holidays: Tues-Fri, 11am-6pm, Sat-Sun, 11am-6pm • **PRICE** Free

HOLLAND PARK ADVENTURE PLAYGROUND 🇫
ADDRESS Kensington High Street, W8

PHONE 0171 603 6956

Ages 5-15 can come any time but on the first Saturday of each month they show them round the colourful equipment. There is smaller-scale equipment in the under-8s area. See also The Great Outdoors.

TRAVEL ⊖ *High Street Kensington or Holland Park* • **HOURS** *Daily, 10am-6pm (sometimes closes for lunch during term-time)* • **PRICE** *Free*

OUTDOOR HANDICAPPED ADVENTURE PLAYGROUNDS ⊟

PHONE 0171 731 1435

There are several playgrounds designed for handicapped children in London, including Charlie Chaplin Playground in Kennington, and Chelsea Playground and Lady Allen Playground in Wandsworth. Phone for details.

SPORTS EXPERIENCE

PHONE 0181 715 5434

With an emphasis on sports, the seven sites in outer London and the Home Counties offer day camps for children aged 4-14 and residential courses for those aged 7-17. Also computer and adventure courses.

PRICES *£199-£234 per week*

ARCHERY

GRAND NATIONAL ARCHERY SOCIETY

ADDRESS Seventh Street, National Agricultural Centre, Stoneleigh, Kenilworth, Warwickshire, CV8 2LG

PHONE 01203 696631

For details of a club and events near you, write to the junior section.

ATHLETICS

AMATEUR ATHLETICS ASSOCIATION

PHONE 0121 440 5000

Information on clubs and meetings near you for children of 7 and over.

CRYSTAL PALACE SPORTS CENTRE

ADDRESS Ledrington Road, SE19

PHONE 0181 778 0131

Hosts major international athletics events (also annual Grand Prix and home to Fulham Rugby League Club).

TRAVEL *Crystal Palace rail*

BASEBALL, BADMINTON, BASKETBALL, NETBALL AND VOLLEYBALL

The following associations will put you in touch with clubs and events near you.

ALL ENGLAND NETBALL ASSOCIATION

PHONE 01462 442344

Details of clubs near you. Try your local authority also.

BADMINTON ASSOCIATION OF ENGLAND
PHONE 01908 568822
Membership scheme with newsletter and annual, for ages 7-16.

BRITISH BASEBALL FEDERATION
PHONE 01482 643551
Teeball is the younger version of baseball for under-10s. Over-10s can start pitching properly with junior baseball. Over 50 junior clubs in leagues around the country.

ENGLISH BASKETBALL ASSOCIATION
PHONE 0113 2326 1166
Promotes basketball for children.

ENGLISH VOLLEYBALL ASSOCIATION
PHONE 0115 981 6324
All ages can play on almost any surface, including the beach. Phone for details of a club near you.

MINI-BASKETBALL ASSOCIATION
PHONE 01223 207213
Under-12s version is very popular. There is also a new version for ages 8-12 which is easier to teach.

BOXING
LONDON AMATEUR BOXING ASSOCIATION
ADDRESS 58 Comber Grove, SE5
PHONE 0171 252 7008
Phone for information on local clubs. Minimum age 11 years. Venues where you can watch boxing include Earl's Court, the Royal Albert Hall and Wembley Arena.

LONSDALE
ADDRESS 21 Beak Street, W1
PHONE 0171 437 1526
Shop selling everything from punch bags and mouth guards to clothes, videos and books. Children's gloves around £20.
TRAVEL ⊖ *Piccadilly Circus or Oxford Circus* • **HOURS** *Mon-Fri, 9am-6pm; Sat, 9am-5pm*

CAMPING
ABBEY WOOD CAMPING AND CARAVAN SITE
ADDRESS Federation Road, SE2
PHONE 0181 311 7708
Open all year. Well equipped with showers, laundry and a shop. Gas available.
TRAVEL *Abbey Wood rail* • **PRICE** *phone for prices*

CAMPING AND OUTDOOR CENTRES
SCOUTS SHOP

ADDRESS 27 Buckingham Palace Road, SW1

PHONE 0171 834 6007

Everything you could possibly need to sleep under the stars.

TRAVEL ⊖ *Victoria* • **HOURS** *Mon-Sat, 9am-5.30pm (Thurs till 7pm); Sun, 10am-4pm*

CRYSTAL PALACE CARAVAN SITE

ADDRESS Crystal Palace Parade, SE19

PHONE 0181 778 7155

A well-equipped site open throughout the year.

TRAVEL *Crystal Palace rail*

LEE VALLEY CAMP SITE

ADDRESS Sewardstone Road, E4

PHONE 0181 529 5689

Right on the edge of **Epping Forest**, the camp site has a small children's play area, a shop, launderette and toilets. Caravans, tents and motor homes.

TRAVEL ⊖ *Walthamstow Central, then bus 215* • **OPEN** *Apr-Oct*

LEE VALLEY CYCLE-CIRCUIT CAMP SITE

ADDRESS Temple Mills Lane, E15

PHONE 0181 534 6085

Camping in 40 acres of parkland as well as the use of the facilities and cycle circuit at the sports centre.

TRAVEL ⊖ *Stratford, then bus 308 or Leyton Tube* • **OPEN** *Mid-Mar to mid-Oct*

TENT CITY HACKNEY

ADDRESS Millfields Road, E5

PHONE 0181 985 7656

Caters for tents and caravans, and has tent with bunk beds for up to 30 people. Showers, cooking facilities, snack bar, terrace.

TRAVEL ⊖ *Liverpool Street* • **OPEN** *Jun-Aug*

CRICKET

Venues where you can watch county and international cricket include Lord's Cricket Ground (tel: 0171 289 1611, see also Behind the Scenes) and the Oval Cricket Ground (tel: 0171 582 6660).

ENGLAND AND WALES CRICKET BOARD

PHONE 0171 286 4405

Most London boroughs run holiday coaching courses, usually for children over 8 years old. Kwick cricket is now played by under-11s at clubs with junior sections, in schools and parks. Designed as a one-hour game, it can be taught easily and organised by parents. Kwick cricket kit available for £49.95 (tel: 0800 214314).

LILLYWHITES
ADDRESS 24 Lower Regent Street, SW1
PHONE 0171 915 4000
Sports department store selling equipment and clothing.
TRAVEL ⊖ *Piccadilly Circus* • **HOURS** *Mon-Wed, Fri, 10am-8pm; Thurs, 10am-9pm; Sat, 9am-7pm; Sun, 11am-5pm*

MCC INDOOR CRICKET SCHOOL
ADDRESS Lord's Cricket Ground, St John's Wood Road, NW8
PHONE 0171 432 1014
Private and group coaching all year round for children aged 8 and over.
TRAVEL ⊖ *St John's Wood*

SURREY COUNTY CRICKET CLUB
ADDRESS The Oval, Kennington, SW8
PHONE 0171 582 6660
Eight- to 10-week, term-time courses for ages 8 and over. Holiday and half-term courses for groups. No experience necessary.
TRAVEL ⊖ *Oval*

CROQUET
THE CROQUET ASSOCIATION
ADDRESS Hurlingham Club, SW6
PHONE 0171 736 3148
Phone for a full list of local clubs and information on croquet.

CYCLING
As anyone who has driven round Hyde Park Corner and nearly knocked over a cyclist will know, cycling in London can be very dangerous. *On Your Bike*, the handbook of the London Cycling Campaign, 3 Stamford Street, SE1 (tel: 0171 928 7220) is a good source of information on safe cycling routes. For details of Cycling Proficiency tests, contact your local town hall.

CYCLIST TOURING CLUB
PHONE 01483 417217
Most bike shops don't hire out kids' bikes, but if your children already have bikes you can still hire one for yourself for a country bike ride. Phone the above number for the Cycle Hire Directory.

LEE VALLEY CYCLE CIRCUIT
ADDRESS Temple Mills Lane, E15
PHONE 0181 534 6085
BMX race track, bikes for hire, coaching, etc. Booking is through schools, but phone for more information.
TRAVEL ⊖ *Stratford, and then bus 308, or* ⊖ *Leyton*

ON YER BIKE
ADDRESS 52-4 Tooley Street, SE1
PHONE 0171 378 6669
A good place to buy or hire a bike, then hop on a train at London Bridge and go for a spin in the countryside. Mountain bikes for hire, but no kids'

bikes or baby seats on adult bikes.
TRAVEL ⊖ *London Bridge* • **HOURS** *Mon-Fri, 9am-6pm; Sat, 9.30am-5.30pm*

DISABLED SPORTS

DISABILITY SPORT ENGLAND

PHONE 0171 490 4910
Information and advice on all sports, from athletics and archery to skiing
and snooker.

FENCING

AMATEUR FENCING ASSOCIATION

ADDRESS 1 Baron Gate, 33 Rothschild Road, W4
PHONE 0181 742 3032
Phone for a full list of clubs with a junior section and events in London.
Minimum age usually 7 years.

LEON PAUL

ADDRESS Unit 1 & 2, Cedar Way, Camley Street, NW1
PHONE 0171 388 8132
Everything you need to fence, from sabres, foils, épées and blades to
masks, jackets, pads and guards.

STREATHAM FENCING CLUB

ADDRESS Dunraven School, Mount Nod Road, SW16
PHONE Nick Stuart 01689 846862
One-hour introductory course available for ages 11-16, leading to the first
British Fencing Association (BFA) award. Private tuition also available.
TRAVEL *Streatham Hill rail*

FISHING

The National Federation of Anglers can provide details of angling clubs
that admit children (tel: 01283 734735). Local libraries and tackle shops
also have lists of clubs near you. Don't spend a fortune on equipment,
especially for beginners and young children. A bamboo pole, a piece of
string, a dog biscuit (if you don't fancy wriggly maggots) and a colander
to catch the fish will do just as well. No fishing licence is necessary for
children under 12 (but parents holding their kids' rods will be doing so
illegally if they themselves have no licence). Licences can be bought in
most tackle shops for fishing in the Thames and canals (the Royal Parks
have a different licence system). For more information contact the Thames
Water Authority (Fisheries Department) on 01734 593333 and for
licences phone the National Rivers Authority on 01734 535000.

BATTERSEA PARK

ADDRESS Albert Bridge Road, SW11
PHONE 0181 871 7530
Angling permits available from the Park Office for fishing in the lake.
TRAVEL *Battersea Park or Queenstown Road rail;* ⊖ *Sloane Square, then
bus* • **OPEN** *Daily, dawn-dusk*

RIVER LEE

Fishing is free from Tottenham to Cheshunt. Details from Thames Water (Lee Division) on 01734 593333

LONDON ANGLERS ASSOCIATION

ADDRESS Forest Road Hall, Hervey Park Road, E17
PHONE 0181 520 7477
Members can fish on 100 miles of water. Phone for details.

RIVER THAMES

All fishing on tidal stretches of the river is free (but you cannot fish round locks or where gardens of private property run down to the river). There are, surprisingly, over 100 different species of fish in the Thames. The first salmon to be caught here was recorded in 1984.

WALTHAMSTOW RESERVOIR

ADDRESS Ferry Lane, N17
PHONE 0181 808 1527
There are six different waters for coarse fishing and three for trout fishing. Whole-day or whole-season permits available at the Gate House for coarse fishing (trout fishing only with whole- or half-day permits). Minimum age 8 years (children under 16 must be accompanied by an adult). Also a very good place for birdwatching.
TRAVEL ⊖ Blackhorse Road or Tottenham Hale • **HOURS** 7.30am to 30 mins after sunset

FITNESS FOR UNDER-5S

CRECHENDO ☺

PHONE 0181 675 6611
Seventeen centres all over London. Crechendo offer stimulating toys, play equipment and soft and hard climbing equipment for ages four months to 5 years, divided into Babyplay, Toddlerplay, Kidsplay and Childsplay. Popular with mothers wanting to socialise while the kids let off steam.

TUMBLETOTS ☺

PHONE Leslie on 0181 777 4332 (London venues); Head Office 0121 585 7003 (venues outside London)
Using specially designed equipment, these 45-minute sessions of active physical play are designed for children from six months to 5 years. Children are encouraged to climb, hang, catch, slide, bounce and jump to improve their balance, co-ordination and general agility.

FLYING

LONDON SCHOOL OF FLYING

ADDRESS Elstree Aerodrome, Elstree, Herts
PHONE 0181 953 4343
Children can learn at any age (as long as they can reach the controls) but it is only at 14 years that the lessons start to count, and they cannot fly solo until the age of 17. The London School of Flying also has clubs at Biggin Hill, Denham, Blackbush, Redhill and Cranfield. As a member you are entitled to use all the clubs.

FOOTBALL

For information on football coaching for children, after-school and holiday clubs and matches in your area, call the Football Association on 0171 262 4542 or the Women's Football Association on 01707 651840.

FOOTBALL IN THE COMMUNITY

Many professional clubs organise soccer training for girls and boys of all ages and abilities, with activities such as weekly after-school or Saturday-morning clinics run by trained coaches, schools programmes, Learning Through Football, work with ethnic minorities, under-privileged children and the disabled. Some schemes are free, others charge up to £1 an hour. The following is a list of clubs participating in the Football in the Community scheme:

ARSENAL FC (tel: 0171 226 2150)
CHARLTON ATHLETIC FC (tel: 0181 850 2866)
CHELSEA FC (tel: 0171 385 01710)
CRYSTAL PALACE FC (tel: 0181 771 5886)
MILLWALL FC (tel: 0171 231 0379)
WEST HAM UNITED FC (tel: 0181 548 2707)
QUEEN'S PARK RANGERS FC (tel: 0181 743 0262)
FULHAM FC (tel: 0171 736 6561)
BRENTFORD FC (tel: 0181 560 2021)
WIMBLEDON FC (tel: 0181 771 1772)

SOCCER SCENE

ADDRESS Carnaby Street, W1
PHONE 0171 437 1966
Boots, balls and shirts for all strips – including foreign ones – to fit adults and children. Also books, magazines and videos.
TRAVEL ⊖ *Oxford Circus* • **HOURS** *Mon-Fri, 9.30am-6pm; Sat, 9.30am-4pm*

WEMBLEY STADIUM

ADDRESS Empire Way, Wembley, Middx
PHONE 0181 902 8833
Wembley Stadium is the venue for FA Cup finals, internationals and other professional games. Guided tours and birthday parties available (see Behind the Scenes and Children's Parties).
TRAVEL ⊖ *Wembley Park*

GOLF

A new set of clubs is expensive but the free-ads paper *Loot* and local papers are always full of second-hand sets at reasonable prices.

GOLF CITY

ADDRESS 13 New Bridge Street, EC4
PHONE 0171 353 9872
Branches in Orpington and Tolworth. Clubs for beginners and pros, bags, trolleys and accessories galore. Free club-fitting service.
TRAVEL ⊖ *Blackfriars* • **HOURS** *Mon-Fri, 9am-5.30pm; Sat, 10am-1.30pm*

GOLF FOUNDATION
PHONE 01920 484044
Provides information on junior starter centres throughout England. Also produces a list of public golf courses in and around London that allow men, women and accompanied children of any age to play on them.

GYMNASTICS
LONDON GYMNASTICS FEDERATION
PHONE 0181 529 1142
Helpful information and a list of local clubs.

HOCKEY AND ICE HOCKEY
See also Ice-skating, below.

BRITISH ICE HOCKEY ASSOCIATION
PHONE 01202 303946
Phone for a list of clubs catering for under-16s.

HOCKEYWISE
PHONE 01908 689290
Phone for details of local clubs and associations and for general advice.

ICE-SKATING
ALEXANDRA PALACE ICE RINK
ADDRESS Alexandra Palace Way, N22
PHONE 0181 365 2121
Although huge, this ice rink is a good place for beginners and potterers.
TRAVEL ⊖ *Wood Green, then bus W3* • **HOURS** *Opening times and sessions vary. Phone for details* • **PRICES** *Adults £4.50, children £3.50 (£3.60/£3 off-peak). Skate hire included. Six-week course of lessons £30*

BROADGATE ICE RINK
ADDRESS Eldon Street, EC2
PHONE 0171 505 4068
London's only outdoor rink, flooded and frozen in winter, is encircled by some wonderful futuristic City architecture. You can watch from one of the bars overlooking it. Ice Christmas Gala event in December. Smallest skate hire: children's size 6.
TRAVEL ⊖ *Liverpool Street* • **HOURS** *Nov-Mar: Mon, noon-3pm; Tues-Thurs, noon-3pm and 4-7.30pm; Fri, noon-3pm and 4-8pm; Sat-Sun, 11am-1pm, 2-4pm and 5-7pm* • **PRICES** *Adults £7, under-12s and concs £4 (includes skate hire). £24 plus £1 skate hire for four 30-min lessons.*

LEE VALLEY ICE CENTRE
ADDRESS Lea Bridge Road, E10
PHONE 0181 533 3151

This vast rink is excellent value for money, and strict supervision on the ice means that troublemakers are soon sorted out. Lessons and under-14s ice hockey available.

TRAVEL *Clapton Pond rail* • **OPEN** *Daily (times vary, phone for details)* •
PRICES *Adults £4.80, children £3.80 (includes skate hire)*

MICHAEL SOBELL ICE RINK ☺

ADDRESS Hornsey Road, N7
PHONE 0171 609 2166
Small but good-value ice rink for ages 4 and over.
TRAVEL ⊖ *Finsbury Park or Holloway Road* • **HOURS** *Opening times vary. Phone for details* • **PRICES** *Adults £2.50, children £1 (includes skate hire). Six-week course of lessons £29*

NATIONAL ICE-SKATING ASSOCIATION OF THE UK LTD

PHONE 0171 253 3824
The Learn to Ice-skate programme is a six-week course for children and adults. Phone for details of participating rinks.
PRICES *Adults £25, children £20*

QUEEN'S ICE-SKATING CLUB ☺

ADDRESS 17 Queensway, W2
PHONE 0171 229 0172
If you want to see serious skaters, as well as wobble about yourself, then central London's most famous rink is well worth a visit. Watch the figure skating from the bar overlooking the ice – it might tempt you to some personal tuition from one of the many full-time instructors. Smallest skates for hire are size 8. Minimum age: 3 years.
TRAVEL ⊖ *Bayswater* • **HOURS** *Mon-Fri, 11am-4.30pm and 7.30pm-10pm; Sat, 10am-noon, 2-5pm and 7-10.30pm; Sun, 10am-12pm, 2-5pm and 7-10pm. Family hours: Mon-Tues, 5-6pm* • **PRICES** *Adults £3.50-£5, children £3-£5, OAPs free. Skate hire £1.20. Children's classes £36 for a 6-week course*

QUEEN'S ICE-SKATING SHOP ☺

ADDRESS 17 Queensway, W2
PHONE 0171 229 0172
Sells skates, accessories and clothing for would-be Torvills and Deans. Will also sharpen blades and convert roller boots into ice skates.
TRAVEL ⊖ *Bayswater* • **HOURS** *Opening times and sessions vary. Phone for details*

SKATE ATTACK

ADDRESS 95 Highgate Road, NW5
PHONE 0171 267 6961
Large selection of ice and roller skates, protective gear, clothing and accessories.
TRAVEL ⊖ *Kentish Town* • **HOURS** *Mon-Sat, 9.30am-6pm; Sun, 10am-1pm*

STREATHAM ICE RINK ☺

ADDRESS 386 Streatham High Road, SW16
PHONE 0181 769 7771
Instruction courses available for under-8s. After-school sessions for under-12s. Popular venue for children's birthday parties. Built in 1931, this was

Britain's first indoor rink. It has recently been refurbished and also offers ice-hockey lessons for children over 8. Minimum age: 3 years.
TRAVEL *Streatham rail* • **HOURS** *Mon-Fri, 10am-4.30pm and 7.30-10.30pm; Sat, 11am-4.45pm and 8-11pm; Sun, 11am-4.45pm and 7.30-10.30pm* • **PRICES** *Adults £4.50, children £3.50, plus £1.50 skate hire*

MARTIAL ARTS

For information on martial arts clubs and tuition for children, contact the British Judo Association, 7a Rutland Street, Leicester LE1 1RB (tel: 0116 255 9669) or the Amateur Martial Arts Association, 120 Cromer Street, London WC1H 8BS (tel: 0171 837 4406).

SHAOLIN WAY
ADDRESS 10 Little Newport Street, WC2
PHONE 0171 734 6391
Shop specialising in judo and karate clothes, videos and books.
TRAVEL ⊖ *Leicester Square or Piccadilly* • **HOURS** *Daily, 11am-7pm*

TIFFIN SPORTS CENTRE
ADDRESS London Road, Kingston upon Thames, Surrey
PHONE 0181 541 3972
Judo and karate classes for ages 7 and over.
TRAVEL *Kingston rail* • **PRICE** *From £4 per session*

MOTOR SPORT

AUTO-CYCLE UNION
PHONE 01788 540519
Children can learn from age 6, but you will have to buy a machine for racing. Phone for details of a club near you.

BRANDS HATCH
ADDRESS Fawkham, Kent
PHONE 01474 872331
Major venue for motor sports. The top events can be quite a crush, so it's more fun for younger children to go off-peak. Phone for dates.
TRAVEL *Swanley rail*

BRITISH MOTOR SPORTS COUNCIL
PHONE 01753 681736
Karting is one of the few motor sports open to under-17s. Phone for details of venues and fixtures, and advice on safety, etc.

PLAYSCAPE PRO-RACING
ADDRESS Hester Road, SW11; Streatham High Road, SW16
PHONE Central reservations 0171 801 0110
Playscape specialises in karting training for children of 8 and over, and safety is its prime concern. Karting is exhilarating, if expensive fun, and your kids will love you for taking them, but don't bring younger siblings as it is not suitable for child spectators. (See also Children's Parties).
TRAVEL *Battersea Park or Queenstown Road rail, then walk; bus 49 or 345 (SW11); Streatham rail (SW16)* • **HOURS** *Children's racing: Mon-Fri, 10am-5pm; Sat-Sun, 9.30am-1.30pm* • **PRICES** *Half-hour test drives £18, 1 hour £30. Cadet School 1st Sat of month, 9.30am-12.30pm, £25*

WIMBLEDON STADIUM

ADDRESS Plough Lane, SW17

PHONE 0181 946 5361

Venue for superstock, hot-rod and banger racing, all of which children seem to love from an early age. Phone for dates.

TRAVEL ⊖ *Tooting Broadway, Wimbledon Park or Wimbledon; Earlsfield rail* • **WHEN** *Aug-May evenings*

MOUNTAINEERING

BRITISH MOUNTAINEERING COUNCIL

PHONE 0161 445 4747

Phone for details of introductory summer courses in rock climbing and mountaineering for children aged 12-16. Also supplies a climbing-wall directory.

MILE END CLIMBING WALL

ADDRESS Cordova Road, E3

PHONE 0181 980 0289

Runs a kids' club on Saturdays and on Fridays after school.

TRAVEL ⊖ *Mile End* • **PRICE** *£5 per session*

ORIENTEERING

For information about local events suitable for children, call the British Orienteering Federation on 01629 734042. Orienteering is fun for all the family. You can divide up into teams or stick together, navigating at your own pace between features marked on special maps. String courses led by costumed characters are popular with toddlers and pre-school children, and there are other courses for ages 8-9 and 9-12. Permanent courses can be found in London at Abbey Wood, SE2, Barnes Common, SW13, **Crystal Palace Park**, SE24, **Finsbury Park**, N4, **Hampstead Heath**, NW3, Lee Valley Park, E4, and **Victoria Park**, E9.

RIDING

The British Horse Society (tel: 01203 414288) deals with general enquiries and can supply a list of riding schools near you. The Pony Club (tel: 01203 696697) runs gymkhanas, summer camps and weekly meetings; phone for your nearest club. Parents of disabled children should phone Riding for the Disabled on 01203 696510 (minimum age is usually 3-4 years).

BARNFIELD RIDING SCHOOL ☺

ADDRESS Parkfields Road (off Park Road), Kingston upon Thames

PHONE 0181 546 3616

The Tiny Tots slot means that children can start riding here from age 2½.

TRAVEL *Kingston rail* • **PRICE** *From £18 for ½ hour private lesson*

BELMONT RIDING CENTRE

ADDRESS The Ridgeway, NW7

PHONE 0181 906 1255

Book well in advance.

TRAVEL ⊖ *Mill Hill East* • **HOURS** *Tues-Fri, 9am-5.30pm and 7pm-9pm; Sat-Sun, 9am-5pm* • **PRICE** *Group children's lessons from £13.50 per person per hour*

DULWICH RIDING SCHOOL

ADDRESS Dulwich Common, SE21
PHONE 0181 693 2944

Lessons for children aged 10 and over, either in outdoor manège or indoor arena.

TRAVEL *West Dulwich rail* • **PRICE** *From £12 for 1 hour lesson*

EALING COMMON RIDING SCHOOL ☺

ADDRESS 17-19 Gunnersbury Avenue, W5
PHONE 0181 992 3808

Lessons from beginners to intermediate for children over 5 years. Under-5s ride ponies. Hacks to Osterley Park on Mondays. Book well in advance.

TRAVEL ⊖ *Ealing Common; bus 83, 112 or 207*

HYDE PARK RIDING STABLES

ADDRESS 63 Bathurst Mews, W2
PHONE 0171 723 2813

Riding in Hyde Park and lessons in two outdoor manèges. Minimum age 5 years.

TRAVEL ⊖ *Lancaster Gate* • **PRICE** *From £22 for 1 hour private lesson*

LEE VALLEY RIDING CENTRE

ADDRESS Lea Bridge Road, E10
PHONE 0181 556 2629

Over 20 horses and ponies to ride in an outdoor manège or indoor riding arena, plus a cross-country course and paddock classes.

TRAVEL ⊖ *Leytonstone* • **PRICES** *Ages 5-7: £7 per 30 mins; ages 7 and over: £14 per hour*

LONDON EQUESTRIAN CENTRE

ADDRESS Lullington Garth, N12
PHONE 0181 349 1345

Large school with covered arena and outdoor manège. Newcomers are assessed before being put in a class.

TRAVEL ⊖ *Mill Hill East* • **PRICE** *From £14 for 1 hour group lesson*

MOTTINGHAM FARM RIDING CENTRE ☺

ADDRESS Mottingham Lane, SE9
PHONE 0181 857 3003

Lovely school with a cross-country course and stream. All lessons held outdoors for ages 3 and over.

TRAVEL *Mottingham rail* • **PRICE** *From £11.50 for 1 hour lesson. Ages 5 and under £6.50 for 20 mins.*

MUDCHUTE FARM RIDING SCHOOL ☺

ADDRESS Pier Street (off Manchester Road), E14
PHONE 0171 515 5901

Lessons in the all-weather manège or riding and jumping in the 32-acre park. One-day courses in equitation and stable management held during

the school holidays, as well as gymkhanas, showjumping and cross-country events. Minimum age 7. Under-7s can have pony rides.
TRAVEL *Island Gardens DLR* • **HOURS** *Sat and Sun, 10.30am or 11.15am* • **PRICE** *From £7.50 for ½ hour lesson*

OEHAMPTON RIDING STABLES
ADDRESS Priory Lane, SW15
PHONE 0181 876 7089
Riding takes place in Richmond Park and there are lessons on Tuesdays and Fridays. Minimum age 7 years.
TRAVEL ⊖ *Richmond* • **PRICE** *From £15-£18 for ½ hour lesson*

OSS NYE
ADDRESS 8 Bathurst Mews, W2
PHONE 0171 262 3791
Early-morning rides on Hyde Park's Rotten Row are especially popular at this 16-horse school. Minimum age 7 years.
TRAVEL ⊖ *Paddington* • **HOURS** *Tues-Fri, 7am-4.30pm; Sat-Sun, 10am-3.30pm* • **PRICES** *Group lessons £25 per person per hour; private lessons £30 per hour*

UZANNE'S RIDING SCHOOL
ADDRESS Brookshill Drive, Harrow Weald, Middx
PHONE 0181 954 3618
Popular school for all kinds of riders, including riding for the disabled. Regular 'own a pony' weeks in summer, when you are lent a pony to look after and ride for a week at the farm. Also Suzanne's Junior School for under-12s (tel: 0181 954 5592).
TRAVEL *Harrow & Wealdstone rail, then bus 258* • **HOURS** *Tues-Fri, 9am-9.30pm; Sat-Sun, 9am-4.30pm* • **PRICES** *Group lessons £17 per person per hour; private lessons £15 for 30 mins, £24 per hour*

RENT PARK EQUESTRIAN CENTRE
ADDRESS Bramley Road, N14
PHONE 0181 363 8630/9005
The centre runs 'own a pony' weeks when you visit the stable daily to look after and ride the pony allocated to you. Also four-day holidays on which you look after a pony and ride twice a day. Phone for full details.
TRAVEL ⊖ *Oakwood tube*

VILLOW TREE RIDING ESTABLISHMENT ☺
ADDRESS Ronver Road, Lee, SE12 0NG
PHONE 0181 857 6438
Large stables with about 40 horses. Lessons for ages 3 and over held in outdoor manège or indoor arena.
TRAVEL *Lee or Grove Park rail* • **PRICES** *£6 per 30 mins, plus 50p for hard hat*

WIMBLEDON VILLAGE STABLES ☺
ADDRESS 24a High Street, SW19
PHONE 0181 946 8579
Great two-hour park and common rides, lots of stable horses for timid first-timers, and the fact that they take children from 2½ years, make this otherwise expensive school very popular and good value for money.
TRAVEL ⊖ *Wimbledon* • **HOURS** *Daily, 8am-5pm* • **PRICES** *Group lessons £19 per hour Tues-Fri; £25 per hour Sat-Sun*

WOODREDON RIDING SCHOOL
ADDRESS Upshire, nr Waltham Abbey, Essex
PHONE 01992 714312
Cross-country courses in the heart of Epping Forest make this a popular venue. The school also has a large covered arena and outdoor manège, and caters for all ages.
TRAVEL ✪ *Loughton or Waltham Abbey rail, then bus 250* • **PRICE** *£15 per hour for children; £19 per hour for adults*

ROLLER-SKATING

Most leisure centres offer some form of roller-skating facilities but you usually have to bring your own skates. Popular parks for roller-skating include **Hyde Park** (street-hockey pick-up games at weekends), **Greenwich Park** (great for downhill grass skating) and **Regent's Park** (Sunday street-hockey pick-up games). The London Association of Skater Hockey can be contacted on 01268 685588.
ALEXANDRA PALACE ROLLER SPEED CLUB, 4 Raleigh Road, Enfield, Middx (tel: 0181 367 0636)

MEADOWSIDE LEISURE CENTRE
ADDRESS Tudway Road, SE3
PHONE 0181 856 0101
Saturday roller hockey for over-12s and under-12s. Family roller-skating open sessions on Sundays, with tuition and grading on Mondays. Also holiday programmes, speed skating, and beginner sessions. Times and prices vary; phone for details.
TRAVEL *Kidbrooke rail* • **HOURS** *Sat & Sun 12.30pm-2pm*

ROAD RUNNER
ADDRESS Unit 2, Lancaster Road, c/o 253 Portobello Road W11
PHONE 0171 792 0584
You can hire in-line skates and arrange lessons from here in nearby Hyde Park. Smallest boot for hire is a children's size 13. Very busy at weekends, so phone to check they have your size.
TRAVEL ✪ *Ladbroke Grove* • **HOURS** *Daily, 10am-6pm* • **PRICES** *£9.50 per day or £16 for 2 days plus £100 deposit (or leave your passport)*

ROEHAMPTON RECREATION CENTRE
ADDRESS Laverstoke Gardens, Roehampton SW15
PHONE 0181 785 0535
TRAVEL ✪ *Putney or bus 72, 74, 85, 170, 265* • **HOURS** *Last Sat of every month, 6.30-8pm roller disco for adults and children* • **PRICES** *Adults £2.50 + 70p, children £2.50 + 50p*

RUGBY UNION
HARLEQUINS
ADDRESS Stoop Memorial Ground, Craneford Way, Twickenham, Middx
PHONE 0181 410 6000, hotline 0839 664414 (50p a minute)
Home to one of London's premier rugby clubs.
TRAVEL *Twickenham rail*

ONDON IRISH RFC

ADDRESS The Avenue, Sunbury-on-Thames, Middx
PHONE 01932 882964
Welcomes all children, and teams range from under-6s to under-19s
(although lack of facilities means girls can only play up to age 12).
TRAVEL *Sunbury rail* • **WHEN** *Sep-Apr: Sun mornings 10am-12.30pm*
• **PRICE** *£40 per year & £10 for an adult associate membership*

ONDON SCOTTISH RFC

ADDRESS Richmond Athletic Ground, Kew Foot Road, Richmond, Surrey
PHONE 0181 332 7112
Openly mainly to children of Scottish parents – boys and girls – from
ages 6-12.
TRAVEL ⊖ *Richmond* • **WHEN** *Sep-Apr: Sun* • **PRICE** *Phone Charlie on 0181
876 5518 for prices and further details*

ONDON WELSH RFC

ADDRESS Old Deer Park, Kew Road, Richmond, Surrey
PHONE 01956 505460
Welsh and non-Welsh boys and girls join teams ranging from under-7s
to under-12s. Holiday and half-term courses. Annual tour to Wales is the
season's highlight. Please phone for full details.
TRAVEL ⊖ *Richmond*

WICKENHAM RUGBY FOOTBALL GROUND

ADDRESS Whitton Road, Twickenham, Middx
PHONE 0181 892 2000
The home of English rugby is host to internationals and other professional
matches. Guided tours available (see Behind the Scenes).
TRAVEL *Twickenham rail*

SKIING AND
SNOWBOARDING

The British Snowboarding Association (tel: 01494 462225) can provide
helpful advice and information on competitions, trips, clubs and camps.
The English Ski Council (tel: 0121 501 2314) also has information on ski
clubs and events. Minimum age for skiing is usually 3 years. Dry ski slopes
in and around London are listed below. Equipment can usually be hired at
the ski centre, but if you are planning a skiing holiday, you can buy or
hire from the specialist shops also listed below.

ECKTON ALPS SKI SLOPE

ADDRESS Alpine Way, E6
PHONE 0171 511 0351
Main slope with mogul field and nursery area. Also snowboarding. Bar,
restaurant, shop. All equipment hire included in the price. **NEARBY: Royal
Docks Water-ski Club** and **Thames Barrier and Visitors' Centre**.
TRAVEL ⊖ *East Ham, then bus 101* • **HOURS** *Sept-Apr, daily, 10am-11pm
(Sat 9.30-11.30am, children only)* • **PRICES** *Adults £8.50 for 2 hours,
children £7.50. Lessons: adults from £18, children from £12. Courses
from £50. Children £8 on Sat (under-6s £4)*

BROMLEY SKI CENTRE
ADDRESS Sandy Lane, St Paul's Cray, Orpington, Kent
PHONE 01689 876812
Main slope with mogul field and nursery area. Also snowboarding lessons.
TRAVEL *St Mary Cray and then bus 51* • **HOURS** *Tues-Thurs, noon-10pm; Fri, 10am-10pm; Sat, 9am-6pm; Sun, 10am-6pm* • **PRICES** *Adults £10 for 2 hours, children £8.50. Three-week course, 2 hours per lesson, adults £56, children £27. Introductory class £5.50*

CRYSTAL PALACE SKI SLOPE
ADDRESS Ledrington Road, SE19
PHONE 0181 778 0131
No recreational skiing as such, but you can book lessons with an instructor. Nursery slope. Children's boots from size 3.
TRAVEL *Crystal Palace rail* • **HOURS** *Mon-Fri, 9am-10pm; Sat, 9am-8pm; Sun, 9am-6pm. Courses from Oct-Mar; Junior Ski Club, Sat and school holidays* • **PRICES** *Adults £25 for 1-hour lesson, children £18, family tickets from £35. Also children's parties with food £8 per head*

HILLINGDON SKI CENTRE
ADDRESS Park Road, Uxbridge, Middx
PHONE 01895 255183
One of the best dry ski centres in the Southeast for skiing and snowboarding lessons and open sessions. One huge main slope, one intermediate, two nursery and one kindergarten. Weekly ski school for children. Also children's parties including one hour's tuition followed by food and drink.
TRAVEL ⊖ *Uxbridge* • **HOURS** *Daily, 10am-10pm (Sat to 6pm)* • **PRICES** *Adults £12 for 2 hours, children £9. Three-week course of 2-hour lessons: adults £60, children £55. Birthday parties £12.50 per head*

LOW PRESSURE
ADDRESS 23 Kensington Park Road, W11
PHONE 0171 792 3134
Popular among hard-core snowboarders, this shop sells everything from the latest boards, clothing and accessories to videos, books and magazines.
TRAVEL ⊖ *Ladbroke Grove or Notting Hill Gate* • **HOURS** *Mon-Sat, 10am-6pm; Sun, 11am-5pm*

SNOWBOARD ASYLUM
ADDRESS 30-2 Southampton Street, WC2
PHONE 0171 240 5316
Sells anything and everything to do with snowboarding – gloves, boots, boards, videos, socks and all major brand names.
TRAVEL ⊖ *Covent Garden or Charing Cross* • **HOURS** *Mon-Wed, Fri, 10am-7pm, Thurs, 10am-7.30pm; Sat, 9.30-6.30pm; Sun, 11.30am-5.30pm*

SWIMMING

Water temperature for under-5s should be 82-4°F (28-9°C). Most indoor pools have mother-and-toddler sessions, special holiday programmes and lessons, so phone your local pool or leisure centre for details. If you have kids who are really serious about swimming, contact the Amateur Swimming Association (tel: 0150 961 8700) or the Royal Life Saving

Society (tel: 01789 773994). There are hundreds of indoor pools in London and the following are just a sample of the more interesting or highly recommended ones.

INDOOR POOLS

THE ARCHES ☺

ADDRESS Trafalgar Road, SE10
PHONE 0181 317 5000
Beach area, water flume, water cannon, volcanic eruptions, bubbling spring. Excellent for even small children (also good soft play gym for under-5s). Café. Crèche and playpens. Family sessions on Friday evenings.
TRAVEL *Maze Hill or Greenwich rail* • **HOURS** *During summer holidays, daily, 10.30am-7 or 9pm; rest of the year, daily 2pm-7 or 9pm* • **PRICES** *Prices vary between £2.05 and £2.70 (peak times) for adults, and £1.25 and £1.70 (peak times) for children*

ARCHWAY LEISURE CENTRE ☺

ADDRESS 14 Macdonald Road, N19
PHONE 0171 281 4105
Water jets, wave machine, water slide, river run, spa pool.
TRAVEL ⊖ *Archway* • **HOURS** *Mon-Fri, 3.30-6.30pm; Sat, 11am-4pm; Sun, 8.30am-4.30pm (school-holiday weekdays, 10am-7pm)* • **PRICES** *Adults £2.90, children £1.50*

BRITANNIA LEISURE CENTRE ☺

ADDRESS 40 Hyde Road, N1
PHONE 0171 729 4485
Tropical setting with beach-style pool, wave machines, fountain and large slide. Summer-holiday sessions with inflatables and floats.
TRAVEL ⊖ *Old Street* • **HOURS** *Mon-Fri, 9am-8.45pm; Sat-Sun, 9am-5.45pm (women-only sessions: Wed, 6-8.45pm)* • **PRICES** *Adults £2.60, children £1.30*

DOLPHIN SWIMMING CLUB ☺

ADDRESS ULU Pool, Malet Street, WC1
PHONE 0181 349 1844
Swimming classes for children of all ages, up to Gold Standard.
TRAVEL ⊖ *Tottenham Court Road* • **HOURS** *Daily, 9am-4pm* • **PRICES** *Eleven individual 30-min lessons for £203.50; 2 in a group £101.75; 5 in a group £62.70. Phone for details.*

FULHAM POOLS ☺

ADDRESS Normand Park, Lillie Road, SW6
PHONE 0171 385 7628
Sloping sides, wave machine, fountain, water slide into separate pool, water toys. Teaching pool. High chairs and café/refreshments. Sessions for disabled children and adults some Sundays 3-5pm. Phone to check times of pool openings and prices.
TRAVEL ⊖ *West Brompton. Wave pool for parents and toddlers only: Mon-Fri, 9.30am-noon*

JUBILEE SPORTS CENTRE ☺

ADDRESS Caird Street, W10
PHONE 0181 960 9629

Weekend afternoon mother-and-baby sessions and family sessions. Crèche.
TRAVEL ⊖ *Queen's Park* • **HOURS** *Mon-Fri, 7am-8pm; Sat-Sun, 8am-4pm* •
PRICES *For tennis: Adults £3/hr, children £1/hr; For miniature golf: Adults £2.80, Children £1*

LATCHMERE LEISURE CENTRE ☺
ADDRESS Latchmere Road, SW11
PHONE 0171 207 8004
Seashore slope into pool, wave machine, toddlers' pool, slide and lots of greenery make this clean, modern pool very popular, especially the baby and toddler classes on Mondays, Tuesdays and Fridays. Playpens and changing mats available. Other clubs and activities for children, from tennis and fencing to judo and gymnastics.
TRAVEL *Clapham Junction rail* • **HOURS** *Mon-Thur, 7am-9.30pm; Fri, 7am-6pm; Sat, 7am-7pm; Sun, 7am-9.30pm* • **PRICES** *Adults £2.20 (off-peak 9am-5pm weekdays), £2.95 (7am-9am, after 5pm), children £1.65 (all hours), under-5s free*

WATERFRONT LEISURE CENTRE ☺
ADDRESS High Street, SE18
PHONE 0181 317 5000
The Wild and Wet Adventure Park has a fitness pool and four themed pools. Safari Oasis has interactive water toys for toddlers and a five-lane slide for over-4s. The Anaconda Serpent Slide has a height restriction of 1 metre. Main pool has wave machines, waterfalls, rapids, jets, hot tub and – on some occasions – costumed entertainers. Lots of special events. Restaurant. Also **Rascals Adventure Centre**.
TRAVEL *Woolwich rail or bus 53, 51, 96 or 54* • **HOURS** *Mon-Fri, 10am-1.30pm and 2-8pm; Sat-Sun, 9am-5pm; Sun family sessions: 6-8pm* •
PRICES *Adults £3.50, children £2.50, family ticket £5*

OUTDOOR POOLS
For a city with such an unpredictable climate, London has a surprising number of outdoor swimming pools.

BROCKWELL LIDO ☺
ADDRESS Brockwell Park, Dulwich Road, SE24
PHONE 0171 274 3088
Lovely 1930s open-air pool, although the water is cold. Toddlers' paddling area and paddling pools for tiny tots on busy days. Café.
TRAVEL ⊖ *Brixton or Herne Hill rail* • **OPEN** *Jun-Sep: daily, 10am-7pm (early-morning swim: 6.45am-10am)* • **PRICES** *£1.50-£3*

FINCHLEY LIDO ☺
ADDRESS Great North Leisure Park, High Road, N12
PHONE 0181 343 9830
Large outdoor pool with paddling pool.
TRAVEL ⊖ *Finchley Central* • **OPEN** *Summer, times vary* • **PRICES** *Adults £2.40, children and concs £1.50 (under-5s free)*

THE OASIS SPORTS CENTRE ☺
ADDRESS Endell Street, WC2
PHONE 0171 831 1804

Central London's only heated outdoor pool is surrounded by a sundeck and is popular with office workers on weekday lunchtimes. Also paddling pool for toddlers and indoor pool.
TRAVEL ⊖ *Covent Garden* • **HOURS** *Mon-Fri, 7.30am-8pm; Sat-Sun, 9.30am-5pm (closed some bank holidays)* • **PRICES** *Adults £2.50, children 85p (under-5s free)*

PARK ROAD POOLS ☺

ADDRESS Park Road, N8
PHONE 0181 341 3567
Heated outdoor pool, toddler pool and grassy slopes. Indoor pool has it own opening times and admission charge. Café.
TRAVEL *Hornsey rail* • **HOURS** *Jun-Sep: 11am-6pm (times and dates vary, phone to check)* • **PRICES** *Adults £3.20, children and concs £1.35*

PARLIAMENT HILL LIDO ☺

ADDRESS Parliament Hill (off Gordon House Road), NW5
PHONE 0171 485 3873
Large pool with changing cubicles, hot showers and somewhere to leave clothes. Shallow end (3 ft) with slide roped off for children and small paddling pool.
TRAVEL *Gospel Oak rail* • **OPEN** *May to late Sep: daily, 7am-6.30pm* • **PRICES** *Adults £1.80, children 90p (under-5s free; free to all, 7-9.30am)*

POOLS ON THE PARK ☺

ADDRESS Old Deer Park, Twickenham Road, Richmond, Surrey
PHONE 0181 940 0561
Indoor and outdoor pools, outdoor toddlers' pool. Admission covers all pools.
TRAVEL ⊖ *Richmond* • **HOURS** *Outdoor pool: early summer to Sep, weather permitting, Mon-Fri, 6.30am-8pm (Wed to 9pm), Sat-Sun, 7am-7pm* • **PRICES** *Adults £2.70, children £2.10 (under-5s free; various concs and season tickets)*

TOOTING BEC LIDO

ADDRESS Tooting Bec Road, SW16
PHONE 0181 871 7198
Huge unheated and often crowded pool. Children's play area with sandpit, grassy area for picnics and sunbathing. Café.
TRAVEL ⊖ *Tooting Bec* • **HOURS** *End of May to Aug: daily, 10am-7.30pm* • **PRICES** *Adults £2.50, children £2*

TENNIS

For details of tennis clubs and coaching for children, call the Lawn Tennis Association on 0171 385 2366. Many parks, recreation grounds and leisure centres have tennis courts, and tennis clubs usually start coaching children at age 7. Look out for Short Tennis courses for 6- to 10-year-olds.

ISLINGTON INDOOR TENNIS CENTRE

ADDRESS Market Road, N7
PHONE 0171 700 1370
Indoor tennis for all ages.

TRAVEL ⊖ *Caledonian Road* • **HOURS** *Daily, 7am-11pm* • **PRICES** *Adults: outdoor courts weekdays £5.70; indoor weekdays £9; weekends £14. Children only (i.e. not 1 adult and 1 child) indoor weekdays £5; indoor weekends £6.80; outdoor £4.70 all week.*

QUEEN'S CLUB
ADDRESS Palliser Road, W14
PHONE 0171 385 3421
You can see all the top male players compete in the Stella Artois Men's Tournament, and it's less crowded than Wimbledon.
TRAVEL ⊖ *Barons Court* • **WHEN** *Mid-Jun*

WESTWAY INDOOR TENNIS CENTRE
ADDRESS 1 Crowthorne Road, W10
PHONE 0181 969 0992
Indoor coaching in Short Tennis for under-9s.
TRAVEL ⊖ *Latimer Road* • **HOURS** *Daily, 7am-10pm* • **PRICE** *£20 for 6-week course*

WIMBLEDON (ALL ENGLAND LAWN TENNIS AND CROQUET CLUB)
PHONE 0181 946 2244
Wimbledon is not necessarily the easiest, cheapest or best way to see the stars if accompanied by young children. If you do want to go to the championships, go early in the competition – tickets are cheaper, crowds are smaller, and you will still see the best players.
TRAVEL ⊖ *Southfields or Wimbledon Park or Wimbledon rail* • **WHEN** *Last week in Jun to 1st week in Jul*

TEN-PIN BOWLING

There are hundreds of clubs in London. The British Ten-pin Bowling Association (tel: 0181 478 1745) will provide a list of venues near you.

TRAMPOLINING

The British Trampolining Federation Ltd (tel: 0181 427 8834) will supply a list of centres. Otherwise try your local sports centre.

WATERSPORTS

British Canoe Federation and Royal Yachting Association (RYA) courses are held at various venues in Surrey during the summer. Summer Safe weeks for ages 8-12 and 12-16 are organised by local authorities and held throughout the summer. Phone your local leisure services department for details. The Amateur Rowing Association (tel: 0181 748 3632) can provide a list of London clubs, most of which take children over 10 years. For a list of canoeing centres in and around London, phone the British Canoe Union on 0115 982 1100. The British Sub Aqua Club (tel: 0151 357 1951) will supply information on local training courses. Children must be able to swim (under-14s usually do snorkelling). The British Water-ski Federation, 390 City Road, EC1 (tel: 0171 833 2855) can supply a list of London clubs and summer residential courses for children. Other centres and associations offering watersports training for children are listed below.

DOCKLANDS SAILING AND WATERSPORTS CENTRE

ADDRESS 235a West Ferry Road, Isle of Dogs, London A14
PHONE 0171 537 2626

Summer courses in July and August in sailing, windsurfing, dragon-boat racing, canoeing and rowing. Sailing every afternoon. Children must be able to swim 50 metres, have the permission of a parent or guardian, and bring a change of clothing, a towel and suitable shoes.

TRAVEL ⊖ *Mile End, then bus D7 or DLR Crossharbour* • **OPEN** *All year, daily. Times vary so phone for full details* • **PRICES** *Children aged 9-18 years £3*

PETER CHIVERS WINDSURFING CENTRE

ADDRESS Gate 5, Tidal Basin Road (west end of Royal Victoria Dock), Newham, E16
PHONE 0171 474 2500

Very friendly venue which runs informal sessions for children to get them into the water. Recommended for ages 7 and over (depending on size). Children begin by getting used to the board itself for a day or two, then the sail is put on.

TRAVEL *Canning Town rail* • **OPEN** *Apr-Oct: Tues-Sun, dawn-dusk; Nov-Mar: Sat-Sun, dawn-dusk* • **PRICE** *Board hire £5 per hour*

PIRATES CASTLE WATERSPORTS CENTRE

ADDRESS Oval Road, NW1
PHONE 0171 267 6605

Club where over-8s can try canoeing.

TRAVEL ⊖ *Camden Town. Phone for full details of opening times, prices and membership details.*

PRINCES WATER-SKI CLUB

ADDRESS Clockhouse Lane, Bedfont, Middx
PHONE 01784 256153

Water-skiing courses varying in length.

TRAVEL ⊖ *Hatton Cross* • **OPEN** *Summer: daily, 9am to dusk* • **PRICES** *Beginners' sessions £45, day course £55, week's course (5 tows per day and use of all club facilities) £195*

ROYAL DOCKS WATER-SKI CLUB

ADDRESS Gate No 16, King George V Dock, Manor Way, E16
PHONE 0171 511 2000

The most flexible water-ski club as far as children are concerned. There is no minimum age as long as the child is fairly confident in the water. Phone in advance for one of the instructors to ski with the child (who in this case can be as young as 3 or 4, depending on size and temperament).

TRAVEL *North Woolwich rail or* ⊖ *East Ham, then bus 101* • **HOURS** *Daily, 10am to dusk (closed Jan-Feb)* • **PRICES** *Non-members (including equipment hire): 4 lessons £52, single lesson £15, day course (5 tows) £50, half-day course (3 tows) £35. (Phone for membership details.)*

ROYAL YACHTING ASSOCIATION

ADDRESS RYA House, Romsey Road, Eastleigh, Hants
PHONE 01703 627400

Governing body for all watersports. Will answer questions and put you in touch with watersports centres in your area. Sailing usually for over-5s only.

HOURS *Mon-Fri, 9am-5pm* • **PRICES** *Adult membership £19 per year; under-18s, £8 per year*

THAMES YOUNG MARINERS
ADDRESS Ham Fields, Riverside Drive, Richmond, Surrey
PHONE 0181 940 5550
Dinghy training offered at all levels, with special courses for children (also orienteering and mountain biking).
TRAVEL ⊖ *Richmond, then bus 371, then a 15 min walk* • **HOURS** *Sailing, canoe/kayak, multi-activity, 9.30am-4.30pm; Adventure week, 9am-5pm* • **PRICES** *For children aged 10-14: Sailing, canoe/kayak, multi-activity: £80/week; for children aged 15-17: adventure week: £100/week*

WESTMINSTER BOATING BASE
ADDRESS Dinorvic Wharf, 136 Grosvenor Road, SW1
PHONE 0171 821 7389
Royal Yachting Association and British Canoeing Union courses for ages 10-23 in canoeing and sailing. Children will be tested for their ability and then put into the correct course.
TRAVEL ⊖ *Pimlico* • **HOURS** *All year, Mon-Thurs, 6pm-9pm; Sun 10am-1pm, 2pm-5pm; adults only on Fri and Sat* • **PRICES** *For either or both courses, 10-23 year old £6/year*

WORKSHOPS

Learn to juggle or speak French, make a film, improve your maths, try your hand at mask-making, pottery or archaeology. See also Museums and Galleries for half-term and holiday activities.

ADVENTURE AND FIRST-AID GROUPS

BADGERS

PHONE 0171 235 5231
The junior division of the St John Ambulance for boys and girls aged 6-10 is rather like Cubs or Brownies, but unlike other youth groups it specialises in learning all about first aid. Following a course called Absolutely Everything, children learn first aid, healthy eating, games, the history of the St John Ambulance, gardening, road safety and communication skills.

GUIDES ASSOCIATION

ADDRESS 17-19 Buckingham Palace Road, SW1
PHONE 0171 794 1181
Activities for girls, with the emphasis on self-development, self-reliance and helping others. Rainbow group for ages 5-7, Brownies for ages 7-10, and Guides for ages 10-14.

ST JOHN AMBULANCE

ADDRESS Edwina Mountbatten House, 63 York Street, W1
PHONE 0171 258 3456
Basic first-aid courses for boys and girls. Ages 6-10 join the Badgers and ages 10-18 join the Cadets.

SCOUTS ASSOCIATION

ADDRESS Baden-Powell House, Queensgate, SW7
PHONE 0171 584 7030
Much the same as the Girl Guides but for boys, with plenty of activities. Beavers for ages 6-8, Cubs for ages 8-10, and Scouts for ages 10-15.

WOODCRAFT FOLK

ADDRESS 13 Ritherdon Road, SW17
PHONE 0181 672 6031
National voluntary youth organisation for boys and girls aged 6 and over.

ARCHAEOLOGY

ENGLISH HERITAGE

ADDRESS Keysign House, 429 Oxford Street, W1
PHONE 0171 973 3000
Junior membership scheme with its own section in the magazine and free entry to English Heritage properties.
PRICE *Annual membership for ages 5-16, £11*

LONDON & MIDDLESEX ARCHAEOLOGICAL SOCIETY

PHONE Karen Fielder at the Museum of London 0171 600 3699
A well-run society with an excellent junior section for children aged 9-16, which organises various activities, workshops and visits on Saturdays and during school holidays.

ARTS AND CRAFT

ART 4 FUN ☺

ADDRESS The Creative Café, 444 Chiswick High Road, W4 5TT
PHONE 0181 994 4100
Workshop for the whole family in a relaxed café where you can paint on ceramics, glass or wood. Buy individually priced items to decorate, have fired and take home.
TRAVEL ⊖ Chiswick Park • **HOURS** Phone for opening times • **PRICES** From £3 for paint and firing

THE ART WORKSHOP

ADDRESS 17 Rosemont Road, NW3
PHONE 0171 431 5696
Activities include sculpture, painting, ceramics and collage. The Mud Club offers after-school clay and sculpture classes. Birthday parties by prior arrangement.
TRAVEL ⊖ Finchley Road

BATTERSEA ARTS CENTRE ☺

ADDRESS Old Town Hall, Lavender Hill, SW11
PHONE 0171 223 2223
Summer school for four weeks in August with extensive classes and workshops for under-5s and under-21s.
TRAVEL Clapham Junction rail • **WHEN** Aug, daily. Also arts and craft workshops every Sat year round • **PRICES** Daily £5 (concs and Young BAC members £4.50), weekly £30 (concs £25)

BETHNAL GREEN MUSEUM OF CHILDHOOD ☺

ADDRESS Cambridge Heath Road, E2
PHONE 0181 980 2415
Open workshops in the art room, where work leaders offer activities for children of 3 and over.
TRAVEL ⊖ Bethnal Green or Cambridge Heath rail • **HOURS** Sat, 10am-5.50pm • **PRICE** Free

CAMDEN ARTS CENTRE

ADDRESS Arkwright Road, NW3
PHONE 0171 435 2643
Saturday workshops and holiday courses for 7- to 16-year-olds include painting, drawing, sculpture, print-making and ceramics. Also Portfolio classes for over-16s to build up a body of portfolio work. Workshops often relate to current exhibitions at the centre.
TRAVEL ⊖ Hampstead • **PRICE** Ten-week half-day workshops £65 (various concs)

CREATIVE WIZ KIDS ☺

PHONE 0171 794 6797

Phone for details of classes in St John's Wood and Hampstead. Art, movement and music classes for children from 6 months to 4 years and after-school clubs for older children. Also customised birthday parties for under-7s (£70). Phone for details.

PRICES *£84-£96 per 12-week term; 12 1-hour sessions £72-£91*

DULWICH PICTURE GALLERY

ADDRESS College Road, SE21
PHONE 0181 693 5254

Seasonal arts workshops, usually for children aged 6-10, based on the gallery's collection of old masters.

TRAVEL ⊖ *West Dulwich* • **WHEN** *Half terms and school holidays*

JACKSON'S LANE COMMUNITY CENTRE

ADDRESS 269a Archway Road, N6
PHONE 0181 340 5226

A wide range of weekly term-time and holiday workshops in dance, arts and craft, drama and more. Phone for details.

TRAVEL ⊖ *Highgate*

LAUDERDALE HOUSE

ADDRESS Waterlow Park, Highgate Hill, N6
PHONE 0181 348 8716

Arts and craft for ages 5-11 on Tuesdays. Drawing and painting for ages 8-15, covering still life, portraiture, figure drawing and landscapes, on Thursdays.

TRAVEL ⊖ *Highgate or Archway* • **HOURS** *Tues and Thurs, 5-6.15pm* • **PRICES** *Tues: £52 per 12-week term, concs £28; Thurs: £50 per 11-week term, concs £26*

LITTLE REMBRANDTS ☺

ADDRESS 16 Brocas Close, NW3
PHONE 0171 722 3199

Half-term and holiday painting workshops for ages 4 and over to paint plaster figurines. Also painting parties for birthdays and special occasions.

TRAVEL ⊖ *Swiss Cottage* • **PRICES** *£6-£15 per 2½-hour session*

PAINT POTS (MONTESSORI) ☺

ADDRESS Chelsea United Reformed Church, Edith Grove (entrance in Slaidburn Street), SW10
PHONE 0171 376 4571 or 0171 792 0433

Three-week August summer school of arts, crafts, music, drama and fun with a different theme each day for children aged 18 months to 2 years, 2-3 and 3-6 years. Also series of weekly classes (bookable per term) for the same age ranges as summer school.

TRAVEL ⊖ *Sloane Square, then bus; NCP car park other side of King's Road* • **PRICES** *Prices vary with age and length of course. Please phone for details.*

ASTRONOMY

BRITISH ASTRONOMICAL ASSOCIATION

ADDRESS Burlington House, Piccadilly, W1
PHONE 0171 734 4145
Monthly meetings from October to June and weekend courses. There is no age limit but members are usually over 6 years old. Phone for details.
TRAVEL ⊖ *Piccadilly Circus*

HAMPSTEAD SCIENTIFIC SOCIETY

ADDRESS Lower Terrace, NW3
PHONE 0171 794 9341; observatory 0181 346 1056
The society has its own observatory, which is open on Fridays and Saturdays on clear nights.
TRAVEL ⊖ *Hampstead* • **PRICES** *Fri-Sat, 8pm*

BRASS RUBBING

ALL-HALLOWS-BY-THE-TOWER

ADDRESS Byward Street, EC3
PHONE 0171 481 2928
A choice of 30 brasses. Price includes all materials and tuition.
TRAVEL ⊖ *Tower Hill* • **HOURS** *Daily, 11am-4.30pm* • **PRICE** *75p-£5 per brass*

LONDON BRASS RUBBING CENTRE

ADDRESS St Martin-in-the-Fields, WC2
PHONE 0171 930 9306
Dozens of replica brasses to rub, including a 7-ft knight.
TRAVEL ⊖ *Leicester Square or Charing Cross* • **HOURS** *Mon-Sat, 10am-6pm; Sun, noon-6pm* • **PRICES** *£2.50-£15 (all materials included)*

CIRCUS

ALBERT AND FRIENDS INSTANT CIRCUS ☺

ADDRESS St Paul's Church, Queen Caroline Street, Hammersmith, W6
PHONE 0181 741 5471
Also in Twickenham. Children learn juggling, stilt walking, tightrope, clowning and unicycle skills, and work towards end-of-term productions. Courses in July and August, ending in a show. Saturday-morning drop-in sessions from £4 per session. All ages from 18 months.
TRAVEL ⊖ *Hammersmith* • **PRICES** *From £40 per term; summer-holiday workshops £15 per day, £70 per week*

CIRCUS UK

ADDRESS Alternative Arts, 47a Brushfield Street, E1
PHONE 0171 375 0441
Learn the art of juggling, stilt walking, acrobatics, body-balancing and trapeze. Half-term, holiday, weekend and summer projects.
PRICE *Free*

JACKSON'S LANE CIRCUS SKILLS WORKSHOP

ADDRESS Jackson's Lane Community Centre, 269a Archway Road, N6
PHONE 0181 341 4421

Drop-in classes with Pizzazz the Clown in unicycling, stilt walking and tightrope for ages 5-8. Also holiday workshops and courses.
TRAVEL ⊖ *Highgate* • **PRICE** *£3.50 per class*

JUNIOR CIRCUS SKILLS ☺

ADDRESS New Peckham Varieties, Havil Street, SE5
PHONE 0171 708 5401
Juggling, stilt walking and plate spinning for ages 4-9 and 10-16.
TRAVEL ⊖ *Oval* • **HOURS** *Fri, 4pm and 5pm* • **PRICE** *£11 per half-term*

COMPUTER STUDIES

COMPUTER WORKSHOPS

PHONE 0171 585 2067
Alison Townsend's computer courses for children aged 4-16 range from ever-popular touch-typing, and simple reading, writing and problem solving for 5- to 6-year-olds, to games, programming and Simulation Strategy for Smart Kids. Alison has an MA in specific learning difficulties and is especially good with children who have dyslexia and dyspraxia. Courses usually held over two days. Phone for details of venue and dates.

FUTURE KIDS ☺

ADDRESS 73 St John's Wood High Street, NW8
PHONE 0171 722 6878
Other venues too. Ages 3-15 can learn graphics, computer skills, desk-top publishing and more. Phone for leaflet and full details.
TRAVEL ⊖ *St John's Wood*

TECHNO KIDS ☺

PHONE 0171 354 9678
Computer courses held after school in schools throughout London (times and prices vary). Children aged 4-15 learn how to use multimedia PCs.

COOKING

LE CORDON BLEU CULINARY INSTITUTE

ADDRESS 114 Marylebone Lane, W1
PHONE 0171 935 3503
Les Petits Cordons Bleus is a series of Saturday-morning workshops for wannabe master-chefs aged 8-14. Also two-day holiday courses.
TRAVEL ⊖ *Marble Arch* • **HOURS** *Sat, 10am-noon* • **PRICES** *£250 per 11-week term; 2-day courses £50*

DANCE

BATTERSEA ARTS CENTRE ☺

ADDRESS Lower Hall, Old Town Hall, Lavender Hill, SW11
PHONE 0171 223 2223 or 01932 847101
Christina Ross Dance runs creative-movement classes for 3-year-olds, and fun ballet and tap for 4-year-olds. Also formal-ballet, modern-dance and tap-dance grade exams from 5 years to adults. Phone for full details.
TRAVEL *Clapham Junction rail*

THE BULL ☺

ADDRESS 68 High Street, Barnet, Herts
PHONE 0181 449 0048
Parents and Toddler Dance for ages 18 months to 3 years creative dance for ages 3-5, after-school dance for ages 6-11. Kathak dance from northern India.
TRAVEL ⊖ *High Barnet* • **PRICE** *All classes £25 per term*

CHISENHALE DANCE SPACE ☺

ADDRESS 64-84 Chisenhale Road, E3
PHONE 0181 981 6617
Tuesday-afternoon and Saturday-morning creative-dance classes for ages 2-15 (divided into age groups). Long waiting list.
TRAVEL ⊖ *Mile End* • **PRICES** *£2.50 (concs £1.50)*

CRAZEE KIDS ☺

PHONE Lisa on 0181 444 5333
Weekly classes in NW3 and N6, covering percussion, creative movement, dance, drama and music, with a wide range of activities for 3- to 5-year-olds.
PRICES *£5.25 per 45-min class; from £55 per term*

DONALD MCALPINE DANCE STUDIO ☺

ADDRESS Longfield Hall, Knatchbull Road, SE5
PHONE 0181 673 4992
Very good, friendly music and movement classes for under-5s.
TRAVEL ⊖ *Loughborough junction rail* • **WHEN** *Tues-Wed afternoon and Sat morning* • **PRICE** *£32 per term. Parents stay for first session.*

GREENWICH DANCE AGENCY ☺

ADDRESS The Borough Hall, Royal Hill, SE10
PHONE 0181 293 9741
Playdance for ages 0-3 and First Steps for ages 3-5. Saturday Movers and Shakers for ages 5-8 and Danszone for ages 8-12.
TRAVEL *Greenwich rail* • **PRICES** *£2.50-£2.75 (concs £1.50-£2)*

HIGHBURY ROUNDHOUSE ☺

ADDRESS 71 Ronalds Road, N5
PHONE 0171 359 5916
Children's classes include under-5s creative dance, ballet and tap.
TRAVEL ⊖ *Highbury & Islington* • **WHEN** *Weekly during term-time* • **PRICES** *Phone for prices*

ISLINGTON DANCE & ARTS FACTORY

ADDRESS 2 Parkhurst Road, N7
PHONE 0171 607 0561
Classes for children aged 12-16, including kit drumming, contemporary dance, visual arts workshop and ballet to grades 3 and 4. Saturday and after-school classes include ballet for ages 5-11 and dance-theatre workshops for ages 8-13 and over-13s.
TRAVEL ⊖ *Caledonian Road* • **PRICES** *£25-£30 per term*

LABAN CENTRE ☺

ADDRESS Laurie Grove, SE14
PHONE 0181 692 4070

Creative-dance classes for 4- to 6-year-olds and 7- to 10-year-olds. Also
Babytone and Toddlertone. Phone for details.
TRAVEL ⊖ *New Cross Gate* • **WHEN** *Sat* • **PRICE** *From £22 per term*

LAUDERDALE HOUSE ☺
ADDRESS Waterlow Park, Highgate Hill, N6
PHONE 0181 348 8716 or 0181 341 2032
Parent and Toddler Dance (Thursday morning). Thursday-afternoon
Creative Dance for ages 3-4, 4-5 and 5-6. Also Thursday afternoon
Creative Dance and Performance for ages 7-11 working towards an end
of term performance.
TRAVEL ⊖ *Highgate or Archway* • **PRICES** *£36 per 11-week term (concs £18)*

MINI MOVERS
ADDRESS Rosslyn Hall, Willoughby Road, NW3
PHONE 0181 458 8519
Classical Greek dance, ballet, jazz and tap, suitable for boys and girls
aged 5-14, no experience necessary.
TRAVEL ⊖ *Hampstead* • **PRICES** *£45-£65 per term*

ROYAL ACADEMY OF DANCING
ADDRESS Vicarage Crescent, SW11
PHONE 0171 223 0091
Classical ballet classes for 5- to 17-year-olds. Children can study for RAD
exams. Also residential and non-residential summer schools for ages 8-12
and 10-14. Entry to classes is by audition only. (The school also supplies
an approved list of teachers.)

ROYAL BALLET SCHOOL
ADDRESS 155 Talgarth Road, W14
PHONE 0181 748 6335
Children who are accepted by this competitive classical-ballet school
receive a full-time general education in addition to ballet classes. Also two
residential summer schools for children aged 10-11 (boys accepted up to
13) and for dancers aged 15-17. Acceptance for junior and senior
summer school by audition only, held January to October.

UNION DANCE SUMMER SCHOOL
ADDRESS Dance Works, 16 Balderton Street, W1
PHONE 0171 734 3262
Week-long summer school with workshops in jazz and contemporary
dance, ballet and tap, for ages 7-11, working with professional dancers.
Also choreographic workshop where children create their own dance, to
be performed at the end of the week. No previous experience necessary.
Book early.
TRAVEL ⊖ *Bond Street* • **WHEN** *Aug* • **PRICE** *£25*

DRAMA
ANNA SCHER CHILDREN'S THEATRE
ADDRESS 70-2 Barnsbury Road, N1
PHONE 0171 278 2101
This is the theatre where the likes of Susan Tully, Pauline Quirke, Linda
Robson and Gary and Martin Kemp trained. Excellent, imaginative
after-school classes for ages 5 and over in improvisation, poetry, stage

technique and theatre production. Long waiting list. Also summer school for ages 6-11 and 12-16. Application forms available Easter.

TRAVEL ⊖ *Angel* • **PRICES** *£5 per session or £20 per week*

BATTERSEA ARTS CENTRE ACTING FACTORY & SUMMER SCHOOL

ADDRESS Old Town Hall, Lavender Hill, SW11

PHONE 0171 223 2223

Acting Up for ages 5-7; Acting Around for ages 8-11; Acting Out for ages 12-15. Summer school for four weeks in August, with extensive classes and workshops for under-5s and under-21s. Half-term, week-long workshops in February and October.

TRAVEL *Clapham Junction rail* • **WHEN** *Acting Up and Acting Around: Sat mornings; Acting Out: Wed, 4.30-6.30pm* • **PRICES** *Acting Up: £30 (concs £25) per term or £3.50 per session; Acting Around: £40 (concs £30) or £4; Acting Out: £40 (concs £30) or £4*

BODEN STUDIO

ADDRESS Intimate Theatre, Green Lanes, N13

PHONE 0181 367 2692

Five-day course in acting, singing and dance for over-7s, culminating in a two-hour show with sound, lighting and live band.

TRAVEL *Palmers Green rail* • **WHEN** *Easter and Aug-Sep* • **PRICE** *£50*

THE BULL

ADDRESS 68 High Street, Barnet, Herts

PHONE 0181 449 0048

After-school club in theatre skills for ages 8-11, with end-of-term show for family and friends. Bull Youth Theatre for ages 11-14, working towards performing children's own devised play (£25 per term). So You Think You're Funny comedy classes for ages 11 and over (£40 per term).

TRAVEL ⊖ *High Barnet* • **HOURS** *After-school club: phone for dates* • **PRICES** *After-school club: £22.50 per term, £2.50 per class*

CAMP BEAUMONT

ADDRESS Eccles Hall, Norfolk

PHONE 01480 456123

Week-long residential summer camp runs every week from July to August. Stage and Screen course for children aged 7-14. Video filming, mime, make-up, singing, costume and more.

GREENWICH AND LEWISHAM YOUNG PEOPLE'S THEATRE

ADDRESS Burrage Road, SE18

PHONE 0181 854 1316

Workshops for ages 11-14, 14-17 and 16-25, covering drama, music and the visual arts.

TRAVEL *Woolwich rail* • **WHEN** *Mon-Fri evenings (term-time only)*

ISLINGTON DANCE & ARTS FACTORY

ADDRESS 2 Parkhurst Road, N7

PHONE 0171 833 4843

Summer courses for ages 7-12 and 13-17, culminating in a performance.

TRAVEL ⊖ *Caledonian Road* • **PRICES** *£35-£45*

LOST THEATRE/EXPERIMENTAL THEATRE

ADDRESS 450 Fulham Road, SW6

PHONE 0171 381 6151 (evenings only)

Workshops leading to performance for under-18s. Some workshops throughout the year for ages 10-13. Phone for details.

TRAVEL ⊖ *Fulham Broadway*

MOUNTVIEW THEATRE SCHOOL

ADDRESS Ralph Richardson Memorial Studios, Clarendon Road, N22

PHONE 0181 889 8110

Saturday activities for ages 6-8 and 9-12 include drama and dance.

TRAVEL ⊖ *Wood Green* • **HOURS** *Sat, phone for times* • **PRICES** *From £40-£50 per term*

NATIONAL YOUTH THEATRE

ADDRESS 443-5 Holloway Road, N7

PHONE 0171 281 3863

For 14- to 21-year-olds. Auditions held in February and March to select cast for plays to be rehearsed and performed during the summer holidays. Applications by December.

TRAVEL ⊖ *Holloway*

THE POLKA THEATRE FOR CHILDREN ☺

ADDRESS 240 The Broadway, SW19

PHONE 0181 543 4888

Six- to 10-week courses for children from 18 months to 12 years. Also Youth Theatre for 13- to 16-year-olds.

TRAVEL ⊖ *Wimbledon* • **PRICES** *Courses £25-£35*

PUPPET CENTRE TRUST

ADDRESS Battersea Arts Centre, Old Town Hall, Lavender Hill SW11

PHONE 0171 223 2223

Everything to do with puppetry, including children's training courses and shop. Bi-monthly magazine. Phone for details.

TRAVEL *Clapham Junction rail*

QUESTORS THEATRE

ADDRESS Mattock Lane, W5

PHONE 0181 567 0011

High-standard amateur theatre. Drama play groups for ages 5-9 with emphasis on imaginative play and role-playing activities. Junior drama workshops after school for ages 10-14, with improvisation and acting exercises. Older children's plays are performed for parents and friends. Long waiting list.

TRAVEL ⊖ *Ealing Broadway*

SAMANTHA GIBLIN'S DRAMA CLUBS

PHONE 0171 231 6083

Venues in SW18 and SW19. Includes Saturday Drama for ages 5-7 and 8-12, Monday Drama for ages 8-11 and Southwest Youth Theatre for ages 12 and over. Phone for details.

PRICES *Sessions £3.25-£7*

SPEAK EASY ☺

ADDRESS Telegraph Hill Centre, Kitto Road, SE14
PHONE 0181 691 1177
Sally Macmillan teaches drama and movement for under-5s, group drama classes for ages 5-16 (divided by age) and small group tuition for honing drama skills for ages 8 and over.
TRAVEL *Nunhead rail* • **PRICES** £25-£40 per term; try-out classes £2.50-£3

STAGECOACH

PHONE 01932 254333
Saturday-morning schools in drama, music, dance and theatre skills. Talented children are invited to audition for stage and television roles through Stagecoach's agency. Phone for details of a school near you.
PRICE £215 per term (siblings half-price)

STAGETALK

ADDRESS Hampstead Meeting House, 120 Heath Street, NW3
PHONE 0181 518 5657 or 0181 531 5211
Holiday drama club for ages 6-11. Games, impro, rehearsals and an end-of-week production in a professional theatre environment.
TRAVEL ⊖ *Hampstead* • **PRICE** £75 per week (reductions for siblings)

THE TREE HOUSE

ADDRESS 18 Furley Road, SE15
PHONE 0171 252 8712
Saturday drama and performance workshops for ages 5-7 and 8-12. Also weekly evening instrument and voice tuition.
TRAVEL *Peckham Rye rail or bus 36, 36B, 27, 12 or 171* • **PRICE** £1

TRICYCLE THEATRE ☺

ADDRESS 269 Kilburn High Road, NW6
PHONE Box office 0171 328 1000
Drama-based, term-time workshops for children from 18 months to 16 years. Past activities have included make your own TV commercial, design your own T-shirt and conduct an orchestra. Booking essential.
TRAVEL ⊖ *Kilburn* • **PRICES** £18 per 10-week term (concs £8)

TRINITY ARTS CENTRE

ADDRESS 170 Gloucester Terrace, W2
PHONE 0171 262 1629
Classes for all ages covering all aspects of drama.
TRAVEL ⊖ *Paddington, Royal Oak or Lancaster Gate* • **PRICES** £30-£63 per term, various concs

UNICORN THEATRE ☺

ADDRESS 6-7 Great Newport Street, WC2
PHONE 0171 836 3334; membership 0171 379 3280
Children can be Erik the Viking or Sherlock Holmes. One-week summer school in August for children of 8 and over to learn stage fighting, clowning, improvisation, script work, mask and mime, make-up, etc. Dance & Drama Club for ages 8-12 and Unicorn Plus for ages 12-16 during term-time. Weekend Unicorn Theatre Club workshops for children aged 4-5, 6-7 and 8-12. Birthday workshops (see Children's Parties). Good facilities and workshops for the disabled.

TRAVEL ⊖ *Leicester Square or Charing Cross* • **PRICES** *Theatre Club workshops from £7.50; birthday workshops £75-£90*

WATERMAN'S ARTS CENTRE
ADDRESS 40 High Street, Brentford, Middx
PHONE 0181 568 1176
Theatre Club on the first three Saturdays of each month (mornings, 9- to 15-year-olds; afternoons, 5- to 8-year-olds) includes drama, improvisation and theatre games. School-holiday workshops covering a wide range of activities.
TRAVEL *Brentford rail* • **PRICES** *£35 per term (£20 concs)*

YOUTH ARTS PROGRAMME
ADDRESS New Peckham Varieties, Havil Street, SE5
PHONE 0171 708 5401
Dance and drama for all ages, all abilities. Youth Drama and Youth Musical Theatre for those keen to pursue career on stage. Also junior drama classes. Phone for term dates and prices.
TRAVEL ⊖ *Oval* • **PRICES** *Most sessions £2-£3*

FILM
CHILDREN'S FILM UNIT
ADDRESS Unit 8, Princeton Court, 55 Felsham Road, SW15
PHONE 0181 785 0350
Film-making for ages 11-18, including acting, camera skills, make-up, script writing, sound and continuity. Also annual full-length movie made in the summer holidays.
TRAVEL *Putney rail* • **WHEN** *Sat* • **PRICES** *membership: £10 per term, workshops £2 each*

LANGUAGES
BUSY BEES
ADDRESS Albercorn Place School, 28 Albercorn Place, NW8
PHONE 0171 286 0923/4785
Runs the A-Scheme for over-6s – holiday English, Maths, French, Latin and Spanish.
TRAVEL ⊖ *Maida Vale or St John's Wood*

LE CLUB FRANCAIS/EL CLUB ESPANOL ☺
PHONE 0181 694 8493 or 01962 714036
Nationwide club runs French and Spanish courses for children aged 3-11. Incorporating games, sports, arts and crafts, cookery and drama, the classes inspire enthusiasm for the language and culture.
PRICE *£4 per hour*

LE CLUB FRERE JACQUES ☺
PHONE 0171 354 0589
Clubs all over London. Times and prices vary; phone for details. Children aged 3-11 learn French through games, songs, rhymes and role playing. All teachers are French.

LE CLUB PETIT PIERROT ☺

PHONE 0171 828 2129

Venues in Belgravia and St John's Wood. French through play using language games, stories, songs, dance and role play for ages 2½-6.
WHEN *Belgravia: Tues and Wed; St John's Wood: Mon and Thurs* • **PRICES** *From £95 per 10-week term*

LE CLUB TRICOLORE ☺

ADDRESS 10 Ballingdon Road, SW11
PHONE 0171 924 4649

Children aged 5-11 learn French through songs, games, role play and activity sheets with qualified language teachers. Venues in Putney, Dulwich, Wimbledon, Hampstead, Chelsea. French Activity Days weekly in holidays for 2- to 11-year-olds in Sloane Square. Also Tricolore Tots, where parents can leave their pre-school children (2-5 years) up to three times a week to learn French, in a totally French-speaking environment. Venues in Chelsea and Wandsworth.
PRICES *After-school sessions: £80 per 10-week term; Sat sessions: £112 per session; activity days: £20 per day; Tricolore Tots: £10 per session*

FRENCH A LA CARTE/SPANISH A LA CARTE ☺

PHONE 0181 946 4777

Venues in SW1 and Wimbledon. Playgroups, songs and games in French or Spanish for ages 3 and over. Phone for list of venues.
PRICES *£40 for 6 week term, 1 hour per week*

IRISH LANGUAGE CLUB FOR CHILDREN

ADDRESS Roger Casement Irish Centre, 131 St John's Way, N19
PHONE 0171 281 7424 or 0171 916 7893

Children from age 5 can hear stories, poetry and songs and play games in the Irish language.
TRAVEL ⊖ *Archway* • **HOURS** *Sat, 2-4pm* • **PRICE** *£40 per 8-week term*

LE PETIT ECOLE ☺

PHONE Nichole Beaumont on 0181 948 6326

French taught by the French for ages 2-12. Games, puppet shows, role playing, songs and a taste of real French life at venues all over London. Phone for full details.

MISCELLANEOUS

PIPPA POP-INS EXCURSIONS AND ACTIVITIES ☺

ADDRESS 430 Fulham Road, SW6
PHONE 0171 385 2458

Children's hotel with particularly good Christmas-holiday activities during December, including visits to shows and films, tobogganing (on snow or grass) at Box Hill in Surrey, pony riding, chocolate making, etc. The nursery is open for New Year's Eve and New Year's Day – the children can celebrate at their own party with pre-recorded chimes from Big Ben at 8pm.
TRAVEL ⊖ *Fulham Broadway* • **PRICES** *£100 per night*

SCIENCE NIGHTS

ADDRESS Science Museum, Exhibition Road, SW7

PHONE 0171 938 9785

Eight- to 11-year-olds, in groups of six accompanied by an adult, can stay the night at the museum and take part in a range of talks, trails, demonstrations and workshops, with storytelling before lights-out at midnight. Book well in advance. See also Museums and Galleries.

TRAVEL ⊖ *South Kensington* • **PRICES** *£18 per child, £20 per adult*

MCA DAY CAMPS

PHONE 0181 520 5599

Activities for children aged 5-15, including archery, hiking, nature walks, arts, crafts and face painting. Phone for details.

MODELLING

CAMERA KIDS MODEL AGENCY

ADDRESS KK Studio, 9 Station Parade, SW12

PHONE 0181 675 4000/4911

If you think your child has what it takes, send two recent snapshots, a covering letter giving child's name, date of birth and brief description and an SAE.

TRULY SCRUMPTIOUS CHILD MODEL AGENCY

ADDRESS The Worx, 16-24 Underwood Street, N1

PHONE 0171 608 3806

As well as being a modelling agency, Truly Scrumptious runs Be a Model for a Day, regular day-long workshops for ages 7-16. Learn about cat walking, hair and make-up tips and commercial casting, have a photo session and take part in a fashion show in front of family and friends.

TRAVEL ⊖ *Old Street* • **PRICES** *£30 per day, 3-day course £80*

MUSIC

Choirs are a good way for children to improve their musical skills and receive ear training. They usually accept children from the age of 8 (they need to be able to read confidently but not necessarily to read music). Some choirs charge a small fee; others entice children with offers of pocket money. Expect a simple audition. Contact your local church for details. There are also many music workshops available for children; some of the best are listed below.

FUN WITH MUSIC

ADDRESS 2 Queensmead, St John's Wood Park, NW8

PHONE 0171 722 9828

Musical appreciation through colouring books and instruments for 3½- to 5-year-olds. Musical story sessions for ages 5-6 and 7-11. Waiting list.

TRAVEL ⊖ *Swiss Cottage* • **PRICE** *From £120 (plus VAT) for 9-week term*

GUILDHALL SCHOOL OF MUSIC AND DRAMA

ADDRESS Silk Street, Barbican, EC2

PHONE 0171 638 1770

Saturday term-time courses for all abilities. Ages 5-8 can take a stringed-instrument preparatory course before joining the junior strings. Musically gifted children aged 8 and over receive individual tuition and orchestral training if they pass the audition.

TRAVEL ⊖ *Barbican*

HONEYWELL SCHOOL ☺

ADDRESS Honeywell Road, SW11
PHONE 0171 223 6369
Daily after-school introduction to jazz for ages 4-12 (and over-12s) through drama, movement and masks, and piano lessons. Phone for full details.
TRAVEL *Wandsworth Common rail*

HORNIMAN MUSIC-ROOM WORKSHOPS

ADDRESS 100 London Road, SE23
PHONE Booking on 0181 699 1872, extn 129
Recorder and general-music workshops, fun-with-music session and Hands On Our Musical Instruments workshops. All ages. Phone for details.
TRAVEL *Forest Hill rail; bus 176 or P4* • **PRICES** *Prices vary but some workshops are free*

ISLINGTON DANCE & ARTS FACTORY

ADDRESS 2 Parkhurst Road, N7
PHONE 0171 607 0561
Classes for children aged 12-16, including kit drumming, contemporary dance, band workshop, visual arts workshop and ballet to Grades 3 and 4.
TRAVEL ⊖ *Caledonian Road* • **PRICE** *From £20 per term*

JANET SODRING SPECTRUM SINGERS ☺

ADDRESS 19 Coombe Road, W4
PHONE 0181 994 8149
Music and action for under-5s, beginners' singing for ages 6-8, solo tuition for ages 9-14, junior choir for ages 9-14. Week-long holiday courses include Create a Show, Top of the Pops, and Captain Noah and His Floating Zoo. Also held in Portobello Road. Phone for details.
TRAVEL ⊖ *Turnham Green*

LEWISHAM ACADEMY OF MUSIC

ADDRESS 77 Watson's Street, SE8
PHONE 0181 691 0307
After-school workshops for under-18s to learn guitar, bass, drums, piano, keyboard and instrument making. Soundbeam Project involves children with disabilities.
TRAVEL ⊖ *New Cross or Deptford rail* • **PRICE** *£5 per month*

LONDON COLLEGE OF MUSIC

ADDRESS Thames Valley University, St Mary's Road, W5
PHONE 0181 231 2304
Saturday-morning music school for ages 4-17, where children can learn one or two instruments, theory and oral work. Range of abilities, from average to highly talented. Bursaries, sponsorships and scholarships available.
TRAVEL ⊖ *Ealing Broadway*

LONDON SCHOOL OF SINGING

ADDRESS 18 Cranhurst Road, NW2
PHONE 0181 452 5502
The school sets very high standards and progress is rapid for children aged 9 and over wanting to sing seriously or for pleasure. Courses

develop voice range, quality and power. Opportunity to enter national singing competitions at various music festivals.
TRAVEL ⊖ *Willesden Green*

MONKEY MUSIC ☺

PHONE 0181 761 7271
Venues all over London. Music and music-making for babies and pre-school children, with action songs and rhythms, games and storytelling.

MUSIC FOR LITTLE PEOPLE

PHONE Rebecca Vicary on 0181 852 0118
Various venues in southeast London. Activities introducing under-5s to singing, ear training, rhythm and reading, with an emphasis on fun. Classes divided into three age groups.
PRICES *£34-£48 per 10-week term*

MUSIC PLAYHOUSE ☺

ADDRESS Tricycle Theatre, Kilburn High Road, NW6
PHONE 0171 328 1000
A musical adventure in rhythm and sound using songs, stories and live music. Ages 3-5.
TRAVEL ⊖ *Kilburn*

TAFELMUSIK ☺

PHONE 0171 376 5201
Venues in Chelsea and St John's Wood. Twelve-week term must be booked in advance (trial lesson available). Creative-music workshops for ages 1-8. Starter sessions for ages 3-8, introducing guitar, recorder, piano and violin. Phone for details.

WATERMAN'S ARTS CENTRE ☺

ADDRESS 40 High Street, Brentford, Middx
PHONE 0181 568 1176
Term-time Pandemonium groups – fun with music for the under-5s.
TRAVEL *Brentford rail* • **WHEN** *Wed, 10.15am (under-2s) and 11.15am (ages 2-4)* • **PRICES** *£2.50 (concs £1.25)*

YOUNG MUSIC MAKERS

ADDRESS William Ellis School, Highgate Road, NW5
PHONE 0958 445246
Classes in guitar, brass and drums, big band and orchestra for ages 5-18.
TRAVEL ⊖ *Kentish Town; Gospel Oak rail* • **PRICES** *£99.50 for a 10-week term of ½ hour private lessons. £29 for a 10-week term of ½ hour group lessons.*

MUSICAL MUSEUMS

FENTON HOUSE, Hampstead Grove, NW3 (tel: 0171 435 3471). ⊖ Hampstead. Open Apr-Oct: Sat-Wed, 11am-6pm; Mar: Sat-Sun, 2-5pm. Free. Merchant's house dating from 1693, home to the Benton Fletcher Collection of early keyboard instruments.
HORNIMAN MUSEUM AND LIBRARY, 100 London Road, Forest Hill, SE23 (tel: 0181 699 1872). Forest Hill rail. Open: Mon-Sat, 10.30am-5.30pm; Sun, 2-5.30pm. Free. Over 6,000 musical instruments from around the world. See Museums and Galleries.

MUSICAL MUSEUM, 368 High Street, Brentford, Middx (tel: 0181 560 8108). ⊖ South Ealing or Gunnersbury, then bus 237 or 267. Open Jul-Aug: Wed-Sun, 2-5pm; Apr-Oct: Sat-Sun, 2-5pm. Adults £3.20, children and concs £2.50, family ticket (2+2) £10. Extensive collection of automatic musical instruments. Send SAE for bookings and details of the 90-minute demonstration tours and fortnightly evening concerts. See Museums and Galleries.

ROYAL COLLEGE OF MUSIC MUSEUM OF INSTRUMENTS, Prince Consort Road, SW7 (tel: 0171 589 3643). ⊖ South Kensington. Open term-time only: Wed, 2-4.30pm. Collections include around 500 keyboard, stringed and wind instruments dating from 1480 onwards.

SELF-DEFENCE
STAND YOUR GROUND
ADDRESS Quindo Centre, 2 West Heath Drive, NW11
PHONE 0181 455 8698
Phone for dates of day courses and workshops. Recommended by the Anti-Bullying Campaign and Kidscape, Quindo offers courses to build self-confidence and develop ways of dealing with bullying. Ages 4-18 divided into three age groups.
TRAVEL ⊖ *Golders Green* • **PRICE** *£65 for a day course and £6 per session*

STAMP COLLECTING
SEE ALSO SHOPPING AND SERVICES

BRITISH PHILATELIC FEDERATION
ADDRESS 107 Charterhouse Street, EC1
PHONE 0171 251 5040
Phone for list of local stamp-collecting clubs and societies, exhibitions, etc. Members receive a free yearbook and there are regular meetings with talks and competitions.

TUTORIAL WORKSHOPS
BUSY BEES ☺
ADDRESS Albercorn Place School, 28 Albercorn Place, NW8
PHONE 0171 286 0923
Holiday activity weeks for ages 3-7: cooking, art, craft, music, drama, outdoor games, party on last day. A-Scheme for over-6s – holiday English, Maths, French, Latin and Spanish (the two schemes can be combined).
TRAVEL ⊖ *Maida Vale or St John's Wood*

THE KUMON MATHS ☺
PHONE 0181 447 9010
Centres all over the country; phone for details. The Kumon method of studying mathematics, which originated in Japan, is best suited to children either more advanced than their classmates or lagging behind, and covers material from basic addition to algebra and calculus. Children (some as young as 2) attend two 20-minute classes a week at one of the 30 centres in London.
PRICE *Enrolment £15 then £38 per month*

HE TUTORIAL SCHOOL

ADDRESS The New Learning Centre, 211 Sumatra Road, NW6
PHONE 0171 794 0321/5328

The New Learning Centre is a school for children aged 6-19 with special needs and behavioural problems, run by Noel Janis-Norton. Short holiday and after-school courses also available to help with anything from revision and school- entrance exams to parenting skills and homework problems. Also Summer Revision Programme courses in academic subjects with an emphasis on study skills, work habits, motivation and self-confidence. After an initial assessment, children are taught by specialists, following individual programmes. Courses are also suitable for dyslexics and children learning English as a second language.

TRAVEL ⊖ *West Hampstead*

SURVIVAL GUIDE

How to find a late-night chemist, join a toddler group or get emergency dental treatment; who to phone when your baby won't stop crying, or your child has eczema, or you need a babysitter; where to get advice on education, legal rights or alternative medicine; all this and much, much more.

ACE (ADVISORY CENTRE FOR EDUCATION)
PHONE 0171 354 8321
Provides free help and advice for parents, students, governors and others in education.
HOURS *Advice line: Mon-Fri, 2-5pm*

ACTION FOR SICK CHILDREN
PHONE 0171 833 2041
Advice and help to enable parents to get the best possible health care for sick children. Also advice on how to prepare children for hospital stays.

ACTIVE BIRTH CENTRE
PHONE 0171 561 9006; mail order 0171 272 0987
Advice on non-invasive active birth. Active Birth is an approach to childbirth which involves practising stretching and movements and being in 'open' and upright positions during labour. Also hires out birthing pools.

ANTI-BULLYING ASSOCIATION
PHONE 0171 378 1446 (answer phone after hours)
Helpline for children who are bullied at school.
HOURS *Mon-Fri, 9.30am-5pm*

ARTSLINE
PHONE 0171 388 2227
Arts advice and information service giving details of places, events and activities, including their accessibility to disabled people.

THE ASSOCIATION FOR ALL SPEECH IMPAIRED CHILDREN
PHONE 0171 236 3632

ASSOCIATION FOR POSTNATAL ILLNESS
PHONE 0171 386 0868
Offers advice for those suffering from postnatal depression.
HOURS *10am-2pm*

ASSOCIATION OF BREAST-FEEDING MOTHERS
PHONE 0181 778 4769
Offers advice and support.
HOURS *Any time before 10pm*

BRITISH PREGNANCY ADVISORY SERVICE
PHONE 0171 637 8962
Advice on all aspects of pregnancy and abortion.

CHILDLINE
PHONE 0800 1111
National 24-hour helpline for kids. Children can phone them with any problem and they have a team of experienced councillors and volunteers who offer support and advice for children. The call is free and totally confidential.

COMPASSIONATE FRIENDS
PHONE 0171 953 9639 (answerphone after hours)
Friendship and understanding for parents in need of help following the
death of a child.
HOURS *Mon-Fri, 9.30am-5pm*

COT DEATH HELPLINE
PHONE 0171 235 1721
Twenty-four-hour helpline with someone to listen and offer advice, information
and reassurance at any time. Run by the Foundation for the Study of Infant
Deaths.

CRUSE
PHONE General information 0181 940 4818; helpline 0181 332 7227
Advice and support in cases of bereavement.
HOURS *Helpline: Mon-Fri, 9.30am-5pm*

DISABLED LIVING FOUNDATION
PHONE 0171 289 6111
Help and information for the disabled, including list of specialist suppliers.

DOWNS SYNDROME ASSOCIATION
PHONE 0181 682 4001
Help and information service.

EPOCH (END PHYSICAL PUNISHMENT FOR CHILDREN)
PHONE 0171 700 0627
An organisation working to change the law relating to the smacking of
children. Useful advice on alternative ways of disciplining your children.

FRES LTD
PHONE 0171 323 4300
Offers advice on wages, contracts and tax when employing nannies.

GINGERBREAD
PHONE 0171 336 8183
The association for single-parent families. Will put you in touch with local
groups. Also organises after-school and holiday activities for children with
a working parent.

HURTWOOD (HANDICAPPED ADVENTURE PLAYGROUND ASSOCIATION)
PHONE 0171 736 4443
Runs specially designed playgrounds for use in holidays and on Saturdays
by handicapped children and their siblings. Also organises youth clubs,
camping trips and holiday play schemes.

HYPERACTIVE CHILDREN'S SUPPORT GROUP
PHONE 01903 725182
Advice and general information.
HOURS *Mon-Fri, 10am-3.30pm*

ISIS (INDEPENDENT SCHOOLS INFORMATION SERVICE)
PHONE 0171 630 8793
Information about and publications on independent schools.
HOURS *Mon-Fri, 8.45am-5.30pm*

KIDSCAPE
PHONE 0171 730 3300
Helpline for parents of bullied children. Advice on assertiveness courses for
the victim. Runs the Stranger Danger campaign.
HOURS *Mon-Fri, 10am-4pm*

LA LECHE LEAGUE
PHONE 0171 242 1278
Advice on breast-feeding. Will put you in touch with a qualified counsellor in your area.

LIBERTY (THE NATIONAL COUNCIL FOR CIVIL LIBERTIES)
PHONE 0171 403 3888
Can give advice on legal rights of children.

MEET A MUM ASSOCIATION (MAMA)
PHONE 0181 665 0357
Help for mothers who are lonely or suffering from post-natal depression.
HOURS *Mon-Fri, 9.30am-2.30pm*

MENCAP (ROYAL SOCIETY FOR MENTALLY HANDICAPPED CHILDREN AND ADULTS)
PHONE 0171 454 0454

MESSAGE HOME
PHONE Freephone 0500 700740
If you have run away and want to get a message home without anyone knowing where you are, you can phone this number, leave a message on the answer phone and it will be passed on.

MIND (NATIONAL ASSOCIATION FOR MENTAL HEALTH)
PHONE 0181 519 2122
Advice of all kinds on mental and emotional problems for people of all ages.

THE MISCARRIAGE ASSOCIATION
PHONE 0131 334 8883
National network of volunteers offering advice and counselling for women who have recently had a miscarriage.

NATIONAL ASSOCIATION FOR GIFTED CHILDREN
PHONE 01908 673677
Advice for parents and teachers of gifted children, plus activities for the children and newsletter four times a year.

NATIONAL ASSOCIATION OF MATERNAL AND CHILD WELFARE
PHONE 0171 383 4541

NATIONAL ASSOCIATION OF VICTIMS' SUPPORT SCHEMES
PHONE 0171 735 9166
Victims of crime are put in touch with a volunteer who will offer emotional and practical support and visit you as soon as possible after the event. They are very good with children who have experienced crimes like burglary.
HOURS *Mon-Fri, 9am-5pm*

NATIONAL ASTHMA CAMPAIGN
PHONE Helpline at local call rate 0345 010203
Specialist asthma nurses on call to help and advise sufferers and parents of sufferers.
HOURS *Mon-Fri, 9am-7pm*

NATIONAL CHILDBIRTH TRUST
PHONE 0181 992 8637
Advice and support to help with most postnatal problems, including breast feeding.

NATIONAL CHILDREN'S BUREAU
PHONE 0171 843 6000
Advice on all aspects of child welfare.

NATIONAL COUNCIL FOR ONE-PARENT FAMILIES
PHONE 0171 267 1361
Advice on all aspects of being a one-parent family; also runs a campaign to improve conditions for them.

NATIONAL ECZEMA SOCIETY
PHONE 0171 388 4097 (answer phone after hours)
Practical advice and moral support.
HOURS *Mon-Fri, 9am-5pm*

NATIONAL SOCIETY FOR THE PREVENTION OF CRUELTY TO CHILDREN (NSPCC)
PHONE 0171 825 2500
Offers advice and help when stress or crisis might be affecting children. Also investigates reports of ill-treatment.

NATIONAL YOUTH AGENCY
PHONE 0116 285 6789
Advice and information on counselling for children and teenagers.

PARENTS ANONYMOUS
PHONE 0171 263 8918
Confidential telephone service for parents who have problems with their babies, toddlers or older children and need emotional support. Staffed by parents and professional workers.
HOURS *Daily, 10am-4pm and 6pm-6am*

PARENTS AT WORK
PHONE 0171 628 3578 or 0171 500 5771
An association that provides information on childcare and will put you in touch with local working-mother groups.
HOURS *Tues-Wed and Fri, 9am-1pm*

PARENT LINE
PHONE 01702 559900 (answerphone after hours)
Helpline for parents under stress. Phone for details of regional help.
HOURS *Mon-Fri, 9am-6pm*

RIDING FOR THE DISABLED
PHONE 01203 696510
Information on riding schools in London and elsewhere.

SAFTA (SUPPORT AROUND TERMINATION FOR FOETAL ABNORMALITY)
ADDRESS 73 Charlotte Street, W1P 1LB
PHONE 0171 631 0285

SAMARITANS
PHONE 0171 734 2800
Look in your local phone directory for your nearest branch. The Samaritans run a 24-hour helpline and are there to listen and offer support to anyone of any age with emotional problems of any kind. Nothing is too trivial, and all calls are confidential (so they won't tell anyone, and you don't even need to tell them your name).

TOXOPLASMOSIS TRUST
PHONE 0171 713 0663 (Mon-Fri 9am-5pm)
For information and advice on toxoplasmosis for pregnant women, send an A4 SAE to 61 Collier Street, London N1 9BE.

TWINS AND MULTIPLE BIRTHS ASSOCIATION (TAMBA)
ADDRESS 41 Fortuna Way, Aylesbury Park, Grimsby, South Humberside, DN37 9SJ
Write for list of local contacts.

INDEX

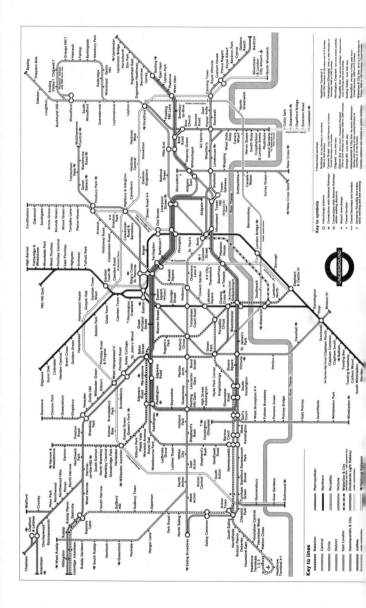